BIBLICA ET ORIENTALIA

(SACRA SCRIPTURA ANTIQUITATIBUS ORIENTALIBUS ILLUSTRATA)

36

ROMAE
E PONTIFICIO INSTITUTO BIBLICO
1980

ANTHONY R. CERESKO, O.S.F.S.
University of St. Michael's College
Toronto

JOB 29-31 IN THE LIGHT OF NORTHWEST SEMITIC

A Translation and Philological Commentary

R O M E
BIBLICAL INSTITUTE PRESS
1 9 8 0

Vidimus et approbamus ad normam Statutorum
Pontificii Instituti Biblici de Urbe

Romae, die *11* mensis ianuarii anni *1979*

Mitchell Dahood, S.I.
Maurice Gilbert, S.I.

TYPIS PONTIFICIAE UNIVERSITATIS GREGORIANAE — ROMAE

To my Parents
Anthony Raymond Ceresko
Mary Elizabeth Tyrie Ceresko

Preface

This volume contains the slightly revised version of a doctoral dissertation submitted in the summer of 1978 to the Biblical Faculty of the Pontifical Biblical Institute in Rome and defended on December 19 of that same year. My thanks are due above all to my director, Rev. Mitchell J. Dahood, S.J. He was a constant source of inspiration and encouragement while the work was in progress. I shall always be grateful for his patient guidance and ready sharing of his time and immense scholarship. To my second reader, Rev. Maurice Gilbert, S.J., I also owe a debt of gratitude. His perceptive comments have helped to enhance the potential usefulness of the work for others. I would like to thank the other members of my examination board, Rev. Luis Alonso Schökel, S.J., and especially Rev. Gian Luigi Prato, who carefully read the manuscript and offered a number of valuable suggestions toward its improvement.

My thanks are due also to my brother Oblates for their support during my years of study, especially Most Rev. William J. Ward, O.S.F.S., who first as Provincial and then as Superior General followed my progress with interest and encouragement.

I must also express my gratitude to the faculty and students of St. Mary's College and SS. Cyril and Methodius Seminary, Orchard Lake, Michigan, especially to the Dean of the latter, Rev. Anthony Kosnik. It was during my three years' sojourn there that a good portion of this present work was completed.

Finally, my thanks are due to my family, especially my parents, brothers, and sisters, who patiently endured my long absences overseas, and who proved of great assistance during the final stages of the work; and last but not least, to my aunt, Helen Ceresko, who prepared the final typescript.

Anthony R. Ceresko
Oblate of St. Francis de Sales

Pentecost 1979
Faculty of Theology
University of St. Michael's College
Toronto, Canada

Table of Contents

Abbreviations

AB = The Anchor Bible.

Aistleitner, *Wörterbuch* = J. Aistleitner, *Wörterbuch der ugaritischen Sprache* (Berlin, 1963).

Alonso Schökel, *Job* = L. Alonso Schökel and J. L. Ojeda, *Job*. Los Libros Sagrados VIII, 2 (Madrid, 1971).

AnOr = Analecta Orientalia.

AOAT = Alter Orient und Altes Testament.

BA = *Biblical Archeologist* (Missoula, MT).

BASOR = *Bulletin of the American Schools of Oriental Research* (New Haven).

BDB = F. Brown, S. R. Driver, C. A. Briggs, *A Hebrew and English Lexicon of the Old Testament* (Oxford, 1906).

*BHK*³ = *Biblia Hebraica*. 3rd edition, eds. R. Kittel and P. Kahle (Stuttgart, 1937).

BHS = *Biblia Hebraica Stuttgartensia*, eds. K. Elliger and W. Rudolph (Stuttgart, 1968-77).

Bib = *Biblica* (Rome).

BibOr = Biblica et Orientalia.

BJ = *Bible de Jérusalem* (1955).

*BJ*² = *Bible de Jérusalem*, 2nd edition (1974).

Blommerde, *NSGJ* = A. C. M. Blommerde, *Northwest Semitic Grammar and Job*. BibOr 22 (Rome, 1969).

BZ = *Biblische Zeitschrift* (Paderborn).

Caquot, *TO* = *Textes ougaritiques, Tome I: Mythes et légendes*, eds. A. Caquot, et al. (Paris, 1974).

CBQ = *Catholic Biblical Quarterly* (Washington, D. C.).

chap(s) = chapter(s).

Chicago Bible = *The Complete Bible: An American Translation*, J. M. P. Smith and E. J. Goodspeed (Chicago, 1939).

col. = column.

CRAIBL = *Comptes rendus de l'Académie des inscriptions et belles lettres* (Paris).

CTA = A. Herdner, *Corpus des tablettes en cunéiformes alphabétiques* (Paris, 1963).

Dahood, *Proverbs* = M. Dahood, *Proverbs and Northwest Semitic Philology* (Rome, 1963).

Dahood, *UHP* = M. Dahood, *Ugaritic–Hebrew Philology*. BibOr 17 (Rome, 1965).

Dahood, *Psalms I* = M. J. Dahood, *Psalms I*. AB 16 (Garden City, N. Y., 1965).

Dahood, *Psalms II*² = M. J. Dahood, *Psalms II*, 2nd edition. AB 17 (Garden City, N. Y., 1973).

Dahood, *Psalms III* = M. J. Dahood, *Psalms III*. AB 17A (Garden City, N. Y., 1970).

Driver–Gray, ICC = S. R. Driver and G. B. Gray, *A Critical and Exegetical Commentary on the Book of Job*, 2 vols. ICC (Edinburgh, 1929).

ed(s). = editor(s).

Fedrizzi, *Giobbe* = P. Fedrizzi, *Gi.obbe* La Sacra Bibbia (Torino-Roma, 1972).

GKC = *Gesenius' Hebrew Grammar*, edited by E. Kautzsch, translated by A. E. Cowley (Oxford, 1910).

Heb. = Hebrew.

ICC = The International Critical Commentary, eds. S. R. Driver, A. Plummer, and C. A. Briggs.

JB = *The Jerusalem Bible*, ed. Alexander Jones (Garden City, N. Y., 1966).

Joüon, *Grammaire* = P. Joüon, *Grammaire de l'hébreu biblique* (Rome, 1923).

JSS = *Journal of Semitic Studies* (Manchester).

KAI = H. Donner and W. Röllig, *Kanaanäische und aramäische Inschriften*, 3 vols. (Wiesbaden, 1962-1969).

K–B, *Lexicon* = L. Koehler – W. Baumgartner, *Lexicon in Veteris Testamenti Libros* (Leiden, 1953).

Kuhnigk, *NSH* = W. Kuhnigk, *Nordwestsemitische Studien zum Hoseabuch*. BibOr 27 (Rome, 1974).

l. = line.

LXX = The Septuagint.

Michel, *Book of Job* = W. Michel, *The Ugaritic Texts and the Mythological Expressions in the Book of Job* (Dissertation for the University of Wisconsin, 1970).

MS(S) = Manuscript(s).

MT = The Masoretic Text.

n. = note.

NAB = *New American Bible* (1970).

NEB = *New English Bible* (1970).

Or = *Orientalia* (Rome).

p. = page(s).

par. = paragraph.

Pesh. = The Peshitta (the Syriac version).

PN = Personal Name(s).

Pope, *Job*[3] = M. H. Pope, *Job*, 3rd edition. AB 15 (Garden City, N.Y., 1973).

RB = *Revue Biblique* (Paris).

Penar, *The Hebrew Fragments of Ben Sira* = T. Penar, *Northwest Semitic Philology and the Hebrew Fragments of Ben Sira*. BibOr 28 (Rome, 1975).

RS = Ras Shamra.

RSO = *Rivista degli Studi Orientali* (Rome).

RSP I = *Ras Shamra Parallels*, vol. I, ed. L. R. Fisher. AnOr 49 (Rome, 1972).

RSP II = *Ras Shamra Parallels*, vol. II, ed. L. R. Fisher. AnOr 50 (Rome, 1975).

RSV = *Revised Standard Version* (1946, 1952).

TEV = *Good News Bible*: *The Bible in Today's English Version*. American Bible Society (New York, 1976).

TM = Tell Mardikh.

Tromp, *Death and the Nether World* = N. Tromp, *Primitive Conceptions of Death and the Nether World in the Old Testament*. BibOr 21 (Rome, 1969).

UF = *Ugarit-Forschungen*. *Internationales Jahrbuch für die Altertumskunde Syrien-Palästinas* (Neukirchen-Vluyn).

Ug. = Ugaritic.

UT = C. H. Gordon, *Ugaritic Textbook*. AnOr 38 (Rome, 1965).

VT = *Vetus Testamentum* (Leiden).

VTSup = Vetus Testamentum, Supplements.

vol(s). = volume(s).

Vulg. = The Vulgate version.

ZAW = *Zeitschrift für die alttestamentliche Wissenschaft* (Berlin).

Introduction

Through the centuries commentators have echoed St. Jerome's characterization of the Hebrew Text of Job, " ut si velis anguillam aut merenulam strictis tenere manibus, quanto fortius presseris, tanto citius elabitur. " [1]   More recently, Professor F. M. Cross, Jr., of Harvard University claims that fifty percent of Job remains unintelligible, [2] while according to Fr. Mitchell Dahood, at least thirty percent of the verses are yet untranslated. [3]   Thus, light from any source which offers to elucidate especially the more important passages of the book should be welcome.

Chapters 29 – 31, called variously " Job's Final Summary of his Cause " (*NAB*), " Perorazione di Giobbe " (Fedrizzi), " Job's Final Survey of his case " (*NEB*), " Plaintes et apologie de Job " (*BJ²*), is one such passage. [4]   M. Gilbert places Job 29:12-17 and Job 31 among the important passages for the moral teaching of the Old Testament.   He cites, for example, *BJ²*'s note on chapter 31:

---

[1] " Incipit Prologus Sancti Hieronymi in Libro Iob, " *Biblia Sacra iuxta Vulgatam Versionem*, vol. I (2nd edition; ed. Bonifatio Fischer; Stuttgart: Würtembergische Bibelanstalt, 1975), p. 731.

[2] In a convocation address at Harvard University in 1958; quoted by M. J. Dahood, review of Jean Lévêque, *Job et son Dieu. Essai d'exégèse et de théologie biblique*, in *Bib* 52 (1971), p. 437.

[3] Dahood, ibid.; idem, " Northwest Semitic texts and textual criticism of the Hebrew Bible, " *Questions disputées d'Ancien Testament. Méthode et Théologie* (ed. C. Brekelmans; Bibliotheca Ephemeridum Theologicarum Lovaniensium 33; Gembloux/Louvain: Duculot et Leuven University Press, 1974), p. 19.

[4] But G. Fohrer prefers a title such as " Job's Speech of Challenge to God " for chaps. 29 – 31 rather than " Job's Concluding Speech ": " God alone can solve Job's problem, as Job had so often wished.   The speeches in Job 29 – 31 move toward the realization of this wish, which finally becomes a reality in the speech of God, although in a way different from that which Job expected "; cf. Georg Fohrer, " The Righteous Man in Job 31, " *Essays in Old Testament Ethics* (*J. Philip Hyatt, In Memoriam*; eds. James L. Crenshaw and John T. Willis; New York: KTAV, 1974), p. 6.

En cette protestation d'innocence, la morale de l'Ancient Testament atteint sa plus grande pureté, au point de préluder directement à la morale évangélique. [5]

G. Fohrer dwells at length on the ethical content of chapter 31 in his essay, " The Righteous Man in Job 31. " He remarks, for instance:

Also, the ethical view of Job 31 refers not only to the external behavior of man like the law, but to his internal intention, the sincerity of which is tested with a precise and infallible standard for religio-ethical motives....

In general, the refining and deepening of ethics, its application to the internal attitude and intention, and its inclination toward that which is fundamental become clear over and over again. [6]

Despite their importance for Old Testament study in general and for the Book of Job in particular, these chapters contain a number of recognized and unrecognized difficulties for translators and commentators. The present study proposes to use the comparative method of Northwest Semitic Philology to make these three chapters of Job more understandable. The Northwest Semitic approach, which depends on Eblaite, Ugaritic, and Phoenician for help in elucidating the text, [7] has proved itself a valuable tool in providing new insights

---

[5] Maurice Gilbert, " Comment lire les écrits sapientiaux de l'Ancien Testament, " *Morale et Ancien Testament* (eds. M. Gilbert, et al.; Lex Spiritus Vitae I; Louvain-la-Neuve: Centre Cerfaux-Lefort, 1976), p. 150. G. Fohrer, " The Righteous Man in Job 31, " p. 13 (quoting A. Weiser, *Das Buch Hiob* [1956]², p. 212), states: " Frequently scholars have called attention to the fact that Job 31 has refined and deepened Wisdom teaching, and have even supposed that it ' attains to the ethical loftiness of the Sermon on the Mount in certain places. ' "

[6] Fohrer, " The Righteous Man in Job 31, " p. 13-14. See also Michael Brennan Dick, " The Legal Metaphor in Job 31, " *CBQ* 41 (1979), p. 37-50; ibid., " Job 31: A Form-critical Study " (unpublished Ph. D. Dissertation, The Johns Hopkins University, 1977).

[7] Dahood in " Northwest Semitic texts and textual criticism of the Hebrew Bible, " p. 19, states: " ... it is the virtual equation of Ugaritic, Phoenician, and Hebrew that will give philologists a chance to reduce the thirty percent unintelligibility of, say Hosea or Job, to more modest proportions .... It seems to me, then, that we should stop producing Hebrew grammars and lexicons and undertake instead to write Northwest Semitic grammars and lexicons that

into and solutions for more difficult selections of Hebrew poetry. Examples of the use of this method have been published in the *Biblica et Orientalia* series of the Biblical Institute Press. Reviews of these works, though often cautious and sometimes critical, nevertheless welcome the insights they have provided. [8]

Marvin Pope's *Anchor Bible* commentary on Job has made extensive use of comparative material from the Ugaritic texts, [9] and the almost seventy page increase of the third edition (1973) over the first edition (1965) of his work consists largely of the results of research which follows this direction. [10] Of fundamental importance in this approach is Anton C. M. Blommerde's monograph, *Northwest Semitic Grammar and Job*. [11] In it, he gathers most of the work done on the Joban text until 1969, especially from the publications of Fr. Mitchell Dahood, and provides a valuable synthesis and bibliography in the section entitled, " Northwest Semitic Grammar and Hebrew. " [12] The

---

will include the grammatical phenomena of Ugaritic, Phoenician, and Hebrew, and give the meaning of the words as they occur in these three Canaanite dialects. "

[8] See, for example, F. I. Andersen's review of W. Kuhnigk, *Nordwestsemitische Studien zum Hoseabuch* (BibOr 27; 1974), in *Bib* 57 (1976), p. 573-575; A. A. Di Lella's review of T. Penar, *Northwest Semitic Philology and the Hebrew Fragments of Ben Sira* (BibOr 28; 1975), in *CBQ* 38 (1976), p. 584-586; D. R. Hillers' review of L. Viganò, *Nomi e titoli di YHWH alla luce del semitico del Nord-ovest* (BibOr 31; 1976), in *CBQ* 39 (1977), p. 576-577. Lester L. Grabbe's dissertation, *Comparative Philology and the Text of Job: A Study in Methodology* (Society of Biblical Literature Dissertation Series 34; Missoula, Mont.: Scholars Press, 1977), came to my attention in the final stages of the preparation of this present study. He treats at some length four passages which we also address (Job 29:18; 30:2,24; 31:39). We have been able only to refer briefly to his discussions in our footnotes. For a response to the methodological questions which he raises, see Dahood's article, " Northwest Semitic texts and textual criticism of the Hebrew Bible, "; Dahood's review of Grabbe's book in *Bib* 59 (1978), p. 429-532; and Gian Luigi Prato's review in *Gregorianum* 60 (1979), p. 173-175.

[9] M. H. Pope, *Job* (AB 15; 3rd edition; Garden City, N. Y.: Doubleday, 1973).

[10] Ibid., p. VII; Mitchell Dahood, S.J., with the collaboration of Tadeusz Penar, " Ugaritic–Hebrew Parallel Pairs, " chapter 2 of *Ras Shamra Parallels I* (ed. Loren Fisher; AnOr 48; Rome: Pontificium Institutum Biblicum, 1972), p. 81, n. 42.

[11] BibOr 22; Rome: Pontifical Biblical Institute, 1969.

[12] Pp. 3-35. Similar partial grammars which collect the results of philological studies of the Hebrew text using the Northwest Semitic approach include

present study builds on these two works, hand in hand with Dr. Walter
Michel's 1970 dissertation, *The Ugaritic Texts and the Mythological
Expressions in the Book of Job.* [13]   The latter offers helpful bibliography
and stimulating suggestions for the solution of many of the problem
verses in Job.

The Northwest Semitic approach has brought to light new elements of Hebrew lexicography, grammar, syntax, style, and mythological background (e.g., the broken construct chain, the break-up
of composite phrases, parallel word pairs, dative suffixes, divine epithets, chiasmus, merismus, delayed identification, etc.). [14]   The present
study collects what has been done thus far on chapters 29-31 using
this approach and suggests new translations for difficult verses. [15]
Reference will also be made to the recently discovered third millennium texts from Tell Mardikh/Ebla in northern Syria where this material touches these chapters from Job. [16]

Briefly, what follows in the present volume includes : (1) a new translation of and philological commentary on Job 29 – 31 ; (2) discussion
of other passages in the Book of Job when a point being made in reference to chapters 29 – 31 is pertinent elsewhere in Job ; (3) a short
summary of the conclusions and possible implications of this study for
the exegesis and understanding of Job's Apology and the Book of
Job as a whole ; (4) and three " Appendixes " (" A Grammar of Job
29 – 31 " ; " Parallel Word Pairs " ; and " Job 29 – 31 and Tell Mar-
dikh/Ebla ") which assemble some of the more pertinent data uncovered in this study.

Mitchell Dahood, S.J., and Tadeusz Penar, " The Grammar of the Psalter, "
in M. Dahood, *Psalms III* (AB 17A ; Garden City, N.Y. : Doubleday, 1970) ;
W. H. Irwin, *Isaiah* 28 – 33 : *Translation with Philological Notes* (BibOr 30 ;
Rome : Biblical Institute Press, 1977), Appendix I, " A Grammar of Isaiah 28-
33 " (p. 163-177).

[13] For the University of Wisconsin, 1970 ; available through Xerox University Microfilms, 300 North Zeeb Road, Ann Arbor, Michigan 48106.

[14] See below " Appendix I : A Grammar of Job 29 – 31 " for a summary
of the elements which this present study has assembled.

[15] The translation of Job 29 – 31 offered herein is largely that of the present
writer. In some cases, the versions of Pope, *Job*[3], and the *RSV* have been
accepted. The following verses reproduce Pope's translation : Job 29 : 2a,3b,
12a ; 30 : 1a,7a,10b,16b,23,25,30b,31 ; 31 : 2,8,9a,12a,20,21a,30b,32,35b,36b,39a.
The following verses repeat the *RSV* : Job 29 : 8a,10a ; 30 : 7a,10a ; 31 : 4.

[16] See below " Appendix III : Job 29 – 31 and Tell Mardikh/Ebla. "

Translation and Commentary on Job 29

Translation of Job 29

1. And Job again took up his poem and said:

2. O that I were as in months past,
       as in the days when God protected me;
3. When he made his lamp shine above my head,
       by his light I walked through darkness.

4. As I was in the days of my prime,
       when God Most High established my family;
5. When the Almighty was still with me,
       my youngsters round about me;
6. When my feet were bathed with cream and balsam,
       when rivers of oil flowed over my legs.

7. When I went storming from the city,
       in the broad place set up my seat,
8. The young men saw me and withdrew,
       while the elders began to stand up;
9. Princes refrained from words
       and put their hand on their mouth;
10. The nobles grew still of voice,
       and their tongue cleaved to their palate.

11. When ear heard me, it blessed me;
       when eye saw me, it testified for me.
12. For I rescued the poor who cried
       and the orphan who had no deliverer.
13. The blessing of him about to perish entered
           my presence,
       and the widow's heart I made joyful.
14. I put on righteousness and it adorned me;
       my robe and my tartan was my justice.

15. Eyes was I to the blind,
    and feet to the lame was I;
16. A father I was to the needy,
    and the cause of one I did not know I
    examined for him;
17. And I broke the jaws of the wicked,
    and from his teeth I cast his prey.

18. And I thought, " Though I perish like its nest,
    I shall multiply my days like the phoenix,
19. My root open to the waters
    and the dew lodging in my branches,
20. My liver fresh within me,
    and my bow renewed in my hand. "

21. To me they listened and waited,
    and kept silent for my counsel.
22. After my speech they did not reply,
    and my word dripped upon them.
23. They waited for it as for the rain,
    and opened their mouth as for the spring rain.

24. When I smiled on them, powerful, they took courage,
    and in the light from my face they did not grow sad.
25. I convoked their assembly and presided as leader,
    and I tented as a king among his troops,
    as a happy man who consoles the grieving.

Commentary on Job 29

Job 29 : 1-3

And Job again took up his poem and said:

O that I were as in months past,
    as in the days when God protected me;
When he made his lamp shine above my head,
    by his light I walked through darkness.

Job 29 : 1

Job. As Marvin Pope notes:

> The name *Ayyāb* > *'Iyyôb̲* is thus well attested as a fairly common name among western Semites in the second millennium B. C. The name may have been chosen for the hero of the story simply because it was an ordinary name. It may be, however, that some ancient worthy bearing that name actually experienced reversals of fortune and became the model of the righteous sufferer. The mention of Job (Ezek xiv 14,20) along with Noah and (the Ugaritic hero) Danel suggests a hero of great antiquity. [17]

Among others, a palace functionary at Ugarit bore the name (*ayab*, son of *gm-*) [18] and the prince of Ashtaroth (*'Ayyāb*) in Bashan around the year 1350 B.C. [19]

again. In his article, " Orthographic Peculiarities in the Book of Job, " David Noel Freedman records *wayyōsep* here as one of the unusual number of defective spellings in the Book of Job. [20] In his concluding remarks he writes,

> The chief implication of the orthographic data with respect to the composition of Job is that the provenance of the book is northern and its date early. Since the Canaanite/Phoenician affinities in poetic style, mythological allusions, vocabulary and syntax have been increasingly recognized by scholars, we may regard the evidence of the orthography as substantiating or corroborating these views. All the evidence fits well with the proposal that Job was a product of the (North) Israelite diaspora some time in the seventh or early sixth century B.C. [21]

---

[17] Pope, *Job³*, p. 6.

[18] Ibid.; cf. *UT* 1035 III : 10, and " *ayab*, owner of a wife (*b'l aṭt*) " in 1077 : 4.

[19] Pope, *Job³*, p. 5 ; J. A. Knudtzon, *Die El-Amarna-Tafeln mit Einleitung und Erläuterungen* (Vorderasiatische Bibliothek 2 ; Leipzig : Hinrich, 1907-1915), p. 816-817 (§ 256).

[20] *Eretz-Israel* 9 (William Foxwell Albright Volume, 1969), p. 37.

[21] Ibid., p. 43. On the date of Job in the seventh or early sixth century B.C., see also Pope, *Job³*. p. xxxii-xl, especially p. xl, " The seventh century B.C. seems the best guess for the date of the Dialogue " ; the bibliography cited

Much of the present study is directed toward uncovering further examples of the " Canaanite/Phoenician affinities in poetic style, mythological allusions, vocabulary and syntax " mentioned by Prof. Freedman.

took up ... and said. Compare the Ugaritic formula *yšu gh yṣḥ* " he lifted up his voice and cried out " which occurs almost forty times in the extant Ugaritic literature. [22]   On the substantive *maśśā᾽* " oracle, utterance " rather than " burden, " see K. Cathcart's discussion of *maśśā᾽ nînĕwēh* " an oracle concerning Nineveh " (Nah 1 : 1). [23]

his poem. Following Pope, who notes on the same opening formula in Job 27 : 1,

> Since parallelism is the very heart of ancient Near Eastern poetics, and every comparison or contrast involves a juxtaposition, the term *māšāl* is about as near as we come ... to the range of meaning carried by our word " poem. " [24]

Job 29 : 2

O that I were. mî-yittĕnēnî, literally, " who would give me?, " the same phrase found again in 31 : 35.   A number of words here in 29 : 1-5 are echoed in the closing verses of chapter 31, and thus may form an inclusion: *'iyyôb* " Job " (29 : 1, 31 : 40), *mî-yittĕnēnî* " who would give me? " (29 : 2, 31 : 35 = *mî yitten-lî*), and the composite divine title *'ēlî* (MT *'ălê*) " Most High " ... *šadday* " Shaddai " (29 : 4-5, 31 : 35 = *śim 'ēlî*, MT *šōmēa' lî* " let the Most High pay attention "... *šadday ya'ănēnî* " let Shaddai answer me ").
   The balance of sound and function of the verbs at the beginning and end here in v 2 (*yittĕnēnî*//*yišmĕrēnî*) with the parallel pair *kĕyarḥē*//

by M. Dahood, *Bib* 52 (1971), p. 438; Francis I. Andersen, *Job: An Introduction and Commentary* (Tyndale Old Testament Commentaries; Downers Grove, Ill.: Inter-Varsity Press, 1976), p. 62-64; Frank Moore Cross, *Canaanite Myth and Hebrew Epic: Essays in the History of the Religion of Israel* (Cambridge: Harvard University, 1973), p. 344, n. 1; J. C. L. Gibson, " Eliphaz the Temanite: Portrait of a Hebrew Philosopher, " *Scottish Journal of Theology* 28 (1975), p. 260.

   [22] Richard E. Whitaker, *A Concordance of the Ugaritic Literature* (Cambridge: Harvard University, 1972), p. 458-459.

   [23] Kevin Cathcart, *Nahum in the Light of Northwest Semitic* (BibOr 26; Rome: Biblical Institute Press, 1973), p. 36-37.

   [24] Pope, *Job³*, p. 190.

kîmê in the center provides a good example of the chiastic word pattern characteristic of so many verses of Job. [25]

months ... days. *RSP* I, II 258 records Job 29:2 as an example of the Ugaritic-Hebrew parallel pair *yrḥ* " months " // *ym* " days "; compare *UT* 49 V : 7-8, *lymm lyrḥm lyrḥm lšnt* " from days to months, from months to years. " Y. Avishur notes a similar collocation in a Phoenician text, *KAI* 43 : 10-12 (*ym md ym ... yrḥ md yrḥ* ; N.B. also *kqdm* " as in olden times " = *kĕyarḥê-qedem* " as in months past ") :

> *lmlqrt ʻl ḥyy wʻl ḥy zrʻy ym md ym wlṣmḥ ṣdq*
> *-lʼ-t- wlʼdmy (bḥd)šm wbksʼm yrḥ md yrḥ ʻd ʻlm*
> *kqdm*

> To Melqart for my life and for the life of my descendants day by day; and for the rightful shoot and for his wife and for his blood on the new moons and on the full moons month by month, forever, as in olden times. [26]

Finally, T. Penar refers to the parallelism *dwr* " generations " // *ywm* " days " in Sir 44 : 7, *šnt* " years " // *yrḥm* " months " in 2 Aqht VI : 28-29, and *yrḥy* " months " // *ymy* " days " here in Job 29:2 as " anticlimactic ": " the latter term, present in the second colon comprises a shorter period of time. " [27]

O that I were as ... as. These three words (*mî yittĕnēnî kĕ ... kĕ*) have been identified in the tablets written in paleo-Canaanite at Tell Mardikh (ancient Ebla). *w/ytn* forms part of a personal name, [28] while *mî + kĕ* appears in the PN *mi-kà-ia* " Who is like YA? " [29]

---

[25] Cf., M. J. Dahood, " Chiasmus in Job : A Text-Critical and Philological Criterion, " *A Light Unto My Path : Old Testament Studies in Honor of Jacob M. Myers* (eds. H. N. Bream, et al.; Philadelphia : Temple University, 1974), p. 119-130.

[26] H. Donner – W. Röllig, *Kanaanäische und aramäische Inschriften* (Wiesbaden : Harrassowitz, 1962, 1964), vol. I, p. 10, vol. II, p. 60-61; Y. Avishur, " Word Pairs Common to Phoenician and Biblical Hebrew, " *UF* 7 (1975), p. 34-35.

[27] Tadeusz Penar, *Northwest Semitic Philology and the Hebrew Fragments of Ben Sira* (BibOr 28; Rome : Biblical Institute Press, 1975), p. 74.

[28] G. Pettinato, " Testi cuneiformi del 3. millennio in paleocananeo, " *Or* 44 (1975), p. 372 (n. 96).

[29] Ibid., p. 372 (n. 89).

as in the days. Note the chiastic word pattern A : B : : B : A in 29 : 2-4, *kîmê 'ĕlôah : nērô : : 'ôrô : bîmê ... 'ĕlôah.* [30] There are a number of other repetitions and word-plays in vv 2-6: *'ălê* " upon " (v 3)/ *'ēlî* " Most High " (v 4 ; MT *'ălê*) ; *'ēlek* " I walked " (v 3)/*hălîkay* " my feet " (v 6) ; *'immādî* " with me " (v 5)/*'ammūday* " my legs " (v 6 ; MT *'immādî*).

Job 29 : 3

When he made his lamp shine. Reading *bahillô*, the yiphil infinitive construct of *hll*, for MT *bĕhillô*. The waw suffix in *bhlw* has created difficulty for translators in the past. Blommerde retains the MT vocalization *bĕhillô* and considers the waw a prospective suffix referring to the following word *nērô* : *bĕhillô nērô 'ălê rō'šî*, literally, " When it began to shine, (i.e.) his lamp, over my head. " [31] *BHK*[3] and *BHS*, following the Targum version, revocalize MT *bĕhillô* to *bahillô*, a contraction of the hiphil construct infinitive phrase *bahăhillô* in which the waw suffix serves as subject, " when *he* made (his lamp) shine. " *bahillô* may indeed be the correct vocalization; however, there is no need to see here a contraction of the hiphil causative form. Rather, the increasing number of Phoenician yiphil causatives identified in Hebrew counsels an openness to the possibility that *bhlw* (vocalized *bahillô*) is a yiphil infinitive phrase, " when he made his lamp shine. " [32] As S. Segert has noted, in a case such as this the yodh ordinarily would not appear in the orthography (*byhlw* > *bhlw*) : " ... in most infinitives preceded by a one-consonantal preposition no marker of the Yiphil is present. The causative was expressed by the vocalization : *lšbt* ' to make quiet ' (cf. Amos 8 : 4 *lašbît* and *lšḥyt* 1QpH 4 : 13). " [33]

his ιamp ... by this ιight. Mention of *yrḥ* (" month "/" moon ") in v 2a suggests that *nērô* " his lamp " in v 3a is the moon rather than the sun : it is by the light (*ιĕ'ôrô*) of the moon that Job can walk through the darkness without stumbling or injuring himself (v 3b).

[30] Cf., A. R. Ceresko, " The Chiastic Word Pattern in Hebrew, " *CBQ* 38 (1976), p. 303-311.

[31] Blommerde, *NSGJ*, p. 108-109.

[32] See, for example, M. Dahood, " Yiphil Imperative *yaṭṭī* in Isaiah 54,2, " *Or* 46 (1977), p. 383-384 ; idem, " Phoenician-Punic Philology, " *Or* 46 (1977), p. 467-468.

[33] S. Segert, *A Grammar of Phoenician and Punic* (Munich : C. H. Beck, 1976), p. 142 (par. 54. 372. 1).

See the fuller discussion of vv 2-3 below under Job 31:26 where the three verses are studied together because of their similar *Wortfeld* (*yārēaḥ, hālal, 'ôr, hālak*).

shine ... walked. This same word pair, *bahillô* (MT *bĕhillô*) " when it shone "//*l'ēlek* " I walked, " occurs again in Job 31:26, *yāhēl* " it brightened "//*hōlēk* " waning. " Although the poet uses the same word pair in both verses, they must be translated differently in order to bring out the nuance of meaning demanded by the context. *hlk* in 29:3, for example, means simply " to walk, to go, " while the stricter parallelism with *hll* " to shine, brighten " (of the moon) in 31:26 calls for the translation " to wane " in order to make clear the merismus (*hll* " to wax "//*hlk* " to wane "). The use therefore of a parallel word pair by the poet does not always imply similarity of context with other passages in which the same word pair occurs. Rather, the use of word pairs imposed strictures on the poet that challenged his grasp of the nuances and his skill in utilizing to the fullest the possibilities inherent in the language. Another example occurs with *ptḥ*//*lyn* in 29:19 and 31:32. The contexts are quite different: roots " opened out " (*pātûaḥ*) toward water and Job " opening " (*'eptāḥ*) his door to the wayfarer, yet the poet employs the same word pair.

light. This root appears in the texts from Tell Mardikh as an element (*ar*) in the personal name *ši-piš-ar* " Shine, O Sun. " [34]

Job 29 : 4-6

> As I was in the days of my prime,
>   when God Most High established my family;
> When the Almighty was still with me,
>   my youngsters round about me;
> When my feet were bathed with cream and balsam,
>   when rivers of oil flowed over my legs.

---

[34] TM. 75. G. 336 (verso) VI : 5 ; cf. G. Pettinato – P. Matthiae, " Aspetti amministrativi e topografici di Ebla nel III millennio av. Cr., " *RSO* 50 (1976), p. 7.

Job 29 : 4

my prime. Following Blommerde; [35] see also Pope's discussion [36] and *ḥōrep* in the new Baumgartner *Lexikon.* [37]   C. H. Gordon relates Ugaritic *ḫprt* " ewes, yearlings " to Hebrew *ḥōrep.* [38]

God Most High. Blommerde revocalizes *'ly* (MT *'ălê* " upon ") to the divine name *'ēlî* and thus uncovers the composite divine name *'ēlî 'ĕlôah* " God Most High. " [39] Pope also reads the divine title *'ēlî* here, but deletes *'ĕlôah* " as a variant rather than a compound. " [40] For further discussion of *'ēlî* " Most High, " see below under Job 31 : 34 and Lorenzo Viganò's chapter, " YHWH l'Altissimo: *yhwh 'l/'ly.* " [41]

established. BHS continues the suggestion of *BHK³* to emend *bĕsôd* to *bĕsôk.* [42] No such emendation is needed if *bswd* is revocalized to *bisôd*, the preposition *bĕ* contracted with the infinitive *yĕsôd* from *yāsad* " to found, establish. " [43] Further, the change from *bĕsôd* to *bĕsôk* would destroy the rhyme between *bĕsôd* in v 4 and *bĕ'ôd* in v 5. [44] Compare also Sir 3 : 9, *brkt 'b tysd šrš* " A father's blessing establishes offspring. " [45]

Job 29 : 6

my feet. *hālîk* is " foot " rather than " steps. " *hălîkay* is thus the dual, " my (two) feet. " [46]

---

[35] *NSGJ*, p. 109.

[36] *Job³*, p. 208-209. The statement of Pope at the top of p. 209, " as applied in Akkadian to green olives, " should be corrected to read, " as applied in Ugaritic to green olives. " He is referring to *UT* 601: (rev) 6, *zt ḫrpnt* " green olives. "

[37] Walter Baumgartner, *Hebräisches und aramäisches Lexikon zum Alten Testament*, vol. I (3rd edition ; Leiden : Brill, 1967), p. 342a.

[38] C. H. Gordon, *Ugaritic Textbook* (AnOr 38 ; Rome : Pontificium Institutum Biblicum, 1965), Glossary 992.

[39] *NSGJ*, p. 109.

[40] *Job³*, p. 209.

[41] *Nomi e titoli di YHWH*, p. 34-62 ; on Job 29 : 4, see ibid., p. 53-54.

[42] See also *Textual Notes on the New American Bible* (eds. Louis Hartman and Myles Bourke ; Paterson : St. Anthony Guild, 1970), p. 377 ; L. H. Brockington, *The Hebrew Text of the Old Testament : The Readings Adopted by the Translators of the New English Bible* (Oxford and Cambridge : University Press, 1973), p. 112.

[43] Blommerde, *NSGJ*, p. 109 ; Pope, *Job³*, p. 209.

[44] M. J. Dahood, review of *The New English Bible*, *Bib* 52 (1971), p. 119-120.

[45] Penar, *The Hebrew Fragments of Ben Sira*, p. 5.

were bathed ... flowed. Dahood reads,
    birḫōṣ hălîkay bĕḥēmâ wĕṣôrî
    ṣôq (MT *wĕṣûr yāṣûq*) *'ămmūday* (MT *'immādî*)
    palgê-šāmen

When my feet were bathed with cream and balsam,
    when rivers of oil flowed over my legs. ⁴⁷

Compare *UT* 'nt II : 31-32 (also *yṣq* // *rḥṣ*),
    yṣq šmn šlm bṣ'
    trḥṣ ydh btlt 'nt

Oil of peace was poured from the bowl,
The Virgin Anath washed her hands. ⁴⁸

The Ugaritic–Hebrew parallel pair *yṣq* " to pour " // *rḥṣ* " to wash "
is found only here in the Hebrew Bible, as also the pair *šmn* " oil " //
ẓrw " balsam " (*wĕṣôrî*, MT *wĕṣûr* // *šāmen*). ⁴⁹ The preposition *bĕ*
of *birḫōṣ* serves double duty in extending its force to the second colon
to govern also the construct infinitive *ṣôq* from *yṣq* " to pour, flow. " ⁵⁰

cream ... oil. This same parallelism occurs in Ps 55 : 22 (*mēḥem'ōt*
" than cream " // *miššemen* " than oil "), " Smoother than cream was
his speech ... His words were softer than oil. " ⁵¹

balsam ... oil. This is the only Hebrew occurrence of the Ugaritic–
Hebrew parallel pair *šmn* // *ẓrw*. ⁵²

---

⁴⁶ M. J. Dahood, " Hebrew–Ugaritic Lexicography II, " *Bib* 45 (1964),
p. 404. See also *'aššūrî* " my foot " below in Job 31 : 7.

⁴⁷ M. J. Dahood, *Ugaritic–Hebrew Philology* (BibOr 17 ; Rome : Pontificium Institutum Biblicum, 1965), p. 60.

⁴⁸ M. J. Dahood, " Some Rare Parallel Word Pairs in Job and in Ugaritic, "
The Word in the World : Essays in Honor of Frederick L. Moriarty, S.J. (eds.
R. J. Clifford and G. W. MacRae ; Cambridge : Weston College, 1973), p. 26.

⁴⁹ Cf., *RSP* I, II, 253 and 561.

⁵⁰ Dahood, *UHP*, p. 60 ; cf. also Blommerde, *NSGJ*, p. 109. On double-
duty prepositions in general see Blommerde, *NSGJ*, p. 25-26 ; Dahood, *Psalms
III*, p. 435-437.

⁵¹ Cf., M. J. Dahood, *Psalms II* (AB 16, 2nd edition ; Garden City, N.Y. :
Doubleday, 1973), 2nd Note on Ps 55 : 22.

⁵² *RSP* I, II, 561.

rivers of oil. Compare *pĕlaggôt nhry* (MT *naḥărê*) " streams of oil " (//*dĕbaš wĕḥem'â* " honey and cream ") in Job 20 : 17. [53]

my legs. In " Hebrew–Ugaritic Lexicography VII, " [54] Dahood discusses the metaphorical use of *'ammūd* " pillar " to designate human legs here (*'ammūday*, MT *'immādî*) and in Job 23 : 10 :

> *kî yāda' derek 'ammūday* (MT *'immādî*)
> *bĕḥānanî kazzāhāb 'ēṣē'*

> Surely he knows the tread of my feet ;
> Should he test me, I would shine like gold.

Job 29 : 7-10

> When I went storming from the city,
>   in the broad place set up my seat,
> The young men saw me and withdrew,
>   while the elders began to stand up ;
> Princes refrained from words
>   and put their hand on their mouth ;
> The nobles grew still of voice,
>   and their tongues cleaved to their palates.

Job 29 : 7

I went. The root *yṣ'* forms part of the personal name, *Ì-ṣa-Yà* " Ya has gone forth, " attested in the third millennium texts found at Tell Mardikh. [55]

storming. Though the general sense of the first colon is clear, *ša'ar* presents a problem, as the LXX testifies by reading instead *šaḥar* " (at) dawn, " and the Qumran Targum by double-translating *š'r* : (*b*)*ṣpryn btr'y qry* " in the mornings at the gates of the city. " [56]   *RSV*

---

[53] M. J. Dahood, " The Phoenician Contribution to Biblical Wisdom Literature, " *The Role of the Phoenicians in the Interaction of Mediterranean Civilization* (ed. W. A. Ward ; Beirut : American University of Beirut, 1968), p. 137-138.

[54] *Bib* 50 (1969), p. 350.

[55] Giovanni Pettinato, " The Royal Archives of Tell Mardikh-Ebla, " *BA* 39 (1976), p. 50.

[56] Michael Sokoloff, *The Targum to Job from Qumran Cave XI* (Ramat-Gan, Israel : Bar-Ilan University, 1974), p. 54-55, 121. The most recent edition of the Qumran Targum to Job is found in *Aramaic Texts from Qumran*, vol. I

and *NAB*'s " to the gate of the city " should be, strictly speaking,
in Hebrew *'ălê-šě'ar-qāret*. But one goes out *from* the city *through*
the gates.

Appealing to the growing appreciation of the Joban poet's use of
the rhetorical figure of merismus, one might revocalize MT *ša'ar* to
šō'ēr, the qal participle of *šā'ar* " to storm, rage. " The two cola of
v 7 then serve to contrast the extremes of Job's behavior in public
which never ceased to inspire the admiration and awe of his fellow
citizens, from his enthusiasm in hurrying out to work to his calm and
serenity when weighty matters were being considered in the assembly.
2 Kgs 6:11 and Isa 54:11 use *š'r/s'r* of someone storm-tossed or
troubled, but the most apt parallel for Job 29:7 is Dan 11:40, " The
king of the north shall storm in (*wěyiśtā'ēr*) upon him with chariots
and horsemen and many ships. "

from the city. Understanding *'ălê* with the sense of " from " ;[57] see
below on Job 30:2 and 4. Compare *KAI* 1:2, *wnḫt tbrḥ 'l gbl* " and
may tranquillity flee from Byblos. " Note the Ugaritic–Phoenician
form of the word for " city " (*qrt*), found in Hebrew only here and
in Prov 8:3; 9:3,14; 11:11.[58]

city ... seat. This same parallelism (*qāret//môšābî*) recurs in *UT* 51
VIII:11-13 (// 67 II:15-16) *qrth* " his city "//*ṯbth* " his residence. "

my seat. *môšāb* in Hebrew as in Ugaritic can mean " seat, throne " as
well as " dwelling "; e.g., *UT* 126 V:24, *ṯb bny lm ṯb(t)km lkḫṯ zblk(m)*
" Be seated, my sons, upon your seats, upon your princely thrones."[59]

in the broad place. The editors of *Textes ougaritiques*[60] compare Job
29:7 to *UT* 2 Aqht V:6-8:

(eds. B. Jongeling, C. J. Labuschagne, A. S. van der Woude; Leiden: Brill,
1976), p. 1-74.
   [57] M. J. Dahood, " Northwest Semitic Philology and Job, " *The Bible in
Current Catholic Thought : Gruenthaner Memorial Volume* (ed. J. L. McKenzie ;
St. Mary's Theology Studies 1 ; New York: Herder and Herder, 1962), p. 68 ;
Pope, *Job³*, p. 210.
   [58] Dahood, " Some Rare Parallel Word Pairs in Job and Ugaritic, " p. 26 ;
Pio Fedrizzi, *Giobbe* (La Sacra Bibbia, ed. S. Garofalo ; Torino–Roma : Marietti,
1972), p. 203.
   [59] Dahood, *UHP*, p. 63.
   [60] A. Caquot, M. Sznycer, A. Herdner, *Textes ougaritiques, Tome I : Mythes
et légendes* (Littératures anciennes du Proche-Orient 7 ; Paris : Cerf, 1974),
p. 427 (n. *s*).

yṯb bap ṯġr
tḥt adrm dbgrn
ydn dn almnt
yṯpṭ ṯpṭ ytm

He sits at the opening of the gate,
Among the nobles who are on the threshing floor.
He judges the case of the widow,
He adjudicates the cause of the orphan. [61]

Dahood suggests that *rĕḥôb* " broad place " is a synonym for *gōren*
" threshing floor, " the open place outside the city gate where the
(royal) court was held and business transacted. [62]

Job 29 : 8

began to stand up. Thus Dahood, who considers *qûm* here as an auxiliary verb denoting inchoate action. [63]   See also below under Job
30 : 28.   The second edition of the *Bible de Jérusalem* (1974) reflects
this function of *qûm.*   Compare the earlier edition's, " et les vieillards
restaient debout, " with *BJ²*'s " les vieillards se mettaient debout. "

Job 29 : 10

The nobles grew still of voice.   Fohrer explains the plural form of *neḥbā'û*
(with a singular subject, *qôl*) as plural by attraction to *nĕgîdîm.* [64]
The analysis here recognizes *nĕgîdîm* as the subject of *neḥbā'û* and
parses *qôl* as an adverbial accusative of specification: literally, " As
to (their) voice, the nobles were silent/hid themselves. " Compare
Job 22 : 9,

   'almānôt šillaḥtā rêqām
   ûzĕrō'ôt yĕtōmîm yidkā'û (MT *yĕdukkā'*)

---

[61] Compare also *yātôm* " orphan, " *'almānâ* " widow, " and *mišpāṭî* " my
justice " of Job 29 : 12-14.
[62] Dahood, " Northwest Semitic Philology and Job, " p. 68 ; Pope, *Job³*,
p. 209-210.
[63] Dahood, ibid. p. 68-69.
[64] Georg Fohrer, *Das Buch Hiob* (Kommentar zum Alten Testament 16 ;
Gütersloh : G. Mohn, 1963), p. 402.   See also Franz Delitzsch, *Das Buch Iob*
(Biblischer Commentar über das Alte Testament IV/2 ; 2nd edition ; Leipzig :
Dörffling und Francke, 1876), p. 378 ; E. Dhorme, *Le Livre de Job* (Paris :
Lecoffre, 1926), p. 383 ; Fedrizzi, *Giobbe*, p. 203.

You have sent away the widows empty-handed
and the arms of the orphans are empty.

(Lit., " as to their hands the orphans are clean/empty "). [65] The
Vulgate similarly treats *něgîdîm* as the subject of *neḥbā'û*: *vocem suam
cohibebant duces.*

Job 29 : 11-14

When ear heard me, it blessed me;
　　when eye saw me, it testified for me.
For I rescued the poor who cried
　　and the orphan who had no deliverer.
The blessing of him about to perish entered my presence
　　and the widow's heart I made joyful.
I put on righteousness and it adorned me;
　　my robe and my tartan was my justice.

This strophe, vv 11-14, recalls Ps 72 which also lists some of the
duties expected of a ruler: N.B., the parallel pair *'šr*//*brk* in Ps 72 : 17
(Job 29 : 11 *wattě'aššěrēnî*, 13 *birkat*); Ps 72 : 12, " If he rescues the
needy crying for aid, and the oppressed who has no helper " //Job
29 : 12 ; the parallel pair *mšpṭ*//*ṣdq* in Ps 72 : 1-2 (*mišpāṭêkā : wěṣidqā-
těkā* :: *běṣedeq : běmišpāṭ*) and Job 29 : 14 (*ṣedeq*//*mišpāṭî*).

Job 29 : 11

ear heard. RSP I,II,565 records this collocation of *'zn* + *šm'* as an
example of the Ugaritic–Hebrew parallel pair *šm' ... udn.* The root
šm' appears in the texts from Tell Mardikh as an element in the personal name *śi-ma-^dgu₅-ra* " Hear O Mountain. " [66]

ear ... eye. This same parallelism recurs in Job 13 : 1, 28 : 21-22,
and 42 : 5.
　　'ōzen and *'ayin* are just two of an entire elenchus of parts of the
body named in vv 9-17: *kap* " palm " and *peh* " mouth " (v 9) ; *qôl*
" voice ", *lašôn* " tongue, " *ḥēk* " palate " (v 10) ; *'ōzen* " ear " and
'ayin " eye " (v 11) ; *'onî* " poor " (v 12 ; paronomasia with *'ayin*
in v 11b) ; *birkâ* " blessing " (N.B. *berek* " knee ") and *lēb* (v 13) ;

---

[65] Cf., Blommerde, *NSGJ*, p. 97.
[66] TM. 75. G. 336 (verso) II : 3 ; cf. Pettinato–Matthiae, *RSO* 50 (1976), p. 6.

'ênayim " eyes " and raglayim " feet " (v 15); mĕtallĕ'ôt " jawbone "
and šēn " tooth " (v 17). Further examples in chapter 29 include
hālîk " foot " and 'ammūd (MT 'immād) " leg " in v 6, yād " hand "
in v 20, peh " mouth " in v 23, and pāneh " face " in v 24. The entire
list of 20 (including repetitions) begins and ends with rō'š " head "
in vv 3 and 25. Dahood has noted a similar proliferation of parts
of the body as an element of style in Ps 110, [67] and W. Irwin remarks
that vv 27-28 of Isa 30 " read like an anatomy book: 'p, kbd, śph,
lšwn, rwḥ, ṣw'r, lḥy. " [68]

Ps 121 offers another example of this poetic technique of unifying
a strophe or chapter by enumerating parts of the body. In this psalm,
each of the four strophes (vv 1-2, 3-4, 5-6, 7-8; cf. NAB, RSV, Chicago Bible, BJ²) mentions a different member: v 1 'ênay " my eyes, "
v 3 raglekā " your feet, " v 5 yad yĕmînekā " your right hand, " and
v 7 napšekā " your soul (throat). "

when ear heard me ... when eye saw me. Blommerde understands the
suffixes of tĕ'aššĕrēnî and wattĕ'îdēnî as doing double duty also for
šāmĕ'â and rā'ătâ respectively. [69]

Job 29 : 12

I rescued ... deliverer. B. Baisas has demonstrated that 'zr (= Ugar.
'ḏr) sometimes has the nuance " to deliver, to save. " The parallelism
of 'ōzēr with mlṭ " to rescue " here has led him to propose Job 29 : 12
as a possible example. [70] For further discussion, see below under
Job 31 : 21.

the orphan. Much of the vocabulary of Job 29 : 12-17 is repeated in
31 : 16-22: ytm " orphan " (29 : 12, 31 : 17,21), 'zr " rescue " (29 :
12, 31 : 21), brk " blessing " (29 : 13, 31 : 20), 'bd " perish " (29 : 13,
31 : 19), 'lmnh " widow " (29 : 13, 31 : 16), lbš " clothe " (29 : 14, 31 : 19),
'yn " eye " (29 : 15, 31 : 16), 'b " father " (29 : 16, 31 : 18), 'bywn " poor "
(29 : 16, 31 : 19), šbr " break " (29 : 17, 31 : 22).

who had no deliverer. Blommerde recognizes the waw in wĕlō'-'ōzēr
lô as a waw explicativum functioning as a relative pronoun. [71] To

---

[67] Psalms III, p. 113.
[68] Irwin, Isaiah 28 – 33, p. 97.
[69] NSGJ, p. 110.
[70] B. Q. Biasas, " Ugaritic 'ḏr and Hebrew 'zr I," UF 5 (1973), p. 51 (n. 97).
[71] NSGJ, p. 110.

Blommerde's discussion and bibliography may now be added *RSP* II,I,3 (on Job 22 : 29) and Dahood. [72]

Job 29 : 13

entered my presence. Pope remarks on this verse, " The preposition *'al* often has this sense (' before, in the presence of ') with verbs meaning ' arrive, ' ' enter, ' or the like. " [73]   Dahood cites *UT* 'nt I : 20f. (//2 Aqht VI : 31), *yšr ġzr ṭb ql 'l b'l bṣrrt ṣpn* " The sweet-voiced youth sings in the presence of Baal in the recesses of Saphon. " [74]   Fedrizzi also accepts the meaning of *'al* here as " before, in the presence of. " [75]

Job 29 : 14

I put on ... it adorned. To the instances of the Ugaritic–Hebrew parallel pair *lbš*//*lbš* listed in *RSP* I,II,331, add Job 29 : 14 (*lābaštî*// *wayĕlabbĕšēnî*, MT *wayyilbāšēnî*) and *UT* 75 II : 47 (*lbš*//*lpš*).

Expressions similar to v 14 here occur in Ps 109 : 18, *wayyilbaš qĕlālâ kĕmaddô* " He clothed himself with cursing as his cloak, " and *UT* 75 II : 47-48, *km lpš dm a(ḫḫ) km all dm aryh* " Like clothing was the abuse of his brothers, like vesture the abuse of his kinsmen. " [76]

it adorned me. Of the modern English versions, Pope's is the closest to the sense of the MT, " I was clothed with righteousness and it with me " ; compare Judg 6 : 34, *wĕrûaḥ yhwh lābĕšâ 'et gid'ôn* " The spirit of Yahweh clothed itself with Gideon. "   Another possibility, suggested by P. Joüon and adopted here, [77] is to revocalize *wayyilbāšēnî* to piel *wayĕlabbĕšēnî* with the meaning " to adorn " ; cf. pual *mĕlūbbāšîm* " arrayed " in 1 Kgs 22 : 10, " (they) were sitting on their thrones arrayed in their robes (*mĕlūbbāšîm bĕgādîm*). "   The use of the same

---

[72] " Northwest Semitic texts and textual criticism of the Hebrew Bible " (on Job 3 : 23), p. 30. See further, Dahood, *Psalms II*[2], 2nd and 3rd Notes on Ps 69 : 36, 3rd and 4th Notes on Ps 72 : 12 ; idem, *Psalms III*, 2nd Note on Ps 107 : 25 and " Grammar of the Psalter, " p. 402.

[73] *Job*[3], p. 212.

[74] " Northwest Semitic Philology and Job," p. 69-70; M. J. Dahood, " Phoenician Elements in Isaiah 52 : 13 – 53 : 12, " *Near Eastern Studies in Honor of William Foxwell Albright* (ed. H. Goedicke ; Baltimore/London : Johns Hopkins, 1971), p. 65-66 (on Isa 52 : 12, 53 : 1). See also Blommerde, *NSGJ*, p. 23, 111.

[75] *Giobbe*, p. 205.

[76] Cf., Dahood, *Psalms III*, 1st Note on Ps 109 : 18.

[77] " Notes philologiques sur le texte hébreu de Job 1, 5 ; 9, 35 ; 12, 21 ; 28,1 ; 28,27 ; 29,14, " *Bib* 11 (1930), p. 324.

verb in the same verse in two different conjugations compares with
ašspr + *tspr* in *UT* 2 Aqht VI : 28-29, *ašsprk 'm b'l šnt 'm bn il tspr
yrḫm* " I will cause you to count years like Baal, like the son of El you
will count months. " See below under Job 31 : 37 (*'aggîdennû* + *nāgîd*).

my robe .. my tartan. The suffix of *wylbšny* does duty also for *me'îl*
(*my* robe) and *ṣānîp* (*my* tartan). [78]

Job 29 : 15-17

> Eyes was I to the blind,
>   and feet to the lame was I ;
> A father I was to the needy,
>   and the cause of one I did not know I examined for him ;
> And I broke the jaws of the wicked,
>   and from his teeth I cast his prey.

Job 29 : 15

was I. *RSP* I,II,51 records Job 29 : 15-16 as an example of the Ugaritic–Hebrew parallel pair *'n*//*'nk*. Dahood comments there, " This
infrequent parallelism in Job 13 : 2 and 33 : 9 may be cited as an argument for the unity of authorship of the main cycle and of the Elihu
speeches. "

to ... to. On this parallelism, *l* " to, for "//*l* " to, for, " see *RSP* I,
II,316.

Job 29 : 16

father. *'b* occurs in the personal name *I š-a-bù* listed in the texts from
Tell Mardikh. [79] Pettinato translates it as " A man is the father. "
However, the Ugaritic–Hebrew root *'wš* " gift " [80] suggests that " Gift
of the Father " is a more accurate version. See also TM. 75. G. 336
(recto) III : 13, *a-bù-ᵈguₛ-ra* " A Father is the Mountain. " [81]

of one I did not know. *lō'-yāda'tî* is a good example of a relative clause
without a relative pronoun. [82]

---

[78] Blommerde, *NSGJ*, p. 111.
[79] Pettinato, *BA* 39 (1976), p. 50.
[80] Dahood, *UHP*, p. 49.
[81] Pettinato–Matthiae, *RSO* 50 (1976), p. 4.
[82] Blommerde, *NSGJ*, p. 34, 111 ; M. J. Dahood, *Psalms* I (AB 16 ; Garden

to the needy ... for him. A prepositional phrase (*lā'ebyônîm* " to the needy ") paralleling a dative suffix (*'eḥqĕrēhû* " I examined for him ") is a device characteristic of the style of Job. Dahood notes its appearance in 3 : 25 ; 6 : 4 ; 15 : 17 ; 20 : 22 ; 32 : 14 ; 33 : 5,33 ; 40 : 30 ; 41 : 20-21. He remarks on 29 : 16,

> Often parsed as the resumptive suffix of *rîb*, *-hû* of *'eḥqᵉrēhû* is preferably construed as the dative of advantage, balancing the preposition *la* of the preceding three cola. The poet achieved variety by employing the dative suffix in the final of four parallel cola. [83]

Job 29 : 17

broke ... cast. This same parallelism occurs in Dan 8 : 7, " and he struck the ram and broke (*wayĕšabbēr*) his two horns ... and he cast him down (*wayyašlîkēhû*) to the ground and trampled upon him "; see also Ex 32 : 19 (*wayyašlēk*//*wayyĕšabbēr*), Deut 9 : 17 (*wā'ašlikēm*// *wā'ăšabbĕrēm*), and Jon 2 : 4 (*watašlîkēnî* + *mišbārêkā*). The presence of this parallel pair (*šbr*//*šlk*) here in 29 : 17 argues against the emendation of *'ašlîk* to *'ešlōp* proposed by *BHK*³, an emendation repeated in the apparatus of *BHS*.

the jaws. On *mĕtallĕʿôt* " jawbone " see Dahood, " Hebrew Lexicography : A Review of W. Baumgartner's *Lexikon*, Volume II. " [84] Compare *UT* 51 VIII : 19,

> *al yʿdbkm kimr bph*
> *klli bṭbrn qnh tḥtan*

> Lest he make you like a lamb in his mouth,
> like a kid you be crushed by the grinding of his teeth. [85]

jaws ... teeth. This same parallelism recurs in Ps 58 : 7.

---

[83] City, N.Y. : Doubleday, 1965), 3rd Note on Ps 35 : 15 ; idem, " Index of Subjects " under " Relative pronoun omitted " in *Psalms II*² (p. 396) and in *Psalms III* (p. 487).

[83] " Northwest Semitic texts and textual criticism of the Hebrew Bible, " p. 32.

[84] *Or* 45 (1976), p. 359.

[85] M. J. Dahood, " The Etymology of *Maltā'ôt* (Ps 58, 7), " *CBQ* 17 (1955), p. 183.

Job 29 : 18-20

> And I thought, " Though I perish like its nest,
>   I shall multiply days like the phoenix,
> My root open to the waters
>   and the dew lodging in my branches,
> My liver fresh within me,
>   and my bow renewed in my hand. "

Job 29 : 18

Lively discussion continues around this verse. Pope in his 3rd edition of *Job* (AB 15, 1973) maintains his interpretation based on the emendation of *qny* " his nest " to *zqny* " my old age, " although he writes, " If ' nest ' is retained here, one should probably, on the basis of parallelism, choose ' phoenix ' rather than ' sand ' in the next line. " [86] Blommerde, who in *NSGJ* (p. 111) adopted Dahood's proposal, [87] has altered his position and now offers this version,

> And I thought : I shall die with my flock,
>   after having multiplied it as the sand of the seas. [88]

The translation here follows Dahood who in his article " *Ḥôl* ' Phoenix ' in Job 29 : 18 and in Ugaritic " has expanded on his earlier treatment of this text. [89] The closing paragraph of that article states,

---

[86] *Job*³, p. 213-214. He translates, " I thought, ' In ripe age I shall expire, / Like sand I shall multiply days. ' "

[87] " Nest and Phoenix in Job 29,18, " *Bib* 48 (1967), p. 542-544.

[88] A. C. M. Blommerde, " The Broken Construct Chain, Further Examples, " *Bib* 55 (1974), p. 550-551.

[89] *CBQ* 36 (1974), p. 85-88. Further bibliography since the publication of Blommerde, *NSGJ*, includes Marvin Pope's review of *NSGJ* in *Bib* 52 (1971), p. 149-150 ; *RSP* I, III, 51 on *ḥl* " phoenix " in Ugaritic ; Dahood, *Psalms III*, 4th Note on Ps 103 : 5 (" Who will imbue your eternity with his beauty, when your youth will be renewed like the eagle's "). *NAB* (1970) opts for the translation " phoenix " and *NEB* (1970) presents it in a footnote as an alternate possibility. Cf. also, Baumgartner, *Lexikon*, vol. I, p. 285b (*ḥôl* II). H. H. Rowley, *Job* (The Century Bible, New Series ; London : Nelson, 1970), p. 239, lists nine modern editors who translate *ḥôl* as " phoenix. " S. Terrien and P. Scherer, " The Book of Job, " *The Interpreter's Bible*, vol. III (New York/ Nashville : Abingdon, 1954), p. 1110, comment, " Furthermore, a good case may be made for the pointing of *ḥwl*, sand, as *ḥûl*, ' phoenix, ' a word which brings a startling image and fits the traditional idea of the *nest* in vs. 18a. " See also *Das Alte Testament* (Einheitsübersetzung der Heiligen Schrift ; Stutt-

For ḥl, " phoenix, " no fully convincing etymology presents itself, which simply means that it joins the long list of words witnessed in only Ugaritic and Hebrew that await convincing etymological explanation. Compare, e.g., ṯlḥn/šlḥn, " table "; ḥrmṯt/ḥrmš, " sickle "; ẓrw/ṣry, " balsam "; ty/šy " gift ". [90]

Those etymological explanations may not be long in forthcoming with the discovery of the large number of proto-canaanite texts from the late third millennium at Tell Mardikh/Ebla in northern Syria. Indeed Dahood's argument in favor of ḥl/ḥôl = " phoenix " finds further support in an as yet unpublished lexical list containing the proto-canaanite word ḥl which the accompanying Sumerian logogram indicates is the name of a species of bird. [91] See also the personal name from Ebla, aḥ-ḥa-lum " My Brother is the Phoenix, " [92] in which " Phoenix " serves as a divine title. [93]

Finally, the collocation of ḥôl with ṭal " dew " in v 19 must be mentioned since it is another link connecting ḥôl to " phoenix. " In his study of the phoenix myth, R. van den Broek devotes an entire chapter to the food of this remarkable animal. [94] He gathers together the various traditions from both classical and judeo-christian sources, and shows that, " Like its periodic death, the food of the phoenix has become the sign of its essential immortality. " [95] In many of the versions of the myth, that food is the life-giving dew from heaven:

gart: Katholischen Bibelanstalt, 1974), " und gleich dem phönix "; L. Alonso Schökel and J. L. Ojeda, *Job* (Los Libros Sagrados VIII, 2; Madrid: Ediciones Cristiandad, 1971), " como el fénix "; *Traduction oecuménique de la Bible* (Paris: Cerf, 1976), " come le phénix. " The latter notes, " Oiseau fabuleux, célèbre par sa longévité et par sa faculté de rejeunissement. " Finally, Lester Grabbe, *Comparative Philology and the Text of Job*, discusses the verse at length and concludes (p. 101): " Several alternate suggestions indeed have merit, but the weight of the evidence available to me favors the phoenix interpretation. "

[90] Dahood, *CBQ* 36 (1974), p. 88.

[91] Dahood, private communication.

[92] TM. 75 G. 336 (recto) V: 3; cf. Pettinato–Matthiae, *RSO* 50 (1976), p. 4.

[93] Cf. Mitchell Dahood, " Ebla, Ugarit and the Old Testament, " *Vetus Testament Supplements* 29 (Congress Volume, Göttingen 1977; Leiden: Brill, 1978), p. 112. Compare the use of ḥl " phoenix " in *UT* 125: 7-8; cf. W. F. Albright, " Baal-zephon, " in *Festschrift Alfred Bertholet* (Tübingen: Mohr, 1950), p. 1-14.

[94] R. van der Broek, *The Myth of the Phoenix according to Classical and Early Christian Traditions* (Etudes préliminaires aux religions orientales dans l'empire roman 24; Leiden: Brill, 1972), Chapter Nine, " The Food ".

[95] Ibid., p. 336.

The Jews, and via them the early Christians saw dew as a special gift of God, dispelling death and nourishing life. This idea is ultimately determined by the geographical and climatological conditions under which the ancient Israelites lived; in the dry Palestinian region life would be impossible without dew. This is why the dew is mentioned in several Old Testament benedictions as one of God's special gifts of grace, and conversely that the absence of dew was taken as one of God's forms of punishment. In Hosea, for instance, dew is an image of God's approval of his people : " I will be as dew to Israel " (*Hosea* xiv. 5). From this it required only a small step to assume that the dead would be revived by the dew. [96]

In Gen 27 : 28, Isaac prays for Jacob, " May God give you of the dew of heaven and of the fatness of the earth (*miṭṭal haššāmayim ûmišmannê hā'āreṣ*), " [97] and in Ps 110 : 3, God is the source of the Israelite king's renewed youth (*ṭal yaldûṭêkā* " the dew of your youth ") :

> When the Holy One appeared he was your Comforter,
>> the dawn of life for you,
>> the dew of your youth. (Dahood)

" Dew " and the theme of renewed life also occur together in Isa 26 : 19,

> But your dead will live,
>> their bodies will rise.
> Arise and sing, O you who dwell in the slime.
> For your dew is the dew of the fields
>> (*kî ṭal 'ûrôt* [MT *'ôrôt*] *ṭallekā*),
> but the land of the Shades will be parched. [98]

See also Ps 133 : 3 :

> Like the dew (*kĕṭal*) of Hermon,
>> which descends upon the mountains of Zion.

---

[96] Ibid., p. 341-342.

[97] Compare *UT* 'nt II : 39, *ṭl šmm šmn arṣ* " dew of heaven, fat of the earth "; cf., *RSP* I, II, 208.

[98] For this translation see Dahood, *Psalms III*, p. L, and *Psalms I*, 3rd Note on Ps 36 : 10. In the latter note he comments, " ... in this text, *'ûrôt*, which is contrasted with ' the land of the Shades,' must signify the Elysian Fields, especially since the context deals with resurrection and immortality. "

For there Yahweh confers
the blessing-
life for evermore (ḥayyîm ʿal-hāʿôlām) !

Dahood remarks on this passage:

> In some texts dew is a symbol of what is refreshing and invigor-
> ating, but in Isa xxvi 19 it symbolizes resurrection and immor-
> tality. The mention of " life for evermore " at the end of
> our verse suggests some allusion to immortality in " the dew
> of Hermon. " [99]

The *a priori* exclusion of the explanation of *ḥôl* as " phoenix " on the
grounds that it implies belief in a resurrection and therefore cannot
possibly be the sense of Job 29: 18 unfairly prejudices the discussion;
e.g., the remarks of Fedrizzi:

> La versione di *ḥwl* con " fenice " non sembra accettabile perché
> la leggenda evocherebbe piuttosto l'attesa della risurrezione
> che il prolungarsi di una vita felice. [100]

The large number of references to resurrection and immortality in the
Psalter, [101] as well as passages in Job itself such as 19: 25-26 [102] demand

[99] *Psalms III*, 1st Note on Ps 133: 3.

[100] *Giobbe*, p. 206; see also Rowley, *Job*, p. 239, " The phoenix is a symbol,
not merely of longevity, but of immortality, and it is impossible that Job
dreamed of this "; likewise Samuel R. Driver and George B. Gray, *A Critical
and Exegetical Commentary on the Book of Job* (International Critical Commentary; Edinburgh: T. and T. Clark, 1929), vol. II, p. 204.

[101] N. B., Dahood, " Death, Resurrection, and Immortality, " in *Psalms III*,
p. XLI-LII.

[102] Dahood suggests for Job 19: 25 (private communication):
I know that my Redeemer is alive again,
and that the Ultimate has risen from
the Dust.
Isa 26: 19 contains this same parallelism *ḥyh*//*qwm* (*yiḥyû*//*yěqûmûn*; cf. the
recent study of M. L. Barré, " New Light on the Interpretation of Hosea VI 2, "
VT 28, 1978, p. 129-141). On *ʿal* " from, " see the discussion under " from
them " in Job 30: 2 and under " plucking ... from the bush " in Job 30: 4.
The same sense of *ḥyh* " to live again, to restore life " occurs in Ps 30: 4; Ps
71: 20; and *UT* 49 III: 2. See also M. Dahood, " Hebrew-Ugaritic Lexicography IX, " *Bib* 52 (1971), p. 346. In *Psalms II²*, 2nd Note on Ps 73: 26,
Dahood renders Job 19: 26a, " Refleshed by him, I will gaze upon God. "

a more open-minded examination of the evidence. With the recognition of the phoenix myth as the background to Job 29:18, the full
force of vv 18-20 becomes clear: at the center of Job's previous happy
existence was the hope that God's favor to him would be unending:
" Diese mit *wā'ōmar* eingeführten Hoffnungen waren selbst ein Bestand-
heit seines ehemaligen Glückes. "[103]

like. Dahood has also identified this sense of *'im* = " as, like " in
Job 3:14, " just like kings (*'im-mělākîm*) and counsellors of the earth."[104]

his nest. The final *-y* of *qinnî* is the third person masculine suffix. [105]

his nest ... the phoenix. An instance of the poetic technique of " delayed identification " used frequently by the author of Job; see the
discussion below on Job 30:1.

Job 29:19

open ... lodging. This same parallel pair, *pātûaḥ//yālîn*, occurs in
Job 31:32, *yālîn* " did not lodge "//*'eptāḥ* " I opened. " See the
remarks above under Job 29:3.

water ... dew. RSP I,II,352 records Job 29:19 as one of two biblical
examples of the Ugaritic–Hebrew parallel pair *mym//ṭl*. [106] The poet
uses the rhetorical figure of merismus in naming the two sources from
which the land is irrigated, the upsurging of water from below the
earth (*māyim*) and the descent of the water from on high (*ṭal*); cf.,
Gen 7:11; Prov 3:20; *UT* 1 Aqht 44-46, *bl ṭl bl rbb bl šr' thmtm bl*

Pope, *Job³*, p. 146-147, remarks on this version of v 26a, " Thus Dahood finds
here expression of ' the doctrine of the creation of a new body for the afterlife. ' This interpretation, if it could be validated, would have considerable
interest as anticipating the climax of Paul's famous discourse on the topic in
I Cor xv. "

[103] Delitzsch, *Das Buch Iob*, p. 384.
[104] " Northwest Semitic texts and textual criticism of the Hebrew Bible, "
p. 26. See also Blommerde, *NSGJ*, p. 25; Dahood, *Psalms III*, p. 68 (on
Ps 106:6).
[105] Dahood, *Bib* 48 (1967), p. 543; Blommerde, *NSGJ*, p. 8. See also the
remarks of L. Boadt, " A Re-examination of the Third-Yod Suffix in Job, "
UF 7 (1975), p. 59-72. J. Gray accepts the third yodh masculine suffix as
proposed by Dahood in Ps 68:31 and 34; cf., J. Gray, " A Cantata of the
Autumn Festival: Psalm LXVIII, " *JSS* 22 (1977), p. 17-18.
[106] The other is Judg 6:38; cf., Dahood, " Some Rare Parallel Word Pairs
in Job and in Ugaritic, " p. 26.

ṭbn ql bʿl " May there be no dew, no rain, no surging of the two deeps, no sweetness of Baal's voice " [107] and 1 Aqht 51 (//55, 200), *pg̱t ṭkmt mym ḥspt lšʿr ṭl* " Pg̱t who shoulders the water (from the well), who gathers the dew from the barley. "

Job 29 : 20

my liver. The context of renewal of life (v 19) and reinvigoration (*ḥdš* and *ḥlp* here in v 20) suggests the more concrete sense of " liver " for *kĕbôdî*, usually translated " my glory. " Job speaks very specifically about what he had believed would be his reward for leading a virtuous life — nothing less than a renewal and continuation of this life even after death. This form, *kābôd*, appears in a number of passages which call for the meaning " liver, innards " and is usually emended to *kābēd* in these passages; e.g., Ps 16 : 9 :

> And so my heart (*libbî*) rejoices,
> my liver (*kĕbôdî*) leaps with joy,
> and my body (*bĕśārî*) dwells at ease. [108]

See also Gen 49 : 6 (*napšî* " I, my soul " //*kĕbôdî* " my liver "); Ps 7 : 6 (*napšî* " me " //*ḥayyāy* " my vitals " //*kĕbôdî* " my liver "); Ps 57 : 8-9 (*libbî* " my heart " ... *libbî* " my heart " ... *kĕbôdî* " my liver "). In other words, *kābôd* (identical in form with *kābôd* " glory ") may represent a biform of *kābēd* " liver "; *kābôd* follows the qatol stative pattern of nouns (GKC 84k) while *kābēd* conforms to the qatel stative pattern (GKC 84g).

This interpretation uncovers the merismus in this verse 20. The two parts of the body mentioned, *kābôd* " liver " (an internal organ) in 20a and *yād* " hand " (an *external* limb) in 20b, express the totality of Job's body. He expects the rejuvenation of his entire physical being.

fresh. G. Pettinato reports that this root, *ḥdš*, appears in a personal name found in the tablets written in paleo-canaanite from Tell Mardikh/Ebla (*é-da-šù*). [109]

my bow. *qešet* " bow " also occurs in the Tell Mardikh tablets (*qà-šù*). [110]

---

[107] Caquot, *TO*, p. 444-445 (n. *i*); Dahood, *Bib* 45 (1964), p. 411.
[108] Dahood, *Psalms I*, p. 86; ibid., the 3rd Note on Ps 7 : 6.
[109] Pettinato, *Or* 44 (1975), p. 372 (n. 92).
[110] Ibid., p. 369.

my bow ... in my hand. Compare *UT* 76 II : 6, *qšthn aḫd bydh* " his bow he took in his hand. "

Job 29:21-23

> To me they listened and waited,
>   and kept silent for my counsel.
> After my speech they did not reply,
>   and my word dripped upon them.
> They waited for it as for the rain,
>   and opened their mouth as for the spring rain.

Many modern translations place vv 21-25 between vv 11 and 12 (e.g., *NAB, NEB, BJ²*, Pope, Fedrizzi, Fohrer). However, neither MSS evidence nor the ancient versions provide any support for this. On the contrary, the most recent indication, the Targum to Job from Qumran from the 2nd century B.C., follows the order of verses in the MT at this point. [111]

Job 29 : 21

To me ... for my counsel. *RSP* I,II,318 records *lî / /lĕmô ʿăṣātî* as an example of the Ugaritic–Hebrew parallel pair *l / /lm*; compare *UT* Krt 101-103 (*l / /lm*), *ybʿr ltn attḥ lm nkr mddth* " Let him lead his wife to another, to a stranger his well-beloved. " With the recognition of this parallel pair here in v 21, the doubts about the proper division of the consonants in this verse may be laid to rest. [112]

To me ... waited. The order of the words *lî ... wĕyiḥĕllû* here in v 21 is reversed in v 23, *wĕyiḥălû ... lî*, forming a chiastic pattern. [113]

waited ... kept silent. This same parallelism (*yḥl / /dmm*) appears in Ps 37 : 7, " Wait (*dôm*) for Yahweh and hope (*wĕhitḥôlēl*) in him "; their collocation is found in Ps 131 : 2-3, Job 30 : 26-27, and Lam 3 : 26.

---

[111] *Le Targum de Job de la Grotte XI de Qumran*, édité et traduit par J. P. M. van der Ploeg et A. S. van der Woude (Leiden : Brill, 1971), p. 40-41 ; Sokoloff, *The Targum to Job*, p. 56-57.

[112] Both *BHK³* and *BHS* cite MSS in the apparatus which read *lĕmôʿăṣātî* ; see also Baumgartner, *Lexikon* vol. II p. 529b.

[113] Cf. Ceresko, *CBQ* 38 (1976), p. 303-311.

Job 29 : 23

They waited. BHS deletes the emendation proposed in *BHK³* of
wĕyiḥălû to *wiḥakkû* (also " they waited "). The A : B :: B : A word
pattern in Job 29 : 21-23 noted above under v 21, *lî* : *wĕyiḥēllû* :: *wĕyiḥălû* : *lî*, confirms the decision of *BHS*.

for it. The continuity between vv 22b and 23a is better served if the
yodh of *lî* in 23a is understood as the 3rd person feminine yodh suffix
with *millâ* " word " as the antecedent : " my word dripped upon them,
They waited for *it* (i.e., the word) as for the rain. " [114]

as for the rain … as for the spring rain. *kĕ* of *kammāṭār* does duty
also for *lĕmalqôš*, as the *lĕ* of *lĕmalqôš* does duty for *kammāṭār*. [115]

Job 29 : 24-25

> When I smiled on them, powerful, they took courage,
>> and in the light from my face they did not grow sad.
> I convoked their assembly and presided as leader,
>> and I tented as a king among his troops,
>> as a happy man who consoles the grieving.

Job 29 : 24

powerful. Revocalizing MT *lō'*, the negative particle, to *lē'* " victorious, powerful, " the adjective from the root *l'y*. [116]
   Pope remarks on this verse, " Comparison of the several modern
versions reveal diverse understandings or misunderstandings of this
couplet. " [117] *l'* vocalized by the Masoretes as the negative particle
lō' seems to be the main source of difficulty. Consideration of two
factors may lead to a possible solution. First, a similar, and equally

---

[114] On the third feminine yodh suffix in Hebrew see M. Dahood, " A Note
on the Third Person Suffix *-y* in Hebrew, " *UF* 4 (1972), p. 163-164 ; idem,
" The Integrity of Jeremiah 51,1, " *Bib* 53 (1972), p. 542. See also " Meetinghouse " under Job 30 : 23 below.

[115] E.g., the Chicago Bible, " They waited for me as for the rain, / And
opened their mouths as for the latter rain. " Cf. Blommerde, *NSGJ*, p. 111 ;
M. Pope, *Bib* 52 (1971), p. 150 ; Dahood, *Psalms III*, Note on Ps 119 : 131.

[116] For a recent discussion and bibliography on this root, see Viganò, *Nomi
e titoli di YHWH*, p. 80-106 ; W. G. E. Watson, " Reclustering Hebrew *l'lyd*-, "
Bib 58 (1977), p. 213-215.

[117] Pope, *Job³*, p. 211.

vexing, phrase ($w\breve{e}l\bar{o}$'-ya'$\breve{a}m\hat{i}n$) appears in Job 39: 24, " Mid rattle
and roar he races, $w\breve{e}l\bar{o}$'-ya'$\breve{a}m\hat{i}n$ $k\hat{i}$-$q\hat{o}l$ $\check{s}\hat{o}p\bar{a}r$ " ($RSV =$ " he cannot
stand still at the sound of the trumpet "). The second consideration
is that both of these passages occur in a military context. Job 39: 24
pictures the cavalry horse's courage and enthusiasm for battle (cf.
Job 39: 19-25), while Job, in 29: 24-25, describes himself as a warrior
king at the head of his troops. In both verses, revocalizing troublesome $l\bar{o}$' " not " to the adjective $l\bar{e}$' " powerful, victorious " uncovers
a word apropos to the situation of combat. The hiphil of 'mn would
then be understood in the absolute sense of " take courage, be confident " (cf. Ex 4: 31), and Job 39: 24 would translate:

> Mid rattle and roar he races,
>   and powerful, he takes courage when the trumpet calls. [118]

In Akkadian, the root ($l\bar{e}$'$\hat{u}$, " able, capable, skilled ") is used as a royal
title for a number of kings, e.g., Salmanasar I (" capable in battle ")
and Asarhaddon (" capable in the fight and in the battle "). [119]

the light of my face. Dahood notes on Ps 4: 7 ('$\hat{o}r$ $p\bar{a}n\hat{e}k\bar{a}$ " the light
of your face "):

> As a sign of beneficence, this phrase is an ancient metaphor of
> frequent occurrence in the El Amarna and Ugaritic correspond-
> ence, as in UT, 1126: 6, *wpn* $\check{s}m\check{s}$ *nr by mid*, " And the face
> of the Sun (i.e., the Pharaoh) shone brightly on me. " [120]

they did not grow sad. The sense of v 24b becomes clear once the
ellipsis is identified. $l\bar{o}$' $yapp\hat{i}l\hat{u}n$ is elliptical for the common Hebrew
expression $l\bar{o}$' $yapp\hat{i}l\hat{u}n$ ($p\breve{e}n\hat{e}hem$) " they did not let their faces fall " =
" they did not grow sad. " Compare Gen 4: 6 in which God asks
Cain, $lamm\hat{a}$ $n\bar{a}p\breve{e}l\hat{u}$ $p\bar{a}n\hat{e}k\bar{a}$ " why has your countenance fallen?, "

---

[118] Compare Job 39: 21, " He paws violently, exults mightily, / He rushes
to meet the fray " (Pope). $b\breve{e}q\hat{o}l$ is parsed as the preposition followed by the
infinitive construct of qwl, a biform of qhl " to call, assemble "; cf. W. F.
Albright, " The High Places in Ancient Palestine, " VTSup 4 (1957), p. 256,
and Dahood, *Psalms II²*, 3rd Note on Ps 95: 7.

[119] M.-J. Seux, *Epithètes royales akkadiennes et sumériennes* (Paris: Letouzez
et Ané, 1967), p. 149-150 ; *The Assyrian Dictionary of the Oriental Institute of the
University of Chicago*, vol. 9 (L) (eds. M. Civil, et al.; Chicago/Glückstadt: Oriental
Institute/J. J. Augustin, 1973), p. 160b ; Viganò, *Nomi e titoli di YHWH*, p. 81.

[120] Dahood, *Psalms I*, 2nd Note on Ps 4: 7.

i.e., "why are you downcast?" *pānîm* already appears in 24b ('*ôr pānay* " the light of my face ") and the poet relies on the echo from it to supply the missing element in the ellipsis (*pĕnêhem*).

The root *npl* occurs in a personal name from Tell Mardikh/Ebla. [121]

Job 29 : 25

This verse provides another example of merismus in expressing the comprehensiveness of Job's leadership role in the community: he presided over the regulation of its internal affairs (v 25a), directed its defense against external enemies (v 25b), and cared for its vulnerable members (25c). Compare Ps 72 and *KAI* 24 (The Kilamuwa Inscription). Andersen remarks:

> While taking this as a figure (*k*- marks a simile), and not as proof that Job was actually king of his people ..., (we note that) the portrait of the king as both soldier and philanthropist is thoroughly Israelite. [122]

I convoked. *bḥr* understood here as the dialectical form of the Canaanite root *pḥr* " to gather, assemble " found frequently in the substantive *pḥr* " assembly " and *mpḥrt* (e.g., UT 51 III: 14-15, *btk pḥr bn ilm* " in the midst of the assembly of the gods "). Dahood has recognized this root, for instance, in 1 Sam 20 : 30 (*bōḥēr* " associating with ") : *yāda'tî kî-bōḥēr 'attâ bĕben-yišay* " I know that you are associating with the son of Jesse. " [123] It also occurs as an element in personal names in the texts from Tell Mardikh; e.g., *Be-sû-pi-ḫir*, which Pettinato renders " (He) has reunited his house. " [124]

their assembly. The parallelism here with *melek* suggests that *derek* has the sense of " dominion, power, assembly (= the place where dominion is exercised). " [125] Dahood finds this meaning of *derek* in Ps 1: 1 (*derek ḥaṭṭā'îm* " the assembly of sinners ") where it parallels

---

[121] Pettinato, *Or* 44 (1975), p. 372 (n. 101).

[122] Andersen, *Job*, p. 234, n. 4.

[123] M. J. Dahood, " Qoheleth and Northwest Semitic Philology, " *Bib* 43 (1962), p. 361 ; Baumgartner, *Lexikon*, vol. I, p. 115b (*bḥr* III).

[124] Pettinato, *BA* 39 (1976), p. 50. See also, ibid., *Ippi-ḫir* " It has been reunited. " Pettinato–Matthiae, *RSO* 50 (1976), record the names *ip-ḫur-ia* (p. 5) and *ip-ḫur-*^dgu₅-ra (p. 7). Additional examples are listed by Pettinato in *Or* 44 (1975), p. 371 : *ip-ḫur-*dKU-RA, *ip-ḫur-*dé-da, and *ip-ḫur-Ma-lik*.

[125] Dahood, *Bib* 45 (1964), p. 404.

'ăṣat rĕšā'îm " council of the wicked " and *môšab lēṣîm* " session of scoffers " (N.B. *yšb* also here in v 25, *wĕ'ēšēb*). [126]

Their assembly... as king. *RSP* I,II,359 records Job 29:25 as an example of the Ugaritic–Hebrew parallel pair *mlk* " kingship " //*drkt* "dominion."

I presided ... as a king. On this parallel pair, cf. *RSP* I,II,360, *mlk* " to reign "//*ytb* " to sit enthroned. "

And I presided as leader. *RSP* I,II,65 compares this construction in Hebrew with *UT* 49 I 37, *wymlk barṣ il klh* " and he ruled upon earth, the god of all of it. "

I tented. The military context implied by *gĕdûd* " troops " suggests this nuance " to tent " for *škn*. Note also the frequent parallelism between *miškān* " dwelling " and *'ōhel* " tent " both in Hebrew and Ugaritic. Dahood remarks on *miškān* in Ps 132:5,

> Where II Sam vi 17 uses *'ōhel*, " tent, " the psalmist employs *miškānōt*, " A dwelling. " Since, however, *'ōhel*, " tent, " and *miškānōt*, " dwelling, " occur frequently in Ugaritic-Hebrew parallelism, the two words may be considered synonymous and even interchangeable. [127]

as king. *mlk* appears in the paleo-canaanite tablets from Tell Mardikh/ Ebla as the title of the Eblaite king Ibbi-Sipis, EN = *malikum*, and as an element in a number of personal names: e.g., *en-na-Ma-lik* " O King (= divine title), be gracious. " [128]

as a happy man. Revocalizing *ka'ăšer* " as one who " to *kĕ'āšēr*. This colon echoes v 11a, " When ear heard me, it blessed me (*watĕ-'aššĕrēnî*), " and 13b " and the widow's heart I made joyful, " and rounds out the merismus expressing Job's former position of importance in the community.

who consoles the grieving. The same expression occurs in Isa 61:2, " Yahweh has anointed me ... to comfort all who mourn (*lĕnăḥēm kol-'ăbēlîm*). " [129]

---

[126] *Psalms I*, 3rd Note on Ps 1:1.

[127] Dahood, *Psalms III*, 6th Note on Ps 132:5. See also *RSP* I, II, 15.

[128] Pettinato, *Or* 44 (1975), p. 366, 370-371.

[129] Pope, *Job³*, p. 212, revocalizes MT *'ăbēlîm yĕnaḥēm* to *'ōbilēm yonḥū-ma* " wherever I guided they were led. " See N. Herz, " Some Difficult Passages in Job, " *ZAW* 20 (1900), p. 63, and *RSP* I, II, 210.

Translation and Commentary on Job 30

Translation of Job 30

1. But now they deride me,
   men younger than I,
   Whose fathers I considered too poor
   to be put with the dogs of my flock.

2. Yes, the strength of their hands —
   what is it to me?
   From them has full vigor fled:
3. For want and sterile hunger,
   gnawing desert or swamp,
   devastation of desolation;
4. Plucking mallow from the bush,
   the very roots of the broom consuming.

5. From the community they are banished;
   they shout after them as a thief,
6. In the most dreaded of ravines to dwell,
   in the holes of the ground and rocks.
7. Among the bushes they bray,
   amidst the nettles they huddle together,
8. A senseless, yes nameless brood,
   thrust out of the town.

9. And now a song for them am I,
   become to them a gibe.
10. They abhor me, keep aloof from me,
    and from my face they spare no spit.

11. Indeed they watch at my door and eye me
    and cast off restraint in my presence.
12. On my right and left,
    they arise who spy on me, they are unrestrained;
    and they heap up against me their roads of ruin.

13. They break up my path,
      they succeed to undo me;
      there is no escape from them.
14. Through a wide breach they come,
      amidst the havoc they arrive.
15. Terror turns on me,
      pursues my dignity like the wind;
      like a cloud, my prosperity disappears.

16. And now my life is drained from me;
      days of affliction seize me.
17. At night my bones are hotter than a caldron;
      those who gnaw me do not rest.
18. With great force he rifles my garment,
      with his hands he loosens from me my tunic.
19. He casts me upon the mud and I perish,
      flung upon the slime and ashes.

20. I cry out to you but you answer me not;
      I present myself but you ignore me.
21. You've become my Tormentor;
      with your powerful hand you make me take cover.
22. You lift me up, O God, you make me ride the wind,
      and sweep victory away from me.
23. I know that you will return me to Death,
      to the Meetinghouse of all the living.

24. ... ... ,
      ... ... ,
25. Did I not weep for the hapless,
      my soul grieve for the poor?
26. When I cried for Good, Evil came;
      when I hoped for Light, came Darkness.
27. My insides seethe and are not silent;
      confronting me are days of affliction.
28. In gloom I go about without an answer;
      I rise in the assembly to cry for help.
29. Brother have I become to jackals
      and companion to ostriches.

30. My skin is blacker than a caldron,
        and my bones are scorched with heat.
31. My harp is turned to mourning,
        my flute to the sound of weepers.

Commentary on Job 30

Job 30 : 1

> But now they deride me,
>   men younger than I,
>   Whose fathers I considered too poor
>   to be put with the dogs of my flock.

These two verses are linked not only syntactically ($ṣĕʿîrîm$ " men younger "...'*ăšer*...'*ăbôtām* " whose fathers "), but also by the break-up between them of two composite phrases ($šĕʿîrê$ $ṣōʾn$ " the little ones of the flock " and '*āb yamîm* " father of days = aged father ").

But now. Job begins the second part of his Apology. Having described his former happy state (chapter 29), he launches into an account of his present woes. *wĕʿattâ* thus carries an adversative sense, " but now, " " now, however. " On the other uses of this expression in the Old Testament, see A. Laurentin, " *Wĕʿattah – Kai nun.* Formule caractéristique des textes juridiques et liturgiques (à propos de Jean 17,5). " [130]

they deride me. Compare this same verb with a different preposition ('*el*) and a different sense three verses earlier (29 : 24): '*eśhaq ʿălēhem* " I smiled on them. " *śḥq* occurs also in Ugaritic (= *ẓḥq*) in *UT* 75 I : 12-13, a text which, as will be seen below, has other parallels with this Chapter of Job:

> *il yẓḥq bm lb*
> *wygmḏ bm kbd*

---

[130] *Bib* 45 (1964), p. 168-197; see also H. A. Brongers, " Bemerkungen zum Gebrauch des Adverbialen *wᵉʿattāh* im Alten Testament, " *VT* 15 (1965), p. 289-299. D. J. McCarthy notes the use of this expression in covenant terminology in *Treaty and Covenant* (Analecta Biblica 21A; Rome: Biblical Institute Press, 1978), see especially p. 214 and 272.

El laughs from his heart
and chuckles from his liver.

On the parallelism *śḥq*//*śûb* of Job 39 : 22 (*yiśḥaq* " he laughs "//
wĕlō'-yāśûb " he does not turn back "), compare the collocation of
these same roots in 2 Aqht VI : 41-42, *tṣḥq 'nt* " Anat laughs " ... *ṭb ly
wlk* " turn from me and be gone ! "

men younger than I. Literally, " those younger than me in days. "
This phrase is echoed by Elihu in 32 : 6 with not a little sarcasm :

> *ṣā'îr 'anî lĕyāmîm*
> *wĕ'attem yĕśîśîm*

> I am young in days
>   and you are venerable men.

ṣḡr appears in Ugaritic parallel to *n'r* " boy " in RŠ 24. 251 : rev.
13-14, *tbky km n'r tdm' km ṣḡr* " You weep like a boy, shed tears like
a child. " Their parallelism in this Ugaritic text accords with their
apparent interchangeability for the author of Job ; cf., especially
nĕ'ārîm " young men "//*wîśîśîm* " elders " of Job 29 : 8 and *ṣā'îr*
" young "//*yĕśîśîm* " venerable men " of Job 32 : 6.

An interesting variant of *ṣĕ'îrîm ... lĕyāmîm* " younger in days "
is seen in Job 15 : 10 where, instead of the prepositional phrase with
lamedh, the poet uses a construct chain *mē'ăbî yāmîm* interrupted by
the second person masculine singular suffix :

> *gam-śāb gam-yāśîś bānû*
> *kabbîr mē'ābîkā yāmîm*

> Yes, the Gray-headed and the Venerable is with us,
>   older than your aged father. [131]

Job 30 : 1 serves as an example of the break-up of this composite phrase
signifying great age, *'ab yāmîm* " father of days " (*lĕyāmîm ... 'ăbôtām*) ;
this is a variant of the epithet of El in Ugaritic, *ab šnm* " father of
years ", e.g., in *UT* 51 IV 24 :

---

[131] The translation follows M.J. Dahood, "Hebrew–Ugaritic Lexicography X,"
Bib 53 (1972), p. 396. On the broken construct chain see Dahood, *Psalms III*,
" Index of Subjects " under " Construct chain with interposing elements " (p.
481) ; D. N. Freedman, " The Broken Construct Chain," *Bib* 53 (1972), p. 534-536.

tgly ḏd il
wtbu qrš
mlk ab šnm

She reaches the territory of El
and enters the abode
of the King, the Father of Years. [132]

Also, the composite phrase *ṣĕ'îrê haṣṣō'n* " the little ones of the flock, "
found in Jer 49 : 20 and 50 : 45, is broken up here in Job 30 : 1 (*ṣĕ'îrîm*
... *ṣō'nî*) ; see also Zech 13 : 7 :

> Strike the shepherd, that the flock (*haṣṣō'n*) may be scattered ;
>   I will turn my hand against the little ones (*'al-haṣṣō'ărîm*).

Finally, the meaning of *ṣ'r* as " to be belittled, disgraced " is
clear from parallelism with *kbd* " to be honored " in Job 14 : 21 :

> His sons achieve honor (*yikbĕdû*) but he never knows ;
>   they are disgraced (*wĕyiṣ'ărû*), but he perceives not (Pope).

This secures the sense of Jer 30 : 19 which exhibits the same parallel
pair :

> *wĕhirbitîm wĕlō' yim'āṭû*
> *wĕhikbadtîm wĕlō' yiṣ'ărû*

> I will increase them, they shall not diminish ;
>   I will raise them to honor, they shall no longer be despised.

Thus *NEB* ; contrast *NAB* (" they will not be tiny ") and *RSV* (" they
shall not be small ").

The " delayed identification " of the subject (*ṣĕ'îrîm*) in the second colon is a poetic device favored by the author of Job. Dahood
discusses it in his first note on Ps 105 : 17, " He sent a man before
them / Joseph sold as a slave " :

---

[132] See Dahood, *Psalms II²*, 3rd Note on Ps 90 : 15. On the break-up of a
composite phrase as a common stylistic device in Canaanite poetry, see E. Z.
Melamed, " Break-up of Stereotype Phrases, " in *Studies in the Bible* (ed. C. Rabin ; Scripta Hierosolymitana 8 ; Jerusalem : Magnes, 1961), p. 115-153. For
examples in the Psalter, Dahood, *Psalms I*, " Break-up of stereotyped phrases "
in the " Subjects Index " (p. 325) ; idem, *Psalms III*, " Break-up of stereotyped phrase " in the " Index of Subjects " (p. 480).

a man ... Joseph. The poet creates suspense by mentioning indefinitely " a man " in the first colon and reserving his specific name " Joseph " to the end of the second colon. The antecedents of this biblical stylistic artifice (see above vss. 3, 6) can be observed in, say, UT 'nt : II : 23-24, *mid tmtḫṣn wt'n ṯḫtṣb tḥdy 'nt,* " Much does she smite and behold, battle and gaze does Anath, " where the subject of the action is not made specific until the last word. See the second Note on Ps 112 : 6. The author of Job is especially fond of this artistic device : cf. Job 6 : 2, 19 : 26, 20 : 23, 22 : 21, 27 : 3, 29 : 18, 34 : 17. [133]

In *UT* 128, El pronounces a blessing on Krt toward the end of which he promises sons and daughters to Krt. The last-born daughter, Octava, will become his heir, according to 128 III : 16, *ṣġrthn abkrn* " I shall make the youngest of them (i.e., the last-born daughter, Octava) the first-born. " [134] C. H. Gordon points out that this same practice of giving one of the younger children the legal status of first-born is witnessed in the patriarchal traditions of Genesis (cf. Gen 27) and 1 Chron 26 : 10 :

> And Hasah, of the sons of Mirari, had sons : Shimri, the chief (for though he was not the first-born (*běkôr*), his father made him chief...). [135]

Thus Job may be comparing his fate to that of a ruler or legitimate successor whom a young usurper (*ṣā'îr*) had dethroned and driven into exile in the marginal areas and among the marginal people of the land (See below under v 3).

I considered too poor. *mā'as* usually has the sense " to reject, " as here. However, Dahood has pointed out two passages in Job (7 : 15-16,

---

[133] Dahood, *Psalms III*, 1st Note on Ps 119 : 141 ; Irwin, *Isaiah* 28 – 33, p. 172.

[134] Compare *ṣġr + bkr* here in 128 III : 16 with Gen 43 : 33 (*běkôr // ṣā'îr*) " And they sat before him, the first-born according to his birthright (*habběkōr kibkōrātô*) and the youngest according to his youth (*wěhaṣṣā'îr kiṣ'irātô*) " (*RSV*).

[135] See also Gen 48 : 14, *ṣā'îr ... běkôr ... bārak* (compare *UT* 128 III : 16-17, *ṣġr + bkr + brk*): " And Israel stretched out his right hand and laid it upon the head of Ephraim, who was the younger (*haṣṣā'îr*), and his left hand upon the head of Manasseh, crossing his hands, for Manasseh was the first born (*habběkôr*). And he blessed (*wayěbārek*) Joseph ... " (*RSV*).

42 : 6) in which the context calls for the privative (piel) meaning, " to prefer, accept " : [136]

Job 7 : 15-16   *wattibḥar maḥănāq napšî*

                môt-m ʿaṣmôtāy (MT *māwet mēʿaṣmôtāy*) *m'sty*

                My neck chooses strangulation,
                I prefer the death of my bones.

Job 42 : 6   *ʿal-kēn ʾm's wĕniḥamtî*

                ʿal-ʿāpār wāʾēper

                Therefore I accept and repent
                upon the dust and ashes.

Job 34 : 33 repeats the Hebrew parallel pair *bḥr*//*m's* of Job 7 : 15-16; see also 2 Kgs 23 : 27; Isa 41 : 9; Jer 33 : 24.

fathers.   Add Job 15 : 10-11 to the Hebrew instances of the word pair *il*//*ab* in *RSP* I,II,30 (*mēʾābîkā* ... *ʾēl*). Compare the collocation here in Job 15 : 10-11, *mēʾābîkā yāmîm* " than your aged father " ... *tanḥūmôt* *ʾēl* " God's replies, " with the Ugaritic phrase *tḥm ṯr il abk* " the message of Bull El, your Father " in *UT* 49 IV : 34. [137]

to be set.   Understanding, with Blommerde, *šît* as a qal passive infinitive (as is the *śîm* in Job 20 : 4). [138]   Blommerde comments,

     ... for mostly the object of *mā'as* is *subject* of the following infinitive, so here *ʾăbôtām* should be subject, not object, of *šît*, which consequently must be parsed as passive. [139]

too poor to be set.   The lamedh of *lāšît* is another in the growing number of examples of the *lamedh comparativum*, [140] first pointed out by Joseph Fitzmyer in Micah 5 : 1:

---

[136] M. J. Dahood, " Hebrew–Ugaritic Lexicography XII, " *Bib* 55 (1974), p. 382.

[137] Also in *UT* 'nt ix II : 17-18; III : 5. On Ug. *tḥm* = Heb. *tanḥūmôt*, see below under Job 30 : 28, and F. J. Moriarty, " Word as Power in the Ancient Near East, " *A Light Unto My Path: Old Testament Studies in Honor of Jacob M. Myers* (eds. H. N. Bream, et al.; Philadelphia: Temple University, 1974), p. 353.

[138] Blommerde, *NSGJ*, p. 89.

[139] Ibid., p. 112.

[140] M. J. Dahood, " Hebrew–Ugaritic Lexicography IV, " *Bib* 47 (1966),

> *wĕ'attâ bêt-leḥem 'eprātâ*
> *ṣā'îr lihyôt bĕ'alpê yĕhûdâ*

And you, O Bethlehem of Ephratha,
    too little to be among the clans of Judah. [141]

Other instances include Ex 1 : 9-10 ; [142] Ezek 16 : 13 ; [143] Nah 1 : 7 ; [144] Ps 30 : 8 ; [145] 119 : 96 ; [146] Prov 24 : 14 ; [147] Cant 1 : 3 ; [148] Qoh 7 : 19. [149]

dogs. Dahood quotes Job 30 : 1 in a note on Ps 68 : 24 apropos the domestication of dogs in the Ancient Near East. He says, in part :

> That the dog was sometimes kept as a pet as early as ca. 1700
> B.C. may be inferred from the Kirta Legend ; cf. UT, 125 : 15-16,
> *kklb bbtk n'tq.* While its sense is not perfectly clear, the asso-
> ciation of *klb*, " dog ", with *bt*, " house, " suggests that dogs
> were kept in the house ....
> That the ancients used watchdogs is perfectly clear from
> Job 30 : 1, " Whose fathers I had disdained / To put with the
> dogs of my flock, " and tolerably clear from UT, Krt : 122-23,
> *zġt klb ṣpr,* " the howling of the watch-dog, " as rendered by
> Ginsberg LKK, pp. 16, 38, and Dahood, *Orientalia* 29 (1960),
> 348. [150]

---

p. 406-407 ; see also Baumgartner, *Lexikon*, vol. II, p. 484b, and M. Dahood, " Hebrew Lexicography : A Review of W. Baumgartner's *Lexikon*, Volume II, " *Or* 45 (1976), p. 341.

[141] J. Fitzmyer, " *lᵉ* as a Preposition and a Particle in Micah 5,1 (5,2), " *CBQ* 18 (1956), p. 12.

[142] M. J. Dahood, " Ugaritic–Hebrew Syntax and Style, " *UF* 1 (1969), p. 21-22.

[143] Dahood, *Psalms I*, 2nd Note on Ps 30 : 8 ; idem, *UHP*, p. 30.

[144] M. J. Dahood, review of G. Gerleman, *Das Hohelied*, in *Bib* 45 (1964), p. 288 ; K. Cathcart, *Nahum*, p. 55.

[145] Dahood, *Psalms I*, 2nd Note on Ps 30 : 8.

[146] Dahood, *Psalms III*, 1st Note on Ps 119 : 96 ; Lorenzo Viganò, *Nomi e titoli di YHWH*, p. 74.

[147] Dahood, *UF* 1 (1969), p. 21-22.

[148] W. F. Albright, " Archaic Survivals in the Text of Canticles, " *Hebrew and Semitic Studies : Presented to Godfrey Rolles Driver* (eds. D. Winton Thomas and W. D. McHardy ; Oxford : Clarendon, 1963), p. 2 ; R. Meyer, review of the foregoing in *Orientalistische Literaturzeitung* 62 (1967), col. 371.

[149] M. J. Dahood, " The Phoenician Background of Qoheleth, " *Bib* 47 (1966), p. 274-275.

[150] Dahood, *Psalms II²*, 3rd Note on Ps 68 : 24.

Job 30 : 2-8

Commentators have remarked on the unity of this rather detailed description of Job's mockers. Fohrer entitles the section, " Ein Lied über die gott- und ehrlosen Landfremden. "[151] The sound patterns in vv 2 and 4, *kōaḥ ... kī lēaḥ* (MT *kālaḥ*) (v 2)//*mallûaḥ ... śiaḥ ... lōḥămīm* (MT *laḥmām*) (v 4), and the inclusion *min-gēw* " from the community " (v 5)//*min-hā'āreṣ* " out of the town " (v 8), delineate further the structure of these seven verses (vv 2-4 / vv 5-8). Within the group formed by vv 2-4, vv 3 and 4 in turn are bound together by the break-up of the expression *ḥeser-leḥem* " lack of bread " (*bĕ-ḥeser ... lōḥămīm*; MT *laḥmām*) which forms an inclusion, and the three successive participles describing the efforts to secure food of these desert-dwellers, *ha'ōrĕqîm* " gnawing, " *haqqōṭĕpîm* " plucking, " and *lōḥămīm* (MT *laḥmām*) " eating. "

The recognition of two motifs which intermingle here can aid the understanding and interpretation of the passage. The first is that of political or social exile into the sparsely populated and sparsely vegetated areas of the land, and the second is the beings who inhabit those areas.

Two key phrases in vv 5 and 8 sound the motif of exile, *min-gēw yĕgōrāšû* " banished from the community " and *nikkĕ'û min-hā'āreṣ* " driven out of the town. " Peckham remarks, for instance, on the use of *grš* in *KAI* 46 : 2 :

> In Hebrew, as in Moabite, it is used most often of the expulsion of " the enemy, " that is, of the actual but intrusive inhabitants of the land, but it can also have the nuance of " banishment " (Gen. 3 : 24, 4 : 14, 21 : 10 ; Jgs. 11 : 2,7), or of dismissal from authority. [152]

William Irwin has pointed out the theme of banishment " into the wilderness " (*battōhû*) as the background of Isa 29 : 21 :

> And all who are intent upon evil will be cut off,
> who fasten guilt on men by slander,
> and for the arbiter in the gate lay snares,
> and thrust into the wasteland the innocent.
> (*wayyaṭṭû battōhû ṣaddîq*).

---

[151] Fohrer, *Das Buch Hiob*, p. 417 ; Driver–Gray, ICC, I, p. 251 ; Fedrizzi, *Giobbe*, p. 207-208.

[152] B. Peckham, " The Nora Inscription, " *Or* 41 (1972), p. 463.

He remarks on the last colon, " This is the third stage in the proceedings ; false accusation and removal of the honest defender are followed by execution of the sentence on the innocent " (i.e., exile into the wilderness). [153]   E. Lipiński has also recognized this motif in *UT* 127 : 57-58 :

> *tqln bgbl šntk*
> *bḥpnk wtʿn*

> May your years pass quickly on the border ;
> the emptiness of your hand may you indeed enjoy.

He notes :

> Le terme *gbl* désigne ainsi un lieu d'exil et le mention des mains vides contient une allusion à la prétension de Yaṣṣib de saisir le sceptre et d'occuper le trône de son père.   La fin de la malédiction paternelle le condamne à l'exil et le prive du droit à la succession royale. [154]

Exile " to the borders " or " to the wilderness " also appears earlier in Job, in 12 : 24-25 :

> He takes away understanding from the chiefs of
>   the people of the land,
>   and makes them wander in a pathless waste
>   (*bĕtōhû lōʾ-dārek*).
> They grope in darkness and obscurity,
>   they wander about like drunken men. [155]

Not only did humans inhabit these regions, those whose physical and oftentimes moral state (cf. Job 24 : 1-12) matched the desolation of their environment.   The ancient near eastern imagination also

---

[153] Irwin, *Isaiah* 28 – 33, p. 64-65.   He compares Amos 5 : 12, *wĕʾebyônîm baššaʿar hiṭṭû* " and thrust the needy from the gate. "

[154] E. Lipiński, " Le bannissement de Yaṣṣib (II Keret VI, 57-58), " *Syria* 50 (1973), p. 38-39.   See also *KAI* 26 A I : 19-21 in which the Phoenician king, Azitawaddu, boasts of his deportation of a conquered population : *wʾnk ʾztwd ʾntnm yrdm ʾnk yšbm ʾnk bqṣt gbly bmṣʾ šmš* " And I, Azitawaddu, subdued them and deported them ; I settled them on the edge of my eastern border " ; cf. also, Obad 7.

[155] On v 25, cf. Blommerde, *NSGJ*, p. 65.   Compare also Ps 107 : 40, " He pours contempt on princes / and makes them wander in trackless wastes (*bĕtōhû lōʾ-dārek*) " (Dahood).

peopled these areas with an assortment of preternatural creatures, as
Isa 34:13-14 witnesses:

> It shall be the haunt of jackals,
>   an abode for ostriches.
> And wild beasts (*ṣiyyîm*; cf. *ṣiyyâ* in Job 30:3)
>   shall meet with hyenas,
>   the satyr shall cry to his fellow;
> Yea, there shall the night hag alight,
>   and find for herself a resting place.   (*RSV*)[156]

UT 75 describes a group of such creatures whom Baal encounters in
the wilderness. Their names, *aklm* " Eaters " and *'qqm* " Devourers "
(I: 27-28,36-37), and their dwelling place in the desert (*mlbr*, I: 21,35),
suggest that this text also must be taken into consideration as part
of the mythological background of Job 30. The philological commentary below discusses the relationship of *ha'ōrĕqîm* and *maš* (MT
'emeš) in Job 30:3 to Ugaritic *'qq* " to devour, rend " and *mšmš* " morass, swamp " (*UT* 75 II: 37,56). Marvin Pope has already noted
the importance of *UT* 75 for the Yahweh Speeches (Leviathan and
Behemoth in chaps. 40 – 41). His long but fascinating note is of
interest also for Job 30. He writes, in part:

> In view of the long recognized mythological and supernatural
> character of Leviathan ... now clearly established by the Ugaritic
> myths, it is in order to question again the interpretation of
> Behemoth as the hippopotamus .... The juxtaposition of Behe-
> moth and Leviathan in Job and in post-biblical texts cited
> above suggests that Behemoth ... had a prototype in pre-Israel-
> ite mythology and that the monsters were connected in some
> ancient myth or played similar roles in different myths.... the
> reference in Enoch to the effect that Behemoth is assigned to
> the wilderness recalls another Ugaritic myth. In the fragmen-
> tary text designated BH (Gordon, *UT* 75), El contrives a dia-
> bolical plot to undo his enemy Baal. Laughing in his heart

---

[156] See also Lev 16:10,22; Isa 13:21; Jer 50:39; Bar 4:35; Tob 8:3;
Matt 4:1; 12:43; Luke 11:24; Otto Böcher, *Dämonenfurcht und Dämonenabwehr: Ein Beitrag zur Vorgeschichte der christlichen Taufe* (Beiträge zur Wissenschaft vom Alten und Neuen Testament 90; Stuttgart: Kohlhammer, 1970),
p. 65-67; W. F. Albright, *Archaeology and the Religion of Israel* (5th edition;
Garden City, N.Y.; Doubleday Anchor Books, 1969), p. 14-15 and note 20.

and chuckling in his liver, El sends out divine handmaids into the wilderness equipped with obstetrical paraphernalia and instructed there to give birth to creatures called "Eaters" (*aklm*) and "Devourers" (*'qqm*). The bovine nature of these monsters is explicit.... As El had planned, Baal goes out into the wilderness and sees these beasts which arouse his instincts as a hunter. Somehow in the attempt to bag them, Baal himself is felled like a bull or a buffalo in a miry swamp and fever racks his body. With Baal thus incapacitated, drought and infertility ensue for a period of seven or eight years. We venture to suggest here, pending further study, that the monstrous bullock of the Ugaritic myths and Behemoth are connected with the Akkadian "bull of heaven" slain by Gilgamesh and Enkidu in the Gilgamesh Epic. [157]

Thus does Job describe his situation here in the opening of Chapter 30. Having removed himself from society (cf. 2:8; 19:13-19), he now sees himself as suffering the fate of those forced to live among the inhabitants, human and otherwise, of "trackless wastes" (12:24), "desert or swamp" and the "devastation of desolation" (30:3). [158]

Job 30 : 2-4

> Yes, the strength of their hands — what is it to me?
>   From them has full vigor fled:
> For want and sterile hunger,
>   gnawing desert or swamp,
>   devastation of desolation;
> Plucking mallow from the bush
>   the very roots of the broom consuming.

---

[157] Pope, *Job*³, p. 321-322. See also *'kl* "devourer" in the Sefire Inscription (I A : 30): *wyšlḥn 'lhn mn kl mh 'kl b'rpd wb'mh* "May the gods send every sort of devourer against Arpad and against its people!"; J. Fitzmyer, *The Aramaic Inscriptions of Sefire* (BibOr 19; Rome: Pontifical Biblical Institute, 1967), p. 14-15.

[158] This motif continues through chapter 30; N.B., the heat (v 17 "my bones are hotter," and v 30 "my bones are scorched"), the thirst (v 12 "dust and ashes"), the desert animals (v 21 "my Tormentor," possibly from *gzr* "to rip, tear"; v 29 "jackals ... the ostrich").

The strength of their hands. Only the Chicago Bible among modern English translations reflects the *casus pendens* of the Hebrew, a nicety of style in Hebrew and Ugaritic pointed out by Dahood in *UT* 2 Aqht VI : 35, *mt mh uḥryt yqḥ* " Man, what will he receive as after life ? " [159] The *casus pendens* also allows for an effective use of assonance to unify this verse and link it with v 4. *gam-kōaḥ* and *kī lēaḥ* (MT *kālaḥ* ; see below) form a semantic inclusion as well as an inclusion of sounds, with the pleasing interplay of the *lamedh* and *mem* in between, *lāmmâ lî ʿālêmô*. v 4 echoes the *kōaḥ/lēaḥ* pattern in *mallûaḥ, śîaḥ* and *lōḥă-mīm* (MT *laḥmām* ; see below).

Note the parallel pair *kōaḥ//mišpāṭ* of Job 9 : 19 and 37 : 23.

what is it to me? This use of *lāmmâ* " why " in a rhetorical question is akin to the rhetorical questions with *lm* in Ugaritic, as discussed by Gordon. [160] He gives *UT* Krt 182 as an example : *lm ank ksp* " What need have I of silver ? " (lit. " Why I silver ? ").

from them. Reading ʿal = " from, " following Blommerde, as also in Job 30 : 4 (See the discussion below under this verse). [161]

has fled. Lexicons usually give the meaning of *ʾābad* as " to destroy, perish, be lost. " In discussing the phrase *ʾābad mānôs mimmennî* in Ps 142 : 5 (" Flight has fled from me "), Dahood proposes the sense " to flee " in certain passages, including Job 30 : 2 :

> In the phrase *ʾābad mānōs* (also in Job xi 20), which is generally rendered by paraphrase rather than by translation, lies a play on words (not unusual in laments) which comes to light when *ʾābad* is identified with Akk. *abātu*, " to flee, " rather than with Akk. *abātu*, " to destroy " .... This sense of *ʾābad* recurs in Ezek xxi 22 (cf. Job xx 8) ; Job xxx 2 ; Prov xxi 28. [162]

George Mendenhall recognizes this meaning of " to flee " for *ʾābad* in Deut 26 : 5 :

---

[159] Compare Ps 103 : 15, *ʾĕnôš keḥāṣîr yāmāyw* " Man, his days are like grass " ; cf. Dahood, *UF* 1 (1969), p. 24. Idem, *Psalms III*, " Index of Subjects " under *casus pendens* (p. 480). See also below in the discussion of Job 31 : 15.

[160] Gordon, *UT*, p. 127.

[161] *NSGJ*, p. 112 ; see also p. 22-23.

[162] Dahood, *Psalms III*, 3rd Note on Ps 142 : 5 ; idem, " Northwest Semitic Philology and Job, " p. 56-57.

Arammī 'ōvēd has the same meaning as *kalbu ḫalqu* in Amarna. Jacob was neither a " wandering Aramean " nor a " Syrian ready to perish. " He was in a fact a " fugitive Aramean " who by flight and stealth cut himself off from the community of which he had been a member.... [163]

See also Lam 3 : 18, " And I said, ' My endurance has fled (*'ābad niṣĕḥî*), my hope from Yahweh. ' " [164]

full vigor. The term *kelaḥ*, occurring only here and in Job 5 : 26, has long puzzled commentators. The parallelism here in Job 30 : 2 with *kōaḥ* " strength " suggests a similar meaning, e.g., " vigor, maturity. " [165] Marvin Pope, following Budde, emends *kalāḥ* to *kōl-lēaḥ* " all vigor. " [166] Dahood and Blommerde explain *kelaḥ* as formed by congeneric assimilation of *kōaḥ* " strength " and *lēaḥ* " vigor. " [167]

The solution adopted here is to revocalize MT *kālaḥ* to *kī lēaḥ*, *lēaḥ* " vigor " parallel to *kōaḥ* and emphatic *kī* (written defectively) paralleling *gam* which serves a similar emphatic function in the first colon. *lēaḥ* occurs in a similar context in Deut 34 : 7, " Moses was a hundred and twenty years old when he died ; his eye was not dim, nor had his vigor departed (*wĕlō'-nās lēḥōh*). " For the parallelism *gam*//*kî* see Job 13 : 16, 31 : 28, 40 : 14. The defective writing (*kī* for *kî*) would not be unusual in Job. [168]

Job 30 : 3

For want. This root occurs in *UT* 49 II : 17-19. Baal's death and absence from earth provoke a famine :

> *npš ḫsrt bn nšm*
> *npš hmlt arṣ*

---

[163] George Mendenhall, *The Tenth Generation* (Baltimore : John Hopkins, 1973), p. 137.
[164] Compare BDB, p. 664a : *'ābad niṣĕḥâ* " my endurance doth vanish. "
[165] E.g., BDB, p. 480 : " firm or rugged strength. "
[166] *Job³*, p. 219.
[167] Dahood, " Northwest Semitic Philology and Job, " p. 56 ; Blommerde, *NSGJ*, p. 12,112. See also Baumgartner, *Lexikon*, vol. II, p. 455 ; contrast L. Grabbe, *Comparative Philology*, p. 43-46.
[168] Freedman, *Eretz-Israel* 9 (1969), p. 35-44.

The appetite of men was lacking,
The appetite of earth's multitudes. [169]

The composite phrase *ḥăsar-lāḥem* " the lack of bread " in 2 Sam
3 : 29, " And may the house of Joab never be without one ... who is
slain by the sword or who lacks bread (*waḥăsar-lāḥem*), " [170] suggests
that the break up of this phrase, *bĕḥeser* " in want " at the beginning
of v 3 and *lōḥămīm* " consuming " (MT *laḥmām*) at the end of v 4,
forms an inclusion.

gnawing. The sense of the dislegomenon *'rq* (Job 30 : 3 and 17) has
caused problems for translators. *NAB* follows the LXX in reading
the Aramaic root *'rq* " to flee " (" they who fled to parched waste-
lands "). However, others (Pope, *RSV*, *NEB*, *BJ*², Chicago Bible)
follow Jerome in the Vulg., who translates *qui rodebant in solitudine*
" who were gnawing in the desert. " *UT* 75 I : 26-27 (see also 36-37)
throws new light on this troublesome verse :

> *kry amt 'pr*
> *'ẓm yd ugrm*
> *ḫl ld*
> *aklm tbrkk*
> *wld 'qqm*

> Dig with your arm the earth,
> With your strong hand the fields.
> Writhe, give birth ;
> Let the Ravagers bring you to your knees,
> Let the Devourers be born. [171]

The parallelism *aklm*//*'qqm* has led most translators to understand *'qqm*
as " Devourers, " and relate it to the Arabic root *'aqqa* " to cut, rend. " [172]
Here too in Job 30 : 3, the context and collocation with *haqqōtĕpîm*

---

[169] Dahood, *Psalms III*, 1st Note on Ps 140 : 10.

[170] See also Isa 51 : 14 ; Ezek 4 : 17 ; Prov 12 : 9.

[171] *wld* " let (them) be born " is parsed as a precative perfect (passive) form
(*UT*, par. 13.28 ; Dahood, *UHP*, p. 38) preserving the primae waw ; it parallels the
jussive *tbrkk* " Let (them) bring you to your knees " (*UT*, p. 72 ; Dahood,
Psalms III, " Index of Subjects " under " Jussive-precative sequence, " p. 484)

[172] Gordon, *UT*, Glossary 1909 ; Theodor Gaster, *Thespis: Ritual, Myth
and Drama in the Ancient Near East* (New York : Henry Schuman, 1950), p. 220
(note on p. 450) ; Caquot, *TO*, p. 341 (n. *k*).

" plucking " and *lōḥămīm* (MT *laḥmām*) " consuming " would lead one
to suspect that in Hebrew *'rq* we have a dissimilated Nebenform of
Ug. *'qq*. Jerome's version of *ha'ōrĕqîm* as *rodebant* " they were
gnawing " would thus receive confirmation. See also M. Sokoloff[173]
who suggests reading the Qumran Targum's *r'yn hwn* (= Heb. *ha'ōrĕqîm*) as " they were pasturing. "[174]

In *Psalms II²*, Dahood suggests that the hapax legomenon *mû'āqâ*
in Ps 66:11 might be another instance of this root *'qq/'rq* :

> Afflicting the thighs, the *mū'āqāh* may be considered a synonym
> of *š°ḥīn*, " boil, inflamation " ... No convincing etymology pre-
> sents itself, though a connection with Ugar. *'qqm//aklm*,
> " devourers " in UT 75 : I : 27,37, might be considered. On
> this hypothesis *mū'āqāh* would signify something like " wast-
> ing, consumption, gnawing. "[175]

Note also that *mû'āqâ* in Ps 66:11 is collocated with *mĕṣûdâ* " the
wilderness, " the same collocation which occurs between Ug. *ṣwd*
" to range, wander " and *'qq* in UT 75 I : 34-37 (*yṣd...'qqm*).

or swamp. Marvin Pope notes concerning v 3c, " This line has been
troublesome, as standard commentaries will show. "[176] *'emeš* is the
principal source of difficulty since its usual significance, " yesterday,
last night, " does not make sense here. Pope translates it as an adverbial accusative, " by night. "

In *UT 75*, cited above in reference to *ha'ōrĕqîm*, the word *mšmš*
occurs (II : 37,56), the exact etymology of which is disputed.[177] The
context, however, suggests a treacherous area such as a deep ditch,
an animal trap, quicksand, or a bog. Thus both Gaster[178] and Driver[179]
propose translating *mšmš* as " miry swamp " ; UT 75 II : 36-37,54-56 :

> *aḫḏ aklm* (*k/w*)
> *npl bmšmš* ...
> *kn npl b'l km ṯr*

---

[173] *The Targum to Job*, p. 124-125.
[174] Contrast van der Ploeg, *Le Targum de Job*, p. 40-41, " (leur) désir était. '
[175] Dahood, *Psalms II²*, 2nd Note on Ps 66:11.
[176] *Job³*, p. 219.
[177] Caquot, *TO*, p. 346-347 (n. *j*).
[178] Gaster, *Thespis*, p. 221 (textual note, p. 450).
[179] G. R. Driver, *Canaanite Myths and Legends* (Old Testament Studies 3 ;
Edinburgh : T. and T. Clark, 1956), p. 72-73.

wtkms hd km ibr [180]
btk mšmš

He seized the Ravagers ( )
He fell into the swamp ...
Thus fell Baal like a bull,
And Hadad collapsed like a buffalo
Into the midst of the swamp.

The context of Job 30 : 3 is similar : the desert (*ṣiyyâ*) and the disle-gomenon *ha'ōrĕqîm* " who gnaw " recall *mlbr* " the desert " and *'qqm* " the Devourers " of *UT* 75. [181] Thus, troublesome *'mš* (MT *'emeš*) may conceal the Hebrew equivalent of Ug. *mšmš*. Revocalizing *'emeš* to *'ō maš*, the defectively written conjunction *'ō* " or " plus *maš* " swamp, " offers a solution for this difficult passage and uncovers the merismus *ṣiyyâ 'ō maš* " desert or swamp " : so ravenous are these creatures that they scour the whole countryside for food, from the most arid desert to the dankest swamp.   A third text which contains this word is a recently published geographic list from Tell Mardikh-Ebla, TM. 75. G. 2231 obv. VI : 15. [182]   The root appears in the place name *gi-maš-maš*ki, which Dahood suggests translating " Valley of the Swamp " or " Bog Valley. " [183]   Thus a word which is hapax in each body of literature studied separately takes on new possibilities of clarification when the three literatures are examined together. [184]

---

[180] For this reading of the text see *CTA*, p. 55 (n. 16), and M. Dietrich, et al., *Die keilalphabetische Texte aus Ugarit. Einschliesslich der keilalphabeti-schen Texte ausserhalb Ugarits, Teil 1 Transkription* (AOAT 24 ; Kevelaer : Butzon und Bercker, 1976), p. 36.

[181] See also the discussion of *šiy* (*UT* 75 I : 22) and *šô'â ûmĕšō'â* below under " devastation of desolation. "

[182] G. Pettinato, " L'Atlante Geografico del Vicino Oriente Antico attestato ad Ebla e ad Abū Ṣalābīkh (I), " *Or* 47 (1978), p. 57.

[183] *gi* would be equivalent to Heb. *gy'* " valley " ; see M. Dahood, " Sti-chometry and Destiny in Psalm 23, 4, " *Bib* 60 (1979), p. 417 (n. 3). *BJ*² comes close to this same interpretation in translating *'emeš šô'â ûmĕšō'â* " ce sombre lieu de ruine et de desolation, " but no explanation of *'emeš* = " ce sombre lieu " is offered.

[184] Dahood, " Ebla, Ugarit and the Old Testament, " *The Month* (August 1978), p. 273, notes : " One should not forget that, while Ebla will elucidate many obscure words in Ugaritic and Hebrew, Ugaritic and the Bible will in turn repay the debt by clarifying numerous words and constructions in Eblaite. Hence the title of this paper is not ' Ebla and the Old Testament, ' but ' Ebla,

devastation of desolation.   In commenting on *šô'â ûměšô'â,* which also
occurs in Job 38 : 27 and Zeph 1 : 15 (all three examples of hendiadys),
Driver and Gray describe the phrase as " the alliterative combination
of two derivatives from the same root expressing the idea of completeness (cf. Is. 29 : 2, Nah 2 : 11, Ezk. 6 : 14, 33 : 29). "[185]   Thus there
is no need to follow the path of *NAB* in emending this line.   Pope
also eschews emendation, noting with Driver and Gray the alliteration : " The alliteration in this line (*'emeš šô'āh ûmšô'āh*) is too striking to be emended."[186]   Finally, another link may be seen between Job
30 and *UT* 75 if Gaster and Driver are correct in their suggestion to
connect *šiy* of *UT* 75 I : 22 with Heb. *šô'â* " desolation, wilderness."[187]

Job 30 : 4

plucking ... from the bush.   Understanding *'al* with the sense of " from "
with Blommerde [188] and Dahood. [189]   (See also *'ālêmô* under v 2 above).
E.g., Dahood notes :

> The sense and syntax of Job 30,4 are noticeably clarified if
> with A. Blommerde ... we recognize the separative force of
> *'ălê* and translate it " from " .... Just as *ḥātāh,* " to snatch, "
> is employed with *min* in Isa 30,14, *laḥtôt 'ēš miyyāqûd,* " to
> snatch fire from the hearth, " but with *'al* in Prov 25,22, *kî
> gehālîm 'attāh ḥôteh 'al rō'šô,* " If you snatch hot coals from
> his head, " so *qāṭap* is used with *min* in Ezek 17,22 *mērō'š yō-
> něqôtāyw rak 'eqṭōp,* " From the topmost branch I shall pluck
> a tender shoot, " but with *'ălê* in Job 30,4. [190]

Ugarit and the Old Testament ' ; the most rapid and solid progress in Ebla studies
will traverse the highway from Ebla to Ugarit to Palestine, and vice versa. "

[185] Driver–Gray, ICC, vol. II, p. 209.   See also the discussion of similar
expressions by Cathcart in *Nahum,* p. 103, and P. Saydon on Job 30 : 3 and
38 : 27, in " Assonance in Hebrew as a Means of Expressing Emphasis, " *Bib*
36 (1955), p. 42.   W. Irwin, *Isaiah* 28 – 33, p. 174, lists passages which he describes as following a " Law of increasing members in alliterative pairs. "

[186] Pope, *Job*³, p. 220.   Contrast *Textual Notes on the New American Bible,*
p. 377 : " omit *'emeš šô'â* : auditory duplication. "

[187] Gaster, *Thespis,* p. 219 (textual note, p. 450) ; Driver, *Canaanite Myths
and Legends,* p. 70-71 ; cf. Caquot, *TO,* p. 339 (n. *c*).

[188] Blommerde, *NSGJ,* p. 22, 112.

[189] Dahood, *Bib* 52 (1971), p. 346-347.

[190] See also the discussion of Job 19 : 25b, *wě'aḥărôn 'al-'āpār yāqûm* " the
Ultimate has risen from the Dust, " above in footnote 102.

BJ[2] rejects the emendation of *'alê* to *wa'ălê* which underlies *BJ*'s version " et les feuilles, " although *BJ*[2] fails to recognize the force of *'alê* as " from " in *'ălê-śîaḥ* here and translates " *sur* le buisson. "

the very roots. The sense seems to demand reading *wĕšoršē* (MT *wĕšōreš*), the defectively written construct plural of *šōreš* " root, " which the LXX early on recognized (plural *rizas*) and which a number of modern versions apparently presuppose (Pope, *RSV*, *NAB*, *BJ*[2], Alonso Schökel). The defective spelling would present no problem in the text of Job.[191] The waw of *wĕšoršē* (MT *wĕšōreš*) is understood in the emphatic sense, thus the translation " very. "[192]

consuming. The context here of " hunger, " " want, " " gnawing, " and especially the parallelism with *haqqōṭĕpîm* favor repointing MT *laḥmām* " their food " to the defectively written active participle *lōḥămîm* " consuming. " This reading tightens the parallelism and uncovers the chiastic structure, participle : complement : : complement : participle,[193] as well as the phenomenon of a shared article. As parallel cola can share prepositions, so parallel words share suffixes and articles ; the definite article of *haqqōṭĕpîm* does double-duty for its partner in the parallelism *lōḥămîm*.[194] See also Deut 23 : 24-25, in which *qṭp* parallels *'kl*, a synonym of *lḥm* :

> When you go into your neighbor's vineyard, you may eat your fill (*wĕ'ākaltā*) of grapes as many as you wish.... When you go into your neighbor's standing grain, you may pluck (*wĕqāṭaptā*) the ears with your hand....(*RSV*)

Dahood notes other texts in which *lḥm* " to consume, to eat " has gone unrecognized :

> Since *'ākal* was the common word " to eat, " MT experienced difficulty with *lāḥam*, the normal verb " to eat " in Ugaritic. Thus the longstanding repointing of MT *laḥmᵉkā* in Obad 7 to *lōḥᵃmekā*, " those who dine with you, " has enjoyed wide ac-

---

[191] Cf. Freedman, *Eretz-Israel* 9 (1969), p. 35-44 ; similarly for *lōḥămîm* (MT *laḥmām*) " consuming " in this same verse.

[192] Cf. Blommerde, *NSGJ*, p. 29.

[193] Dahood, " Chiasmus in Job : A Text-Critical and Philological Criterion, " p. 119-130. The chiasmus is reinforced by the rhyme, *haqqōṭĕpîm* : *'ălê* : : *šoršē* : *lōḥămîm*.

[194] Dahood, *Psalms III*, 2nd Note on Ps 121 : 6.

ceptance since it supplies both a parallel to preceding *'anšê*
šᵉlōmekā and a subject for the following verb *yāśîmû*. A similar
solution commends itself in Job 3,24, *kî lipnê lōḥᵃmay* (MT
laḥmî) *'anḥātî tābō' wayyittᵉkû kammayim ša'ᵃgōtāy*, " Even in
front of those dining with me sobbing comes upon me, and my
groans pour out like water " .... *UT*, 3 Aqht obv. 29, *yṯb llḥm*,
" he sits down to dine ", prompts a repointing in Isa 47,14,
'ên gaḥelet lōḥᵃmîm (MT *laḥmām*) *'ûr lāšebet negdô* " There is
no ember for the diners, no hearth to sit in front of. " [195]

Job 30 : 5-8

From the community they are banished ;
    they shout after them as a thief,
In the most dreaded of ravines to dwell,
    in the holes of the ground and rocks.
Among the bushes they bray,
    amidst the nettles they huddle together,
A senseless, yes nameless brood,
    thrust out of the town.

As vv 2-4 stress the nutrional deprivation of this group, vv 5-8
describe the poverty of their shelter. The inclusive function of *min-gēw*
" from the community " (v 5) and *min-hā'āreṣ* " out of the town " (v 8)
was noted above in the introduction to this section (vv 2-8). The
two terms, *gēw* " community " and *'ereṣ* " city, " emphasize the completeness of their expulsion from society. *'ereṣ* refers more to the
physical city with its walls and buildings, while *gēw* encompasses the
contact with their fellow men, the human " community, " from which
they have been excluded.

Job 30 : 5

from the community. The proximity of *min-gēw* in v 5 to *min-hā'āreṣ*
in v 8 suggests that *hā'āreṣ* has the meaning here of " city " [196] and
that these two cola act as an inclusion for vv 5-8 :

---

[195] Dahood, *Or* 45 (1976), p. 343. Contrast G. I. Davies, " A New Solution to a Crux in Obadiah 7, " *VT* 27 (1977), p. 484-487.
[196] See below under Job 30 : 8.

(5a) *min-gēw yĕgōrāšû*
From the community they are banished.
(8b) *nikkĕ'û min-hā'āreṣ*
Thrust out of the town.

NAB's proposal to emend *min-gēw* to *min-gôy* " from among men "
is unnecessary. Although *gēw* here is a hapax in Hebrew with the
sense of " community, " its appearance in Phoenician with this meaning (*KAI* 60 : 2,5,7,8 ; 164 : 3) [197] supports the reliability of the Hebrew
text ; e.g., *KAI* 60 : 7-8 :

> *lkn yd' ḥṣdnym k yd' hgw lšlm ḥlpt 'yt*
> *'dmm 'š p'l mšrt 't pn gw*

Thus that the Sidonians will know that the community knows
how to pay the wages of men who do service in the presence
of the community.

they are banished. *grš* is another word which occurs also in Phoenician, in the Nora Stone (*KAI* 46 : 2) : *btršš wgrš h'* " from Tarshish
he was driven. " [198]
    The collocation here of *grš* (v 5) and *škn* (v 6) recalls their paral-
lelism in Gen 3 : 24, " He (God) drove out (*wayĕgāreš*) the man ; and
at the east of the garden of Eden he placed (*wayyaškēn*) the cherubim " ;
see also Ps 78 : 55 (*wayĕgāreš* / /*wayyaškēn*).

Job 30 : 6

In the most dreaded of ravines. Most translators connect hapax *'ārûṣ*
of *ba'ărûṣ* with an arabic root for " slope, gully. " ICC, for example,
renders the phrase, " In a gully of the wadis. " [199] BDB is probably
more accurate in deriving it from Heb. *'rṣ* (Ug. *'rẓ*) " to fear, dread "

---

[197] And also in *KAI* 17 : 1, according to J. T. Milik, in his review of *Les
papyrus araméens d'Hermopoulis et les cultes syrophéniciens en Egypte perse,*
in *Bib* 48 (1967), p. 572-573. He translates *lrbty l'štrt 'š bgw hqdš* " A ma mai-
tresse, à Astarté qui réside entre la gent des Saints, " and rejects the characterization of *bgw* as " an aramaism " : " On comprend *gw* comme un aramaïsme
ce qui est gratuit et sans aucun parallèle dans l'épigraphie phénicienne. "
[198] Peckham, *Or* 41 (1972), p. 459. See also his remarks quoted above in
the introduction to this section, Job 30 : 2-8.
[199] Driver–Gray, ICC, vol. I, p. 253 ; vol. II, p. 210. Pope, *RSV*, *NEB*,
all have " gully " ; *NAB* has " slope. "

and in recognizing here the adjective + genitive construction (*ba'ărûṣ + nĕḥālîm*) expressing the superlative, " in the most dreaded of ravines. "[200] Compare Ezek 28:7 (and 30:11; 31:12; 32:12): *'ārîṣê gôyim* " the most terrible of the nations " (*RSV*).[201]

to dwell. Compare the collocation of *mal'āk* " messenger " ... *škn* " to inhabit " in Job 4:18-19 (*ûbĕmal'ākāyw ... šōkĕnê*) with the parallelism of these same roots in *UT* 51 VII:44-45, *yštkn//ilak*. Note also the Hebrew parallel pair *škn//yšb* in Job 15:28 (*wayyiškôn//lō'-yēšĕbû*) and 29:25 (*wĕ'ēšēb//wĕ'eškôn*).

ravines. Numerous references are made in the course of this commentary to parallel word pairs which appear both in Job and in Ugaritic literature. This might be the appropriate point at which to quote Dahood's comment on the large number of Ugaritic parallel pairs attested only in Job, including the word here *nḥl* " torrent, ravine " as it appears in Job 20:17 parallel to *peleg* " stream ":[202]

> If (Cyrus) Gordon is correct when maintaining that " Nowhere does the proximity of Hebrew and Ugaritic manifest itself more plainly than in pairs of synonyms used parallelistically in both languages, " then special significance must be attached to those pairs occurring *only* in Job and Ugaritic.[203]

the ravines ... the ground. This same parallelism (reversed), *naḥal// 'āpār*, occurs also in Job 22:24, a verse now made clearer by recognition of three elements of Northwest Semitic, the infinitive absolute continuing a chain of finite verbs (*šît*), a compound preposition (*bĕṣûr*, " upon, " lit. " on the back of "), and the break-up of a composite phrase (*beṣer-'ôpîr* " gold of Ophir "):

> And if you set on the dust gold
> and upon the wadis Ophir.

---

[200] BDB, p. 792a; see GKC, par. 133h.

[201] Dahood discusses further examples in Deut 33:19 (*ṭĕmûnê ḥôl* " the most hidden treasures of the sand "), Isa 35:9 (*pĕrîṣ ḥayyôt* " the most violent of the wild beasts "), and the inverted construct chain *'ōrāḥôt* (MT *'orḥôt*) *pārîṣ* " the most rugged of paths " in Ps 17:4, in his article " Deuteronomy 33,19 and *UT*, 52:61-63, " *Or* 47 (1978), p. 263-264.

[202] See also *nhq* in Job 30:7 and its parallelism with *g'h* in Job 6:5.

[203] Dahood, *RSP* I, p. 82.

BHS repeats the suggestion of *BHK³* to emend *wĕšît* to *wĕšattā* "and (if) you set." However, the numerous examples of an infinitive absolute continuing a finite verb (N.B., *tāšûb ... tarḥîq* in v 23)²⁰⁴ suggest that MT *wĕšît* mat be left unchanged and parsed as an infinitive absolute.

Similarly, modern versions fail to recognize in *bĕṣûr* the compound preposition formed from *bĕ* "in, on" + *ṣûr* "back" (= Ug. *ẓr* "back"). In *UT* 51 VIII : 5-6, *'l* "on" parallels the compound *lẓr* "upon" (= *l* + *ẓr*; compare *'al* // *bĕṣûr* here in Job 22 : 24): *ša ġr 'l ydm ḫlb lẓr rḥtm* "Lift up the mountain on your hands, the hill upon your palms."

Finally in *bāṣer ... 'ôpîr*, we may have the break-up of the composite phrase *beṣer 'ôpîr* "gold of Ophir"; compare *ketem 'ôpîr* "gold of Ophir" in Job 28 : 16, Ps 45 : 10, Isa 13 : 12.

in the holes. The preposition *bĕ* in the first colon (*bă'arûṣ nĕḥālîm* "in the most dreaded of ravines") does double duty governing also *ḥōrê 'āpār wĕkēpîm* "in the holes of the ground and rocks" of the second colon.²⁰⁵

ḥōr "cave, hole," may appear in Ugaritic, in RŠ 24.247, according to Ch. Virolleaud: *ḫr apm* = "nostrils."²⁰⁶

Job 30 : 7

among ... amidst. The parallelism *bên* // *taḥat* suggests that *taḥat* here has the sense of "among, amidst." Ug. *tḥt* can also have this meaning, e.g., in 2 Aqht V : 6-7, *ytb bap ṯġr tḥt adrm dbgrn* "He sits at the edge of the gate, among the nobles who are on the threshing floor." Marvin Pope also recognizes *tḥt* = "among" in Job 34 : 26:

> *taḥat-rĕšā'îm sĕpāqām*
> *bimqôm rō'îm*
>
> As criminals (lit. "among, in the place of") he strikes them down
> In a public place.²⁰⁷

Ezek 10 : 2 repeats the parallelism *bên* // *taḥat* (*'el-bênôt* // *'el-taḥat* // *mibbênôt*): "Go in among (*'el-bênôt*) the whirling wheels underneath

---

²⁰⁴ Dahood, *Psalms III*, p. 425.
²⁰⁵ Driver–Gray, ICC, vol. II, p. 210.
²⁰⁶ Gordon, *UT*, Glossary 998. See also Cathcart, *Nahum*, p. 108.
²⁰⁷ Pope, *Job³*, p. 259; Dahood, "Northwest Semitic Philology and Job," p. 71; idem, *RSP* I, II, 101.

(*'el-tahat*) the Cherub; fill your hands with burning coals from between (*mibbênôt*) the Cherubim. "

they bray. *nāhaq* occurs only here and in Job 6 : 5 in the Bible:

> *hăyinhaq-pere' 'ălê-deše'*
> *'im yig'eh-ššôr 'al-bĕlîlô*
>
> Does the ass bray over his grass
> The bull bellow over his fodder?[208]

Compare *hăyinhaq*//*yig'eh* with the same parallelism in *UT* Krt 120-
123 (*nhqt* " braying " //*g't* " lowing ") :

> *lqr ṯigt ibrh*
> *lql nhqt ḥmrh*
> *lg't alp ḥrṯ*
> *zǵt klb ṣpr*
>
> Because of the roar of his bull,
> Because of the braying of his donkey,
> Because of the lowing of his plow ox,
> Because of the barking of his watch dog.[209]

Job 30 : 8

A senseless, yes nameless brood. Literally, " Sons of a fool, yes sons
of no name. " The repetition *bĕnê ... gam-bĕnê* is similar to the construction with the emphatic waw pointed out by Blommerde in Job
in which " a word of the first stich is repeated at the beginning of the
second one, but now reinforced by emphatic waw ... "; e.g., *šām ...
wĕšām* in Job 3 : 17:

> *šām rĕšā'îm ḥādĕlû rōgez*
> *wĕšām yānûḥû yĕgî'ê kōaḥ*
>
> There the rich stop striving
> there indeed they rest tired of wealth.[210]

gam performs a similar emphatic function here in Job 30 : 8.
Wolfgang Roth suggests that *nābāl*, " senseless one, fool " may

---

[208] Blommerde, *NSGJ*, p. 47.
[209] *RSP* I, II, 378.
[210] Blommerde, *NSGJ*, p. 29 and 39.

have the meaning here of " outcast, " which certainly accords with
the motif of exile in vv 2-8 discussed above. [211]

nameless. The positive form of *běnê běli-šēm* " sons of no name "
occurs in Phoenician in the Karatepe Inscription (*KAI* 26 III : 12-13),
'dm 'š 'dm šm " a man who is a man of a name, " i.e., an ordinary
citizen in contrast to *rznm* " princes " or *mlkm* " kings. "

thrust. For this sense of *nk'*, a biform of *nkh* " to strike, smite, thrust, "
see 1 Sam 2 : 14, " And he would thrust (*hikkâ*) (it) into the pan, or
kettle, or cauldron, or pot " (Likewise 1 Sam 19 : 10).

out of the town. *'rṣ* appears in Phoenician with the sense " city, city-
state " : *ṣdn 'rṣ ym* " Sidon, City by the Sea. " A number of passages in Hebrew call for this same meaning, as Dahood first pointed
out in Prov 31 : 23,

> Her husband is known at the gates,
> From his sitting with the elders of the city
> (*'im-ziqnê-'āreṣ*). [212]

The (distant) parallelism of v 5a and v 8b, *min-gēw yĕgōrāšû* " banished
from the community " // *nikkĕ'û min-hā'āreṣ* " thrust out of the town, "
suggests that *'rṣ* should be translated here also as " city, town. "

Job 30 : 9-10

> And now a song for them am I,
>   become to them a gibe.
> They abhor me, keep aloof from me,
>   and from my face they spare no spit.

A " distant parallelism " (*wĕ'attâ śāḥăqû*, v 1 // *wĕ'attâ nĕgînātām*,
v 9 ; see below) joins these two verses to the opening verse of Chapter
30. The twin motifs of " mocking " and " spitting " recall a similar
collocation of ideas in *UT* 51 III : 13 (*qlṣ* " revile " + *wpṭ* " spit ") :

[211] " NBL, " *VT* 10 (1960), p. 402-403. But see G. Gerleman, " Der Nicht-
Mensch, Erwägungen zur hebräischer Wurzel *NBL,* " *VT* 24 (1974), p. 153-154.
[212] Mitchell Dahood, S.J., *Proverbs and Northwest Semitic Philology* (Rome :
Pontificium Institutum Biblicum, 1963), p. 62-63 ; idem, *Bib* 44 (1963), p. 297-
298 ; idem, *Bib* 47 (1966), p. 280 ; idem, *Psalms II²*, 2nd Note on Ps 74 : 20 ;
van Dijk, *Ezekiel's Prophecy on Tyre*, p. 52-53 ; Cathcart, *Nahum*, p. 141 ; Irwin,
Isaiah 28 – 33, p. 153-155.

> *wydd wyqlṣn*
> *wqm wywpṭn*
> *btk pḫr bn ilm*

And he began to revile,
He proceeded to spit
In the midst of the assembly of the gods.

The latter passage invites comparison with the Qumran Manual of
Discipline (VII : 13) :

> *w'yš 'šr yrwq 'l twk mwšb*
> *hrbym wn'nš šlšm ywm*

And the man who spits into the midst
of a session of the elders shall be
punished thirty days. [213]

Job 30 : 9

And now a song. Many commentators have remarked on *wĕ'attâ*
" and now " which harks back to *wĕ'attâ* in v 1. But none of them
has noted the phenomenon of " distant parallelism " which strengthens
the connection between these two verses. [214]   The two roots parallel
in Lam 3 : 14 (*śĕḥōq* " a joke " //*nĕgînātām* " a song for them "),

> *hāyîtî śĕḥōq lĕkol-'ammî*
> *nĕgînātām kol-hayyôm*

I am a joke to the whole people,
a song for them all day long. [215]

are distantly parallel in Job 30 : 1 and 9 (*wĕ'attâ śāḥăqû* " And now they
deride " //*wĕ'attâ nĕgînātām* " And now a song for them ").

a song for them. Following Blommerde, who understands the suffix
of *nĕgînātām* here and in Lam 3 : 14 as datival :

---

[213] M. Burrows, *The Dead Sea Scrolls of St. Mark's Monastery*, vol. II,
fascicle 2 (New Haven : American Schools of Oriental Research, 1951) ; A. R. C.
Leaney, *The Rule of Qumran and its Meaning* (New Testament Library ; London : SCM, 1966), p. 198, 206-207.

[214] *RSP* I, p. 80-81.

[215] Reading the yodh of *'ammî* as an archaic genitive ending and the suffix
of *nĕgînātām* as datival.

The parallelism with *lāhem lĕmillâ* seems to indicate that the
genitive suffix in *nĕgînātām* serves as a dative; similarly in
Lam 3:14 *nĕgînātām//sĕḥōq lĕ.* [216]

a gibe. BHS has wisely deleted the emendation of *lĕmillâ* to *lĕmāšāl*
(based on Job 17:6) suggested in the apparatus of *BHK³*. Note also
mll in the Azitawaddu Inscription (*KAI* 26 B/C II:16-17), *mtmll ...*
ldnnym " one speaking derisively of the Danunians. " [217]

Job 30:10

they abhor me. Note the Hebrew parallel pair *tᶜb* " to abhor "//*'hb*
" to love " in Job 19:19; Jer 14:10; Ps 119:163.

• *keep aloof.* The collocation here of *rḥq* " to be distant " (v 10, *rāḥăqû*)
and *ᶜyn* (MT *ᶜnh*) " to see, eye " (v 11, *wîᶜînūnî*, MT *wayĕᶜannēnî*) recalls
the parallelism of these same verbs in *UT* ᶜnt IV:83-84 (*yᶜn//šrḥq*):

> *hlk aḫth bᶜl yᶜn*
> *tdrq ybnt abh*
> *šrḥq aṯt lpnnh*
> *št alp qdmh*

The coming of his sister Baal eyes,
The approach of his father's offspring.
He removes the women from his presence,
He sets an ox before her. [218]

and from my face. Some translators understand *mippānay* as " in
my presence, before me. " [219] This is certainly possible, in which
case *min* here has the sense of " in " (compare *lipnay*), [220] and an in-

---

[216] Blommerde, *NSGJ*, p. 112.

[217] Dahood, *Bib* 44 (1963), p. 71-72; Blommerde, *NSGJ*, p. 112. See
also Sefire III:2, *ymll mln lᶜly* " and who utters evil words against me " (Fitzmyer, *The Aramaic Inscriptions of Sefire*, p. 96-97, 104-105).

[218] For the parallelism *šrḥq//št*, compare Job 22:23-24, *tarḥîq ... wĕšît.*

[219] *RSV* " at the sight of me "; *BJ²* " devant moi "; Duhm, *Das Buch
Hiob*, p. 142, " vor mir. "

[220] See Blommerde, *NSGJ*, p. 22, 100-101, on Job 23:12, *mēḥēqî* (MT
mēḥuqqî) *ṣāpantî 'imrê-pîw* " In my bosom I treasured the words of his mouth. "
Driver–Gray, ICC, vol. II, p. 211, refer to Lev 19:32, *mippĕnê šêbâ tāqûm*
" In the presence of an elder you shall rise. " Further on *min* = " in, " cf.
Dahood, *Psalms II²*, 2nd Note on Ps 68:27.

teresting parallel pair comes to light with *min* employed with two different meanings in the same verse, *min* " from " // *min* " in. " However, comparison with Job 17 : 6, *wĕtōpet lĕpānîm 'ehyeh* " And I am he in whose face they spit, " argues in favor of the present translation. See also Isa 50 : 6, *pānay lō' histartî mikkĕlimmôt wārōq* " My face I did not turn away from ignominy and spittle " [221] and Ps 71 : 7, *kĕmôpet hāyîtî lĕrabbîm* " as an object of spitting was I to the rabble. " [222]

they spare.   U. Cassuto recognizes this word in *UT* 'nt III : 15, *ḥšk 'ṣk 'bṣk* " Spare your rod, your club. " [223]

Job 30 : 11-15

> Indeed they watch at my door and eye me
> > and cast off restraint in my presence.
>
> On my right and left,
> > they arise who spy on me, they are unrestrained;
> > and they heap up against me their roads of ruin.
>
> They break up my path,
> > they succeed to undo me;
> > there is no escape from them.
>
> Through a wide breach they come,
> > amidst the havoc they arrive.
>
> Terror turns on me, .
> > pursues my dignity like the wind;
> > like a cloud, my prosperity disappears.

A new section begins with v 11. Job now describes himself as under siege by a nameless army of attackers. [224] Their identity is revealed finally in v 15 with *ballāhôt* " Terror, " one of the numerous epithets of the netherworld. [225]

---

[221] Dahood, *Psalms I*, 2nd Note on Ps. 10 : 11.

[222] On Job 17 : 6, Ps 71 : 7, see Dahood, *Bib* 55 (1974), p. 390-391.

[223] Compare Prov 13 : 24, *ḥôśēk šibṭô śōnē' bĕnô* " Who spares the rod hates his son "; U. Cassuto, *The Goddess Anat*, p. 126 ; also, Aistleitner, *Wörterbuch*, p. 109 (no. 983).

[224] Fedrizzi, *Giobbe*, p. 209.

[225] See below under *ballāhôt* " Terror " in 30 : 15. G. Fohrer, *Das Buch Hiob*, p. 419, comments on v 12, " Unter der ' Brut ' sind daher nicht mehr die Spötter, sondern die Scharen der Krankheitsdämonen, der unheilbringenden Kräfte und der Mächte des Unglücks zu verstehen .... "

With the recognition of the sense of *twr* " watch " in v 11 and *rgl* " spy " in v 12, the imagery becomes clearer. The poet proceeds through the various stages in the storming of a city beginning with the scouting and spying of its defenses (v 11), the encirclement and construction of the siege ramps (v 12), the isolation of the city from sources of supply and assistance (v 13), and finally the breach of the walls (v 14) and defeat (v 15).

Job 30 : 11

they watch ... and eye me. Dahood's suggestion to read here the roots *twr* " to roam, explore " and *'yn* " to eye, see " (*kî yātūrû petaḥ wî'înūnî* " They spy at my door and eye me " ; MT *kî yitri* [Ketiv *ytrw*] *pittaḥ wayĕ'annēnî*) [226] finds confirmation in *UT* 76 II : 27-28, where these same two roots also occur in parallel (line 28, *wt'n*//*tr*) :

> *wtšu 'nh wt'n*
> *wt'n arḥ wtr blkt*

> She lifts up her eyes and sees,
> She sees a cow and roams in walking.

1 Sam 18 : 9 offers a similar use of the denominative verb *'yn* " to look suspiciously, hostilely at " : " And Saul eyed (*'ōwēn*) David from that day on. " The same idea is echoed in Job 31 : 9, " If I lurked at my neighbor's door (*'al-petaḥ rē'î*), " and Gen 4 : 7, *lapetaḥ ḥaṭā't rōbēṣ* " Sin is the demon (lit. the Croucher) at the door. "

These two motifs of the " evil eye " (*'yn* " to eye hostilely ") and of beings, human and otherwise, lurking at one's door (*petaḥ*) recur in the Phoenician Inscriptions from Arslan Tash. [227] Frank Cross and Richard Saley describe the first inscription (*KAI* 27) as an incantation placed over the doorway of a house to ward off evil spirits :

> The conjurations require that the demons of the night time depart, disappear, fly from room, house, door entrance....

---

[226] Dahood, *Bib* 55 (1974), p. 386. *yātūrû* for *yātûrû* is another example of defective spelling in Job ; cf. Freedman, *Eretz-Israel* 9 (1969), p. 35-44.

[227] F. M. Cross and R. Saley, " Phoenician Incantations on a Plaque from the Seventh Century B.C. from Arslan Tash in Upper Syria, " *BASOR* 197 (February 1970), p. 42-49 ; T. Gaster, " A Hang-Up for Hang-Ups : The Second Amuletic Plaque from Arslan Tash, " *BASOR* 209 (February 1973), p. 18-26 ; F. M. Cross, " Leaves from an Epigraphist's Notebook, " *CBQ* 36 (1974), p. 486-494.

The incantation strongly suggests the function of the plaque.... it is a device to protect the house, especially its entrance. Moreover, the shape of the plaque and the hole drilled through it suggest strongly that it was hung up in a doorway where it could be seen by the demons attempting an entrance. [228]

The second inscription contains two incantations. One of the beings against whom the first incantation is directed is called *rb ʿn* " Big-Eye " and the second incantation begins, *brḥ ʿyn bdr*, which Cross translates, " Flee, O ' Eyer ' (with the evil eye), from (my) house. " [229] Compare also Job 7 : 8b, *ʾênêkā bî wĕʾiyyĕnunî* (MT *wĕʾenennî*) " Your eyes are against me and annihilate me, " [230] 16 : 9c *ṣārî yilṭôš ʿênāyw lî* " He sharpens his blade, his eyes are fixed upon me," [231] and 27 : 19b *ʿênāyw pāqaḥ wĕʾiyyĕnennû* (MT *wĕʾenennû*) " He fixes his gaze and annihilates him. " [232]

watch ... cast off. This same collocation (*twr ... šlḥ*) occurs in Num 13 : 2, *šĕlaḥ-lĕkā ʾănāšîm wĕyātūrû ʾet-ʾereṣ kĕnaʿan* " send out men to spy out the land of Canaan " ; [233] on " spy out the land " (*wĕyātūrû ʾet- ʾereṣ*) compare *UT* 51 V : 83, *wtr arṣ* " and she roams the earth " (//2 Aqht VI ; 46 : ʿnt V : 13). [234]

at my door. *petaḥ* (MT *pittaḥ*) shares the suffix of its parallel in the second colon, *mippānay* " in my presence. " On the absence of the preposition with *petaḥ*, consult Joüon, *Grammaire*, par. 126h.

eye ... in my presence. The collocation here of the roots *ʿyn* " eye " and *panîm* " face " recalls the Ugaritic–Hebrew parallel pair *ʿn*//*pnm*. Compare Jer 16 : 17, " For my eyes (*ʿênay*) are upon all their ways ; they are not hid from my presence (*millĕpānāy*) nor is their iniquity concealed from my eyes (*minneged ʿênāy*), " and *UT* ʿnt IV : 83-84 (*ʿn ... pnn*) :

> *hlk aḫth bʿl yʿn*
> *tdrq ybnt abh*
> *šrḥq aṯt lpnnh*

---

[228] Cross and Saley, *BASOR* 197 (February 1970), p. 48.
[229] Cross, *CBQ* 36 (1974), p. 488-489.
[230] Cf., Blommerde, *NSGJ*, p. 106.
[231] Ibid., p. 77.
[232] Ibid., p. 105.
[233] See also Num 13 : 16,17 ; 14 : 36.
[234] C. Virolleaud, *La légende phénicienne de Danel* (Mission de Ras Shamra 1 ; Paris : Paul Geuthner, 1936), p. 216 (n. 1) ; Caquot, *TO*, p. 174 (n. *i*).

The coming of his sister Baal eyes,
The tread of his father's offspring.
He removes the women from his presence. [235]

Phoenician provides some further examples; e.g., *KAI* 10 : 10 and 16
(*l'n ... l'n ... pn*) :

(10)   *ḥn l'n 'lnm wl'n 'm 'rṣ z*
       favor in the eyes of the gods and
       in the eyes of the people of this city.
(16)   *'t pn kl 'ln gbl*
       before the face of all the gods of Byblos.

See also *KAI* 60 : 5 and 8.

in my presence.   Add the collocation of *pny* " face " ... *ymyn* " right
hand " here in Job 30 : 11-12 to the instances of the Ugaritic–Hebrew
parallel pair *pnm//ymn* in *RSP* I,II,461.

Job 30 : 12

   This analysis of the stichometry of v 12 reveals the ascending
pattern of the accents (2 /3 /4) as well as of the syllable count (6 : 8 : 10).

On my right.   *BHK*[3] suggests emending *'al-yāmîn* " on the right "
to *'al-yĕmînî* " on my right, " a proposal not repeated by *BHS*.   In
Ugaritic and in Hebrew, the suffix may be omitted with names of parts
of the body. [236]

and left.   *BHK*[3] and *BHS* both record that numerous manuscripts
read *prḥh* rather than *prḥḥ*.   A possible solution thus emerges for this
crux interpretum if one vocalizes *prḥh* as *pĕraḥâ*, the conjunctive particle
pa " and " plus the feminine singular absolute *raḥâ* " palm, hand. "
   An increasing number of examples of the particle *pa* " and " in
Hebrew have been identified, and Dahood points to one in particular
in Job which also occurs in the context of battle imagery (16 : 14) :

---

[235] Some other Hebrew examples of this parallel pair include Jer 40 : 4;
Ps 17 : 2 ; Job 11 : 19-20 ; 17 : 5-6 ; 21 : 8 ; 24 : 15.
[236] Blommerde, *NSGJ*, p. 10 ; Dahood " Index of Subjects " under " Suffix
omitted with name of part of body " in *Psalms II*[2] (p. 398) and *Psalms III*
(p. 488).

yiprĕṣēnî pārōṣ (MT *pereṣ*) *'al pānay* (MT *pĕnê*)
pārōṣ (MT *pereṣ*) *yārūṣ 'ālay kĕgibbôr*

He breaches me with a breach in front of me,
And charging, he charges me like a warrior. [237]

The poet thus uses a different conjunctive device in each of the three
cola of v 12 : *pa* in the first colon, asyndeton in the second colon (" My
detractors rise up, let loose "), and *waw* in the third.

raḥâ " palm, hand " occurs in Ugaritic (*rḥ* II) in the feminine
dual form parallel to *ydm* " hands " in *UT* 51 VIII : 6 (//67 V : 14) : [238]

ša ǵr 'l ydm
ḫlb lẓr rḥtm

Lift up the mountain on your hands,
The hill upon your palms.

Koehler–Baumgartner have identified the root in Hebrew in Isa 30 : 24,
raḥat, which they define as " winnowing shovel " and compare to
Ug. *rḥtm* " two palms. " [239] Here in Job 30 : 12, in parallelism with
yāmîn " right hand, " *raḥâ* is probably best taken in a contrastive
sense " left hand. " Compare *yād* " left hand "//*yāmîn* " right hand "
elsewhere in both Hebrew and Ugaritic. [240] With the recognition of
raḥâ " (left) hand ", the imagery of v 12 is clarified. The context is
definitely that of battle, and not reminiscent of a courtroom scene as
an isolated *'al-yāmîn* " on my right " has led some commentators to
suggest. Fedrizzi, for example, writes :

La versione propone l'imagine degli accusatori (cfr. il testi-
mone in 16,8 e lo stare " alla destra " per accusare, Sal. 109,6 ;
Zacc. 3,1) che insolentiscono per rovinare l'onore di Giobbe. [241]

---

[237] Dahood, *Bib* 51 (1970), p. 393-395. For further bibliography and examples of the particle *pa* " and, " cf. Blommerde, *NSGJ*, p. 32-33 ; Dahood, *Psalms
III*, p. 410 ; Kuhnigk, *NSH*, p. 26,88 ; *RSP* I, p. 174.

[238] Gordon, *UT*, Glossary 2315.

[239] K-B, *Lexicon*, p. 888 ; Dahood, *Bib* 53 (1972), p. 388-389. See also *UT*
49 II : 33-34, *bišt tšrpnn brḥm tṭḥnn* " with fire she burns him, with millstones
she grinds him. "

[240] Dahood, *Psalms III*, p. 449.

[241] Fedrizzi, *Giobbe*, p. 209 ; Dhorme, *Le Livre de Job*, ad locum. Contrast
the note in *BJ*² on v 12 : " Job compare les injures qu'il a subies au siège et à
l'assaut d'une ville. "

who spy on me. E. Kissane first proposed reading the word *raglay* in another sense than " foot " : " The key to the difficulty is to regard the noun as meaning ' slander ' instead of the usual meaning ' foot.' " [242] The collocation with *twr* " to roam, watch " in v 11 suggests rather to understand *rgly* here as *rōgĕlay* " those who spy on me, " the qal participle of the denominative verb *rāgal* " to search out, to spy. " Both *twr* and *rgl* are used in this sense of reconnoitering the Promised Land in Num 13 : 16, " the men whom Moses sent to spy out (*lātûr*) the land, " and Num 21 : 32, " And Moses sent to spy out (*lĕraggēl*) Jazer. " See also Deut 1 : 24 (*wayĕraggĕlû* " and they spied it out ") and 33 (*lātûr lākem māqôm* " to seek you out a place "). Although the denominative verb *rgl* appears in these passages in the piel conjugation, there are instances of it in the qal, e.g., Ps 15 : 3. [243]

they are unrestrained. Repointing MT *šillēḥû* to *šūllĕḥû*, the 3rd person plural pual. Compare Prov 29 : 15 (*NEB*) " a boy who runs wild (*naʿar mĕšūllaḥ*, pual participle) " and Gen 49 : 21 " Nephtali is a hind let loose (*šĕlūḥâ*, qal passive participle). "

their roads of ruin. As Pope notes, siegeworks are being referred to, the ramparts which an attacking army raises against the wall of a besieged city ; cf., Job 19 : 12 and *sōlălâ* " siege mound. " But another motif is operative here. Those attacking Job are none other than the minions of Death, as suggested by *'êd* " ruin, " which is associated elsewhere in Job with the netherworld context, e.g., in 18 : 12 :

> The Ravenous One confronts him,
> Calamity (*'êd*) ready at his side. [244]

Compare also *'ōraḥ lō'-'āšûb* " the way of no return " in Job 16 : 22.

---

[242] E. J. Kissane, *The Book of Job : Translated from a Critically Revised Hebrew Text with Commentary* (Dublin : Richmond Press, 1939), p. 191, *BJ*² also identifies the sense of *rgl* " to spy (épier) " but it emends the text in the process : " On lit *wayeraggelû shalwî* ' épie si je suis tranquille ' au lieu de *weraglay shillehû*, litt. ' ils ont jeté mes pieds. ' "

[243] Dahood, *Psalms I*, 1st Note on Ps 15 : 3 ; idem, *Psalms II*², 5th Note on Ps 56 : 7.

[244] Dahood, *Psalms I*, 2nd Note on Ps 38 : 18, 2nd Note on Ps 18 : 19 ; idem, *Psalms III*, 6th Note on Ps 116 : 10 ; Pope, *Job*³, p. 132 ; Tromp, *Death and the Nether World*, p. 164.

Job 30 : 13

They break up. There is no need to emend hapax *nts* to *nātaṣ* " to
pull down, break down " now that the root *nts* (related to *ntṣ*, and
probably with the same sense) is attested in *UT* 68 : 4, *its anšq* (b)*htm*
" I will break up, I will burn the (hou)se. "[245] The translators of
Textes ougaritiques remark on this passage :

> '*its* : nous rapprochons ce terme énigmatique de l'hapax hé-
> braïque *nâtas,* " défoncer " (Job 30,13), apparenté à *nâtaṣ,*
> " detruire, abattre " (Virolleaud, Driver).[246]

my path. Some manuscripts and ancient versions read the plural
nĕtîbôtay " my paths. "[247] Retaining the singular here, however,
preserves the rhyme and play on words with *nĕdibātî* " my dignity "
in v 15. Dahood has remarked on the possible interplay between
these two words since *ndbty* " my dignity " of Job 30 : 15 has been
read *ntbty* " my path(s) " by some manuscripts and the Syriac. On
the basis of this interplay he proposes translating Prov 12 : 28,

> On the road of righteousness there is life,
>   and on the path of nobleness (*wĕderek nĕtîbâ*)
> is immortality.[248]

In Judg 5 : 6, *BHS* repeats the suggestion of *BHK*[3] to delete *'ŏrāḥôt*
of *'ŏrāḥôt 'ăqalqallôt* " the winding roads, " where it is parallel with
wĕhōlĕkê nĕtîbôt " the wayfaring men. " This same parallelism (*'orḥî*
" my way "//*nĕtîbôtay*) in Job 19 : 8,

> He has blocked my way (*'orḥî*) so that I cannot pass,
> He puts darkness upon my path (*nĕtîbôtay*) (Pope),

and their collocation here in Job 30 : 12-13 (*'orḥôt ... nĕtîbatî*) argues
against such a move.[249]

---

[245] Caquot, *TO*, p. 135.

[246] Ibid., p. 135 (n. *h*) ; Pope, *Job*[3], p. 221.

[247] *NEB* follows this reading ; cf. Brockington, *The Hebrew Text of the Old
Testament*, p. 113.

[248] *RSP*, I, p. 84 (n. 48).

[249] MT in Judg 5 : 6 is further supported by the A : B :: B : A word pattern,
'ŏrēḥôt (MT *'ŏrāḥôt*) : *wĕhōlĕkê* :: *yēlĕkû* : *'ŏrāḥôt* ; see Ceresko, *CBQ* 38 (1976),
p. 306-307.

my path ... breach. These two words collocated here in vv 13-14 *(nĕtî-bātî ... pereṣ)* are parallel in Isa 58 : 12 where the idea being expressed presents quite a contrast to Job 30 : 13-14 :

> You shall be called the repairer of the breach *(pereṣ),*
> the restorer of streets *(nĕtîbôt)* to dwell in. *(RSV)*

they further. *yōʿîlû* offers yet another example of the unusual number of *scripta defectiva* in Job. D. N. Freedman comments :

> There are four examples of the Hiphil of *yʿl* in Job, of which two are defectively written...
> Elsewhere there are in MT 19 examples of the Hiphil of *yʿl,* all of which have the full spelling. The only two cases of contracted spelling in the Bible occur in Job. [250]

there is no escape. The *BHS* apparatus retains the emendation of *ʿzr* " to help " to *ʿṣr* " to hinder " advised by the apparatus of *BHK³.* *NAB, RSV, BJ²* all follow this suggestion. Pope and *NEB* avoid changing the text by appealing to the arabic cognate of *ʿzr* which can be used in the opposite senses of " help " and " hinder. "

Dahood and, more fully, B. Baisas, [251] however, have demonstrated that *ʿzr* in certain contexts and especially when used with the preposition *min* (or *bĕ* or *lĕ* when employed with that meaning as, for example, *lĕ* here) has the sense of " rescue, save " : " Normally signifying ʿ to help,ʾ *ʿḏr* denotes ʿ to rescue, liberate fromʾ when employed with the preposition *b,* ʿ from, ʾ in Ugaritic or *min* in Hebrew. " [252] They appeal to *UT* 3 Aqht (rev) 12-14, where *ʿḏr* parallels *plṭ* " to save, rescue " :

> *w (   ) aqht wplṭk*
> *bn (dnil) wʿḏrk*
> *byd btlt (ʿnt)*

> Then (call) Aqht to save you,
> Daniel's son to liberate you
> From the hand of the Virgin Anath.

If the preposition *lĕ* of *lāmô* is understood as " from " (see below) in this verse, then *ʿzr* " to save, rescue " fits the context perfectly.

---

[250] Freedman, *Eretz-Israel* 9 (1969), p. 37-38. The four occurrences in Job are 15 : 3 *(yôʿîl)* ; 21 : 15 *(nôʿîl)* ; 30 : 13 *(yōʿîlû* for fully written *yôʿîlû)* ; and 35 : 3 *(ʾōʿîl* for *ʾôʿîl).*

[251] Baisas, *UF* 5 (1973), p. 41-52 ; on Job 30 : 13, see p. 43.

[252] Dahood, *Psalms III,* Note on Ps 108 : 13.

The Qumran Targum supports this interpretation with *wpṣ' l' (lhw)n*
" and a savior (they did) not (have), " [253] and P. Grelot in his review
of van der Ploeg's edition of 11QtgJob [254] proposes a restoration
which agrees with our rendering of the MT: *wpṣ' l' ('yty ly mnhw)n*
" et il n'(y a personne qui me) sauve (d'eu)x. "

The translation adopted here is based on the revocalization of
'ōzēr to the substantive *'ēzer* " escape, rescue. " See, for example,
Isa 30 : 5, in which *'ēzer* parallels *y'l* in an A + B + A pattern (*yôʿîlû*
+ *lĕʿēzer* + *lĕhôʿîl*): " All are humiliated on account of a people who
profit them nothing (*lōʾ yôʿîlû*), neither as help nor as aid (*lōʾ lĕʿēzer*
wĕlōʾ lĕhôʿîl). [255]

from them. Understanding the preposition *lĕ* of *lāmô* with the sense
of " from, " as, for example, in Job 36 : 3, *'eśśāʾ dēʿî lĕmērāḥôq* " I
shall fetch my knowledge from afar. " [256]

Job 30 : 14

through a wide breach. Compare Job 16 : 14 discussed above under
v 12 :

> *yiprĕṣēnî pārōṣ* (MT *pereṣ*) *ʿal pānay* (MT *pĕnê*)
> *pārōṣ* (MT *pereṣ*) *yārūṣ ʿālay kĕgibbôr*

> He breaches me with a breach in front of me,
> And charging, he charges me like a warrior.

kĕpereṣ may be a scribal error for *bĕpereṣ* " through a (wide) breach. "
This reading finds some support in the Ugaritic–Hebrew parallel pair
b//tḥt which would be uncovered (*RSP* I,II,101 ; cf. Job 20 : 12 ; 26 : 8 ;
34 : 26) and in the beth which the Qumran Targum has here. [257]

---

[253] Sokoloff, *The Targum to Job*, p. 58-59. See also, van der Ploeg, *Le Targum de Job*, p. 42-43, " tandis qu'(ils) n'(ont) personne qui (les) sauve. "

[254] *Revue de Qumran* 8, 29 (1972), p. 109 ; but see B. Jongeling, " La Colonne XVI de 11QtgJob, " *Revue de Qumran* 8, 31 (1974), p. 415-416.

[255] The translation follows Irwin, *Isaiah 28 – 33*, p. 74-75. On the A +
B + A pattern see Dahood, *UF 1* (1969), p. 32-33.

[256] Cf. Blommerde, *NSGJ*, p. 125. On *lĕ* " from " see further, ibid., p. 21 ;
Dahood, *Bib* 47 (1966), p. 406 ; idem, *Psalms III*, p. 394-395.

[257] At the beginning of Job 30 : 14, the Qumran Targum reads *btqp šḥny*
" In my strong boil/Strongly my boils " ; cf. Sokoloff, *The Targum to Job*, p. 58-
59, 125.

they come. '*th* occurs also in Job 3 : 25 where, as here, it preserves the original yodh (*wayye'ĕtāyēnî* in 3 : 25; *ye'ătāyû* in 30 : 14). Dahood remarks on this phenomenon in 3 : 25 :

> The preservation of the original -*y* in *y'tyny* (cf. Ugar. *tity*) assumes particular significance because in the next verse *šlwty* preserves the original third radical -*w*, as in Ugar. *ašlw* " I shall take my ease. " Perhaps only here in the Bible does one encounter in successive verses two weak verbs preserving the original third radical. [258]

The Hebrew parallel pair '*th* " to come " // *bw'* " to enter " in Job 3 : 25 recurs in Deut 33 : 2; Isa 41 : 22-23,25; Micah 4 : 8; and Prov 1 : 27 where it forms an A + B + A pattern (*bĕbō'* + *ye'ĕteh* + *bĕbō'*). [259]

amidst. On this sense of *taḥat* " under, among " see the discussion of *taḥat ḥārûl* " amidst the nettles " in v 7.

the havoc. The root here is *š'h* I " to destroy, be desolate " rather than *š'h* II " to roar, be in an uproar. " See Isa 47 : 11 in which *š'h* " destruction " parallels *hōwâ* " disaster " (N.B. *lĕhawwātî* " my undoing " in Job 30 : 13) :

> Disaster (*hōwâ*) shall fall upon you,
>   which you shall not be able to expiate;
> and ruin (*šô'â*) shall come on you suddenly,
>   of which you know nothing.

Compare also Nah 1 : 5-6 which echoes the collocation here in Job 30 : 13-14 of *nts* " to break up " ... *š'h* " havoc, destruction " : " The earth is laid waste (*watiššā'*; MT *watiššā'*) before him ... the rocks are broken up (*niteṣû*) before him. " [260]

The netherworld connotations of this root are clear in the substantives *šā'ôn* " Destruction " and *maššû'ôt* " Ruin " used as appelatives for the abode of the dead. See, for example, Ps 40 : 3, " He drew me up from the pit of Destruction (*mibbôr šā'ôn*), " [261] and Ps 73 : 18-19

---

[258] Dahood, " Northwest Semitic texts and textual criticism of the Hebrew Bible, " p. 32.

[259] On the A + B + A pattern, see Dahood, *UF* 1 (1969), p. 32-34. Examples of this pattern in Job include 10 : 1, 22; 15 : 30.

[260] Cathcart, *Nahum*, p. 31, 53.

[261] Dahood, *Psalms I*, 1st Note on Ps 40 : 3.

in which *š'h* is collocated as here (Job 30 : 14-15) with *ballāhôt* " Terrors " :

> Surely to Perdition you will transplant them,
>   making them fall into Destruction (*lĕmaššû'ôt*).
> How quickly they will belong to Devastation,
>   utterly swept away by Terrors (*min-ballāhôt*). [262]

they arrive.   The parallelism with *ye'ĕtāyû* " they come " and comparison with *UT* 127 : 4-5, *tgly wtbu nṣrt tbu pnm 'rm* " They arrived and entered the enclosures, they entered inside the cities, " suggest that the hapax legomenon here *hitgalgālû* derives from *gly* " to arrive, penetrate " rather than *gll* " to roll. " [263]   Recognition of the Ugaritic-Hebrew parallel pair *gly* " to arrive, penetrate "//*ba* " to enter " [264] permits a better balance between the cola in Job 41 : 5 :

> Who can penetrate (*mî-gillāh*) inside his covering?
>   his double coat of mail, who can enter (*mî yābô'*)? [265]

Other verses in Job in which *gly* has this nuance include 3 : 22,

> Who rejoice in the end (*gêl*; MT *gîl*),
>   and are glad when they reach the grave, [266]

and 20 : 28,

> The flood shall reach (*yigel*) his house,
>   the rushing waters in the day of his wrath. [267]

Job 30 : 15

Terror.   Understanding the ending -*ôt* of *ballāhôt* as the Phoenician singular ending -*ōt* and therefore the subject also of *tirdōp*, which

---

[262] Idem, *Psalms II²*, p. 187.

[263] Idem, " Northwest Semitic texts and textual criticism of the Hebrew Bible, " p. 30.

[264] *RSP* I, II, 142.   To the examples listed there add Job 38 : 16-17, *hăbā'tā ... hănigĕlû.*

[265] Ibid.

[266] Dahood, " Northwest Semitic texts and textual criticism of the Hebrew Bible, " p. 30.   Contrast Grabbe, *Comparative Philology*, p. 38-41.

[267] See also Dahood, *Bib* 43 (1962), p. 224-225, for *gly* " to reach " in Ruth 3 : 7.   Other possible examples are noted by Pope, *El in the Ugaritic Texts*, p. 64-65.

consequently requires no change in its vocalization as second person feminine singular *yqtl*.[268]

In vv 11-14 Job has been describing his plight in terms of a city under siege by unnamed enemies. Here in v 15 at the end of this description these foes are identified. They are none other than the minions of Mot (= Death), the god of death and the netherworld, " the King of Terrors (*melek ballāhôt*) " (Job 18:14). In his chapter entitled " The Names and Epithets of Sheol, " N. Tromp remarks on Job 18:11-14, in which *ballāhôt* " terror(s) " occurs twice:

> Bildad's description of the portion of the wicked is particularly instructive: he is in darkness (vv. 5 f.), his feet trip and are thrown in the net (vv. 7 ff.). The text proceeds:

> > Roud about TERRORS affright him,
> > and harry him at every step.
> > Let the Hungry One face him,
> > with Death stationed at his side.
> > His skin is gnawed by disease;
> > Death's first-born feeds on his limbs.
> > He is snatched away from his comfortable tent
> > and haled before the King of TERRORS. (Pope)

> This text shows that the infernal terrors originate from Death himself: this panic is a certain symptom of his sway and announces the coming of his Kingdom.[269]

turns. Revocalizing the hapax hophal form *hohpak* to *hahăpōk*, the niphal infinitive absolute. For the sense, compare 1 Sam 4:19, " She gave birth because her pangs had come upon her (*kî-nehepkû 'ālêhā ṣîrêhā*). " The new Baumgartner *Lexikon* records Esther 9:1 as another example of the niphal infinitive absolute as a stand-in for the normal finite form, *wĕnahăpōk hû'* " but it had been changed. "[270] Niphal *hpk* recurs again in v 21, *tēhāpēk* " you have turned into. "

---

[268] On *ballāhôt* as the Phoenician form of the feminine singular in Job 18:14 and 27:20, see Blommerde, *NSGJ*, p. 11,85. See also van Dijk, *Ezekiel's Prophecy on Tyre*, on *ballāhôt* " terror, " in Ezek 26:21; 27:36; 28:19.

[269] Tromp, *Death and the Nether World*, p. 74. Further on Job 18:11-14, see Pope, *Job*³, p. 134-136; Sarna, *JBL* 82 (1963), p. 315-318. On *ballāhôt* " Terrors " in Ps 73:19 (//*baḥălāqôt* " Perdition " //*lĕmaššû'ôt* " Desolation "// *lĕšammâ* " Devastation "), see Dahood, *Psalms II*², 5th Note on Ps 73:19.

[270] Baumgartner, *Lexikon*, vol. I, p. 243b. For further examples of this

pursues. Phoenician feminine singular *ballāhôt* provides the subject for *tirdōp* " pursues "; thus there is no necessity for the suggested emendation of *tirdōp* to the niphal *tērādēp* in the apparatus of *BHS*. [271]

pursues ... disappears. These two roots are also parallel in Isa 41 : 3, *yirdĕpēm ya‘ăbôr šālôm* " he pursues them, he passes on safely. "

my dignity. *nĕdibātî* is another example of defective orthography in Job. [272] The other two instances of this noun in the Bible are written fully (Ps 51 : 14 *nĕdîbâ*, Isa 32 : 8 *nĕdîbôt*).

On the possible relationship between *nĕtîbâ* and *nĕdîbâ*, see the discussion above under v 13.

The parallelism here *nĕdibātî* " my dignity " / / *yĕšū‘ātî* " my prosperity " reverses that of Ps 51 : 14, *yiš‘ekā* / / *nĕdîbâ*.

wind ... cloud. This same parallelism, *rûaḥ* " wind " / / *‘āb* " cloud, " recurs in Qoh 11 : 4 and 1 Kgs 18 : 45.

my prosperity. On this nuance of *yĕšû‘a* " salvation, prosperity, victory, " see S. Mowinckel. [273]

Job 30 : 16-19

> And now my life is drained from me ;
>   days of affliction seize me.
> At night my bones are hotter than a cauldron ;
>   those who gnaw me do not rest.
> With great force he rifles my garment,
>   with his hands he loosens from me my tunic.
> He casts me upon the mud and I perish,
>   flung upon the slime and ashes.

This section, introduced by the third repetition of *wĕ‘attâ*, continues Job's description of his sufferings. He speaks of God in the third person in contrast to the following vv 20-23 in which God is addressed in the second person singular.

---

phenomenon see J. Huesman, " Finite Uses of the Infinitive Absolute, " *Bib* 37 (1956), p. 271-295, and the indexes to Dahood, *Psalms I-III*, under " Infinitive absolute. "

[271] *RSV* follows this reading : " my honor is pursued as by the wind. "
[272] Freedman, *Eretz-Israel* 9 (1969), p. 35-44.
[273] *He That Cometh* (trans. G. W. Anderson ; Oxford : Blackwell, 1956), p. 47 ; also Dahood, *Psalms I*, 5th Note on Ps 36 : 7 ; Pope, *Job³*, p. 222.

Job 30 : 16

And now. The refrain *wĕʿattâ* of vv 1 and 9 is again repeated, rein-
forcing the contrast between Chapters 29 and 30. *BHS* omits the
suggestion of the apparatus in *BHK³* to delete *wĕʿattâ* as a dittography
for *yĕšūʿātî* at the end of v 15. The evidence from the Qumran Targum (*wkʿn* " and now " = MT *wʿth*) supports this decision of *BHS*. [274]
Contrast this with the drastic rearrangement of the MT which *NAB*
undertakes: *wĕʿattâ* is omitted as a dittography of *yĕšūʿātî* (v 15);
v 16b is omitted as a dittography of vv 18b and 27b; and v 16a is
transposed after v 26. [275]

my life is drained from me. In *UT* 125 : 34-35, Keret orders his son
not to repeat the news of his mortal illness to his sister Octavia lest
she weep too violently over his death:

> *al tšt bšdm mmh*
> *bsmkt ṣat npš*

> Let her not pour out upon the fields her waters,
> Upon the highlands the issue of her throat.

Terence Collins in his article, " The Physiology of Tears in the Old
Testament, " describes the physical process and imagery involved
here:

> Distressing, external circumstances produce a physiological
> reaction in a man, which starts in his intestines and proceeds
> to affect his whole body, especially the heart. This physiological
> disturbance is actually a change in the physical composition
> of the inner organs, a general softening up, which initiates an
> outflow of the body's vital force. This outflow proceeds through
> the throat and eyes, and issues in the form of tears which are
> nothing less than the oozing out of the body's vital substance.
> The immediate consequence is that the subject is left weak and
> exhausted... [276]

Job's *nepeš* here in v 16 probably has the more material sense of
" throat. " Compare Lam 2 : 12c which describes the weeping of the

---

[274] Sokoloff, *The Targum to Job*, p. 58-59, 212.
[275] The order of verses at the end of chapter 30 thus reads in *NAB*: 25,26,
16a,27b,17,28,29,30,31; cf. *Textual Notes on the New American Bible*, p. 377.
[276] *CBQ* 33 (1970), p. 18.

children of Jerusalem who are victims of the famine brought on by
the siege of the city: *běhištappēk napšām 'el-ḥêq 'immōtām* " While
their *npš* is poured out in their mothers' laps. "   Collins comments:

> The pouring out of the *npš* is taking place on two levels.   It is
> their life force being spent in weeping for hunger.   It is also
> the substance of their throats being poured out, just as the
> poet's liver is poured out in vs. 11b, in the form of tears. [277]

'al of *'ālay* thus has the force of " from " discussed above under vv 2
and 4 : Job's tears/vital force pours out *from* him rather than " upon "
or " within " him, as most modern translations have, understanding
v 16a in a less material sense. [278]   Ps 142 : 4a provides a good parallel,
běhit'aṭṭēp 'ālay rûḥî " as my spirit ebbs from me " ; [279] see also v 15c
above and v 22b below (" success slips from me ").

Although the initial *wě'attâ* indicates that v 16 begins a new section, it is bound to the previous section by an A : B : : B : A word pattern which extends over vv 15 and 16, *hhpk* (MT *hāhěpak*): *'ālay*:
kě: : *kě*: *'ālay*: *tištappēk.* [280]

my life.   G. Pettinato remarks in " The Royal Archives of Tell Mardikh-Ebla, "

> The bilingual vocabularies mentioned earlier make an essential
> contribution to the Northwest Semitic lexicon of the 3rd mil-
> lennium.   Many words hitherto attested only in the Old Ak-
> kadian inscriptions and the pre-Sargonic onomastica, and often
> erroneously considered to be East Semitic, are now more accu-
> rately assigned to the West Semitic branch documented at
> Ebla. [281]

---

[277] Ibid., p. 25.   See also 1 Sam 1 : 15, *wā'ešpōk 'et-napšî lipnê yhwh* " I
have been pouring out my soul before Yahweh, " and Dahood, *Psalms I*, 1st
Note on Ps 42 : 5.

[278] E.g., Pope, *Job³*, " My soul within me is emptied " ; likewise *RSV*, the
Chicago Bible, *BJ²*.   *NAB* apparently saw that the context calls for translating
'al as " from " here.   *NAB*'s version reads, " my soul ebbs *from* me, " and the
Textual Notes on the New American Bible (p. 377) give no indication that
any other preposition than *'al* is understood here.

[279] Dahood, *Psalms III*, p. 316 and the 1st Note on Ps 142 : 4.

[280] Cf. Ceresko, *CBQ* 38 (1976) p. 303-311.

[281] *BA* 39 (May 1976), p. 50.

Among the examples he lists is *nu-pù-uš-tu-um* " life " (= Heb. *nepeš*).

is drained ... seize. Job 16 : 12-13 collocate these same two verbs (*wě'āḥaz ... yišpōk*).

seize. This verb is attested in the paleo-canaanite texts from Tell-Mardikh. [282]

days. vv 16 and 17 form the merismus " days of affliction ... At night. " Job's suffering is continuous ; he is allowed no respite either by day (v 16) or by night (v 17).

Job 30 : 17

At night. The reference to nighttime evokes an atmosphere of dread and apprehension. Delitzsch suggests that the gnawing pains are here personified, [283] and Fohrer remarks, " ... so kommt ihm der heftige Gliederschmerz vor, der mit fieberhaften Erscheinungen verbunden sein kann und nachts besonders quält. " [284] Frank Cross and R. Saley remark concerning the Arslan Tash tablet, " Each (incantation) is directed against demons who go abroad in darkness. " [285]

night ... rest. The collocation of *laylâ* and *škb* here in v 17 recalls a theme which Northwest Semitic often employs : " ... the bedroom was a proper place for the expression of emotions most deeply felt. " [286] In the privacy of his own bedroom Job finds no respite. Even there his enemies attack. He is not allowed the comfort of night's silence and solitude.

my bones. The proximity of *'ăṣāmay* " bones " with *'ōṣem* " strong " (below in v 21) here hould be compared with this same paronomasia in Ps 139 : 15-17 (*'āṣmî*, MT *'oṣmî* and *'āṣĕmû*). [286a] In his introductory remarks on Ps 139, Dahood speaks of " literary and semantic rap-

---

[282] Pettinato, *Or* 44 (1975), p. 372 (n. 97).

[283] Delitzsch, *Das Buch Iob*, p. 398.

[284] Fohrer, *Das Buch Hiob*, p. 419.

[285] Cross and Saley, *BASOR* 197 (February 1970). p. 48. For *lāylâ* used as an epithet of the Netherworld, see Dahood, *Psalms III*, the Notes on Ps 139 : 11 ; Michel, *Book of Job*, p. 75-78 ; Tromp, *Death and the Nether World*, p. 95-98.

[286] Dahood, *Psalms III*, 2nd Note on Ps 149 : 5 ; idem, *Psalms I*, 3rd Note on Ps 4 : 5.

[286a] See also Job 21 : 23-24 (*bě'eṣem* and *'aṣmōtayw*). On *'aṣmî* " my bones " (MT *'oṣmî*) in Ps 139: 15, see Dahood, *Psalms III*, 1st Note on Ps 139: 15.

prochements with the Book of Job " which lend " substance to the view that ascribes the psalm (139) to the same literary ambience as Job. "[287] This is another example of such rapprochements.

are hotter than a cauldron.   Reading *nōqĕdū mēʿĕlî* for MT *niqqar mēʿālāy.* *nqr* "to bore, dig out " (e.g., Judg 16 : 21 *wayĕnaqqĕrû ʾet-ʿênāyw* " they gouged out his eyes ") does not fit the context, and John Gray has recently proposed emending MT *niqqar* to *niqqad* from *yqd* " to burn. "[288] This suggestion finds support in two ancient versions. A. Rahlf's edition of the LXX follows the codex Vaticanus in reading *sygkḗkautai* " are inflamed "[289] and the Qumran Targum of Job has *grmy ydwn* " my bones burn. "[290] This accords with Dahood's repointing of *mēʿālāy* " from upon me " to *mēʿĕlî* " than a cauldron, " recognizing in *mʿly* the cognate of the Arabic *ġly* " to seethe, boil. "[291] This same word recurs in a similar context below in v 30, where it is again col- located with *ʿṣm*:

> *ʿôrî šāḥar mēʿĕlî* (MT *mēʿālāy*)
> *wĕʿaṣmî-ḥārâ minnî-ḥōreb*
>
> My skin is blacker than a cauldron,
>   and my bones burn with heat. [292]

Compare also Ps 102 : 4b (N.B., *ʿṣm + yqd*), *wĕʿaṣmôtay kĕmôqēd niḥārû* " My bones burn like a brazier. "[293]

my bones ... do not rest.   Job 20 : 11 (*ʿaṣmôtay ... tiškāb*) and 33 : 19 (*ʿăṣāmāyw ... miškābô*) repeat this collocation of *ʿṣm* and *škb*.

---

[287] Dahood, *Psalms III*, p. 285 ; A. Glasner, " Psalm 139 and the Identifica- tion of Its Author, " *Beth Mikra* 60 (Jerusalem : Israel Society of Biblical Research, October-December, 1974), English Summary on p. 166.

[288] Although it is probably better to vocalize *nqd* (MT *nqr*) as *nōqĕdū*, the defectively written 3rd person plural perfect niphal of *yqd*. See J. Gray, " The Massoretic Text of the Book of Job, the Targum and the Septuagint Version in the Light of the Qumran Targum, " *ZAW* 86 (1974), p. 345 ; Dahood, *Bib* 57 (1976), p. 270.

[289] Rahlfs, *Septuaginta*, vol. II, p. 319.

[290] Sokoloff, *The Targum to Job*, p. 58-59 ; van der Ploeg, *Le Targum de Job*, p. 42-43.

[291] See Dahood, *Psalms I*, 2nd Note on Ps 12 : 7, for the discussion of *ʿĕlî* " crucible " in Ps 12 : 7 and Prov 27 : 22 ; Gray, *ZAW* 86 (1974), p. 345, also accepts this interpretation of *ʿly* " caldron " here in v 17 and below in v 30.

[292] Dahood, *Psalms I*, 2nd Note on Ps 37 : 20.

[293] Idem, *Psalms III*, p. 8 and 11.

Job 30 : 18

Pope comments, " This verse is so beset with difficulties that some interpreters (e.g., ICC) do not attempt a translation. "[294] Our solution takes as its starting point Dahood's version suggested in *RSP* I (p. 249):

> With great force he searches my garments,
> With his hands he draws tight my tunic.

With great force. This composite phrase, *běrāb-kōaḥ*, is used of God in Pss 33 : 16; 147 : 5; Job 23 : 6; and Isa 63 : 1. It is broken up in Josh 17 : 17, *'am rab 'attâ wěkōaḥ gādôl lāk* " You are a numerous people and you have great power. "[295]

he rifles. The usual significance of *ḥpś* in the hithpael " let oneself be searched for = disguise oneself " does not fit the context. An examination of its use in the other intensive conjugation, the piel (e.g., Gen 31 : 35 *wayěḥappēś* " he searched carefully "), and the hapax niphal in Obad 6,

> *'ēk neḥpěśû 'ēśāw*
> *nib'û maṣpūnāyw*

> How Esau has been pillaged,
> his treasures sought out ! (*RSV*)

suggests an English equivalent such as " rifle, ransack, plunder " for *yitḥappēś* of Job 30 : 18.

my garment ... my tunic. *RSP* I,II,330 lists Job 30 : 18 among the occurrences of the Ugaritic-Hebrew parallel pair *lbš*//*ktnt*.

my garment ... loosens. This collocation of *lěbûśî ... yě'azzěrēnî* (MT *ya'azrēnî*; see below) should be added to the examples of the Ugaritic–Hebrew parallel pair *lpš ... mizrtm* recorded in *RSP* I,II,340.

with his hands. The consonantal text, long obscured by the masoretic pointing of this phrase, *kěpî kūtāntî* " like the mouth (collar) of my tunic, " now yields sense with the recognition of two points of North-

---

[294] *Job³*, p. 223.
[295] See also Isa 40 : 26, *mērōb 'ônîm wě'ammîṣ kōaḥ* " By the greatness of his might and because he is strong in power " (*RSV*).

west Semitic grammar known from the Phoenician and Ugaritic texts :
the double-duty preposition and the third masculine singular yodh
suffix. The repointing of *kĕpî* to *kappay* reveals the dual construct
of *kap* " hand " with the third masculine yodh suffix, paralleling *bĕrāb-
kōaḥ* and sharing its preposition : " with his hands. " This same
parallelism occurs in Judg 6 : 14, " Go with this great power of yours
(*bĕkōḥăkā*) and save Israel from the hand of Midian (*mikkap midyān*). "
In v 21 below Job uses a similar expression in reproaching God, *bĕʿōṣem
yādĕkā* " with your powerful hand. "

he loosens from me. A. Blommerde's revocalizing of MT *wayyeʾsōr* in
Job 12 : 18 to the privative piel form *wayyĕʾassēr* makes sense of an
otherwise unclear verse :

> *môsēr* (MT *mûsar*) *mĕlakîm pittēaḥ*
> *wayyĕʾassēr* (MT *wayyeʾsōr*) *ʾēzôr bĕmotnêhem*

> He unties the belt of kings
> and loosens the girdle from their loins.

He comments :

> Thus understood the two stichs form a good parallel ; the loss
> of the girdle is indeed a sign of humiliation, cf. Job 12,21b ;
> Isa 5,27 ; and Gordon's discussion of belt-wrestling, with special
> reference to 2 Sam 2,21, " take his belt (*ḥăliṣātô*) for you. "[296]

A similar solution commends itself for Job 30 : 18. To make sense
of the second colon, Pope proposes emending *ʾzr* to *ʾḥd* " to grasp. "[297]
However, by parsing *yʾzrny* as a privative piel *yĕʾazzĕrēnî* (MT *ya-
ʾazrēnî*) " he loosens " with the dative suffix (" from me "), a clear
image emerges. As in vv 19, 21 and 22 below, Job accuses God of
doing physical violence to him. Job's reaction here to God's humil-
iating despoilation of the clothes off Job's back contrasts sharply
with the Job of the Prologue (1 : 20) :

> Naked I came from my mother's womb,
> And naked shall I return there.

---

[296] Blommerde, *NSGJ*, p. 63. For the discussion of beltwrestling see C. H.
Gordon, " Belt-Wrestling in the Bible World, " *Hebrew Union College Annual*
23 (1950-1951), p. 131-136.

[297] *Job*³, p. 223.

Yahweh gave, Yahweh took away.
Blessed by Yahweh's name. (Pope)

Job 30 : 19

He casts me. hōrānî is one of the four defectively written forms out
of eight examples of the hiphil of *yrh* in Job. This contrasts with the
rest of the MT of whose sixty examples, nine are defectively written. [298]

upon the mud ... slime. For lě " upon " see Blommerde. [299] W. Michel discusses the netherworld implications of ḥōmer and 'āpār in Job [300]
and translates ḥōmer in v 19 as if it were a place-name for the netherworld: " He (God) throws me into the Clay (Mud). " He notes:

> Blommerde took *l* in the sense of '*l* " upon " .... But ḥmr
> is taken (here) as a name of the underworld, " the Mire, " and
> therefore *l* " into " is retained. Cf. Job 4 : 19; U. Cassuto,
> *Genesis* I, 104 f. [301]

ḥōmer also parallels 'āpār in Job 4 : 19; 10 : 9; 27 : 16.

and I perish, flung. Some translators want to lengthen the first colon
by inserting an expressed subject (e.g., hēn 'ēl). Pope remarks, for
example, " This line is too brief, consisting only of two short words.
We follow Moffatt and *RSV* in supplying the unexpressed subject
as ' God. ' " [302] Indeed, the masoretic word division and pointing
yields the rather colorless wā'etmaššēl kě " and I am become like "
presenting still another drawback to the present reading of the verse.
The approach adopted here is to follow a slightly different word division and revocalization of wā'etmaššēl kě to wā'ettōm (m)ūšlak " and
I perish, flung (into the slime and ashes). " The result offers a more
vigorous image as well as a more balanced accent pattern (3/3) and
syllable count (9 : 7). wā'ettōm, from the common root *tmm* " to be
completed, finished, to perish, " and mūšlak, the hophal participle
from *šlk* " to throw, " share the consonant mem, a phenomenon documented by Blommerde [303] and W. Watson. [304] *šlk* (wattūšlěkî, 2nd

---

[298] Freedman, *Eretz-Israel* 9 (1969), p. 38.
[299] *NSGJ*, p. 113.
[300] Michel, *Book of Job*, p. 72-73.
[301] Ibid., p. 426 (n. 606).
[302] Job³, p. 223; see also *NEB* and Driver–Gray, ICC, vol. II, p. 217.
[303] *NSGJ*, p. 4.

feminine singular imperfect hophal) appears in a similar context in
Ezek 16:5:

> No eye pitied you, to do any of these things out of compassion
> for you; but you were cast out (*wattūšlĕkî*) on the open field,
> for you were abhorred, on the day that you were born. (*RSV*)

V 19 now reveals another contrast with the Job of the Prologue
(see the discussion under " he loosens from me " in the preceding
verse), based on a play on the root *tmm*. Job the " blameless " (*tām*,
Job 1:1,8; 2:3) in God's sight here becomes the Job who " perishes "
(*wā'ettōm*) at the hand of that same God.

upon the slime and ashes. The preposition *lĕ* of *laḥōmer* " upon the
mud " in the first colon does double duty for *'āpār wā'ēper* in the
second colon.

The same parallelism *'pr* " slime " // *'pr* " ashes " recurs in Job
42:6.

Job 30: 20-23

> I cry out to you but you answer me not;
>   I present myself but you ignore me.
> You've become my Tormentor;
>   with your powerful hand you make me take cover.
> You lift me up, O God, you make me ride the wind,
>   and sweep victory away from me.
> I know that you will return me to Death,
>   to the Meetinghouse of all the living.

Job moves from speaking about God in the third person to addressing him directly in the second person singular. Job's language is
shockingly harsh, accusing God of being his " Tormentor, " an epithet
ordinarily reserved for the figure of Death (see below under v 21),
and charging him with acting like a cruel bully who seems intent only
on making sport of his victims (vv 21b-22) before finally finishing
them off (v 23).

These are the only verses in these three chapters 29 – 31 in which
Job speaks directly to God, and significantly, they stand almost at

304 W. Watson, " Shared Consonants in Northwest Semitic, " *Bib* 50 (1969),
p. 525-533; idem, " More on Shared Consonants, " *Bib* 52 (1971), p. 44-50.

the center of this final " Apology, " 45 verses preceding and 48 verses
following this strophe. Job's speech reaches one of its high points:
he berates God as " El the Cruel One " (*'akzārî ...'ēl*, MT *'el*) and
dwells on his own sufferings (" me " is repeated eight times within
the four verses).

Although *bĕʻōṣem yādĕkā* " with your powerful hand " echoes
bĕrāb-kōaḥ " with great force " and *kappay* (MT *kĕpî*) " with his hands "
of v 18 joining vv 20-23 with vv 16-19, the sound pattern within these
four verses also serves an internal unifying function: *tûšiwwâ* of v 22
recalls *'ăšawwaʻ* of v 20 and the striking repetition of the first person
suffix — *taʻănēnî, titbōnēn bî, lî, tašaṭminnî* (MT *tiśṭĕmēnî*), *tiśśāʼēnî,
ûtĕmōgĕgēnî, tĕśîbēnî* — stresses Job's preoccupation with himself and
his own afflictions.

The place of v 24 is unclear since the translation continues to be
a problem. However, the return to the third person in *yišlaḥ* " he
stretches forth " indicates that v 24 belongs with what follows rather
than with the series of direct addresses in the preceding four verses.

Job 30 : 20

cry out ... answer.   Job 19 : 7 also collocates these two verbs (*'ēʻāneh
+ 'ăšawwaʻ*).

answer ... pay attention. This parallelism, *taʻănēnî*//*wattitbōnen*,[305] recalls
the collocation of these same words in *UT* 51 V : 120-125 (*wyʻn ... bn*):

> *wyʻn kṯr wḥss*
> *šmʻ laliyn bʻl*
> *bn lrkb ʻrpt ...*
> *wyʻn aliyn bʻl*

> And answers does Kothar-and-Hasis,
> " Hear, O Victor Baal !
> Perceive, O Rider of the Clouds !... "
> And replies does Victor Baal.

I present myself. For this nuance of *ʻmd,* see, for example Ex 18 : 13,
" and the people presented themselves (*wayyaʻămōd*) before Moses
from morning until evening. "[306]

---

[305] See also 23 : 5, *yaʻănēnî* + *wĕ'ābînâ*.
[306] K–B, *Lexicon*, p. 712a ; see also Job 4 : 16.

In *RSP* I,I,38, A. Schoors points to *'md* in discussing J. Obermann's interpretation of Ugaritic *nṣbt il* " I stand before El " a phrase
reminiscent of *'āmadtî* " I present myself " here in Job 30 : 20 :

> In his (Obermann's) opinion *nṣb* = Akk *nazâzu*, " to stand. "
> The verb here would be used in the specific sense of " standing
> before a deity as a suppliant " (cf. Heb. *'md*).... The Ugaritic
> verse would be intended to denote : " I stand fast by, I trust
> in, I rely on, El. " [307]

'md and *'nh* are collocated in Job 32 : 16 (*'amĕdû*, *'ānû*), as are *'md*
and *byn* in 37 : 14 (*'ămōd wĕhitbônēn*).

I present myself but you ignore me. Lit., " I present myself but you
do not pay attention to me, " understanding the *lō'* of *wĕlō' ta'ănēnî*
in the first colon as doing duty also for *titbōnēn*. Pope's translation,
" You stand and look at me, " is based on the Syriac version. [308] Both
the departure from the MT and the blandness of this interpretation,
which contrasts with the usual liveliness of Job's style, argue against
Pope's resort to emendation. The parallelism between the first and
second colon calls for the negative with *titbōnen*. Among the modern
versions, Fedrizzi, *BJ²*, and Driver–Gray, ICC recognize this and all
three appeal to the Vulgate and/or one manuscript. [309] Apparently
Jerome realized the double-duty function of the negative *lō'* in the
first colon, whose force extends to the parallel verb in the second colon.
In his Note on Ps 9 : 19, Dahood comments on this usage : " The use of
double-duty negatives (as well as double-duty suffixes, prepositions,
conjunctions, etc.) characterizes Canaanite poetic style. " [310] The failure
by translators to recognize the double-duty force of *lō'* in v 20a could
be due to the intervening *'āmadtî* at the beginning of v 20b. Although
the double-duty negative usually occurs with parallel verbs which
follow one another directly, Dahood has pointed out at least one other

---

[307] Cf. J. Obermann, " An Antiphonal Psalm from Ras Shamra, " *JBL*
55 (1935), p. 39-40.
[308] *Job³*, p. 223. *NAB* translates, " you stand off and look at me. "
[309] E.g., Fedrizzi, *Giobbe*, p. 211, reads, " mi presento e tu non badi a me, "
and notes, " *tu non badi*, leggendo *wĕlō' titbōnen* con la Vlg e il Ms de Rossi
593. Il TM non ha la negazione. "
[310] Dahood, *Psalms I*, Note on Ps 9 : 19 ; idem, *Psalms II²*, 3rd Note on Ps
75 : 6 ; idem, *Psalms III*, " Index of Subjects " under " Double-duty negatives "
(p. 482).

example, also in Job (15 : 30), in which a colon intervenes between the two cola governed by a single negative :

> *lō' yāsûr minnî-ḥōšek*
> *yōnaqtô těyabbēš šalhābet*
> *wěyāsûr běrewaḥ* (MT *běrûaḥ*) *pîw*

He will not escape from the Darkness,
His shoots the Flame will wither,
Nor will he escape from its massive mouth. [311]

Job 30 : 21

my Tormentor. In vv 20-23, Job is pointing an accusing finger directly at God and calling him by the title " the Tormentor " [312] which elsewhere is used of personified Death. W. A. van der Weiden, for instance, understands *'akzārî* as an epithet of " Death " (" le Cruel, " the Cruel One) in Prov 17 : 11,

> *'ak-měrî yěbakkeš-rā'*
> *ûmal'ak 'akzārî yěšūllaḥ-bô*

Le rebelle cherche sûrement le mal
Eh bien, un messager du Cruel sera envoyé contre lui,

and Jer 30 : 14,

> *kî makkat 'ôyēb hikkîtîk*
> *mûsar 'akzārî*

Parce que je t'ai frappé par le coup de l'Ennemi,
Avec le châtiment du Cruel. [313]

W. Michel comments on the relationship between Yahweh and " Death " in Job :

> The evidence that Yahweh is the ultimate reason for human misery and death is overwhelming in the book of Job. The

---

[311] Dahood, *Bib* 50 (1969), p. 343.

[312] Michel also capitalizes " Tormentor " in his translation, recognizing its pointed use here as a divine title ; cf. Michel, *Book of Job*, p. 209 and 426 (n. 607).

[313] W. A. van der weiden, *Le Livre des Proverbes : Notes philologiques* (BibOr 23 ; Rome : Biblical Institute Press, 1970), p. 55.

emphasis on this aspect of Yahweh is out of proportion to any other subject.

Yahweh is the lord and master of his creation, including death and the underworld. He is not only the cause of life but also the cause of diminished life, of sickness and finally death ....

Yahweh as " the Victor " over chaos powers and death does not therefore break the powers of death, but incorporates them into his arsenal. [314]

He states further that, " Quite a few terms reveal his (Yahweh's) hostile and deadly actions toward man, " and among these he lists *'kzr* " Tormentor " of Job 30 : 21. [315]

W. van der Weiden proposes Heb. *gāzar* " to cut into pieces " as the possible etymology of *'akzār*:

> ... dans le texte ougaritique 52,23.58.61 nous trouvons le mot *agzrm*: il s'agit des " Dieux Gracieux " qui sont décrits dans les lignes 62-76 comme des " voraces ": ils ont un appétit insatiable. Driver, Aistleitner et Gordon n'ont pas relié la racine *gzr* de *agzrm* à l'hébreu *gāzar* " découper un morceau avant de le dévorer, " comme en Is 9,19. Peut-être pourrait-on, trés prudemment, se demander si nous n'avons pas en *'akzārî* un cas de dissimilation, de sorte qu'il serait à relier à la racine *gāzar*, comme *bazar* et *pazar*; oug. *ṭpd* et hebr. *šapat*. [316]

This etymology for *'akzār* would fit in well with the theme of the " gnawers " above in vv 3 and 17 (*ha⁹ōrĕqîm, wĕ⁹ōrĕqay*).

with your powerful hand. This exact expression (*bĕ⁹ōṣem yādĕkā*) occurs in *UT* 75 I : 24 (*⁹ẓm yd*), where it is collocated with *⁹pr* (N.B. *kā⁹āpār* in v 19):

---

[314] Michel, *Book of Job*, p. 54-55.

[315] Ibid., p. 55.

[316] van der Weiden, *Le livres des Proverbes*, p. 55-56; a different etymology (Arabic *qḏr* " dirty, uncouth ") is proposed by C. Rabin, " Three Hebrew Terms from the Realm of Social Psychology, " VTSup 16 (1967), p. 223-224. On *agzrm* in *UT* 52, see also P. Xella, *Il Mito di ŠḤR e ŠLM : Saggio sulla mitologia ugaritica* (Studi Semitici 44; Rome : Istituto di Studi del Vicino Oriente, Università di Roma, 1973), p. 58-59, 138-149.

kry amt 'pr
' ẓm yd ugrm

Dig with your arm the dust,
With your strong hand the fields.

bě'ōṣem yādĕkā distantly parallels *bĕrāb-kōaḥ* of v 18 on two counts.
First, *'ṣm* and *rb* have already been identified as a Ugaritic–Hebrew
parallel pair in *RSP* I,II,516; e.g., *UT* 'nt I : 12, *bk rb 'ẓm* " a beaker
large, mighty, " and Isa 31 : 1, *kî rāb* " so numerous "//*kî 'āṣĕmû
mĕ'ōd* " so very many. " [317]   Second, *kōaḥ* and *'ōṣem* are parallel in
Deut 8 : 17 (*kōḥî wĕ'ōṣem yādî* " my power and the might of my hand ").

you make me take cover.   Reading consonantal *tśṭmny* as šaphel of
ṭmn " to hide, " i.e., " to cause someone to hide, take cover " (*tašaṭminnî*).   Applying this same solution to *wyśṭmny* of Job 16 : 9a (i.e.,
= šaphel of *ṭmn*) elicits an acceptable translation from a troublesome
verse : *'appô ṭarap wayašaṭminnî* (MT *wayyiśtĕmēnî*) " His anger rages
and he makes me take cover. "

Blommerde recognized *ṭmn* in *nṭmynw* of Job 18 : 3, and offered
the version *niṭmannû* (MT *niṭmînû*) *bĕ'ēnēkā-m* " must we hide from
your sight ? " [318]   He parses the form *niṭmannû* as niphal.   A better
explanation might be to read *nṭmynw* as *naṭmînû*, the first person plural
imperfect hiphil with an internal accusative (" hide ourselves ") and
an archaic -*û* ending. [319]   For the motif of hiding oneself in the presence of a dignitary, cf. Job 29 : 8.   See also Job 14 : 13,

O that you would hide me in Sheol,
        conceal me till your anger withdraws,

and Isa 2 : 10, " hide (*wĕhiṭṭāmēn*) in the Dust before the terror of
Yahweh. "

Job 30 : 22

For this translation, see Dahood, " Hebrew–Ugaritic Lexicography XII. " [320]

---

[317] Irwin, *Isaiah* 28 – 33, p. 109, 177.
[318] *NSGJ*, p. 83.   Contrast Grabbe, *Comparative Philology*, p. 72-74.
[319] M. Dahood, private communication ; on the internal hiphil, cf. Dahood,
Psalms III, " Grammar of the Psalter, " p. 389.
[320] *Bib* 55 (1974), p. 386-387.

You lift me up. The word *na-se*$_{II}$ appears a number of times in an administrative tablet from Tell Mardikh.[321]   G. Pettinato remarks, " *na-se*$_{II}$ (SIG) lo interpretei come semitico e non sumerico, accostandolo all'ebraico *nāsī*. "[322]

You lift me up ... make me ride. These same verbs (*tiśśā'ēnî//tarkibēnî*) are also parallel in *UT* Krt 74-76 (165-168):

> *rkb tkmm ḥmt*
> *ša ydk šmm*
>
> Straddle the shoulders of the wall,
> Lift up your hands heavenward.

O God. The repointing of consonantal *'l* from the preposition *'el* (= MT) to *'ēl* (vocative, " O God ") follows a suggestion first made by Blommerde[323] and taken up by Dahood.[324]   Although Job is obviously speaking of God in vv 18-19 and addressing him directly beginning in v 20, he does not explicitly identify the object of his complaints until here in v 22. On this poetic device of " delayed identification, " see the remarks above under Job 30 : 1.

sweep ... away from me. Failure to recognize the datival function of the suffix of *ûtĕmōgĕgēnî* has resulted in confusion in the attempts to deal with this verse.   For example, Pope must emend *tūšiwwâ* " victory " to *tĕšū'â* " tempest " (used as an accusative of means " with a tempest ") in order to retain an accusative sense for the suffix (" You toss *me* about ").   But parsing the suffix as datival (" from me "), one may conserve MT *tūšiwwâ* and its accusative status and recognize the sentiment expressed earlier in Job 6 : 13, *wĕtūšiyyâ nidḥâ mimmenî* " and victory has been put out of my reach. "[325]   See also Job 30 : 15c above: *ûkĕ'āb 'ābĕrâ yĕšū'ātî* " like a cloud, my prosperity disappears. "

victory. On *tūšiwwâ* and its sense of " victory, " Dahood comments: Witnessed only in Ugaritic and Hebrew, *tūšiyāh* occurs twelve

---

[321] TM. 75. G. 336 (obv) VI : 5 ; (rev) I : 10 ; III : 1 ; IV : 4,6,8,10,13 ; V : 2 ; VÍII : 2 ; cf. Pettinato–Matthiae, *RSO* 50 (1976), p. 1-30.

[322] Ibid., p. 12 (n. 19).

[323] *NSGJ*, p. 68.

[324] *Bib* 55 (1974), p. 386-387.

[325] Ibid. ; on *mûg* used with the dative suffix in Isa 64 : 6, see Dahood, *Or* 45 (1976), p. 347-348.

times in the Bible; the fact that six of these occurrences are in Job sheds welcome light on the lexical background of this book, especially since the nuance " victory " encountered in several texts corresponds to Ugaritic usage; see Pope, *Job*[3], p. 93. [326]

For the other five instances of *tūšîyyâ*, the author of Job uses the lamedh yod form of $\sqrt{w\check{s}y}$. [327]   Here in 30 : 22, he employs the lamedh waw form, *tūšiwwâ*. Compare *šālwatî* ($\sqrt{\check{s}lw}$) of Job 3 : 26 with *yišlāyû* ($\sqrt{\check{s}ly}$) of 12 : 6, and *wĕhayyātî* ($\sqrt{hyh}$) of Job 6 : 2 with *lĕhawwātî* ($\sqrt{hwh}$) of 30 : 13.

The collocation of *tûšiyyâ* " success " and *nimhārâ* " brought to a quick end " (*RSV*) in Job 5 : 12-13 reflects the similar collocation of *tšyt* " success " and *mhrm* " (quick, skilled) troops " of *UT* 'nt II : 27-28.

Job 30 : 23

you will return me. Pope [328] and Dahood [329] rightly emphasize the force of *tĕšîbēnî* " cause to turn back, return (transitive sense) " as opposed to translators who apparently miss the implication of hiphil *šûb*; e.g., *RSV* " bring, " *NEB* " hand me over, " Fedrizzi " mi conduci, " Vulg. *trades me*. The author of Job evokes the image of Mother Earth. From the slime (*'āpār*) of her fertile womb are formed all living creatures and to that slime they will inevitably return. [330]   Gregory of Nanzianzus (d. 390 A.D.), for example, reflects this motif in his *Orationes* (33 : 9) :

---

[326] *Bib* 55 (1974), p. 387. For the other five occurrences and further remarks on *tūšîyyâ*, see also Pope, *Job*[3], p. 43 (on Job 5 : 12b).

[327] Gordon, *UT*, Glossary 812, gives *wšy** as the root of Ugaritic *tšyt*. Dahood has identified this root in Hebrew in Ps 55 : 16 (*wašaya* = Heb. *wašah*); cf. *Psalms II*[2], 1st Note on Ps 55 : 16.

[328] *Job*[3], p. 223; see also p. 16 (on Job 1 : 21).

[329] *Psalms III*, 2nd Note on Ps 116 : 8; also Alonso Schökel, *Job*, p. 144, " Ya sé que me devuelves a la muerte. "

[330] On the frequency of this theme in the OT, see Tromp, *Death and the Nether World*, p. 79; ibid., chapter 2.2, " Dust (*'āpār*), " p. 85-91; ibid., chapter 3.2, " Terra *Mater* (various terms), " p. 122-124. See also Holman, *BZ* 14 (1970), p. 71; Dahood, *Psalms III*, 4th Note on Ps 104 : 29, 6th Note on Ps 139 : 15; Pope, *Job*[3], p. 16.

The sky is the common possession of all men.... and the one and the same earth; the earth which is our mother and our grave, from which we were taken and to which we shall return. [331]

Death. Pope takes *māwet* as "the proper name of the ruler of the infernal region, Mot." [332] Dahood's ascription of a local meaning to *māwet* because of the synonymy with *bêt mô'ēd* "the meeting house" appears preferable. [333]

Death ... the living. In both Hebrew and Ugaritic *mwt* and *ḥy* are frequently collocated; cf. *mt//ḥy* in *RSP* I,II,372.

Meetinghouse. Tromp discusses the use of *bêt* as a synonym for the underworld in his chapter, "Names and Epithets of Sheol: Local Aspects." He concludes:

> The evolution of the use and meanings of *byt* finally comes to an end in *byt mw'd*; here all graves are melted together in one vast reality as appears in Jb 30,23.... [334]

On the netherworld implications of *mô'ēd*, see Dahood's discussion of *'ēdâ* "(nether) assembly" in "Hebrew–Ugaritic Lexicography VII"; [335] in *UT* 137 : 19-20, for example, *pḫr m'd* "the gathering of the assembly"//*ǵr ll* "the Mountain of the Night" both designate the abode of the dead.

Recognition of the netherworld background of *'ēdâ* serves to clarify Job 16 : 7:

> *'ak-'attâ hal'ēnî haššamôt* (MT *hel'ānî hăšimmôtā*)
> *kol-'ădātî wtqmṭny* (MT *watiqmĕṭēnî*)

> Even now Devastation overpowers me,
> her whole company indeed lays me low.

---

[331] *The Later Christian Fathers* (ed. Henry Bettenson; Oxford Paperbacks 293; London: Oxford University Press, 1970), p. 102.

[332] *Job*[3], p. 223.

[333] *Psalms III*, 2nd Note on Ps 116 : 8. On the local meaning of *māwet* see Dahood, *Psalms I*, Note on Ps 6 : 6; idem, *Psalms II*[2], 3rd Note on Ps 56 : 14 and Note on Ps 88 : 6; idem, *Bib* 48 (1967), p. 435-436; Tromp, *Death and the Nether World*, p. 96 (n. 76); Michel, *Book of Job*, p. 413 (n. 563).

[334] *Death and the Nether World*, p. 79.

[335] *Bib* 50 (1969), p. 348.

MT *hăšimmôtā* has confused translators because it introduces a second person singular verb into a third person context. Proceeding from the parallelism with *'ēdâ* " (nether) clan, company, " one can repoint it as Phoenician-style feminine singular *haššamôt* " Devastation, " an epithet of Sheol. [336] The yodh of *'ĕdātî* becomes the third feminine singular suffix whose antecedent is feminine *haššamôt*. [337] *hal'ēnî* (MT *hel'ānî*) parses as a hiphil infinitive absolute of *l'h* " to prevail, overpower " with a first person singular suffix. [338] The transfer of *wtqmṭny* to v 7 marks no innovation, since many modern translations read the passage this way (e.g., Driver–Gray, ICC; Pope; *NAB*; *BJ*). Failure to appreciate the emphatic function of the waw in *wtqmṭny*, parallel to *'ak* of the first colon, apparently caused the displacement of *wtqmṭny* to the beginning of v 8. The syllable count for v 7 thus stands at a balanced 9//9 (10).

A dislegomenon in the Bible (its other occurrence is in Job 22 : 16), *qmṭ* is generally connected with Heb. *qmṣ* " to take, grasp (a handful). " However, its parallelism with *l'h* " to prevail, overcome " in v 7 invites comparison with Ugaritic *qmṣ* which is collocated with *l'y* " to overcome " in *UT* Krt 33-35 :

> *šnt tluan wyškb*
> *nhmmt wqmṣ*

> Sleep overcomes him and he lies down,
> A heavy sleep, and he reclines.

H. L. Ginsberg relates Ug. *qmṣ* to Akk *kamaṣu* and translates it " and he reclines. " [339] Associating *wtqmṭny* of Job 16 : 7-8 then with Ug. *qmṣ* " to recline, lie down, " one may point it as a piel (*watĕqammĕṭēnî*) or hiphil (*wataqmīṭēnî*) and translate " lays me low. " For a similar

---

[336] On *šammâ* " Devastation, " see Dahood, *Psalms II²*, 3rd Note on Ps 73 : 19. The four epithets of the netherworld mentioned by Dahood in *Psalms III*, 4th Note on Ps 140 : 11, are all Phoenician feminine singulars in *-ōt*.

[337] Dahood, *UF* 4 (1972), p. 163-164, mentions two further examples of the feminine yodh suffix in Job 3 : 10 ; 19 : 17. See also, idem, *Bib* 53 (1972), p. 542.

[338] On *l'h* " to prevail, " see Dahood, *Bib* 47 (1966), p. 408. Another possibility is to understand " God " as the unexpressed subject of *hal'ēnî* (MT *hel'ānî*) and *haššamôt* as an accusative of means : " Even now he (God) overcomes me with Destruction. "

[339] Ginsberg, *The Legend of King Keret*, p. 14, 35. See also Dahood, " Ugaritic Lexicography, " p. 99-100.

theme, see Prov 26 : 26, *šā'ôn* " Destruction " // *qāhāl* " the (nether) Assembly " :

> His hatred will be exposed in Destruction,
> his wickedness will be revealed in the Assembly. [340]

I know ... the living. This same collocation (*yāda'tî ... ḥay*) occurs also in *UT* 49 III : 8 (*yd' + ḥy*) : *wid' kḥy aliyn b'l* " For I know that Victor Baal lives. "

Job 30 : 24-31

> ...   .   ,
>   ...   .   ,
> Did I not weep for the hapless,
>   my soul grieve for the poor?
> When I cried for Good, Evil came;
>   when I hoped for Light, came Darkness.
> My insides seethe and are not silent;
>   confronting me are days of affliction.
> In gloom I go about without an answer;
>   I rise in the assembly to cry for help.
> Brother have I become to jackals
>   and companion to ostriches.
> My skin is blacker than a caldron,
>   and my bones are scorched with heat.
> My harp is turned to mourning,
>   my flute to the sound of weepers.

BJ², **RSV**, **NEB**, and the Century Bible [341] group these eight verses together. The repetition of certain words and motifs within this section argues in favor of the unity of this series of verses. Vv 25 and 31 repeat the verb *bkh* " to weep " (*bākîtî, bōkîm*); *yôm* " day " of v 25 (*liqšēh-yôm* " hapless, " lit. " the hard of day ") appears also in v 27 (*yĕmê-'ōnî* " days of affliction "); and *lĕqôl* " the sound " (v 31) echoes *baqqāhāl* " in the assembly " (v 28). The motif of darkness recurs three times: *'ōpel* " Darkness " (v 26), *qōdēr* " gloom " (v 28), and *šāḥar* " black " (v 30); and Job mentions four parts of his body

---

[340] van der Weiden, *Le Livre des Proverbes*, p. 144-145.
[341] Rowley, *Job*, p. 249.

within six verses (25-28): *napšî* " my soul " (v 25), *mēʿay* " my insides "
(v 27), *ʿôrî* " my skin " and *ʿaṣmî* " my bones " (v 30). V 24 remains
problematic, but the switch to the third person in *yišlaḥ*, in contrast
to the direct address of the verbs in vv 20-23, indicates that it belongs
to what follows (vv 25-31) rather than with what precedes.

Job 30 : 24

I find the Hebrew of this verse unintelligible; translations generally resort to emendation to make sense of it. *RSV* renders it:

> " Yet does not one in a heap of
>   ruins stretch out his hand,
>   and in his disaster cry for help ? "

and notes, " Heb(rew) obscure. "

Job 30 : 25

Did I not. *'im-lō'* does double-duty, extending its force over the second colon, as noted by F. Delitzsch[342] and Driver–Gray, ICC.[343]

weep ... grieve. *ʿgm* is a hapax in the Bible, though some connect it
with *'gm* in *'agmê-nāpeš* " sad (of soul) " in Isa 19: 10.[344] M. Dietrich
and O. Loretz recently brought *ʿgm* to light in *UT* Krt 27, the passage
describing King Keret when he cries himself to sleep in sorrow over
the death of his heirs:[345]

> *yʿrb bḥdrh ybky*
> *bṭn ʿgmm wydmʿ*
>
> He entered his chamber to weep;
> While repeating his griefs he shed tears.

---

[342] Delitzsch, *Das Buch Iob*, p. 404.
[343] Driver–Gray, ICC, vol. II, p. 219.
[344] K–B, *Lexicon*, p. 9b, 679b. Dahood gives other examples of roots in
which the interchange of initial laryngals has occurred; e.g., *'gl* " drop " of
Job 38 : 28 (*'eglê ṭāl* " drops of dew ") and *ʿgl* " to be round "; Heb. *'ĕgôz* " nut "
and Ug. *ʿrgz*. Cf. Dahood, *Bib* 57 (1976), p. 270.
[345] M. Dietrich–O. Loretz, " Der Prolog des Krt-Epos (CTA 14 I 1-35), "
Wort und Geschichte: Festschrift für Karl Elliger zum 70. Geburtstag (eds. H. Gese
and H. P. Rüger; AOAT 18; Neukirchen-Vluyn: Neukirchener Verlag, 1973),
p. 34-35.

Although Dietrich and Loretz cite Hebrew *'gm* of Job 30:25, they fail to mention the significant justaposition of *'gm* with *bky* in the Krt text. The two roots juxtaposed in Krt 26-27 (*ybky ... 'gmm*) stand parallel in Job 30:25 (*bākîtî//'āgĕmâ*). This would have secured their reading of *'gmm* [346] in Krt 27 as well as added another set to the growing list of Ugaritic–Hebrew parallel pairs: "The author of Job balances two verbs that are juxtaposed in Ugaritic. This unique biblical parallelism elucidates the close nexus between Job and Northwest Semitic literature."[347]

Job 30 : 26

Good ... Evil ... Light ... Darkness. The proposed translation derives from Michel's interpretation of this verse:

> I cried for the good (health, life, the Good
>   One?), but the Evil One came,
> I hoped for the Light (Sun, life, God?), but
>   the Gloom came.[348]

Dahood has argued that *ṭôb* "the Good One" is a divine epithet in Prov 13:21, where it parallels *rāʿâ* "the Evil One," as here in v 26:

> The Evil One will pursue sinners,
>   but the Good One will reward the just.[349]

This epithet appears in at least one other place in Job, in 22:21, as shown by Blommerde, *bāhem tĕbûʾātĕkā* (MT *tĕbôʾātĕkā*) *ṭôbâ* "then your gain will be the Good One."[350] The proto-canaanite texts from ancient Ebla also witness *ṭwb* as a divine title, e.g., *tù-bí-sí-piš* "my good is Shapash."[351]

---

[346] Gordon, *UT*, p. 250, reads *rgmm*, and A. Herdner, *CTA*, p. 62, has *-gmm*. Cf. Herdner's n. 5 and the discussion of Dietrich and Loretz cited in the preceding note.

[347] Thus Dahood, *RSP* I, II, entry 107 on *bky//qbr* of Job 27:15. The quote holds true of *bky//'gm* as well.

[348] Michel, *Book of Job*, p. 210 and 427 (n. 611).

[349] *Ephemerides Theologicae Lovanienses* 44 (1968), p. 53.

[350] Blommerde, *NSGJ*, p. 98. For further examples and discussion see Dahood, *Psalms III*, 2nd Note on Ps 104:28; Kuhnigk, *NSH*, p. 104-105, 154-155.

[351] TM. 75. G. 336 (recto) VII:6; cf. Pettinato–Matthiae, *RSO* 50 (1976), p. 5; see also Pettinato, *Or* 44 (1975), p. 370.

For *rāʿ* as an epithet of personified Death, see Dahood on Ps
140 : 12 (3rd Note) [352] as well as the discussion of Prov 13 : 21 in the
preceding paragraph, where *ṭôb* " the Good One " // *rāʿâ* " the Evil
One. " [353]

The use of *'ôr* " the Sun " as a divine title is well documented.
Dahood, for example, translates Ps 112 : 4,

> In the Darkness (*ḥōšek*) will dawn
> the Sun (*'ôr*) for the upright. [354]

In his third Note on this verse, he points to other examples of this
title, including Job 24 : 13. J. Holman also has a full discussion of
'ôr " Sun " (= divine title) in his treatment of Ps 139 : 11. [355] Note
also this name of one of the kings of Ebla, *Ar-Ennum* " the Light is
mercy. " [356]

The feminine form of *'ōpel* " darkness " appears in Jer 23 : 12
as an epithet of the netherworld :

> And so their way shall be like Perdition (*ḥălaqlaqqôt*) to them ;
> they shall be thrust into Darkness (*'ăpēlâ*) and fall into it. [357]

In other texts, e.g., Job 10 : 22, *'ōpel* describes the milieu of Sheol
and often parallels *ḥōšek*, itself a frequent synonym for the abode
of the dead. [358]

Michel could very well be correct when suggesting that *ṭôb* and
'ôr here refer specifically to God and that *rāʿ* and *'ōpel* directly point
to death and Sheol, especially if one looks back to v 23, for instance.
However, the text does not make it clear whether Job is specifying
God and Death explicitly. The translation thus reflects this ambiguity
by capitalizing the four terms, " Good, " " Evil, " " Light, " " Darkness, " but omitting the definite article for each.

---

[352] *Psalms III*, p. 306.
[353] See also Dahood, *Psalms III*, 2nd Note on Ps 144 : 10 ; Sabottka, *Zephanja*, p. 128-129, on Zeph 3 : 15, where *rāʿ* " der Böse " = Baal.
[354] *Psalms III*, p. 126-128.
[355] *BZ* 14 (1970), p. 56-57. Sabottka, *Zephanja*, p. 108 (n. 26), lists also
Isa 10 : 17 ; 60 : 1.
[356] Pettinato, *BA* 39 (1976), p. 47.
[357] Dahood, *Psalms I*, 2nd Note on Ps 35 : 6.
[358] Tromp, *Death and The Nether World*, p. 95-98, 140-144 ; Michel *Book
of Job* (" The Underworld as Darkness and Gloom "), p. 75-78.

I cried for ... I hoped. W. Michel's proposal to read here *qwh* " to
cry out " rather than *qwh* " to wait for " is adopted here. [359] The
context suggests a more dynamic activity than simply " waiting for, "
as vv 20 (*'ăšawwa'* " I call "), 25 (*'im-lō' bākîtî* " Did I not weep "),
and 28 (*'ăšawwēa'* " cry for help ") indicate. Michel would also read
qwh " to cry out " in Job 3 : 9 and 17 : 3 ; see his discussion in the note
in Job 3 : 9, *yĕqaw-lĕ'ôr wā'ayin* " Let it cry out for the Light (Sun)
but there is none. " [360] In Ps 130 : 5, *qwh* " call " parallels *yḥl* " wait
for " as here in Job 30 : 26. [361] Another candidate for *qwh* " to cry
out " is Isa 59 : 9, which echoes Job 30 : 26 :

> *nĕqawweh lā'ôr wĕhinneh ḥōšek*
> *lingōhôt bā'ăpēlôt nĕhallēk*

> We cry out for the light and behold, darkness,
>   for brightness, but we walk in gloom.

The parallelism between " crying out " and " waiting, hoping " occurs
also in Ps 69 : 4, " I am wearied by my crying (*bĕqār'î*) ... as I wait for
(*mĕyaḥēl*) my God, " and Ps 119 : 147 (*wā'ăšawwē'â* " I cried for help " //
yiḥālti " I waited ").

Job 30 : 27

Dahood has directed attention to the importance of chiasmus as
a stylistic technique in Job. [362] Here the grammatical chiasmus (subject : predicate :: predicate : subject) is reinforced by the chiasmus of
sound (*mē'ay* : *dāmmî* :: *qiddĕmūnî* : *yĕmê-'ōnî*). [363] Contrast *NAB*'s rearrangement of this passage. [364]

my insides seethe and are not silent. V 27a implies that Job's intestines
are the source of his mournful plaints (v 25 *bākîtî* " I weep, " v 26
qiwwîtî " I call out, " v 28 *'ăšawwēa'* " I cry out "). Driver and Gray

---

[359] *Book of Job*, p. 427 (n. 611).

[360] Ibid., p. 256 (n. 50).

[361] Dahood, *Psalms III*, 1st Note on Ps 130 : 5.

[362] " Chiasmus in Job : A Text-Critical and Philological Criterion, " p. 119-130.

[363] See also the chiasmus and play on the roots *m'ṭ* // *ṭ'm* in Job 15 : 11 ;
cf. Dahood, " The Phoenician Contribution to Biblical Wisdom Literature, "
p. 125-126.

[364] " 30, 26 : Followed by vv 16a.27b.17b.27a.28. " *Textual Notes on the
New American Bible*, p. 377.

point to *mēʿay* in Isa 16 : 11, *mēʿay* ... *kakkinôr yēhĕmû* " my innards
moan like a lyre, " and 63 : 15, *hămôn mēʿêkā* " the tumult of your
innards. "[365] In his article, " The Physiology of Tears in the Old
Testament, " Terence Collins remarks on this phenomenon : " The
same violent physical disturbance of the intestines which causes tears
to flow also produces the noise which accompanies them. "[366] *UT*
127 : 26 witnesses a similar concept, *wywsrnn ggnh* " his innards instruct
him "; see also *UT* 51 VII : 47, *yqra mt bnpš h ystrn ydd bgngnh* " Mot
called from his throat, the Beloved ... from his innards. "[367]

confronting me are. *qiddĕmūnî* offers another example of the defective
orthography typical of Job.[368]

Job 30 : 28

without an answer. Translators show uncertainty regarding *bĕlō'
hammâ.* Pope, *RSV*, *NAB*, and Alonso Schökel[369] understand *hammâ*
as " sun " (= " with no sun "), while Driver–Gray, *NEB*, Fedrizzi,[370]
and *BJ*² emend the phase to *bĕlō'-nehāmâ* " uncomforted, friendless. "
But neither group is fully satisfied with the resulting version; e.g.,
Driver–Gray in the ICC comment, " It must be admitted that *bl'
hmh* yields an ambiguous and unsatisfactory sense. "[371]
    Relating *hammâ* to Ugaritic *thm* " word, message, " which C. H.
Gordon associates with the Arabic root *hmm* " to decree, "[372] offers
a third possibility. Dahood has posited this root elsewhere in Job
with the more particular nuance of " answer, reply "; e.g., in 15 : 11,
tanhūmôt 'ēl " God's replies " //*dĕbārō* (MT *wĕdābār*) " his word " and in
21 : 2, *tanhûmōtaykem* (MT *tanhûmōtêkem*) " my replies to you " //*millātî*
" my speech. "[373] He recognizes the verbal form *nhm* (a homonym of

---

[365] Driver–Gray, ICC, vol. I, p. 260.
[366] *CBQ* 33 (1971), p. 37-38.
[367] The Ugaritic enclitic particle, *m'*, used with the imperative (e.g., *UT*
127 : 40-42, *yšu gh wyṣh šm' m' lkrt* " he lifts up his voice and cries, ' Listen,
O Keret ' "), may be related etymologically to Hebrew *mēʿîm* " insides, intestines. "
[368] See Freedman, *Eretz-Israel* 9 (1969), p. 35-44.
[369] Alonso Schökel, *Job*, p. 145.
[370] Fedrizzi, *Giobbe*, p. 213.
[371] Driver–Gray, ICC, vol. II, p. 220.
[372] *UT*, Glossary 2542, cites Ullendorf in *Or* 20 (1951), p. 271.
[373] " The Phoenician Contribution to Biblical Wisdom Literature, " p. 125-
126, 144 (n. 16). For further comments on Job 15 : 11, see Dahood, *Bib* 55

nḥm " to comfort ") in Job 21 : 34, in which *tĕnaḥămûnî* " you reply
to me " balances *tĕšûbōtêkem* " your answers. "[374]   Zech 10 : 2 parallels *hebel yĕnaḥēmûn* " they reply nonsense " and *waḥălōmôt haššāw
yĕdabbērû* " they tell false dreams. " To Dahood's list of examples
may be added Job 16 : 2-3, which also collocates *nḥm* and *dbr* :

> I have heard many such things;
>   wearisome oracles (*mĕnaḥamê ʻāmāl*) are you all,
> Have windy words (*dibrê-rûaḥ*) a limit ?[375]

In his contribution to the Jacob Myers *Festschrift*, Frederick Moriarty
accepts the suggestion that Ug. *tḥm* underlies *tanḥūmôt* of Job 15 : 11. [376]
He finds particular significance in the parallelism *tanḥūmôt*//*dābār* and
the link thus established between Ug. *tḥm* and Heb. *dābār*.   On *tḥm*
in *UT* 51 : IV : 41-42, for instance, he comments :

> ... the text joins in parallelism " word " (*tḥm*), " wisdom, "
> and " life, " an early association of concepts which is note-
> worthy in view of later developments in biblical literature :

> *tḥmk il ḥkm*
> *ḥkmt ʻm ʻlm*
> *ḥyt ḥẓt tḥmk*

> Your word, O El, is wise,
> Your wisdom is unto eternity,
> Lucky life is your word. [377]

The thought of Job 30 : 28 thus echoes v 20 : Job's numerous queries
for some hint of explanation from God (a divine " message, " Heb.
dābār, Ug. *tḥm*) are met only with silence.

(1974), p. 382 : *hamĕ'aṭ mimmĕkā tanḥūmôt 'ēl ûdĕbar lĕ' ṭ'mk* (MT *wĕdābār
lā'aṭ 'immāk*) " Are God's replies too meager for you / or does the word of
the Almighty disgust you ? "

[374] *tĕnaḥămûnî* of 21 : 34 thus forms an inclusion with *tanḥūmôt 'ēl* " God's
replies " of 21 : 2.

[375] Compare *dbr 'ml* of Prov 24 : 2, *wĕ'āmāl śiptêhem tĕdabbērnâ* " and their
lips talk mischief. "

[376] Moriarty, " Word as Power in the Ancient Near East, " p. 353.

[377] Ibid., p. 353-354.   On Ugaritic *tḥm*/Hebrew *dābār*, see also H. Cazelles,
" Positions actuelles dans l'exégèse du Pentateuque, " *De Mari à Qumran* :
Festschrift J. Coppens (ed. H. Cazelles ; Bibliotheca Ephemeridum Theologicarum
Lovaniensium 24 ; Gembloux : Duculot, 1969), p. 41.

I rise ... to cry for help. '*ăšawwēa*' is parsed as a subjunctive expressing purpose after *qamtî*. The lack of the waw before '*ăšawwēa*' accords with both Hebrew and Ugaritic usage; see Dahood's discussion of this construction in Ps 39:5. [378]

Job 30 : 29

jackals ... ostriches. The Hebrew parallel pair *tannîm*//*bĕnôt ya'ănâ* occurs also in Isa 13:21-22; 34:13; Mic 1:8; Lam 4:3.

brother ... friend. RSP I,II,18 records this Ugaritic–Hebrew parallel pair *aḫ*//*r'*. '*ḫ* "brother" also appears as an element in personal names in the texts from Tell Mardikh; e.g., *aḫ-ḫa-lum*, which Dahood proposes means "(my) brother is the Phoenix." [379]

Job 30 : 30

Note the sound pattern of this verse: the triple '*ayin*, the triple *mem*, and the three-fold repetition of the *ḥēth–rēsh* sequence, *šāḥar*, *ḥārâ*, *ḥōreb*.

my skin ... my bones. The parallelism '*ôr*//'*eṣem* occurs in Mic 3:3; Job 10:11; Lam 3:4.

than a caldron. The masoretic pointing of *m'ly* as *mē'ālāy* obscures the noun '*ĕlî* "caldron, crucible" proposed by Dahood for this verse and for Ps 12:7, *kesep ṣārûp be'ĕlî* (MT *ba'ălîl*) "silver purged in a crucible." [380] For the meaning of '*ĕlî* he points to its parallelism with *maktēš* "mortar" in Prov 27:22. The sense and *Wortfeld* of Ps 102:4b is strikingly similar: *wĕ'aṣmôtay kĕmôqēd niḥārû* "my bones burn like a brazier." [381]

scorched. *ḥrr* "to burn, be hot" occurs several times in Ugaritic, appearing in a context not unlike that of v 30 in *UT* 75 II:38-39, *anpnm yḥr* (...) *bmtnm yšḫn* "His face is flushed, in his loins he is

---

[378] *Psalms I*, 1st Note on Ps 39:5. See also idem, *Psalms II²*, 1st Note on Ps 88:11; idem, *Psalms III*, 2nd Note on Ps 102:14, in which *qûm* + the subjunctive expresses purpose.

[379] VTSup 29 (1978), p. 112; cf. TM. 75. G. 336 (recto) V:3 in Pettinato-Matthiae, *RSO* 50 (1976), p. 4.

[380] *Psalms I*, 2nd Note on Ps 12:7.

[381] Dahood, *Psalms III*, p. 8.

feverish. "[382]   V 30 characterizes Job's sickness in terms of *ḥrh* " to
burn, be scorched " (= Ug. *ḥrr*), while Job 2 : 7 uses *šĕḥîn* " foul pox "
(= Ug. *šḫn* " be feverish, " parallel to *ḥrr* in *UT* 75 II : 38-39 cited
above) to describe his affliction. [383]

with heat.   *ḥōreb* " heat " and *rtḥ* " to seethe, boil " (v 27), used here
for Job's sickness, appear together in Sir 43 : 3 to describe the burning
action of the sun : *bhṣhyrw yrtyḫ tbl lpny ḥrbw my ytklkl* " At noon it
seethes the land ; who can withstand its heat ? "[384]

Job 30 : 31

mourning ... weepers.   The roots *'bl* and *bkh* are parallel in Neh 8 : 9
(*'al-tit'abbĕlû wĕ'al-tibkû*) and collocated in Gen 37 : 35 ; Deut 34 : 8 ;
2 Sam 19 : 2 ; Esth 4 : 3.   If Gordon is correct in linking Ug. *ablm*
of *qryt ablm* in *UT* 1 Aqht 163, 165 to Heb. *'bl* " to mourn, "[385] then
note its collocation with *bky* beginning six lines later in 1 Aqht 171-172
(*bkyt*), 173 (*ybk*), and 177 (*ybk*).

my harp ... my flute.   Gen 4 : 21 and Job 21 : 12 repeat this parallelism *kinnôr* " harp "//*'ûgāb* " flute. "   *kinnôr* appears in several
Ugaritic texts[386] among which *UT* 602 : 3-6 resembles the context of
Job 21 : 12, especially in the repetition of the four roots : *rqd* " to
dance, " *tp* " drum, " *knr* " lyre, " and *ṭb* in the sense of " merry " :[387]

UT 602 : 3-6   *d yšr w yḏmr*
                       bknr w ṯlb
                       btp w mṣltm
                       bm rqdm dšn
                       bḫbr kṯr ṭbm

                       Who sings and chants
                       With lyre and lute,
                       With drum and cymbals,

---

[382] Ibid., 3rd Note on Ps 102 : 4.
[383] See also Pope, *Job³*, p. 21 (on Job 2 : 7).
[384] Vattioni, *Ecclesiastico*, p. 231.
[385] *UT*, Glossary 27 ; also, Aistleitner, *Wörterbuch*, p. 3 (no. 21) : " Es sind
aber auch andere Etym. möglich. "
[386] Gordon, *UT*, Glossary 1274.   See also Dahood's comments in *Psalms I*,
3rd Note on Ps 49 : 5.
[387] For the nuance of *ṭb* " merry " see Dahood, *Or* 39 (1970), p. 377.

Among the plump dancers,
Amid the merry companions of Koshar. [388]

Job 21 : 11b-13a　*wĕyaldêhem yĕraqqēdûn*
yiśʾû kī-tōp (MT *kĕtōp*) *wĕkinnôr*
wĕyiśmĕḥû lĕqôl ʿûgāb
yĕballû baṭṭôb yĕmêhem
Their children dance,
They take up both drum and harp, [389]
And rejoice to the sound of the flute.
They pass their days in merriment.

Dahood adopts the LXX and Targum reading of *ʿûgābīm*, "reed-pipes, flutes," for Masoretic *ʿăgābîm* in Ezek 33 : 32. [390] On closer examination, the word-play mentioned by him, *ʿăgābîm* "applause" (v 31) / / *ʿăgūbîm* (MT *ʿăgābîm*) "flutes" (v 32), [391] proves to be part of a larger A : B : : B : A chiastic word pattern extending over vv 31-32 : *wĕšāmĕʿû ʾet-dĕbārêkā ... yaʿăśû : ʿăgābîm bĕpîhem : : ʿăgūbîm yĕpeh : wĕšāmĕʿû ʾet-dĕbārêkā wĕʿōśîm.* [392]

[388] Translation follows Dahood and Penar, *RSP* I, p. 168.

[389] There is no need to follow the emendation suggested in the *BHS* apparatus of *kĕtōp* to *bĕtōp*. One may vocalize *ktp* as *kī-tōp*, reading *kī* as the emphatic particle (written defectively) and translating "*both* drum and harp."

[390] *Bib* 44 (1963), p. 531-532.

[391] Ibid., p. 532 (n. 1).

[392] On the A : B : : B : A word pattern in Hebrew involving paronomasia see Ceresko, *CBQ* 38 (1976), p. 309-311, and J. S. Kselman, "Semantic-Sonant Chiasmus in Biblical Poetry," *Bib* 58 (1977), p. 219-223.

Translation of Job 31

1. I made a covenant in His presence —
   never would I gaze upon the Virgin.
2. What is God's allotment from above,
   Shaddai's heritage from on high?
3. Is it not calamity for the wicked,
   and disaster for evildoers?
4. Does he not see my ways
   and number all my steps,
5. Whether I have walked toward an idol,
   or my foot hastened after a fraud?
6. Should he weigh me on honest scales
   God would know my full weight.
7. If my foot has strayed from the way,
   or my heart followed after my eyes,
   or a spot stuck to my hands,
8. May I sow and another eat,
   and my offspring be uprooted.

9. If my heart has been lured by a woman,
   and at my neighbor's door I lurked,
10. May my wife grind for another,
    and over her may others bend;
11. For that were licentiousness,
    which itself is criminal iniquity,
12. A fire that devours to Perdition,
    destroying all my gain.

13. If I despised the claim
    of my slave or my slave girl
    when they complained against me,
14. Then what would I do if God punished me;
    if he called me to account, what could I answer him?

15. The Victor — he who made me in the belly made him,
    and he created us in the womb — the Unique.

16. If I have held back any desire of the poor,
    or the eyes of the widow caused to fail,

17. While I ate my portion alone,
    but the orphan ate none of it.

18. For from his youth he was raised by me as by his father,
    and from his mother's womb I guided him.

19. If I saw one perishing for lack of clothing,
    or a poor man without covering,

20. If his loins did not bless me
    warmed by the fleece of my sheep;

21. If I raised my hand against the orphan,
    when I saw his acquittal at the gate.

22. Let my shoulder-blade fall from my shoulder,
    and my arm be broken from its socket.

23. For a dread to me is God's hand,
    and the raising of it I cannot bear.

24. I put not my confidence in gold,
    nor called fine gold my security.

25. I gloated not when my wealth was great,
    when my hand attained abundance.

26. I gazed not on the light as it brightened —
    the moon, that is, waning in splendor;

27. Nor was my heart secretly seduced,
    that my hand wafted a kiss from my mouth.

28. That also is criminal iniquity,
    for I would betray God on high.

29. I have not gloated at my foe's ruin,
    nor been elated when evil overtook him;

30. I have never let my mouth offend,
    seeking his life with a curse.

31. The men of my household have not said,
    " O that we might feast on his flesh ! "

32. The stranger did not sleep in the street;
    my door I opened to the traveler.

ۈ× (33.) If I hid my rebellious acts from you in the Earth,
                concealing my guilt in Hades;
       34. If I feared the rabble clamor,
                and the scorn of the clans terrified me,
                so that I kept silent and did not go out the door.

ۈ× (35.) O that the Most High would pay attention to me!
                Behold my signature, let Shaddai answer me,
                and my Opponent write an indictment.
       36. Surely on my shoulder I would wear it,
                I would bind it on like a crown.
       37. The number of my steps I would tell him;
                like a prince I would approach him.

×ۈ (38.) If because of me my land cried out,
                and in unison its furrows wept;
       39. If I ate its yield without paying,
                or the life of its workers snuffed out;
       40. Instead of wheat let thistles sprout,
                instead of barley, let fire come upon it.

       Ended are the words of Job.

Commentary on Job 31

W. Michel and G. Fohrer both offer suggestions for the structure
of Chapter 31. Michel groups the following sets of verses together
according to subject matter: vv 1-4 (Other Gods; Covenant with himself); 5-8 (Idols); 9-12 (Woman, neighbor); 13-15 (Slave); 16-22 (Poor);
23-25 (Wealth); 26-28 (Idolatry); 29-34 (Enemy, Stranger); 35-37
(God; Covenant with God); 38-40 (Land; Workers). He comments:

> According to this arrangement Job denies that he has ever
> committed a sin against God (three times he denies that he
> has committed the crime of idolatry, 3 for emphasis?), or against
> man (seven different groups of people are mentioned, 7 for per-
> fection?), he denies also of having sinned against nature, against
> his land, property and wealth. [393]

---

[393] Michel, *Book of Job*, p. 437 (n. 648).

Fohrer would divide the entire chapter into two parts. The first part contains nine strophes enumerating twelve sins: strophe one, lust (vv 1-4); strophe two, double-dealing (vv 5-6) and greed (vv 7-8); strophe three, adultery (vv 9-12); strophe four, disregard of the right of slaves (vv 13-15); strophes five and six, hardheartedness toward the poor (vv 16-23); strophe seven, reliance on riches (vv 24-25) and superstition (vv 26-28); strophe eight, hatred of enemies (vv 29-30) and lack of hospitality (vv 31-32); strophe nine, dissimulation (vv 33-34) and exploitation of the land (vv 38-40). The second, shorter part of Chapter 31 has only one strophe (vv 35-37; Fohrer places these verses at the end of the chapter, after vv 38-40). [394]

Our study of this chapter leads us to propose an eleven-fold division of the verses, ten strophes dealing with various types of sin of which Job declares himself innocent, plus his final plea (vv 35-37): strophe one, idolatry (vv 1-8); strophe two, adultery (vv 9-12); strophe three, mistreatment of servants (vv 13-15); strophe four, disregard of the poor, the orphan, and the widow (vv 16-18); strophe five, selfishness which leads to injustice toward others (vv 19-21; vv 22-23 are a curse which serves as a climax for the previous two strophes, vv 16-18, 19-21); strophe six, trust in riches and idols rather than in God (two aspects of the same sin; vv 24-28); strophe seven, hatred of enemies (vv 29-30); strophe eight, lack of hospitality (vv 31-32); strophe nine, dishonesty (vv 33-34); strophe ten, Job's final plea (vv 35-37); strophe eleven, exploitation of the land (vv 38-40). Job's climactic plea for a hearing before God (vv 35-37) does not come at the end of the chapter but is inserted between the ninth and tenth declarations of innocence. This point of style which has parallels elsewhere in Job is discussed below under vv 35-37. The reasons for this eleven-fold division are included in the treatment of each group of verses.

The poet uses inclusion as a means of giving a larger overall unity to this chapter. Certain phrases which appear at the beginning are repeated toward the end of the chapter. *kol-ṣĕʿāday yispôr* " he numbers all my steps " of v 4 is echoed by *mispar ṣĕʿāday* " the number of my steps " in v 37 (i.e., four verses from the end). The roots *ʼkl* and *yṣʼ* of v 8 (*yōʼkēl* " may he eat, " *ṣeʼĕṣāʼay* " my offspring ") occur again in vv 39-40 (*ʼākaltî* " I ate, " *yēṣēʼ* " may it grow, spring forth "). *yipt … libbî* " my heart has been lured " of v 27 reiterates *niptâ libbî* " my heart has been lured " of v 9. Finally, *kî-hûʼ* (Ketib) … ʿāwōn

[394] Fohrer, *Das Buch Hiob*, p. 427-428.

pĕlîlîm " For that ... criminal iniquity " of v 11 is repeated in v 28 (i.e., the thirteenth verse from the end of the chapter), *gam-hû' 'āwōn pĕlîlî* " That also is criminal iniquity. "

Job 31 : 1-8 (Strophe One)

> I made a covenant in His presence —
>> never would I gaze upon the Virgin.
> What is God's allotment from above,
>> Shaddai's heritage from on high?
> Is it not calamity for the wicked,
>> and disaster for evildoers?
> Does he not see my ways
>> and number all my steps,
> Whether I have walked toward an idol,
>> or my foot hastened after a fraud?
> Should he weigh me on honest scales
>> God would know my full weight.
> If my foot has strayed from the way,
>> or my heart followed after my eyes,
>> or a spot stuck to my hands,
> May I sow and another eat,
>> and my offspring be uprooted.

This first part of Chapter 31 deals with idolatry; see especially the remarks on vv 1 and 5, which in the past have been misunderstood as treating respectively of unchaste thoughts and dishonesty. Of the modern versions, only the Chicago Bible groups these verses together as a unity. The curse in v 8 which ends this section employs the roots *'kl* " to eat " and *šrš* " to uproot " (piel) which the statement of calamity at the end of the next section repeats (*tō'kēl* " devours " and *tĕšārēš* " uprooting, destroying " of v 12). Turning away from God to put one's trust in idols for the prosperity of field and progeny leads to the uprooting and destruction of both.

To pull together this section, the poet " gathers up " in v 7 three words which had appeared earlier in vv 1-5. Thus *lĕ'ênāy* " in His presence " of v 1, *dĕrākāy* " my ways " of v 4, and *hālaktî* " I walked " of v 5 are repeated together in v 7 (*haddārek, 'ênay, hālak*).

Job 31 : 1

in His presence. Almost all translations understand *lĕʻênāy* "with my eyes." This expression, "to make a covenant with one's eyes," is hapax and the exact sense is not clear. A more satisfactory reading may be to take *lĕʻênāy* as "in His presence," understanding the yodh suffix as third person singular rather than first person.[395] The phrase occurs in this sense in legal contexts in reference to witnesses in whose presence an agreement is made; e.g., "'I give you the field, and I give you the cave that is in it; in the presence of the sons of my people (*lĕʻênê bĕnê-ʻammî*) I give it to you'" (Gen 23 : 11, *RSV*; see also Gen 23 : 18).

never would I. As noted by Pope[396] and Driver–Gray,[397] *mâ* has a negative force here; thus LXX (*kai ou*), Vulgate (*ut ne*), Fedrizzi, *NEB*, Alonso Schokel, BJ². Contrast the emendation to *mēhitbônēn* suggested in *BHK*³ and continued is *BHS*. Cognizance of the potential negative sense of *mâ* serves to clarify Prov 20 : 24. *NAB* translates:

> *mēyhwh miṣĕʻădê-gāber*
> *wĕʾādām mâ-yyābîn darkô*

> Man's steps are from the Lord;
> how, then, can a man understand his way?

Does the suffix of *darkô* refer to *yhwh* or to *ʾādām*? To avoid ambiguity, *NAB* adds an explanatory footnote[398] and *NEB* paraphrases *darkô* "the road he travels." If *mâ* is understood here in its negative sense, the parallelism becomes more precise and the ambiguity disappears:

> From Yahweh are a man's steps,
> thus a mortal knows not his own destiny.[399]

---

[395] On the third person singular yodh suffix, see the bibliography above in footnote 105.

[396] Pope, *Job*³, p. 228.

[397] Driver–Gray, ICC, vol. II, p. 222.

[398] "Man is dependent upon God and cannot fully foresee his own course."

[399] Dahood, private communication; see also M. Dahood, "The Emphatic Double Negative *m'yn* in Jer 10 : 6-7," *CBQ* 37 (1975), p. 458-459, and idem, *Or* 45 (1976), p. 347.

never. The waw of *ûmâ* serves an emphatic function, thus the translation " never. " Blommerde has pointed out a similar case in Job 31 : 30, " I really did not permit (*wĕlō'-nātattî*) my palate to sin. " [400]

gaze upon. Andrée Herdner has recently published a Ugaritic text, a prayer to Baal in time of danger, which provides further insight into this verse. [401] The introductory formula reads :

kgr 'z tǵ(r)km
(q)rd ḥmytkm
'(n)km l(b)'l tš'un
yb(')lm

Si un fort attaque votre po(r)te,
    (Un pui)ssant, vos murailles,
Vous élèverez vox ye(ux) vers (Ba)al :
    " O Ba(a)l ... " [402]

The import of verses such as Job 31 : 1 and 26 thus becomes clearer. Fixing one's eyes upon the idol or manifestation of a god (e.g., v 26) was a cultic act of worship or supplication. Several passages in the Psalter provide even closer parallels : Ps 121 : 1, *'eśśā' 'ēnay 'el-hehārîm* " I raise my eyes to the Mountain "; [403] Ps 123 : 1, *'ēlêkā nāśā'tî 'et-'ēnay hayyōšĕbî baššāmāyim* " I raise my eyes to you, who are enthroned in heaven "; Ps 139 : 20, *'ăšer yō'mĕrū kol-mĕzimmâ* (MT *yō'mĕrūkā limzimmâ*) *nāśū' laššāw' 'ārîk* (MT *'ārêkā*) " Because they gaze upon every figurine, raise their eyes to vanities arrayed "; [404] Ps 101 : 3, *lō' 'āśît lĕneged 'ēnay dĕbar bĕliyyā'al* " I have never set before my eyes any worthless object. " [405] In the Akkadian acrostic poem, the

---

[400] *NSGJ*, p. 115. An analogous usage is emphatic *kî + lō'*, as in Ps 125 : 3, " The scepter of the wicked will surely not rest (*kî lō' yānûaḥ*) "; cf. Dahood, *Psalms III*, 2nd Note on Ps 125 : 3.

[401] Andrée Herdner, " Une prière à Baal des Ugaritains en danger, " *CRAIBL* (1972), p. 693-703.

[402] Ibid., p. 694.

[403] Dahood, *Psalms III*, p. 199 ; in his 3rd Note on this verse he comments, " *the Mountain.* Probably designating both Yahweh's celestial abode and Yahweh himself.... "

[404] Ibid., 2nd, 3rd, 4th Notes on Ps 139 : 20.

[405] Ibid., 3rd Note on Ps 101 : 3 : " *any worthless object.* Probably an idol, since it is something held up to view... "; cf. Ezek 18 : 6, *wĕ'ênāyw lō' nāśā' 'el-gillûlê bêt yiśrā'ēl* " (But if) he does not raise his eyes to the idols of the house of Israel. "

" Babylonian Theodicy, " in which many see rapprochements with the form and content of Job, [406] the protagonist employs similar terminology in protesting his piety : " Dans mon enfance, je me suis tourné vers l'ordre du dieu ; avec prostration et oraison j'ai regardé la déesse. " [407]   The irony of Job 30 : 20 and 31 : 1 now emerges : even though God does not look upon Job's plight (30 : 20, $l\bar{o}$' ... *titbōnen bî* " you ignore me "), Job does not turn from God and " look upon " (31 : 1, *ûmâ 'etbônēn*) any pagan idol.

the Virgin.   *bĕtûlâ* here $=$ Ugaritic *btlt 'nt* " the Virgin Anat, " Baal's sister and consort.   W. Michel calls attention to a suggestion advanced in 1928 [408] that this verse deals with idolatry and that *bĕtûlâ* refers to the *virgo coelestis*, Ishtar-Astarte-Venus : " But is it not conceivable that the poet would begin this catalogue of negative sins with one of the worst sins he could think of, namely idolatry ? " [409]   Indeed, as Blommerde has shown, v 5 (see below) deals specifically with idolatry, *šāw'* $=$ " an idol " and *mirmâ* $=$ " a fraud, " [410] and further on in this chapter (v 26), Job foreswears idolatrous worship of the moon. The author of Job reinforces his allusion to *btlt 'nt* " the Virgin Anat " by alluding to one of her titles, *b'lt šmm rmm* " mistress of the highest heaven " [411] in the following v 2 : *nahălat šadday mimmĕrōmîm* " the inheritance of Shaddai from on high. "   This ancient title appears also in Job 16 : 19, *baššāmayim* " in heaven "//*bammĕrômîm* " on high. " [412]   The Virgin Anat (*btlt 'nt*) is further associated with the

---

[406] Pope, *Job*[3], p. LXIV-LXVII ; Lévêque, *Job et son Dieu*, vol. I, p. 23-25.

[407] Strophe VII, line 3 ; the translation is that of E. Dhorme, " Ecclésiaste ou Job ? " *RB* 32 (1923), p. 15, as quoted by Lévêque, *Job et son Dieu*, p. 25. For an Egyptian parallel see Helmer Ringgren, *The Faith of the Psalmist* (Philadelphia : Fortress, 1963), p. 124, n. 7 (in reference to Ps 127 : 4).

[408] George Jeshurun, " A Note on Job XXX : 1 (sic), " *Journal of the Society of Oriental Research* 12 (Toronto, 1928), p. 153-154.   The title of this article as it appears in *JSOR* is apparently a misprint ; it should read, " A Note on Job XXXI : 1. "

[409] Michel, *Book of Job*, p. 429 (n. 616).

[410] Blommerde, *NSGJ*, p. 113.

[411] Gordon, *UT*, Glossary 1291a.

[412] Cf. M. J. Dahood, " Hebrew–Ugaritic Lexicography III, " *Bib* 46 (1965), p. 313.   On the divine title *rāmîm* " Exalted One " in Job 21 : 22, see Blommerde, *NSGJ*, p. 94, and Pope, *Job*[3], p. 160.   Dahood discusses the title in the Psalter in *Psalms II*[2], 2nd Note on Ps 78 : 69 ; idem, *Psalms III*, 2nd Note on Ps 148 : 1.   To his list of passages from Job in the latter note (Job 16 : 19 ; 22 : 12 ; 25 : 2) add Job 38 : 33-34 (*šāmāyim ... hătārîm*).

" heights of Saphon " *mrym ṣpn* in *UT* 51 IV : 18-19 ; V : 82,85. Note also the parallelism here, *lĕʿênāy* " in His sight " // *ʿal-bĕtûlâ* " upon the Virgin, " which may be a pun on the name *btlt ʿnt*.

Job disclaims idolatry and not unchaste thoughts and looks. The contextual problems much discussed by commentators [413] vanish and proposals to emend *bĕtûlâ* to *nĕbālâ* (e.g., Pope) or to transpose this verse become unnecessary. [414] Finally, *btlt* and *knr* (cf. *kinnōr* of 30 : 31) are collocated in *UT* 603 II : 5-6, *trḥṣ ydh btlt ʿnt … tiḫd knrh bydh* " Washes her hands does Virgin Anat … She takes her lyre in her hand. "

Job 31 : 2

allotment … heritage. The Hebrew parallel pair *ḥēleq* // *naḥălâ* occurs frequently either directly paralleled or collocated. In Job alone it occurs three times : here in 31 : 2, in 20 : 29, and in 27 : 13 (*ḥēleq* // *wĕnaḥălat*).

from above … from on high. The parallelism here, *mimmā́ʿal* " from above " // *mimmĕrōmîm* " from on high, " gives added strength to Pope's eschewing the emendation of *ʿim-ʾēl* to *mēʾēl* in Job 27 : 13, as proposed, for example, by the *BHS* apparatus :

> *zeh ḥēleq-ʾādām rāšāʿ ʿim-ʾēl*
> *wĕnaḥălat ʿārîṣîm miššadday yiqqāḫû*
> This is the wicked's portion from God,
> the tyrant's inheritance from Shaddai.

" The context clearly indicates that the sense of the preposition *ʿim* is here ' from ' rather than ' with, ' " and he quotes *UT* 2065 : 14-17

---

[413] E.g., Alonso Schökel, *Job*, p. 146. Pope, *Job³*, p. 228-229, points to Sir 9 : 5 in which the first colon uses the same expression as Job 31 : 1b : *bbtwlh ʾl ttbwn pn twqš bʿwnšyh* " At a virgin do not look, / Lest you be trapped in sin with her. " However, the context there clearly calls for an interpretation warning against unchastity, as the following vv 6-9 indicate. After discussing the suggestion of Jeshurun and Michel, Pope notes (p. 229), " If the virgin in question here (Job 31 : 1b) is the Queen of Heaven whose licentious worship Job has forsworn, vowing not to look at her even as he avoided looking to the sun and moon as objects of worship, then the difficulties considered at the beginning of this note (on Job 31 : 1b) vanish. "

[414] *NAB* puts v 1 before v 9 ; cf. *Textual Notes on the New American Bible*, p. 377. *NEB* inserts v 1 between vv 5 and 6 ; cf. Brockington, *The Hebrew Text of the Old Testament*, p. 113.

as a clear example of *'m* meaning "from": (*i*)*rš 'my mnm iršt k dḫsrt wank aštn liḫy* "Ask of me whatever you wish that is lacking and I will send it to my brother." [415] See also *UT* 2009 II: 3-4, *š(al) išal 'mk ybl šd* "I am asking from you the produce of the field."

Job 31 : 3

wicked ... evil. The parallelism *'awwāl* "wicked" // *'āwen* "evil" here and in Job 11 : 14 (*'āwen* // *'awĕlâ*) [416] serves to clarify the parallelism in Jer 4 : 15-16 :

> *kî qôl maggîd middān*
> *ûmašmîa' 'āwen mēhar 'eprāyim*
> *hazkîrû laggôyim hēnnâ* (MT *hinnēh*)
> *hašmî'û 'ōl* (MT *'al*) *yĕrûšālaim*

Hark a voice announcing from Dan,
  and divulging the evil from Mount Ephraim.
Mention these things, O nations,
  divulge the wickedness of Jerusalem.

The note in *BHK³* to read *bĕ* (following the LXX and Vulgate) or *lĕ* (Syriac) for the preposition *'al* reflects the difficulties translators have had with this passage. [417] Repointing the preposition *'al* to the substantive *'ōl* "wickedness" provides a complement for the imperative *hašmî'û* and uncovers the parallel pair *'āwen* // *'ōl*, witnessed in Job 11 : 14, 31 : 3. [418]

---

[415] Pope, *Job³*, p. 191; Dahood, *UHP*, p. 32; idem, *Psalms II²*, 4th Note on Ps 85 : 5. In *UT* 2065 quoted here, *šyt*, may have the sense of "prepare" rather than "send": *wank aštn liḫy* "I will prepare it for my brother"; compare Heb. *šyt* in Jer. 51 : 39 (BDB, p. 1011b.).

[416] Further occurrences include Isa 59 : 3-4 (*'awĕlâ ... 'āwen*); Ps. 125 : 3,5 (*bĕ'awĕlātâ ... hā'āwen*): Prov 22 : 8 (*'awĕlâ* // *'āwen*).

[417] The *NEB* translator apparently felt the need of a substantive here and supplied "the doom": "Tell all this to the nations, proclaim the doom of Jerusalem." No note justifying this translation is provided in Brockington, *The Hebrew Text of the Old Testament*, p. 199.

[418] MT *hnh* is repointed *hēnnâ* "these things," the 3rd feminine plural pronoun used in the oblique case; for further comments on Jer 4 : 16, see M. J. Dahood, "Jeremiah 5, 31 and *UT* 127 : 32," *Bib* 57 (1976), p. 108. On *'ōl* (MT *'al*) "injustice, wickedness" in Prov 10 : 12, see M. J. Dahood, "Una coppia di termini ugaritici," *Bibbia e Oriente* 15 (1973), p. 253-254; see also the discussion of Job 14 : 16 below under Job 31 : 4.

Recognition of this parallel pair also bears on the reading of Job 22 : 15. The presence of the parallel pair ʿôl-m (MT ʿôlām) [419] / / ʾāwen supports Tur-Sinai's reading of this verse:

> haʾōraḥ ʿôl-m (MT ʿôlām) tišmôr
> ʾăšer dārĕkû mĕtê-ʾāwen

> Will you keep to the way of wickedness
>   which evil men have trod? [420]

Job 31 : 4

Comparison of Job 31 : 4 with Job 14 : 16 may offer a solution for the latter:

> kî ʿattâ ṣĕʿāday tispôr
> lĕʾ (MT lōʾ) tišmôr ʿōl (MT ʿal) ḥaṭṭāʾtî

> Because now you count my steps,
>   O Victor, you observe the malice of my sins. [421]

Pope remarks, " The two halves of this verse are not congruent. The almost identical verse in xxxi 4 shows that both lines have to agree, that one cannot be positive and the other negative. " [422] His solution is to insert a negative in the first colon, following the Syriac version:

> Then you would (not) count my steps,
> Nor be alert for my sins.

But this contradicts Job's statement later in 31 : 4 (see also Job's title for God in 7 : 20, nōṣēr hāʾādām " Man-Watcher "). A simpler solution is to revocalize MT lōʾ to lĕʾ " O Victor. " The positive sense fits the context better and accords with Job's affirmation of God's omniscience in 31 : 4. In 14 : 16, Job is chiding

---

[419] The northern contracted form of ʾāwel " wickedness, " plus an enclitic mem.

[420] N. H. Tur-Sinai, *The Book of Job : A New Commentary* (revised edition ; Jerusalem : Kiryath Sepher, 1967), p. 342 ; contra Pope, *Job*³, p. 166, who accepts Dahood's proposal that Ug. ǵlm (= Heb. ʿlm) " to grow dark " is the root in question : " Do you mark the dark path. " Cf. Dahood, " Northwest Semitic Philology and Job, " p. 65-66.

[421] Compare Viganò, *Nomi e titoli di YHWH*, p. 97 (n. 287) : " allora conteresti i miei passi, / o Vincitore, spieresti il mio peccato. "

[422] Pope, *Job*³, p. 109.

the Mighty One (*lē'*) for wasting his time in keeping close account of all Job's petty faults. MT *'al* is revocalized '*ōl* " malice " (*'ōl ḥaṭṭā'tî* " the malice of my sins "); see the discussion of Jer 4 : 16 above under Job 31 : 1. The two terms parallel here in Job 14 : 16, *ṣĕ'āday* " my steps" // *'ōl* (MT *'al*) "malice," are collocated in 31 : 4 (*lĕ'awwāl ... ṣĕ'āday*).

see ... count. This Hebrew parallel pair occurs also in Job 28 : 27 (*rā'āh* // *wayĕsappĕrāh*).

my ways ... my steps. This same parallelism (*dĕrākāy* // *ṣĕ'āday*) appears elsewhere in Ps 37 : 23 (*miṣ'ădê* // *wĕdarkô*), Job 34 : 21 (*darkê* // *ṣĕ'ā-dāyw*), Prov 16 : 9 (*darkô* // *ṣa'ădô*), and Prov 20 : 24 (*miṣ'ădê* // *darkô*).

The collocation of *ṣa'ad* here with *hālak* of v 5 (*hālaktî*) recalls the parallelism of these two roots in Job 18 : 7-8 (*ṣa'ădê ... yithallāk*), Prov 4 : 12 (*bĕlektĕkā ... ṣa'ădekā*), Prov 30 : 29 (*ṣā'ad* // *lāket*) and Lam 4 : 18 (*ṣĕ'ādênû ... milleket*).

Job 31 : 5

Whether I walked. Although most versions see no close continuity between vv 4 and 5, [423] the four key words, *dĕrākāy* " my ways, " *ṣĕ'āday* " my steps, " *hālaktî* " I walk, " *raglî* " my feet, " suggest that the two verses should be read together (N. B. the comments on the parallel word pair *ṣa'ad* (4b) // *hālak* (5a) in the preceding note). Previous commentators connected vv 5 and 6 because of the association they saw between *šāw'* " deceit, " *mirmâ* " fraud " and *mō'znê-ṣedeq* " just scales. " E.g., *JB* notes on v 5, relating it logically to v 6 : " Fraud in barter or in the market. Job, appealing to the law of retaliation, asks that he himself be justly weighed. " But if *šāw'* and *mirmâ* are taken rather as referring to idolatry (see the following note), then the emphasis can shift to the logical movement of thought from vv 4 and 5 (God's complete knowledge of Job's conduct) to v 6 (a challenge to God for a fair trial).

toward an idol ... after a fraud. Dahood first suggested that *šaw'* and *mirmâ* should be taken in the concrete sense of " idol, figurine, fraud " here. [424] This accords with Job's foreswearing of idolatry at

---

[423] *RSV* and *NEB* have a space between them and *NAB* puts v 5 between vv 6 and 7.

[424] Dahood, *UHP*, p. 31 ; idem, *Psalms III*, 2nd Note on Ps 139 : 20 ; Blommerde, *NSGJ*, p. 113 ; Holman, *BZ* 14 (1970), p. 218.

the beginning of this first strophe (v 1). Dahood also proposed that
'*im* here has a directional sense, " toward. " He cites *UT* Krt 124
in which this same verb-preposition combination (*hlk* '*m*) appears :
lk '*m krt* " Go to Keret ! " [425]

walked ... hastened. This same set of parallel verbs (*hlk*//*ḥwš*; this
parallelism is a hapax legomenon in the Bible) appears twice in Ugaritic. One occurrence is *UT* 'nt x IV : 7, *dl ylkn ḥš barṣ* " that he (not)
go quickly into the netherworld. "   *UT* 51 VI : 16-18 may be another
instance, if the proposed restoration found in Whitaker's *Concordance*
is correct :

> (*ḥš*) *bhth tbnn*
> (*ḥš*) *trmm hklh*
> *y(tl)k llbn w'ṣh*
> *l(šryn) mḥmd arzh*

> Quickly is his house built,
> Quickly is his palace raised.
> He brings from Lebanon and its wood,
> From Sirion its choicest cedar. [426]

The *Assyrian Dictionary*, vol. 6, reports that an Assyrian lexical list
equates the two words (*ḫa-a-šu* = *a-la-ku*) found parallel here in Job. [427]

Job 31 : 6

Should he weigh me. This follows Blommerde, who sees the first colon
as a conditional clause without a morphological indicator. [428] *JB*
understands the verse in the same sense :

---

[425] Dahood, *UHP*, p. 32 ; accepted by Pope, *Job³*, p. 230. Note also *UT*
2060 : 15-16, '*my ... ltlk* " You have not come to me. "

[426] Whitaker, *A Concordance of the Ugaritic Literature*, p. 266 ; Driver,
Canaanite Myths and Legends, p. 98. Compare *UT* 51 V : 113-115, *ḥš bhtm*
k(tr) ḥš rmm hk(lm) ḥš bhtm tbnn ḥš trmm hklm " Hasten, Koshar, the house,
hasten to raise the palace. May the house quickly be built, may the palace
quickly be raised. " The verbs *bny* and *r(y/w)m* here in *UT* 51 V : 113-115,
VI : 16-18 are apparently 3rd masculine plurals with *t*-preformative ; see Dahood,
Psalms II², 3rd Note on Ps 68 : 3 ; idem, *Psalms III*, " Grammar of the Psalter, "
p. 387.

[427] *The Assyrian Dictionary of the Oriental Institute of the University of
Chicago*, vol. 6 (Ḫ), p. 146b.

[428] *NSGJ*, p. 34, 114.

If he weighs me on honest scales,
    being God, he cannot fail to see my innocence.

This verse also exhibits the technique of " delayed identification " ; the subject of *yišqĕlēnî* is not explicitated until the second colon (= *'ĕlôah* " God " ; see the discussion above on Job 30 : 1). *NAB* and *NEB* both ignore this stylistic nicety by transferring " God " to the first colon in their versions of this verse.

on honest scales. *RSP* I,II,606 lists Job 31 : 6 (*šql ... m'znym*) as an example of the Ugaritic–Hebrew parallel pair *tql ... mzn* (cf. *UT* 2100 : 1). Amos 8 : 5 (*šeqel//mō'zĕnê mirmâ*) can be added to the Hebrew instances cited there.

my full weight. Dahood argues that congruity of metaphor favors the rendering of *tūmmātî* as " my full weight " rather than " my innocence. " [429] N.B. ICC's comment on Job 1 : 1 (*tām wĕyāšār*):

> ... (Job's) is a character that seeks its ends openly, along the one true path, not like the *'ikkeš* trickily, by crooked and devious paths ; or, in a figure used by the writer himself, the *tām*, or *perfect* man, is one whose character is full-weight: " let me be weighed in correct scales that God may recognize my integrity, " i.e. that I am full weight (31 : 6). [430]

The Hebrew parallel pair *ṣedeq//tūmmâ* occurs also in Job 9 : 20 ; 12 : 4 ; 22 : 3 ; 27 : 5-6.

A. R. C. Leaney compares Job 31 : 6 with a passage from the Qumran " Manual of Discipline " (IX : 12):

> These are the statutes for the instructor for him to walk in them, with everyone who lives according to the rule of each time and the weight of each man (*wlm šql 'yš w'yš*). [431]

Finally, G. Pettinato reports the appearance of this root *tmm* in the paleo-canaanite texts from ancient Ebla, *tam-mim* " perfect, " in TM 74 G. 121 (recto) I : 1. [432]

---

[429] M. Dahood, " Congruity of Metaphors, " *Hebräische Wortforschung* (Festschrift Walter Baumgartner ; VTSup 16 ; Leiden : Brill, 1967), p. 47-48 ; Blommerde, *NSGJ*, p. 114.

[430] Driver–Gray, ICC, vol. I, p. 4.

[431] Leaney, *The Rule of Qumran and Its Meaning*, p. 228, 230.

[432] Pettinato, *Or* 44 (1975), p. 369 (n. 49).

Job 31 : 7

my foot. The frequent parallelism of *'āšūr* with parts of the body, here *libbî* " my heart " (note also *'ênay* and *kappî* in the same verse), suggests in these cases the more concrete sense " foot, leg " (N.B., LXX *ho poús mou* for *'aššûrî*). Dahood, for example, points to Ps 17 : 5 *'ăšūray* " my legs " // *pĕ'āmāy* " my feet " and Pss 40 : 3, 73 : 2 *raglay* " my feet " // *'ăšūray* " my legs. " [433] Compare also the thought and *Wortfeld* of Job 23 : 10-11 :

> *kî-yāda' derek 'ammûday* (MT *'immādî*)
> *bĕḥānanî kazzāhāb 'ēṣē'*
> *ba'ăšūrô 'āḥăzâ raglî*
> *darkô šāmartî wĕlō'-'āṭ*

> Surely he knows the tread of my feet ;
>> should he test me, I would shine like gold.
> My foot held to his path,
>> I kept his way without deviating. [434]

The similarity of vocabulary of Sir 4 : 16-19 (v 16 *hlk*, v 17 *lb*, v 18 *'šr*, v 19 *nṭh* and *m'ḥry*) to Job 31 : 7 favors F. Zorell's translation of *'šr* " to walk, tread " in *"šrnw* (v 18) in contrast to the more common interpretation " make happy " (*NAB, NEB, RSV*) : [435]

> 18.   *'šwb "šrnw wglyty lw mstry*
> 19.   *'m yswr wnṭwtyhw wysrtyhw b'swrym*
>>   *'m yswr m'ḥry 'šlyknw w'sgyrnw lśddym*
> 18.   I will again guide him
>>   and reveal to him my secrets.
> 19.   If he deviates then I will turn from him [436]
>>   and detour him into the Prison.

---

[433] Dahood, *Psalms I*, 1st Note on Ps 17 : 5. Further examples include Ps 17 : 11 ; Hab 3 : 16. See also *hālîk* " foot " rather than " step " under Job 29 : 6 above.

[434] On *'ammûday* (MT *'immādî*) " my feet, " see Dahood, *Bib* 50 (1969), p. 350.

[435] F. Zorell and L. Semkowski, *Lexicon Hebraicum et Aramaicum Veteris Testamenti* (Rome : Pontificium Institutum Biblicum, *reeditio photomechanica* 1968), p. 87.

[436] Understanding the suffix of *nṭwtyhw* as datival, " from him. " The text follows Vattioni, *Ecclesiastico*, p. 23.

If he turns from after me
  I will crush him
  and close him up in Destruction.

Although *atr b'l* in *UT* 67 VI: 24-25 (//62 : 7) is generally understood as a place name, [437] it may allude to a title of Baal:

> *my lim bn dgn*
> *my hmlt atr b'l*

> Woe, O peoples of Dagon's son.
> Woe, O multitudes of Atr-Baal.

W. F. Albright admits of two possible interpretations of the goddess
Asherah's name *rbt atrt ym*: " The Lady Who Traverses the Sea, "
or " The Lady Who Treads on the Sea (Dragon) ":

> It has been plausibly suggested that Yam was the sea-dragon
> rather than the literal sea. Both explanations are perhaps
> equally tenable. Yahweh also appears as " treading on the
> back of Yam " (Job 9 : 8). [438]

Since Baal also defeated Yam (*UT* 68), *atr b'l* " Leader Baal " (?)
may represent an adaptation of Asherah's title to Baal and a variant
of the more common *aliyn b'l* " Victor Baal. " Isa 9 : 15 illustrates
this nuance of '*šr* (piel) " to lead " and *ûmĕ'ūššārāyw mĕbūllā'îm* may
be meant as a pun on *atr b'l*:

> *wayyihyû mĕ'aššĕrê hā'ām-hazzeh mat'îm*
> *ûmĕ'ūššārāyw mĕbūllā'îm*

> For those who lead this people lead them astray,
>   and those who are led by them are swallowed up. (*RSV*)

Finally, Duane Christensen has identified '*šr* " to march " in
Num 21 : 15b, but he errs in suggesting the deletion of either '*šr* or
nth. [439] The parallel with Job 31 : 7 is obvious:

---

[437] Gordon, *UT*, Glossary 424.
[438] W. F. Albright, *Yahweh and the Gods of Canaan* (Garden City, N.Y.:
Doubleday Anchor Books, 1969), p. 121 (n. 24).
[439] D. L. Christensen, " Num 21 : 14-15 and the Book of the Wars of Yahweh, " *CBQ* 36 (1974), p. 359-360.

'ašūr (MT *'ăšer*) *nāṭâ lěšebet 'ār*
wěniš'an ligbûl mô'āb

His [440] foot turned toward the seat of Ar,
He leaned toward the border of Moab.

my foot ... my heart. The parallelism *libbô* " his heart " // *'ăšūrāyw*
" his feet " of Ps 37 : 31, *libbēnû* " our heart " // *'ăšūrênû* " our feet "
of Ps 44 : 19, and *'ăšūrē* (MT *'ăšer*) *hî'* " the feet of her " // *libbāh* " her
heart " of Qoh 7 : 26, [441] repeat that of Job 31 : 7 and recall the collocation of these two roots in *UT* 49 II : 8-9, 29-30 :

> *klb arḫ l'glh*
> *klb ṭat limrh*
> *km lb 'nt aṯr b'l*

> Like the heart of a wild cow for her calf,
> Like the heart of a wild ewe for her lamb,
> Such was the heart of Anath toward Baal.

my foot ... after. The collocation *'aššūrî ... 'aḥar* in v 7 echoes the
Ugaritic–Hebrew parallel pair *uḫryt* " afterlife " // *aṯryt* " destiny, happiness " of 2 Aqht VI : 35-36 :

> *mt uḫryt mh yqḥ*
> *mh yqḥ mt aṯryt*

> Man will not receive an afterlife.
> Man will not receive happiness. [442]

spot. More commonly spelled *mûm*, this form *m'ûm* occurs here and
in Dan 1 : 4. The suffix of *mûmô* in Prov 9 : 7 is probably datival,
balancing the *lô* in the first colon :

> *yōsēr lēṣ lōqēaḥ lô qālôn*
> *ûmôkîaḥ lěrāšā' mûmô*

---

[440] No possessive pronoun is needed with parts of the body ; cf. Blommerde,
NSGJ, p. 10.

[441] Dahood, *Bib* 47 (1966), p. 275-276. Compare also Ps 10 : 6, " He says
to himself (*bělibbô*), ' I will not stumble, / forever happy (*'ăšer*, MT *'ăšer*) without misfortune, ' " ; cf. Dahood, *Psalms I*, Note on Ps 10 : 6.

[442] *RSP* I, II, 20. For this version of 2 Aqht VI : 35-36, see Dahood, *Or*
45 (1976), p. 347.

Who corrects a scoffer gets for himself abuse,
    and he who reproves the wicked, a stigma is his (lit. " to
    him ").

Compare the Vulgate (v 7b), *qui arguit impium, generat maculam sibi.*

Job 31 : 8

J. Krašovec has studied the rhetorical figure of merismus in the Bible. [443] Job 31 : 8 offers an example of a double merismus hinging on the double parallelism, *zrʿ*//*ʾkl* and *zrʿ*//*šrš*. [444] In the first parallelism, *zrʿ* " to sow, plant " and *ʾkl* " to eat " represent the two extremes in the agricultural cycle, from the initial steps in the process to the end product. The two terms of the second parallelism, on the other hand, *zrʿ* " to sow, plant "//*šrš* " to uproot, " encompass the range of possibilities in which agricultural activity can issue. A planting (*zrʿ*) may result in anything from an abundant crop, to a poor one, to the uprooting (*šrš*; by an enemy, animals, insects, etc.) and resulting total loss of the crop.

sow ... eat. *RSP* II,I,15 records this Ugaritic–Hebrew parallel pair and lists two Hebrew instances, Job 31 : 8 and Isa 55 : 10, to which may now be added Gen 1 : 29 (*zōrēaʿ zeraʿ ... lĕʾoklâ*); Gen 47 : 24 (*lĕzeraʿ*//*ûlĕʾāklĕkem*); Lev 25 : 22 (*ûzĕraʿtem*//*waʾăkaltem*); Lev 26 : 16 (*ûzĕraʿtem*//*waʾăkālūhû*); Hag 1 : 6 (*zĕraʿtem ... ʾākôl*).

The context of the Ugaritic example of this parallel pair (*UT* 49 II : 33-37 : *tdrʿnn*//*ltikl*) makes an interesting comparison with Job 31 : 8-12 :

> *bi št tšrpnn*
> *brḥm tṯḥnn*
> *bšd tdrʿnn*
> *širh ltikl ʿṣrm*
> *mnth ltkly nprm*

---

[443] Krašovec, *Der Merismus im Biblisch-Hebräischen und Nordwestsemitischen.*
[444] M. Dahood, in his review of N. C. Habel, *The Book of Job*, in *Bib* 57 (1976), p. 268, discusses another example of double merismus in Job 40 : 20 : " If one renders (Job 40 : 20) literally ' For they bring him the produce of the hills, and all the wild beasts of the plain who gambol there ', one recovers the double merismus. This extraordinary beast is both herbivorous and carnivorous : he devours the *grass* of the *hills* and the *beasts* of the *plain.* "

> With fire she burns him,
> With millstones she grinds him,
> In the field she sows him;
> His flesh the birds eat,
> His members the flying ones consume.

Ug. *bišt* " with fire " = *'ēš* of v 12 ; Ug. *ṭṭḥnn* " she grinds him " = *tiṭḥan* of v 10 ; Ug. *tdr'nn* " she sows him " //*ltikl* " indeed (they) eat " = *'ezrĕ'â*//*yō'kēl* of v 8.

May I sow ... my offspring. The collocation of *'ezrĕ'â* " May I sow " with *ṣe'ĕṣā'ay* " my offspring " recalls the parallelism of these two roots in Isa 44 : 3 (*zar'ekā*//*ṣe'ĕṣā'êkā*) ; 48 : 19 (*zar'ekā*//*wĕṣe'ĕṣā'ê*) ; 61 : 9 (*zar'ām*//*wĕṣe'ĕṣā'êhem*) ; 65 : 23 (*zera'*//*wĕṣe'ĕṣā'êhem*) ; Job 5 : 25 (*zar'ekā*//*wĕṣe'ĕṣā'êkā*) ; 21 : 8 (*zar'ām*//*wĕṣe'ĕṣā'êhem*).

May I sow ... be uprooted. These two roots appear as parallel in Isa 40 : 24, *bal-zōrā'û* " scarcely sown " //*bal-šōrēš* " scarcely taken root. " This same parallelism is found in Phoenician where both *zr'* and *šrš* = " children " (See below, " and my offspring be uprooted "). *KAI* 43 : 15-16 provides a good example :

> *wn'm ykn ly wlzr'y*
> *wskrn mlqrt*
> *(wskr l)n'm šrš*

> And may grace be mine and my descendants';
> and may Melqart remember me,
> (and may he be mindful for) the good of my offspring. [445]

See also *KAI* 14 : 11-12, *zr' mml(k)t h' 'm 'dmm hmt 'l ykn lm šrš lmṭ wpr lm'l* " ... the descendance of that king or those men. May there not be for them a root below nor fruit above. "

eat. *'kl* appears as a paleo-canaanite root in the bilingual vocabularies discovered at Tell Mardikh, *a-kà-lum*. [446]

and my offspring be uprooted. This follows the lead of those scholars, represented by Pope, who understand *ṣe'ĕṣā'ay* in sense of " children " : " In these, and in other cases, the context and parallelism indicate

---

[445] Cf. *KAI*, vol. II, p. 62 (note on *KAI* 43 : 16).
[446] Pettinato, *BA* 39 (1976), p. 50.

that the reference (of *ṣe'ĕṣā'ay*) is to human progeny.... Human beings may be 'uprooted' as well as plants. " [447]

The word *šrš* " root " itself appears in the figurative sense of " offspring, children " in Ugaritic, Phoenician (see above under " May I sow ... be uprooted "), and Hebrew. [448] *RSP* I,II,116, for example, records its parallelism with *bēn* " son " in both Hebrew (Job 5 : 3-4) and Ugaritic (2 Aqht I : 19-20, etc.).

Job 31 : 9-12 (Strophe Two)

> If my heart has been lured by a woman,
>   and at my neighbor's door I lurked,
> May my wife grind for another,
>   and over her may others bend ;
> For that were licentiousness,
>   which itself is criminal iniquity,
> A fire that devours to Perdition,
>   destroying all my gain.

A number of modern translations treat these four verses as a unit. [449] Job claims innocence of the sin of adultery, and the section ends with *'kl* " eat, devour " and *šrš* " uproot, " echoing the end of the first series of verses (1-8); in both cases, idolatry and adultery, Job's curse deals with the destruction of progeny.

Job 31 : 9

my heart has been lured. This same expression occurs below in 31 : 27, *wayyipt ... libbî* " my heart has been lured "; see also Deut 11 : 16; Hos 7 : 11.

lured ... woman. These two roots are paralleled in Prov. 9 : 13, *'ēšet kĕsîlût* " Dame Folly " // *pĕtiyôt* (MT *pĕtayyût*) " Simpleton. " [450] See also Judg 14 : 15.

lured ... I lurked. These two verbs in parallelism here are collocated in Prov 1 : 10-11 (*yĕpattûkā ... ne'erbâ*).

---

[447] *Job*[3], p. 230.
[448] E.g., *šrš* " offspring " // *nṭ'* " progeny " in Sir 3 : 9; cf. Penar, *The Hebrew Fragments of Ben Sira*, p. 5.
[449] E.g., *RSV*, Fohrer, Chicago Bible, Delitzsch, Michel, ICC, Fedrizzi.
[450] Cf. van der Weiden, *Le Livre des Proverbes*, p. 90.

The chiastic structure of the verse's syntax (verb : prepositional phrase : : prepositional phrase : verb) is reinforced by the chiastic word pattern involving the two first person singular suffixes, the twice-repeated preposition ʿal, and the paronomasia niptâ/petaḥ (niptâ libbî : ʿal : : ʿal : petaḥ rēʿî). [451]

by ... at. This Ugaritic–Hebrew parallel pair is recorded in *RSP* I,II,418 (ʿl//ʿl). Employing the same preposition in the same verse with different senses (here ʿal " by " //ʿal " at ") is not uncommon; compare Ps 118 : 6 :

> Yahweh is for me (lî), I fear not;
>   what can man do against me (lî)? (Dahood) [452]

by a woman. Although a number of versions recognize ʿal as expressing agency with a passive verb here (Pope, *NEB*, King James, *BJ*²), none of the modern lexicons or grammars discusses this usage; e.g., Joüon remarks, " Les prépositions *avec un verbe passif* pour indiquer l'auteur de l'action.... On trouve, avec les nuances différentes, *min, b, l.* " [453] In his article, " Le Complément d'Agent après un Verbe Passif dans l'Hébreu et l'Araméen de Qumrân, " [454] J. Carmignac points to two examples of an ʾl of agency with a passive verb, [455] but he nowhere refers to its use in either biblical Hebrew or the Hebrew of Qumran. Besides the instance here in Job 31 : 9, one might also list Zeph 2 : 11 " Yahweh will be feared by them (nôrāʾ yhwh ʿălêhem) "; Ps 71 : 6 " By you have I been supported (ʾālêkā nismaktî) from the womb " (Dahood); and Ps 96 : 4 " Feared is he by all the gods (nôrāʾ hûʾ ʿal-kol-ʾĕlōhîm). "

woman ... neighbor. The frequent occurrence of the phrase ʾēšet rēʿekā " your neighbor's wife " in the context of the commandment condem-

---

[451] Cf. Ceresko, *CBQ* 38 (1976), p. 303-311; especially p. 309-311 on paronomasia.

[452] This poetic device is not limited to prepositions; on the use of the same word with different senses as an element of Hebrew poetry, see Dahood, *Psalms III*, 6th Note on Ps 138 : 2, and the " Index of Subjects " under " Same word with different meanings " (p. 487-488).

[453] Joüon, *Grammaire*, par. 132c; see also GKC, par. 121f, and Rudolph Meyer, *Hebräische Grammatik* (Sammlung Göschen, Band 763-765; Berlin : Walter de Gruyter, 1966-1972), vol. III, p. 84 (par. 109.3.a.).

[454] *Revue de Qumran* 9, 35 (1978), p. 409-427.

[455] Ibid. p. 416.

ning adultery suggests that this verse represents an example of the
break-up of a composite phrase; e.g., Ex 20 : 17 :

> lō'-taḥmōd 'ēšet rē'ekā
> You shall not covet your neighbor's wife. [456]

The two components of the technical term *'ēšet rē'ekā* are distrib-
uted over the two cola of v 9, *'iššâ ... rē'î*. [457]

Job 31 : 10

grind for another. Although most modern translations follow the
MT, [458] there has been some question as to whether *tiṭḥan* was originally
vocalized *tiṭṭāḥēn* (niphal) " may (she) be abused. " The apparatus
of *BHK*[3] suggests this reading, which at first glance seems to give a
better parallelism between the first and second cola. [459] However,
recognition of the rhetorical figure of merismus here supports the
MT. In naming two of a wife's chief roles, the poet is, in effect, implying all facets of her relationship with her husband ; e.g., *TEV*'s
free rendering, " then let my wife fix another man's food / and sleep
in another man's bed. " Job thus expresses the wish that, as a result
of the curse, his wife would be at the service of others continually,
day and night. [460]

others. The free interchange of plurals in *-m* and plurals in *-n* is
characteristic of the author of Job ; e.g., 15 : 3 *millîm* and 15 : 13
millîn ; *'ăḥērîn* here in 31 : 10 and *'ăḥērîm* in 34 : 24.

bend. The single instance of this verb in Ugaritic where it partially
parallels *qwm* (*UT* 76 II : 17-18), *lpnnh ydd wyqm lp'nh wkr' wyql*
" In her presence he proceeds to rise, / At her feet he bows down to
prostrate, " should be compared with Job 4 : 4 which collocates these
same two roots (*yĕqîmûn ... kōrĕ'ôt*) :

---

[456] See also Lev 20 : 10 ; Jer 29 : 23 ; Ezek 18 : 6,11,15 ; 33 : 26 ; Prov 6 : 29.
[457] Ruth 2 : 14 represents an example in prose. The usual term *pat-leḥem*
" a morsel of bread " (Gen 18 : 5 ; also Judg 19 : 5 ; 1 Sam 28 : 22 ; 1 Kgs 17 : 11)
is split into its component parts which become the complements of two parallel
verbs : *wĕ'ākalt min-halleḥem wĕṭābat pittēk baḥōmeṣ* " Take some bread and
dip your morsel into the wine. "
[458] Pope, *NAB, RSV, NEB, BJ*[2].
[459] Compare the Vulgate, *scortum sit alterius* " may she be the whore of
another. " Cf. Driver–Gray, ICC, vol. I, p. 265 ; vol. II, p. 223.
[460] Cf. Krašovec, *Der Merismus*, p. 1-4.

kôšēl yĕqîmûn millêkā
ûbirkayim kōrĕʿôt tĕʾammēṣ

Your words encouraged the faint,
    braced tottering knees. (Pope)

Job 31 : 11

licentiousness. As Pope remarks, *tdmmt* " lewdness " (the Ugaritic cognate of Heb. *zimmâ*), is used " in reference to some shameful misdeed committed by the slave girls at a divine feast " (*UT* 51 III: 17-22) : [461]

    ṯn dbḥm šna bʿl
    ṯlṯ rkb ʿrpt
    dbḥ bṯt w dbḥ dnt
    wdbḥ tdmm amht
    kbh bṯt ltbṯ
    wbh tdmmt amht

Two banquets hates Baal,
Three, the Rider of Clouds :
A banquet of shame and a banquet of quarrelling
And a banquet of maidservants' lewdness.
For in this shame is seen
and in this maidservants' lewdness.

Compare *tdmm amht* " maidservants' lewdness " with Job 31 : 11 and 13, *zimmâ* " licentiousness " ... *waʾămātî* " my maidservant. "

    The two terms paralleled in the Ugaritic text, *bṯt* " shame " // *tdmm* " lewdness, " are distantly parallel in Ezek 16 : 52 and 58 (*bôšî* // *zimmātēk*) : [462]

    V 52   *wĕgam-ʾatt bôšî ûśĕʾî kĕlimmātēk*
              " So be ashamed, you also, and bear
              your disgrace ... "

    V 58   *ʾet-zimmātēk wĕʾet-tôʿăbôtayik ʾatt nĕśāʾtîm*
              " You bear the penalty of your lewdness
              and abomination ... "

---

[461] Pope, *Job³*, p. 231.
[462] N.B. *pillalt laʾăḥôtēk* (v 52), which E. A. Speiser, " The Stem *PLL* in Hebrew, " *JBL* 82 (1963), p. 304, translates, " You have caused reassessment in favor of your sister " ; compare *pĕlîlî* " assessable, criminal " of Job 31 : 11.

criminal iniquity. The *BHS* note on this expression, " constructio
mixta ex *'āwōn pĕlîlî* et *'āwōn pĕlîlîm,* " is unnecessary if the mem of
pĕlîlî-m (MT *pĕlîlîm*) is recognized as the enclitic particle. [463]   E. A.
Speiser in his article, " The Stem *PLL* in Hebrew, " argues for the
basic meaning " to assess or reckon " for this root, and he translates
'āwōn pĕlîlî of Job 31:28 " an assessable transgression. " [464]

This root appears in the Ebla tablets in the form of a divine title
(" the Mediator, the Arbiter ") in the personal name *i-da-pa-lil* " the
Mediator knows. " [465]   Compare 1 Sam 2:25: " If a man sins against
a man, God would be his arbiter (*ûpilĕlô 'ĕlōhîm*); but if a man sins
against Yahweh, who can intercede for him (*mî yitpallel-lô*)? "

The " criminal iniquity " (*'āwōn pĕlîlî*) of v 11 refers to sexual
sins (*zimmâ*; cf. vv 9 and 10).   Compare, for example, Lev 20:14:
" If a man takes a wife and her mother also, it is wickedness (*zimmâ*);
they shall be burned with fire (*bā'ēš*; cf. *'ēš* of Job 31:12), both he
and they, that there might be no wickedness (*zimmâ*) among you. "
The " criminal iniquity " (*'āwōn pĕlîlî*) of 31:28, on the other hand
is idolatry (see the discussion below on vv 26-27).

Job 31:12

Some modern versions bracket verses 11 and 12 indicating thereby
that these two verses are a " gloss " which has made its way into the
text (*TEV*, Alonso Schökel, Fedrizzi, *NEB*).   But the 2nd Century
B.C. targum of Job found at Qumran clearly includes these verses. [466]

A fire that devours. The " fire " which " devours " (*'ēš ... tō'kēl*) can
serve as an instrument of God's wrath, as in Job 1:16, " ' Lightning
fell (*'ēš 'ĕlōhîm nāpĕlâ*) from heaven and burned the sheep and the
boys and consumed them all (*watō'klēm*).' " [467]   Job 15:30 shows

[463] Pope, *Job³*, p. 232.
[464] *JBL* 83 (1963), p. 304.   He remarks on p. 306, " It is precisely this
element of consideration or calculation that links together all the forms and
uses of the stem *pll* in Hebrew. "
[465] TM. 75. G. 336 (rev) I:12; cf. Pettinato–Matthiae, *RSO* 50 (1976),
p. 6. Note also the comments of M. Dahood in VTSup 29 (1978), p. 104-105.
[466] van der Ploeg, *Le Targum de Job*, p. 46-47; Sokoloff, *The Targum to
Job*, p. 62-63, 127.
[467] The two roots paralleled here, *nāpĕlâ*//*watō'klēm*, are collocated in *UT*
75 II:36-37: *aḫd aklm k* (- - -) *npl bmšmš* " he seized the Devourers ... he falls
into the morass. "

that fire also has the eschatological function of punishing evildoers in Sheol:

> lō' yāsûr minnî-ḥōšek
> yōnaqtô tĕyabbēš šalhābet
> wĕyāsûr bĕrewaḥ (MT bĕrûaḥ) pîw

> He will not escape from Darkness
>   his offshoot Flame will wither,
>   nor will he escape its (i.e., 'ereṣ " the netherworld's ";
>   cf. v 29) massive mouth. [468]

The reference to 'ăbaddôn " Perdition " indicates that the eschatological sense predominates here in v 12. [469]

This expression, " the fire (that) devours " ('ēš ... tō'kēl), occurs five times in Job (1 : 16 ; 15 : 34 ; 20 : 26 ; 22 : 20 ; 31 : 12) recalling the same phrase in *UT* 75 I : 10 *kiš tikln* " like a fire they devour " (also *UT* 51 VI : 25,27,30).

Perdition.   Nicolas Tromp remarks on this term:

> *Abaddon*. (Place of Destruction). Although grammatically an abstract noun meaning " devastation, destruction " (Joüon 88 Mb), this word is always used concretely for " place of destruction, " i.e. the nether world. [470]

In Job 26 : 6 it parallels Sheol (šĕ'ôl / /la'ăbaddôn) and in 28 : 22 *māwet* " Death ":

> 'ăbaddôn wāmāwet 'āmĕrû
> bĕ'oznēnû šāma'nû šimĕ'āh

> Perdition and Death say,
>   " We have heard rumor of it. " (Pope) [471]

---

[468] Dahood, *Psalms III*, 2nd Note on Ps 140 : 11.

[469] On the motif of infernal fire, see Penar, *The Hebrew Fragments of Ben Sira*, p. 29 ; e.g., Sir 9 : 8, *b'd 'šh (h)šḥtw rbym wkn 'hbyh b'š tlhṭ* " Through a woman many have been pitted, / and thus her lovers are in the scorching fire. " See also Tromp, *Death and the Nether World*, p. 191.

[470] Tromp, *Death and the Nether World*, p. 80.

[471] These roots are partially parallel in Job 4 : 20-21 (*yō'bēdû / /yāmûtû*).

UT Krt 7-8 parallels *rpa//abd, umt* (- - -) *rpat bt mlk itdb* " The clan (- - -) is weakened, the house of the king has perished "; whereas Job 26 : 5-6 collocates them (*hārĕpā'îm ... la'ăbaddôn*) :

> *hārĕpā'îm yĕḥôlālû*
> *mittaḥat mayim wĕšōknēhem*
> *'ārôm šĕ'ôl negdô*
> *wĕ'ên kĕsût la'ăbaddôn*

> The Shades beneath writhe,
> Terrified are the Waters and their denizens.
> Naked is Sheol before him,
> Perdition has no cover. (Pope)

destroying all my gain. Ps 52 : 7 offers the only other occurrence of this verb (*šrš*) in the piel :

> *wĕyissāḥăkā mē'ōhel*
> *wĕšērešĕkā mē'ereṣ ḥayyîm*

> May he pluck you from your tent,
> and snatch your sons alive from the earth ! (Dahood)

Commenting on this version of *šērešĕkā*, Dahood remarks : " Etymologically, it is a denominative verb from *šōreš* in its metaphorical meaning ' offspring, scion ' .... " [472] The " gain " referred to here, therefore, is not just material " income " (cf. Pope), but more importantly, the curse involves the destruction of one's posterity. [473] The emendation of *tĕšārēš* here to *tĕraššēš* " to rage " accepted by *NEB* [474] weakens the force of this curse considerably since the nuance of the loss of children which *tĕšārēš* implies is lost. [475] In 15 : 34, for example, Eliphaz describes the fate of the wicked in terms similar to 31 : 12, destruction of descendance :

---

[472] Dahood, *Psalms II²*, 7th Note on Ps. 52 : 7. See also the discussion of *šrš* " be uprooted " under Job 31 : 8 above.

[473] This is evident in the chiastic structure of the Prologue in which the dearest of Job's possessions, his children (1 : 2), is mentioned first. The climax of Job's calamities is the death of the children (1 : 19). This chiastic structure can be schematized as follows — son and daughters (v 2) : sheep and camels : oxen and she-asses (v 3) : : oxen and she-asses (v 14) : sheep and camels (vv 16-17) : sons and daughters (vv 18-19).

[474] Brockington, *The Hebrew Text of the Old Testament*, p. 113.

[475] N.B., LXX has *ek rizōn apōlesen*.

kî 'ădat ḥānēp galmûd
wĕ'ēš 'ākĕlâ 'oholê-šōḥad

For an impious gang is impotent,
Fire devours the tents of the briber. (Pope)

Also, the only other occurrence of *tĕbû'nâ* in Job in 22:21 probably
refers to a person (God) rather than goods:

hasken-nā' 'immô ûšĕlām
bāhem tĕbû'ātĕkā (MT *tĕbô'ātĕkā*) *ṭôbâ*

Come to terms with him and make a covenant,
then your gain will be the Good One. [476]

   Job 31:12 repeats the parallel pair *'kl* // *šrš* of 31:8. The same
roots are collocated in Job 36:30-31 (*wĕšoršê ... 'ōkel*).

Job 31:13-15 (Strophe Three)

If I despised the claim
of my slave or my slave girl
when they complained against me,
Then what would I do if God punished me;
if he called me to account, what could I answer him?
The Victor — he who made me in the belly made him,
and he created us in the womb — the Unique.

   In defending his just treatment of his servants, Job also affirms
the oneness of mankind and the uniqueness of its Creator; thus wealth
and position do not free one from the obligation to deal justly with
all human beings.

Job 31:13

   The reading of this verse as a tricolon (syllable count 5:6:6)
avoids the imbalance of the Masoretic punctuation (11:7) and modern
versions such as Pope (7:10). It also makes clearer the parallelisms
'abdî // *wa'ămātî* and *mišpaṭ* // *bĕrîbām*.

---

[476] Blommerde, *NSGJ*, p. 98; cf., v 20b, *wĕyitrām 'ākĕlâ 'ēš* " Their sur-
plus the fire burns. "

the claim ... when they complained. The paralleling of *mišpaṭ//bĕrībām* here by the poet merits notice because of its bearing on the inter- pretation of Job 37:23. 2 Sam 15:4 offers a prose example (*rîb// mišpaṭ*): *wĕʿālay yābôʾ kol-ʾîš ʾăšer-yihyeh-llô-rîb ûmišpāṭ wĕhiṣdaqtîw* " Then every man with a suit or a cause might come to me, and I would give him justice " (*RSV*). Isa 1:17 serves as an example from poetry :

> *šipṭû yātôm*
> *rîbû ʾalmānâ*

> Defend the fatherless,
>> plead for the widow.   (*RSV*) [477]

On the basis of this parallelism, which was familiar to the Joban poet as 31:13 testifies, Dahood argues for the repointing of *wĕrōb-ṣĕdāqâ* " abundant justice " to *wĕrib-ṣĕdāqâ* " the cause of justice " in Job 37:23. [478] The parallel pair *mišpaṭ//rîb* now emerges :

> *šadday lēʾ* (MT *lōʾ*) *mĕṣāʾnūhû*
> *śaggîʾ-kōaḥ ûmišpāṭ*
> *wĕrib-ṣĕdāqâ* (MT *wĕrōb-ṣĕdāqâ*)
> *lēʾ* (MT *lōʾ*) *yĕʿanneh*

> We have found Shaddai the Omnipotent,
>> pre-eminent in power and judgment,
>> and the cause of justice the
>>> Omnipotent makes triumphant. [479]

Note the chiastic word pattern, with the word-play *rʾh* " to see "//*yrʾ* " to fear, " of vv 21-24 – *rāʾû* " they see " : *nôrāʾ* " fearful " : *lēʾ* (MT *lōʾ*) " the Omnipotent " :: *lēʾ* (MT *lōʾ*) " the Omnipotent " : *yĕrēʾûhû* " they fear him " : *yirʾeh* " he sees. " Job 33:12-13 presents the same idea and also includes an A:B::B:A word pattern involving a play on roots- *ʾeʿĕnekā* " I will answer " : *yirbeh* " is greater " :: *rîbôtā* " you contend " : *yaʿăneh* " conquers " :

---

[477] Also Ex 23:6; 1 Sam 24:16; Ezek 44:24; Mic 7:9.

[478] Compare also the *wĕhiṣdaqtîm* in 2 Sam 15:4 above.

[479] M. Dahood, review of P. Fedrizzi, *Giobbe*, in *Bib* 55 (1974), p. 288. The paleo-canaanite texts from Tell Mardikh contain the root *śgʾ* (cf., *śaggîʾ-kōaḥ*, " Shaddai ... pre-eminent in power ") as part of the personal name *ši-ga-Da-mu* " Damu is exalted "; cf. Pettinato, *Or* 44 (1975), p. 369 and 372 (n. 98).

In this you are not right, I will answer you;
  God is greater than man.
Why do you contend with him?
For in all his causes the Victor conquers. [480]

Job 13:18-19 (*mišpāṭ ... yārîb*); 23:6-7 (*yārîb ... miššōpṭî*); and 29:14-16 (*mišpāṭî ... wěrib*) all collocate these same two roots.

my slave or my slave girl. The parallel pair '*bd* " slave "//*bn amt* " son of a handmaid " is recorded in *RSP* I,II,404 (*UT* Krt 55-56, 127-128, etc.), along with two Hebrew instances (Pss 86:16; 116:16). The parallelism here, '*abdî*//*wa'amāti*, could be included in the Hebrew examples, as well as Job 19:15-16 (*wě'amhōtay ... lě'abdî*).

  '*bd* appears in a number of personal names in the tablets from Tell Mardikh/Ebla; e.g., *eb-du-*ᵈ*Ra-sa-ap* " Servant of Rasap. " [481]

Job 31:14

what ... if ... if ... what. The Vulgate reproduces the chiasmus in this verse (*ûmâ : kî :: wěkî : mâ*):

  Quid enim faciam, *cum* surrexit ad iudicandum Deus?
    et *cum* quaesierit, *quid* respondebo illi?

This poetic device is lost in *NEB*'s translation:

  What should I do *if* God appears?
  What shall I answer *if* he intervenes? [482]

could I do ... could I answer. This same parallelism ('*śh*//*šwb*) recurs, for example, in Job 10:9:

  Remember that you made me ('*ăśîtānî*) like an earthen vat,
    and that you will return me (*těšîbēnî*) to dust. [483]

---

[480] For further discussion of this passage see A. R. Ceresko, " The A : B :: B : A Word Pattern in Hebrew and Northwest Semitic, with Special Reference to the Book of Job, " *UF* 7 (1975), p. 86.

[481] Pettinato, *BA* 39 (1976), p. 50.

[482] Ceresko, *UF* 7 (1975), p. 85.

[483] This version follows Blommerde, *NSGJ*, p. 118; Dahood, *Bib* 45 (1964), p. 408-409.

See also Job 9 : 12 (*yěšíbennû ... ta'ǎśeh*) and 23 : 13 (*yěšíbennû ... way-yā'aś*).

punished me ... called me to account. The parallelism *pqd//nqm* of Jer 15 : 15,

> *yhwh zākěrēní ûpāqědēní*
> *wěhinnāqem lí mērōděpay*

> Yahweh, remember me and visit me,
>   and take vengeance for me on my persecutors,

suggests that Dahood is correct in his proposal to read here *yiqqôm* " he punished, took vengeance " (*//yipqōd* " he calls me to account ") for MT *yāqûm* " he rises. " [484] One may point to LXX *ean etasin mou poiēsetai* " when he prepares my trial " to support this proposal. Indeed, *'bd* " slave, " *'mh* " slave girl, " and *nqm* (MT *qwm*) " punish " of Job 31 : 13-14 echo strongly the law in Ex 21 : 20 :

> And if a man strikes his slave (*'abdô*) or his slave girl (*'ǎmātô*) with a rod and he dies under his hand, he shall be punished (*nāqōm yinnāqēm*).

Compare also the collocation *mišpaṭ* " claim " ... *yiqqôm* (MT *yāqûm*) " he punishes " of vv 13-14, with the parallelism *špṭ//nqm* in 1 Sam 24 : 13, " May the Lord judge (*yišpōṭ*) between me and you, may the Lord avenge me (*ûněqāmaní*) upon you. "

Finally, the suffixes needed with *yiqqôm* (MT *yāqûm*) and *yipqōd* (" punished *me* ... called *me* to account ") may be supplied by the subjects of *'e'ěśeh* and *'ǎšíbennû* by what Blommerde refers to as the " extension of the idiom of the double duty suffix. " [485]

Job 31 : 15

The Victor. Reading MT *hǎlō'* " did not " as the divine title *hālē'* " the Victor. "

The Victor ... the Unique. Translators generally recognize in *'eḥād* a divine appellative ; e.g., " the same One " (Pope, *NAB*), " the (one) same God " (*NEB*, *BJ²*). Blommerde argues that this divine title

---

[484] *Bib* 52 (1971), p. 346. See also *pqd//nqm* in Jer 5 : 9,29 ; 9 : 8.
[485] *NSGJ*, p. 10, 114.

appears as part of the composite title *lē' 'eḥād* " The Mighty One alone "
in Job 14 : 4 :

> *mî-yittēn ṭāhôr mĕṭummā'* (MT *miṭṭāmē'*)
> *lē'* (MT *lō'*) *'eḥād*

> Who can make the impure clean?
> The Mighty One alone. [486]

Further, L. Sabottka proposes this same composite title in Mal 2 : 15,
where it combines with " der Erschaffer " *'ōśeh* (MT *'āśâ* ; N.B., *'ōśēnî*
" he who made me " here in v 15a and *'āśîtā* " you established " of
Job 14 : 5) :

> *wĕlē' 'eḥād 'ōśeh ûšĕ'ēr rûaḥ lô*
> (MT *wĕlō' 'eḥād 'āśâ ûšĕ'ār rûaḥ lô*)

> Denn der Mächtige, der Einzige, ist der Erschaffer ;
> so ist sein der Leib und der Geist. [487]

Here in Job 31 : 15, the poet has broken up this composite divine name
lē' 'eḥād " the Unique Victor, " and recognition of its now parallel
components reveals the chiastic word order of this verse : A : B : C : : C' :
B' : A'. [488] All three of these verses (Mal 2 : 15 ; Job 14 : 4 ; 31 : 15)
deal with God's might and creative power.

Gordon proposes the divine appellative *'eḥād* " the Unique " in
Deut 6 : 4, Zech 14 : 9, and Job 23 : 13. [489] His discussion of Zech
14 : 9 (*wĕhāyâ yhwh lĕmelek 'al-kol-hā'āreṣ bayyôm hahû' yihyeh yhwh
'eḥād ûšĕmô 'eḥād* " And Yahweh will become king over all the earth ;
on that day Yahweh will be unique, for his name is ' the Unique ' ")
would have benefited from a comparison (N.B., *aḥdy, mlk, arṣ*) with
UT 51 : VII : 49-51 :

> *aḥdy d ymlk 'l ilm*
> *lymru ilm w nšm*
> *d yšb' hmlt arṣ*

---

[486] Ibid., p. 69-70.

[487] Sabottka, *Zephanja*, p. 17-18.

[488] See, for example, Dahood, " Chiasmus in Job : A Text-Critical and
Philological Criterion. "

[489] C. H. Gordon, " His Name Is ' One, ' " *Journal of Near Eastern Studies*
29 (1970), p. 198-199. On Deut 6 : 4, see also *RSP* I,II,566.

He alone will be king over the gods
to feed gods and men,
to satisfy the multitudes of the underworld. [490]

Finally, W. Kuhnigk recognizes *yāḥīd* (MT *yaḥad*) " the Unique "
in Hos 11 : 7, where it is collocated with *l'h* " to be strong, victorious "
as here in Job 31 : 15. [491]

he who made me made him. The divine title *'ōśēh* " Creator, Maker, "
mentioned in the preceding note in Sabottka's rendering of Mal 2 : 15,
occurs in Job 35 : 10 in compound with *'ĕlôah* : *'ĕlôah 'ōśāy* (N.B., *'ēl*
here in 31 : 14). The breakup of this compound in Job 4 : 17,

Can mortal be just before God (*mē'ĕlôah*)?
A man pure to his Maker (*mē'ōśēhû*)?

enabled Blommerde to recognize the repetition of this title two verses
later in 4 : 19: *yidkĕ'û millipnê 'ōśā(m)* (MT *yĕdakkĕ'ûm lipnê-'āś*)
" would then they ... be pure before their Maker? " [492] Further
examples in Job occur in 5 : 9, *'ōśeh gĕdōlôt* " Doer of great deeds "
(N.B., *'ēl//'ĕlōhîm* in v 8); 32 : 22, *'ōśēnî* " my Maker "; 37 : 5, *'ēl//*
'ōśeh gĕdōlôt; 40 : 19, *hā'ōśô* " his Maker. "

Two different metaphors are possible when the verb *'śh* describes
God's creative activity. *'śh* with the sense " to make, produce "
sometimes exhibits fertility overtones; e.g., Gen 41 : 47, " During the
seven plenteous years the earth brought forth (*watta'aś hā'āreṣ*) abun-
dantly " (*RSV*), and Hab 3 : 17, " And the fields produce (*lō' 'āśâ*)
no grain. " [493] On the other hand, the author of Ps 139 uses *'śh* " to
oppress, squeeze " for the image of God as a potter forming man from
clay (15) :

Since I was nipped off (*'ūśśêtî*) in the Secret Place,
kneaded in the depths of the nether world. [494]

---

[490] On *UT* 51 VII : 49-51, see R. Coote, " Ugaritic *ph(y)* ' see ', " *UF* 6
(1974), p. 1-5.

[491] Kuhnigk, *NSH*, p. 134-138.

[492] *NSGJ*, p. 41-42.

[493] W. F. Albright, " The Psalm of Habakkuk, " *Studies in Old Testament
Prophecy* (T. H. Robinson Festschrift; ed. H. H. Rowley; Edinburgh: T. and
T. Clark, 1950), p. 13.

[494] Dahood, *Psalms III*, 3rd Note on Ps 139 : 15.

This ambiguity creates difficulties for the interpretation of *šd* '*šy* in *UT* 1079 : 7,10,14. Should it be associated with '*šh* " to make, produce " (" fertile, productive field ") [495] or with '*šh* " to squeeze, oppress " (and therefore " plowed field ") ? [496]

in the belly ... in the womb. W. Michel notes :

> It is quite possible that the parallel words *bṭn*//*rḥm* are used by the poet to play with several images. *bbṭn* may refer to the belly of the mother (cf. 1 : 21, where a similar situation exists) and *brḥm* to Mother Earth, or the underworld.... [497]

See also the discussion above under " you will return me " in Job 30 : 23.

made him ... he created us. Two solutions offer themselves for the problematic Masoretic vocalization of *yĕkūnennû*, which seems to read " he created him " while the context calls for the first person plural suffix " he created us " (*yĕkōnĕnēnû*). F. Delitzsch accepts the massoretic vocalization and explains it as a pilel form + first person plural suffix, the resulting three nun's contracted to two. [498] Brockington revocalizes the form to the hiphil + first person plural suffix, *wayĕkīnēnû*. [499] Both solutions are possible since *kwn* can mean " to create " in either the pilel or the hiphil. It appears in the pilel parallel to '*šh* (as here in v 15) in Ps 119 : 73, *yādêkā* '*āśûnî wayĕkônĕnûnî* " your hands made me and fashioned me "; also Deut 32 : 6, where it parallels *qnh* " to create, " *hălō'-hû' 'ābîkā qānekā hû' 'āśĕkā wayĕkōnĕnekā* " Is he not your father who created you; is he not your Maker, who brought you into existence? " [500] But in Jer 10 : 12 (= 51 : 15), '*šh* balances hiphil *kwn* : '*ōśēh 'ereṣ bĕkōḥô mēkîn tēbēl bĕḥokmātô* " He who made the earth by his power, who created the world by his wisdom. " See also Job 15 : 35, in which *kwn* (hiphil) parallels *hārâ* " to conceive " and *yālad* " to give birth " :

---

[495] E.g., Gordon, *UT*, Glossary 1929a.
[496] E.g., Sabottka, *Zephanja*, p. 137. See also Dahood, *Proverbs and Northwest Semitic Philology*, p. 14.
[497] Michel, *Book of Job*, p. 431 (n. 627).
[498] Delitzsch, *Das Buch Iob*, p. 413.
[499] Brockington, *The Hebrew Text of the Old Testament*, p. 113.
[500] Reading the waw of *wayĕkōnĕnekā* as a relative particle. On the Ugaritic–Hebrew Parallel pair *qny*//*kwn* see *RSP* I, II, 493.

hārōh 'āmāl wĕyālōd 'āwen
ûbiṭnām tākîn mirmâ

Pregnant with pain, he gives birth to evil;
Their womb forms deceit.

Further examples of *kwn* (hiphil) " to create, bring into being " appear
in Pss 65 : 10 ; 74 : 16 ; Prov 8 : 27 (cf., *'śh* in 8 : 26). [501]
The Ugaritic use of *kwn* parallels that of the Hebrew ; both the
L form and Š form can mean " to form, create. " Compare *kwn* (L)
in *UT* 76 III : 5-7 with *kwn* (Š) in *UT* 126 V : 25-28 :

76 III : 5-7 : *wy'ny aliyn (b'l) lm*
                k qnyn 'l(m)
                kdrd<r> dyknn

And Victor Baal replied to them,
" Indeed our begetter is the Eternal,
indeed the Everlasting is he who
brought us into being. " [502]

126 V : 25-28 : *(a)nk iḫtrš w(   ) škn aškn*
                 ydt (m)rṣ gršt zbln
                 (M)oi, je façonnerai et je créerai sûrement
                 celle qui chasse la (ma)ladie,
                 celle qui exorcise le mal. [503]

Besides the four instances discussed above (here in Job 31 : 15 ;
also Deut 32 : 6 ; Ps 119 : 73 ; Jer 10 : 12 = 51 : 15), the Hebrew parallel
pair (or collocation) *'śh*//*kwn* occurs in Gen 41 : 32 ; 43 : 16-17 ; Ex
8 : 22 ; Num 23 : 1-2,29-30 ; Deut 13 : 15 ; 17 : 4 ; 1 Kgs 2 : 24 ; Isa 9 : 6 ;
45 : 18 ; Jer 33 : 2 ; 51 : 12 ; Amos 4 : 12 ; Ps 8 : 4 ; 33 : 14-15 ; 90 : 17 ;

---

[501] Dahood, *Psalms II²*, 8th Note on Ps 65 : 10, 1st Note on Ps 74 : 16 ;
idem, " Proverbs 8,22-31. Translation and Commentary, " *CBQ* 30 (1968),
p. 517.

[502] For the text and translation see Dahood, *CBQ* 30 (1968), p. 515.

[503] Thus Caquot, *TO*, p. 566 (n. *e*, *f*), and Aistleitner, *Wörterbuch*, no. 1335
(p. 151-152).   *TO*'s interpretation *ḥrš* " façonner "//*kwn* (Š) " créer " is reinforced by the collocation of these same two roots in Isa 40 : 20, " He seeks out
a skillful craftsman (*ḥārāš ḥākām*) to set up (*lĕhākîn*, ' form, create '?) an image
that will not move. " See also M. Dietrich, O. Loretz, J. Sanmartín, " KUN-Š
und ŠKN in Ugaritischen, " *UF* 6 (1974), p. 47-53 ; N.B. p. 52 (§ 2.19).

99 : 4 ; 101 : 7 ; Job 27 : 17-18 ; 28 : 26-27 ; Prov 16 : 3,12 ; 20 : 18 ; 1 Chron 15 : 1 ; 28 : 7 ; 2 Chron 12 : 14 ; 26 : 14-15 ; 35 : 6.

Job 31 : 16-18 (Strophe Four)

> If I have held back any desire of the poor,
>> or the eyes of the widow caused to fail,
> While I ate my portion alone,
>> but the orphan ate none of it.
> For from his youth he was raised by me as by his father,
>> and from his mother's womb I guided him.

With *NAB* and Delitzsch, [504] we consider these three verses a unit, describing Job's attitude toward the poor, the widow, and the orphan (cf. the discussion of *dl*//*ytm*//*almnt* below).   It ends with *beṭen* (*mib-beṭen*) " from the womb " as does the previous unit : *babbeṭen* of v 15.

Vv 16-18 form the first strophe in the larger unit of 16-23.   Vv 16-18 and 19-21 both treat of a similar subject, one's duty toward the more helpless members of society (the poor, the widow, the orphan, etc.) ; vv 22-23 climax the unit with a curse.   The play on words *'ăkalleh* " (I) caused to fail " (v 16)//*'ûkāl* " I could (not) bear " (v 23) may be meant as an inclusion for this larger section.

Job 31 : 16

withheld … caused to fail. Ezek 31 : 15 repeats this parallelism, *wā-'emnaʿ* " and I will restrain "//*wayyikkālĕ'û* " and (they) shall be stopped. "

any desire.   Recognition of the A : B : : B : A word pattern of vv 16-17, *mēḥēpeṣ : 'ăkalleh : : wĕ'ōkal : mimmennâ*, [505] in which the *min* of *mē-ḥēpeṣ* parallels partitive *min* of *mimmennâ* " (none) of it, " confirms ICC's suggestion to understand the *min* of *mēḥēpeṣ* also as partitive ; [506] thus the translation " *any* desire. "

the poor … the orphan. Dahood compared this same parallelism in Ps 82 : 3, *šipṭû-dal wĕyātôm* " Judge the poor and the orphan, " to the

---

[504] *Das Buch Iob*, p. 413-414.
[505] Note the play on the roots *kly*//*'kl* (see below under " caused to fail … I ate "); cf. Ceresko, *CBQ* 38 (1976), p. 309-311.
[506] Driver–Gray, ICC, vol. II, p. 225.

collocation of these roots in *UT* 127 : 48-49, *dl ... ytm*. [507] Note also *'āwel* " wickedness " of Ps 82 : 2 and *bǵlt* " into wickedness " of *UT* 127 : 45.

the poor ... the widow ... the orphan (*v* 17). *RSP* I,II,153 compares Job 31 : 16-17 to *UT* 127 : 48-50, in which the same parallelism occurs, *dl / /ytm / /almnt* :

> *ltdy ṯšm 'l dl*
> *lpnk tšlḥm ytm*
> *b'd kslk almnt*

> You do not drive away those who plunder
>   the infant of the poor,
> Nor give food to the orphan before you,
> Nor to the widow behind you. [508]

This accusation made by *Yṣb* against his father, King Keret, closely parallels Job's denial here of withholding sustenance from the widow and the orphan (N.B., vv 16b-17).

the eyes ... caused to fail. This expression has its literal counterpart in *UT* 125 : 25-27 (*tkl ... 'nk*) :

> *al tkl bn qr 'nk*
> *my* [509] *rišk udm't*

> Do not deplete, my son, the fount of your eyes,
>   the waters of your head with tears.

Compare also Job 11 : 20, *wĕ'ênê rĕšā'îm tiklênâ* " But the eyes of the wicked will fail, " and 17 : 5 *wĕ'ênê bānāyw tiklênâ* " and the eyes of his children will fail. "

caused to fail ... I ate. This collocation of the roots *klh ... 'kl* may be added to the other examples listed in *RSP* I,II,26 of *akl /kly*.

---

[507] *Psalms II*², 1st Note on Ps 82 : 3.

[508] This same parallelism *'l dl* " the infant of the poor " / /*ytm* " orphan " occurs in Job 24 : 9, *yātôm* " orphan " / /*'ūl*-(MT*'al*)*'ānî* " the suckling of the poor " ; cf. Pope, *Job*³, p. 175.

[509] The Ugaritic has *mḫ*; on this emendation of *mḫ* to *my*, see Gordon, *UT*, p. 21 and Glossary 1451.

RSP II,I Suppl 1 comments on the play on the roots *'kl – klh –
hlk* in Jer 30:16. Job 7:9 also exhibits the parallelism *klh//hlk,
kālâ 'ānān wayyēlak* " A cloud evaporates and vanishes "; compare
UT 1 Aqht 195-197 (*hlk ... kly*):

> *tmrn alk nmrrt*
> *imḫṣ mḫṣ aḫy*
> *akl mkly 'l umty*

May they strengthen me that I may go strengthened.
I will strike him who struck my brother,
I will destroy him who destroyed the infant of my mother.

the widow ... the orphan (*v* 17). Cf. *RSP* I,II,40 for *almnt//ytm*, and
262 for *ytm//almnt*. Compare Job 29:12-13, *wĕyātôm ... 'almānâ.*

Job 31 : 17

The poet pulls together vv 16 and 17 not only by common theme
but by rhetorical devices as well. The play on *'ăkalleh* " I caused
to fail "//*'ōkal* " I ate "//*'ākal* " he ate " was mentioned above under
Job 31:16 (" caused to fail ... I ate "). Note also the rhyme *'almānâ*
(v 16) – *mimmennâ* (v 17).

The parallel group *dallîm//'almānâ//yātôm* may contain a fourth
element in *libaddî* " I alone. " Passages such as *UT* Krt 96-97 (184-
185), *yḥd bth šgr almnt škr tškr* " The solitary man closed up his house,
the widow hired herself out, " and Ps 68:6-7,

> *'ăbî yĕtômîm*
> *wĕdayyan 'almānôt*
> *'ĕlōhîm bimĕʿôn qodšô*
> *'ĕlōhîm môšîb yĕḥîdîm baytāh*

Father of the fatherless and defender of the widows
Is God from his holy habitation.
God who established a home for the solitary (Dahood),

suggest that the *yaḥîd*, " the solitary man, " was sometimes included
in the list of those exposed to possible mistreatment. [510]   Job may be

---

[510] Dahood notes on Ps 68:7, " *the solitary.* As some commentators (e.g.,
Rosenmüller) have observed, the term *yᵉḥîdîm*, ' solitary ones, ' here denotes
those in exile from their home or fatherland. "

playing on this theme by reversing it : he does not disclaim the solitude which would have classed him with the widow and the orphan and thus vulnerable to oppression. Rather, he disclaims the reprehensible solitude which arises from greed and selfishness.

ate ... ate. " We must grow accustomed to the idea that repetition was a hallmark of Canaanite poetry. " [511] Translations in general tend to obscure this peculiar trait of Hebrew poetry, except the more consciously literal ones such as *RSV*. Even the LXX eschews the repetition of *'kl* in the two cola of v 17, *ephagon//metedōka.* [512]

Compare Job 20 : 20b-21a (*ḥmd//'kl*),

> *baḥămûdô lō' yĕmallēṭ*
> *'ên-śārîd lĕ'oklô*

> From his desire he could not escape,
>   nothing survived his ravening. [513]

to *UT* 75 I : 36-38 (*akl ... ḥmd*): *ymġy aklm wymza 'qqm b'l ḥmdm yḥmdm* " He approaches the Devourers and reaches the Renders; Baal indeed covets them. "

Job 31 : 18

The Northwest Semitic approach has provided the solution for this formerly troublesome verse. [514] The only emendations necessary in the version offered here are two simple revocalizations : that of MT *gĕdēlanî* to *guddĕlanî*, the pual of *gādal* with the first person singular dative of agent suffix (" he was raised by me "), [515] and that of MT *minnĕ'ûray* to *minnĕ'ûrēy* (" from *his* youth "). The yodh suffixes of *minnĕ'ûrēy* (MT *minnĕ'ûray*) and *'immî* are third person singular, " from *his* youth " and " of *his* mother, " and do double duty for

---

[511] *RSP* I, p. 77-78 (II Intro 6a).

[512] See also Pope, " ate "//" shared "; *NEB* " eaten "//" shared "; *BJ*², " manger "//" partager "; *NAB*, " ate "//"no share. " Add this instance in Job 31 : 17 to the list of examples of *'kl//'kl* in *RSP* I, II, 23.

[513] *bĕ* of *baḥămûdô* has the sense here of " from, " as was seen by *NEB*, " he cannot escape (from) his own desires. " On *bĕ* = " from, " see Blommerde, *NSGJ*, p. 19, and Dahood, *Psalms III*, " Grammar of the Psalter, " p. 391-393.

[514] See Blommerde, *NSGJ*, p. 115, for bibliography.

[515] Compare Ps 144 : 12 : *'iśśēr* (MT *'ăšer*) *bānênû kinĕṭi'îm mĕguddālîm bin'ûrêhem* " May he bless our sons like plants, carefully trained from their youth "; cf., Dahood, *Psalms III*, 1st and 2nd Notes on Ps 144 : 12.

kĕ'āb, " as by *his* father," and *'anḥennâ*, " I guided him," respectively.
The *-nh* of *'anḥennâ* functions as the verbal energic ending (N.B.,
the rhyme with *mimmennâ* of v 17) balancing *kî* of the first colon.

The presence of the Phoenician 3rd person singular masculine
suffix in yodh should occasion no surprise in the context of vv 18-21.
Dahood has already pointed out [516] that *minnĕ'ûrēy* " from his youth "
equals Phoenician *lmn'ry* " since his youth " in the Kilamuwa Inscription (*KAI* 24 : 12). Further comparison between this inscription (esp.
lines 10-13) and Job 31 : 18-21 reveals even more parallels :

> *w'nk lmy kt 'b*
> *wlmy kt 'm*
> *wlmy kt 'ḥ*
> *wmy bl ḥz pn š*
> *šty b'l 'dr*
> *wmy bl ḥz pn 'lp*
> *šty b'l bqr*
> *wb'l ksp wb'l ḥrṣ*
> *wmy bl ḥz ktn lmn'ry*
> *wbymy ksy bṣ*
> *w'nk tmkt mškbm lyd*
> *whmt št nbš*
> *km nbš ytm b'm*

But I was for one a father,
      and I was for another a mother,
      and I was for a third a brother.
And the one who had never seen the face of a sheep
      I made the owner of a flock ;
And the one who had never seen the face of an ox
      I made the owner of a herd,
      and the owner of silver and the owner of gold.
The one who had never seen a tunic from his youth,
      in my own days was clothed with byssos.
I held the *Mškbm* by the hand,
      and they showed a disposition
      like the orphan's disposition toward its mother. [517]

---

[516] Ibid.
[517] The metrical arrangement of the text follows Terence Collins, " The
Kilamuwa Inscription — a Phoenician Poem," *Die Welt des Orients*, Band
VI (1971), p. 187.

In addition to the same theme, the concern of a man in authority for the welfare of those most vulnerable to mistreatment, note the following verbal parallels between the Phoenician and Hebrew passages: *'b* " father " (*KAI* 24 : 10) = *kĕ'āb* " as by his father " (Job 31 : 18); *'m* " mother " (line 10,14) = *'immî* " his mother " (v 18); *lmn'ry* " from his youth " (l. 12) = *minnĕ'ûrēy* " from his youth " (v 18; N.B., the 3rd masculine yodh suffix in both cases); *ksy* " was clothed " (l. 12) = *kĕsût* " covering " (v 19); *lyd* " by the hand " (l. 13) = *yādî* " my hand " (v 21); *ytm* " orphan " (l. 13) = *yātôm* " orphan " (v 21).

father. Compare the parallelism *'āb* " father "//*hôlîd* " gave birth " of Job 38 : 28 to the collocation of the same roots in *UT* Krt 151-152 (297-298), *ab ... wld*: *dbḥlmy il ytn bḍrty ab adm wld špḥ lkrt* " (She) whom El gave me in my dream, the Father of mankind in my vision, that a scion may be born for Keret. "[518]

father ... his mother. Verse 18 reverses the usual order of this Ugaritic–Hebrew parallel pair, *'m*//*'b*; cf., *RSP* I,II,47.

Both of these roots turn up in the paleo-canaanite texts from Tell Mardikh. On *'āb* " father, " see above under Job 29 : 16. G. Pettinato reports that *ù-mu-mu* (= Heb. *'mm* " mother ") is among the words appearing in a bilingual vocabulary.[519]

I guided. *nḥh* occurs in a similar context of guiding the helpless in Qoh 4 : 1:

> And look at the tears of the oppressed (*hā'ăšûqîm*)
> who have no consoler (*mĕnaḥēm*),
> And from the grip of their powerful oppressors (*'ōšĕqêhem*)
> they have none to free them (*manḥēm*; MT *mĕnaḥēm*).[520]

Job 31 : 19-21 (Strophe Five)

> If I saw one perishing for lack of clothing,
> or a poor man without covering,

---

[518] Reading *wld* as qal passive with the primae waw preserved; cf. Gordon, *UT*, p. 85.

[519] *BA* 39 (1976), p. 50.

[520] Note the double play on words *hā'ăšûqîm*//*'ōšĕqêhem* and *mĕnaḥēm* (from *nḥm* " to console ")//*manḥēm* (from *nḥh* " to lead, free "; MT *mĕnaḥēm*); for further discussion of this verse, see Dahood, *Bib* 47 (1966), p. 271-272.

If his loins did not bless me
   warmed by the fleece of my sheep;
If I raised my hand against the orphan,
   when I saw his acquittal at the gate.

Each of these verses begins with the particle *'im* " if, " and *'er'eh*
" I saw " of v 21b forms an inclusion with *'er'eh* " I saw " of 19a. The
verses describe the selfish attitude which leads to unjust actions toward
others. This attitude can be either passive in nature whereby one
simply ignores the plight of the helpless (vv 19-20), or it can be active,
as v 21 so vividly depicts.

Job 31 : 19

If I saw one perishing. Cf., the Mesha Stone (*KAI* 181 : 7, *w'r'* / / *'bd*):
w'r' bh wbbth wyšr'l 'bd 'bd 'lm " I gloated over (triumphed over) him
(i.e., Omri) and his house, and Israel perished, perished forever. "
Job looks with pity (*'er'eh*) upon one who is perishing (*'ôbēd*), whereas
King Mesha looks with pleasure (*r'h* + *b*) upon the eternal ruin (*'bd*
'lm) of his enemy Israel.
   Job 20 : 7 also offers an interesting parallel (*yō'bēd* / / *rō'āyw*):

kĕgelălô lāneṣaḥ yō'bēd
rō'āyw yō'mĕrû 'ayyô

He will perish forever like his own dung;
   those who have seen him will say, " Where is he ? " (*RSV*)

See also Job 4 : 7-9 (*'ābād ... rā'îtî ... yō'bēdû*). The parallelism *w'r'* / / *'bd*
in *KAI* 181 : 7 and *yō'bēd* / / *rō'āyw* of Job 20 : 7 argues in favor of
" perishing " as the proper nuance of *'ôbēd* here in 31 : 19 rather than
" wanderer " of *NAB*, Fedrizzi (" viandante "), Alonso Schökel (" va-
gabundo "), and Fohrer [521] (" einer ohne Kleid unherirrte ").

I guided (v 18) ... perishing. These two words collocated here, *'anḥen-*
nâ " I guided " (v 18) ... *'ôbēd* " perishing, " parallel one another
in 12 : 23, where they are used to contrast God's seemingly arbitrary
actions toward different peoples :

---

[521] *Das Buch Hiob*, p. 424.

maśgî' laggôyim wayĕ'abbĕdēm
šōṭēaḥ laggôyim wayyanḥēm

Some nations he raises, then makes them perish (in Sheol),
Other nations he disperses, then leads them (into Paradise). [522]

perishing ... bless. The composite phrase, *birkat 'ōbēd* " the blessing
of him about to perish " of Job 29 : 13, is broken up here in Job 31 : 19-20
'ōbēd " one perishing " ... *bērăkûnî* " did (not) bless me. "

clothing ... covering. RSP I,II,339 records this Ugaritic–Hebrew parallel
pair both here (*lĕbûš//kĕsût*) and in Job 24 : 7 (*lĕbûš//kĕsût*). The
Ugaritic example collocates the two words (*UT* 67 VI: 16,31): *lpš*
yks mizrtm " For clothing he is covered with a double loincloth. "

Job 31 : 20

his loins. D. N. Freedman has noted the omission of the yodh before
the 3rd masculine singular suffix in this masculine dual noun. MT
normally preserves the vowel letter ; e.g., *ḥălāṣāyw* of Isa 5 : 27 in
contrast to *ḥălāṣāw* here. [523]

by the fleece. The verb from this root *gzz* " to shear, " appears in *UT*
1153 : 4-5, where it parallels *ṭbḥ* " to slaughter " : *ṭbḥ š(h) bkl ygz ḥḥ šh*
" he slaughtered his sheep, in each (house ?) *ḥḥ* sheared his sheep. "
Compare Isa 53 : 7 (N.B., *ṭbḥ//gzz + šh*): *kaśśeh laṭṭebaḥ yûbāl ûkĕ-*
rāḥēl lipnê gōzĕzêhâ " Like a lamb he was led to the slaughter, like
a ewe before her shearers. "

warmed. In *UT* 1 Aqht 40-41, this root (*ḥmm*) parallels *qṣ* " summer
fruit " (*bḥm//bqṣ*) :

    'rpt bḥm un yr
    'rpt tmṭr bqṣ

A rain cloud in the heat of the season,
A cloud which showers upon the summer fruit.

Compare Gen 8 : 22 (*ḥōm//qayiṣ*): " While the earth remains, seedtime
and harvest, cold and heat, summer and winter, (*wĕqōr wāḥōm wĕqayiṣ*
wāḥōrep), day and night, shall not cease " (*RSV*).

---

[522] Following Blommerde, *NSGJ*, p. 64.
[523] Freedman, *Eretz-Israel* 9 (1969), p. 41.

Job 31 : 21

against the orphan. *NEB* and *NAB* emend MT *'al-yātôm* " against
the orphan " to *'ălê-tām* " against the innocent "; [524] both *BHK³*
and *BHS* propose this reading in their apparatus. Neither versional
(LXX *orphanō̧*; Vulg. *pupillam*) nor MSS evidence supports such an
emendation. Rather, this verse appears to be an echo of 29:12 f.,
and thus the traditional rendering should be retained. Comparison
of the *Wortfeld* of 29:12f. and 31:21 makes this clear, especially when
it is seen that *'ōzēr/'ezrâ* " acquitter/acquittal " in both cases refers
to the orphan:

>   *kî 'ămallēṭ 'onî mĕšawēa'*
>   *wĕyātôm wĕlō' 'ōzēr lô*

>   For I rescued the poor who cried,
>   the fatherless who had no acquitter. [525]

See also *'ōbēd/'ôbēd* " one perishing " (29:13 and 31:19), *birkat* "blessing "/*bĕrăkûnî* " (they) blessed me " (29:13 and 31:20).

my hand ... his acquittal. The translation of this verse is that offered
by Dahood in *RSP* II,I,46, where he records the Ugaritic–Hebrew
parallel pair *yd//'ḏr.* [526] The yodh suffix of *'ezrātî* is understood as
3rd person singular, " his (i.e., the orphan's) acquittal. " Cf., *UT* 3
Aqht " rev. ": 12-14 (*'ḏr + yd*):

>   *w(qra) aqht wyplṭk*
>   *bn dnil wy'ḏrk*
>   *byd btlt 'nt*

>   And (call) Aqhat that he might save you,
>   Danel's son, that he might rescue you
>   from the grasp of Virgin Anat. [527]

---

[524] Brockington, *The Hebrew Text of the Old Testament,* p. 113; *Textual
Notes on the New American Bible,* p. 377. The first edition of *BJ* translated
v 21a " contre un innocent " and noted, " ' innocent ' corr.; ' orphelin ' hebr. "
The second edition has returned to the MT, " contre un orphelin. "

[525] For " his (i.e., the orphan's) acquittal " in 31:21 and *'zr* " to acquit,
liberate, " see the discussion in the following note (" my hand ... his acquittal ").

[526] Ps 10:14 (*bĕyādekā + 'ôzēr*) and Ps 119:173 (*yādĕkā + lĕ'ozrēnî*) may
be added to his list of Hebrew examples.

[527] For the restoration of *w(qra)* see Baisas, *UF* 6 (1974), p. 41 (n. 4).

Taking this Ugaritic passage with its paralleling of *plṭ* " to save " and
'ḏr " to rescue, " Bienvenido Baisas has studied the Hebrew usage of
cognate *'zr*, ordinarily rendered " to help " by the lexicons. [528] He
concludes that Hebrew *'z(ḏ)r* normally retains its general sense " to
help " except when it appears (1) with prepositions meaning " from "
(*b* in Ugaritic; *min* = *lĕ* and *bĕ* in Hebrew), (2) in parallel with
synonymous " saving roots, " or (3) in contexts which favor the translations " save, deliver. " In these three cases, " it conveys a more
specific and emphatic concept which is best rendered by the words
' rescue, ' ' liberate. ' " [529] Baisas identifies the occurrences of *'z(ḏ)r*
in Job 29 : 12; 30 : 13; 31 : 21 as examples of this more specialized
sense. [530] For 31 : 21, he argues :

> The use of the *'zr* I* meaning (= " save, liberate, acquit ") in
> this text produces a sense more consistent with the context :
> Job shows no arrogance at the liberation of the fatherless from
> his unjust accusers and oppressors. This text ought to be seen
> together with Job 5 : 4 and 29 : 12.... [531]

The reason for this motif in Job 31 : 21 is found in v 23 :

> For a dread to me is God's hand,
> and the raising of it I cannot bear. [532]

Note also the play on words *'ezrātî* (v 21) /*wĕ'ezrō'î* (v 22).

the orphan ... his acquittal. Ps 10 : 14 also collocates these two terms
(*yātôm* + *'ôzēr*; N.B., *bĕyādekā* in v 14a and *yhwh 'ēl nĕśā' yādekā*
" Yahweh God, lift up your hand " in v 12) :

> *rā'itāh kî 'attâ 'āmāl wāka'as*
> *tabît lātēt bĕyādekā*
> *'ālêkā ya'ăzōb hēlekā yātôm*
> *'āttâ hāyîtā 'ôzēr*

---

[528] E.g., William Holladay, *A Concise Hebrew and Aramaic Lexicon of the
Old Testament* (Grand Rapids : Eerdmans, 1971), p. 270.
[529] Thus R. A. F. MacKenzie, as quoted by Baisas, *UF* 6 (1974), p. 52.
[530] Baisas, ibid., p. 43, 45, 47.
[531] Ibid., p. 45.
[532] Ibid., p. 45 (n. 43).

See for yourself the misery, and the sorrow behold,
  since you give them from your own hand!
To you entrusts himself the unfortunate, the fatherless,
  you be his helper (acquitter?)! [533]

the orphan ... at the gate.   UT 2 Aqht V: 6-8 provides an interesting
parallel:

  yṯb bap ṯġr
  tḥt adrm dbgrn
  ydn dn almnt
  yṯpṭ ṯpṭ ytm

He takes his seat at the opening of the gate
  among the noblemen who are at the threshing floor.
He decides the case of the widow,
  he judges the lawsuit of the orphan.

Textes ougaritiques recognizes this parallel in comparing this passage
to Job 29:12 and 31:21. [534]   See also 1 Kgs 22:10; Prov 31:23;
Ruth 4:1.

Job 31 : 22-23

Let my shoulder-blade fall from my shoulder,
  and my arm be broken from its socket.
For a dread to me is God's hand,
  and the raising of it I cannot bear.

These two verses are the curse which concludes the larger unit
of vv 16-23 (Strophe Four, vv 16-18, and Strophe Five, vv 19-21).
As was mentioned above in the introduction to Strophe Four, the play
on words *'ăkalleh* " (I) caused to fail " (v 16)/*'ûkāl* " I could (not)
bear " (v 23) may act as an inclusion for this larger section which deals
with one's duty toward the more helpless members of society.   The
merismus " fall " (*npl*, v 22a)//" rise " (*nś'*, v 23b) serves to unify the
two verses; see below under " the raising of it " (v 23) for a fuller
discussion.

---

[533] The translation follows Dahood, *Psalms I.*
[534] Caquot, *TO*, p. 427 (n. *s*).

Job 31 : 22

shoulder-blade. The sequence *yādî ... kĕtēpî* of vv 21-22 " If I raised
my hand ... Let my shoulder-blade fall " reverses the order of *ktp//bn
ydm* in *UT* 68 : 14 and 16 :

> *hlm ktp zbl ym*
> *bn ydm ṯpṭ nhr*

> Strike the shoulder of Prince Sea,
>   the chest (lit. " between the hands ") of Ruler River. [535]

fall ... be broken. With the recognition of this same parallelism (reversed) in *UT* 137 : 7-9, *ṯbr//npl*, another set enters the growing list
of Ugaritic–Hebrew parallel pairs. The Ugaritic pair and the Hebrew
pair (v 23) both appear as part of a curse formula :

> *yṯb(r ḥrn y ym*
> *yṯbr ḥrn) ri šk*
> *'ṯtrt (šm b'l qdqdk)*
> *(——)t mṭ tpln bg(bl)*

> May Hauron break, O Yam,
> May Hauron break your head,
> Aṭṭrt Name-of-Baal, your skull ...
> ... may the staff fall in Byblos. [536]

Compare *UT* 1 Aqht 108-109, in which *ṯbr* parallels *qll*, a synonym of
npl " to fall " :

> *b'l yṯbr diy hmt*
> *tqln tḥ p'ny*

> May Baal break their pinions.
> May they fall at my feet. [537]

Hebrew *šbr//npl* occurs in a context analogous to the curse formula,
i.e., the results of a curse or disaster ; e.g., Ezek 27 : 34 :

---

[535] Cf. *RSP* II, I, 29.
[536] On the restoration of this passage, see *CTA*, p. 7, N.B. notes 2 and 3.
[537] And the parallel passages, lines 114-116, 122-124, 128-130, 136-138,
142-144.

'attā nišbart miyyam-m bĕma'ămmaqqê-m yām
(MT *'et nišberet miyyammîm bĕma'ămaqqê māyim*)
ma'ărābēk wĕkol-qĕhālēk bĕtôkēk nāpālû

Now you are wrecked by the sea,
  by the depths of the sea.
Your wares and all the crew
  in you have perished. [538]

Further instances of this parallelism and collocation include Deut 9:
17-18; 1 Sam 4:18; Isa 8:15; 21:9; 30:13; Jer 51:8; Ezek 6:6-7;
30:17-18,22; 31:12; Dan 11:26; 2 Chron 14:12.

The four-fold repetition of *nāpal* in Job 1:15-20 intensifies the
drama of the succession of disasters which befall Job and his family:
v 15 " the Sabeans fell upon " (*tippōl*); v 16 " lightning fell " (*nāpĕlâ*);
v 19 " it (the house) fell " (*wayyippōl*); culminating in Job's self-hum-
bling before God (v 20) *wayyippōl 'arṣāh wayyištāḥû* " He fell on the
ground and worshipped. "   This same parallel pair, *npl//ḥwy*, occurs
also in UT 137:14-15:

l p'n il al tpl
al tštḥwy pḫr m'd

At the feet of El do not fall,
Do not worship the gathering of the assembly. [539]

ICC recognizes the fixed nature of this combination and notes further
instances in Josh 5:14; 2 Sam 1:2; 9:6; 14:4; Ruth 2:10; 2
Chron 20:18. [540]   Other examples include 1 Sam 20:41; 25:23;
2 Kgs 4:37. The New Testament continues the combination with the
word pair *piptō* + *proskyneō* in Matt 2:11, *kai pesontes proskynēsan*
" and falling down, they worshipped him "; see also Matt 4:9; 18:26;
1 Cor 14:25; Rev 4:10; 5:14; 7:11; 11:16; 19:4,10; 22:8.

shoulder.   L. Sabottka remarks, " Es (i.e., *šĕkem*) bezeichnet den oberen
Teil des Rückens zwischen den Schulterblättern (*ktp*); vergleiche dazu
Job 31,22. " [541]

---

[538] Cf. van Dijk, *Ezekiel's Prophecy on Tyre*, p. 50, 89-90; however, understanding *bĕ* of *bĕ'amaqqê-m* as causal " by " (//causal min of *miyyam-m*).

[539] See also *UT* 137:30-31, *tpl//tštḥwy*.

[540] Driver–Gray, ICC, vol. I, p. 18.

[541] Sabottka, *Zephanja*, p. 117.   See also Zorell, *Lexicon*, p. 379: " Homo
habet duos *kātēp*, unum *šĕkem*.

my arm ... from its socket. An explanation of *'ezrō'î miqqinnāh* (MT
miqqānâ) goes hand in hand with a solution to *qn ḏr'* in *UT* 67 VI : 19-22
(//62 : 3-5) :

> *yḥdy lḥm w dqn*
> *yṭlṭ qn ḏr'h*
> *yḥrṭ km gn ap lb*
> *k'mq yṭlṭ bmt*

> He lacerates cheeks and chin,
> He furrows his armpit ;
> He plows like a garden his chest,
> Like a valley he furrows his back. [542]

Although there is general accord that *qnh* means " socket, shoulder-
joint " in Job 31 : 22 (e.g., *RSV*, ICC, Michel, *NEB*, *JB*), translators
disagree on its etymology. Some connect it with *qāneh* " reed " with
the transferred sense " humeral bone, upper arm, elbow, " [543] but
Gordon, Driver, and U. Cassuto propose a separate root. [544] A more
straightforward solution presents itself in *qēn* " nest " : the " nest of
the arm " (Ug. *qn ḏr'*) is nothing other than the armpit or shoulder
socket. This satisfies both the Ugaritic and the Hebrew contexts
without stretching the sense of *qāneh* " reed " or necessitating the
proposal of a new root. *miqqānâ* of v 22 should thus be repointed
to *miqqinnāh* " from its socket. "

'ezrô'î with the prothetic aleph in contrast to *zĕrôa'* of 38 : 15
(and 40 : 9) accords with the style of the author of Job who alternates,
for example, *kap* " hand " in 13 : 21 with *'ekep* " hand " in 33 : 7. [545]

my arm be broken. *zĕrôa'* " arm " + *šābar* " to break " is a frequent
combination in Hebrew ; for example, Job 38 : 15b, *ûzĕrôa' rāmâ tiššābēr* " The upraised arm is broken " and Ps 10 : 15 *šĕbōr zĕrôa' rāšā'*

---

[542] The first to recognize this was Andrée Herdner, " Remarques sur ' La
déesse 'Anat, ' " *Revue des études semitiques–Babyloniaca* (1942-1945), p. 49.
For further bibliography cf. Michel, *Book of Job*, p. 432-433 (n. 632).
[543] See the discussions of Pope, *Job³*, p. 234-235, and Driver–Gray, ICC,
vol. II, p. 226.
[544] Gordon, *UT*, Glossary 2245 ; Driver, *Canaanite Myths and Legends*,
p. 144 (n. 5) ; U. Cassuto, *A Commentary on Exodus* (translated by Israel Abrahams ; Jerusalem : Magnes Press, The Hebrew University, 1967), p. 343-344.
[545] Dahood, *Bib* 44 (1963), p. 293.

" Break the arm of the wicked. " Dahood compares the latter with
UT 1 Aqht 108, *b'l yṯbr diy hmt* " May Baal break their wings. " [546]

Job 31 : 23

A dread to me. Compare Isa 19 : 16, *ûpāḥad mippĕnê tĕnûpat yad-
yhwh ṣĕbā'ôt 'ăšer-hû' mēnîp 'ālāyw* " And (Egypt will) tremble with
fear before the hand which the Lord of hosts shakes over them " (*RSV*;
N.B., *'im hănîpôtî ... yādî* " If I raised my hand " of Job 31 : 21).

God's hand. The phrase *'ēlay 'êd 'ēl* has called forth a variety of suggested emendations. [547] But the present consonantal text yields sense
once one recognizes *'yd = yād* " hand " with a prothetic aleph. [548]
The poet used the *'yd* with the aleph for the sake of the alliteration:
'ēlay 'êd 'ēl ... 'ûkāl. A number of examples of *'ad* " hand " have
already been identified; for example, W. Kuhnigk reads Hos 11 : 4
(*'adēm* " mit beiden Händen " for MT *'ādām*),

> *baḥăbālay 'adēm* (MT *bĕḥablê 'ādām*)
> *'emšĕkēm*
> *ba'ăbōtôt 'ahăbâ*
>
> Mit meinen Seilen, mit beiden Händen
> zog ich sie,
> mit Stricken der Liebe. [549]

Besides leaving the consonantal text unaltered, this solution for v 23
suits the context well; in v 21 Job denies having raised his hand (*yādî*)
against the orphan out of fear of what God's hand (*'yd 'ēl* in v 23) would
do to him in return. H. H. Rowley comments, " What restrained
Job from exploiting his power over others was his dread of the power
of God, who was ever present to his thoughts. " [550]

---

[546] *Psalms I*, 1st Note on Ps 10 : 5.

[547] E. g., Brockington, *The Hebrew Text of the Old Testament* (*NEB*), p. 113,
'elay 'êd 'ēl < 'el 'ad 'elay " But the terror of God was heavy on me "; *Textual
Notes on the New American Bible*, p. 377, (*kî paḥad*) *'ēl 'ālay* " For the dread
of God will be upon me "; Fedrizzi, *Giobbe*, p. 217, *paḥad 'ēl ye'ĕtâ 'ēlāy* " il
timore di Dio veniva su di me. "

[548] Cf. Ugaritic *'id*, a biform of *yd*; Gordon, *UT*, Glossary 1072. See also
Baisas, *UF* 6 (1974), p. 45 (n. 43).

[549] Kuhnigk, *NSH*, p. 126, 132. See also Dahood, *Psalms I*, 3rd Note
on Ps 17 : 4; idem, *Psalms II²*, 3rd Note on Ps 68 : 19; idem, *UHP*, p. 13.

[550] Rowley, *Job*, p. 257.

yad 'ēl occurs elsewhere in Job in 19:21, *yad-'ĕlôah nāgĕ'â bî* " the hand of God has struck me " and 27:11, *'ôreh 'etkem bĕyad-'ēl* " I will teach you of God's power. " See further, *yad yhwh* in Job 12:9 and *bĕ'ōṣem yādĕkā tśṭmnny* " with your strong hand you make me take cover " above in 30:21; also Job 1:11; 2:5; 6:9; 13:21; 33:7 and Ex 9:3; Deut 2:15; 1 Sam 5:6,11. Job 23:2b reads *yādî kābĕdâ 'al-'anḥātî* " his hand is heavy in spite of my groaning. " [551] Blommerde compares this with *UT* 54:11-13, *wyd ilm p kmtm 'z mid* " and the hand of El is here like death, very strong. " [552]

the raising of it. Revocalizing MT *miśśĕ'ētô* " before his majesty " (*śĕ'ēt* " majesty, dignity ") to *maś'ētô* " the raising of it, " i.e., of God's hand (*maś'ēt* " raising, lifting "). In v 21 Job denies having raised his hand (*'im-hănîpôtî ... yādî*) against the orphan, lest God raise his hand (*'ēd 'ēl ... maś'ētô*) against him in return. Compare, for example, Ps 141:2,

> May my prayer be ever set
>   as incense before you,
> The uplifting of my palms (*maś'at kappay*)
>   as an evening sacrifice. (Dahood)

and *UT* Krt 75, *śa ydk śmm* " Lift up your hands towards heaven. " [553]

Job 31:22a " Let my shoulder-blade fall " and 23b " the raising of it " form a merismus: the two extremes represented by " falling " and " rising " encompass all the possible evils which Job could call down upon himself in curse. This same parallelism (*nś'*//*npl*) occurs also in Ps 106:26:

> So he raised (*wayyiśśā'*) his hand against them
>   to fell (*lĕhappîl*) them in the desert. (Dahood)

---

[551] Following Blommerde, *NSGJ*, p. 99, who understands the yodh suffix of *yādî* as 3rd person masculine singular, " his (God's) hand. " This meaning of *'al* " in spite of, despite " is frequent in Job. Its appearance in both the Dialogues (10:7; 16:17; 23:2) and the Elihu Speeches (34:6) provides another indication of the linguistic affinities between these two sections and may have some bearing on the discussion of common authorship; cf., Dahood, *Bib* 52 (1971), p. 438.

[552] Blommerde, *NSGJ*, p. 99.

[553] See also *UT* Krt 167-168 (*nśa ydh śmmh*); 51 VIII:5 (*śa ǵr 'l ydm*); 52:37 (*yd + nśa*).

The masculine singular suffix of *maś'ētô* (MT *miśśĕ'ētô*) indicates
that the antecedent *'ēd* " hand " represents one of the rare examples
of *'yd/yd* as masculine; cf. also Ex 17:12, *wîdê mōšeh kĕbēdîm* " the
hands of Moses were heavy. " [554]

Job 31:24-28 (Strophe Six)

I put not my confidence in gold,
 nor called fine gold my security.
I gloated not when my wealth was great,
 when my hand attained abundance.
I gazed not on the light as it brightened —
 the moon, that is, waning in splendor;
Nor was my heart secretly seduced,
 that my hand wafted a kiss from my mouth.
That also is criminal iniquity,
 for I would betray God on high.

RSV, Delitzsch, *TEV*, and Fedrizzi also treat vv 24-28 as a unit.
Whether one trusts primarily in riches (vv 24-25) or in idols (vv 26-27),
one is in either case putting God in second place and thus is guilty
(v 28). ICC, for instance, notes on vv 24-25, " Job repudiates the
idolatry of wealth as in (verse) 26 another form of idolatry. " [555]

Job 31:24

I put not ... called. The parallelism of these roots here (*śamtî / /'āmartî*)
recalls their collocation in Job 22:22:

qaḥ-nā' mippîw tôrâ
wĕśîm 'ămārāyw bilbābekā

Take instruction from his mouth,
 and write down his words in your heart. [556]

---

[554] On the frequent concurrence in Ugaritic and Hebrew of the same noun in
both masculine and feminine gender, see Dahood, *Psalms III*, Note on Ps 104:22.

[555] Driver–Gray, ICC, vol. I, p. 268. See also Fedrizzi, *Giobbe*, p. 218.
BJ²'s note on v 26 reads, " Après le culte de Mammon, celui des astres. " Andersen, *Job*, p. 243, remarks, " But the avoidance of cupidity may be linked
with idolatry (verses 26f.), with verse 28 as the common guilt. "

[556] On *śîm* = " to write " see Dahood, *Psalms II²*, 4th Note on Ps 56:9;
idem, *Bib* 53 (1972), p. 399. Another example of this parallelism is Job 7:
12-13, *tāśîm ... 'āmartî*.

gold.   *UT* 137 : 18-19 (//35) and 'nt III : 43-45 mention a motif the recognition of which may help to clarify certain biblical texts.   These two passages indicate that Baal's dominant role within the divine assembly also implied possession of a certain horde of gold, the booty from his victory over his various adversaries.   In *UT* 137 : 18-19, " Sea " (*ym*) threatens El :

> *tn b'l w'nnh*
> *bn dgn art m pdh*

> Surrender Baal and his attendants,
> The Son of Dagan, that I may inherit his gold. [557]

In 'nt III : 43-45, the goddess Anat declares :

> *imtḫṣ ksp itrt ḫrṣ*
> *ṭrd b'l bmrym ṣpn*

> I shall smite for the silver,
> I shall inherit the gold
> of him who drove Baal
> from the heights of Saphon.

Although the full significance of this theme is not clear, the recognition of it in Job 37 : 22, for instance, throws new light on the passage :

> *miṣṣāpôn zāhāb ya'ăteh* (MT *ye'ĕteh*)
> *'ēl* (MT *'al*) *'ĕlôah nôrā' hôd*

> He brings gold from Zaphon,
>   the Most High God, awe-inspiring in majesty.

The repointing of *ye'ĕteh* " he /it comes " to hiphil *ya'ăteh* " he brings " was suggested by Dahood. [558]   For the reading *'ēl* (MT *'al*) " the Most High ", cf. Blommerde. [559]   The following verse, 37 : 23, twice refers to God as " the Victor " (*lē'*; MT *lō'*) :

---

[557] Caquot, *TO*, p. 130 (n. *r*), comments, " La possession de l'or semble avoir joué un rôle, que nous saisissons mal, dans les mythes ougaritiques. "

[558] " Seminar in Ugaritic–Hebrew Style and Syntax, " Fall Semester 1973-1974, Pontifical Biblical Institute.   For a similar understanding of this verse, cf. Viganò, *Nomi e titoli di YHWH*, p. 54.

[559] *NSGJ*, p. 132.   However, the Masoretic vocalization of *'al* " Most High " may be correct.   Note the PN from Tell Mardikh, *a-lu-a-ḫu* " The Most

We have found Shaddai the Omnipotent,
     pre-eminent in power and judgment,
     and the cause of justice the Omnipotent makes trium-
     phant. [560]

A symbol of this victory is the possession of the horde of gold on
Mount Zaphon. [561]
     The root *ktm* " gold " appears in the tablets from Tell Mardikh
as *ku₈-tim*. [562]   In commenting on the frequency of the divine name
Ya as an element in the personal names listed in these tablets, [563]
Dahood suggests that some of the gentilic nouns in *-y* in Ugaritic [564]
may actually be personal names containing the divine element " Ya. "
An example he offers is *aktmy* (*UT* 321 IV : 10) which he translates
" I consider Ya my fine gold " ; [565] compare Job 22 : 25,

     Let Shaddai be your gold,
     Silver piled high for you (Pope),

and Job's friend Eliphaz (*'ĕlîpaz* " My God is fine gold ").

gold ... fine gold.   These two terms also parallel one another in Prov
25 : 12, *nezem zāhāb waḥălî-kātem* " ring of gold and ornament of fine
gold, " and in Lam 4 : 1, *zāhāb//ketem* ; Job 28 : 16-17 collocates them,
bĕketem ... zāhāb. In the latter passage, Job 28 : 16-19, an A : B :
C :: C : B : A chiastic pattern includes *ketem* as one of its elements,
*lō'-tĕsŭlleh : bĕketem : 'ôpîr : lō' -ya'arkennâ :: lō' -ya'arkennâ : bĕketem ṭā-
hôr : lō' tĕsŭlleh.* [566]

my confidence ... my security. Job 8 : 14 contains this same parallelism, *kislô//mibṭaḥô.*

High is a brother " (TM. 75. G. 336 rev. I : 7) ; cf. Pettinato-Matthiae, *RSO*
50 (1976), p. 5.   Compare the Hebrew–Phoenician name *'aḥîrām* " My brother
is exalted " ; see Dahood, VTSup 29 (1978), p. 102-103.
     [560] Cf. Dahood, *Bib* 55 (1974), p. 288.
     [561] = the golden palace of Baal? Cf. Pope, *Job³*, p. 286-287.
     [562] Pettinato, *Or* 44 (1975), p. 369 (n. 44) and p. 371 (n. 83).
     [563] E. g., *Mi-kà-Il/Mi-kà-Yà, En-na-Il/En-na-Yà, Iš-ra-Il/Iš-ra-Yà* ; cf.
Pettinato, *BA* 39 (1976), p. 48.
     [564] Cf. Gordon, *UT*, p. 61-62.
     [565] Dahood, VTSup 29 (1978), p. 105-107.
     [566] Cf. Ceresko, *CBQ* 38 (1976), p. 303-311.

Excursus on p-nun Verbs in Job

The presence of the root *śîm* in this verse provides the opportunity to discuss a number of passages in Job where the context suggests that *nšm* " to breathe, pant " is the root that should be read rather than *śîm* " to put, place, " as the present Masoretic vocalization implies. Dahood, for instance, has proposed repointing MT *yāśîm* " he puts " of Job 40 : 23 to *yaśśîm* (hiphil of *nšm*) " he makes to froth " :

yartîaḥ kassîr měṣûlâ
yām yaśśîm kammerqāḥâ

He makes the deep seethe like a pot,
The sea to froth like a crucible. [567]

He comments,

The revowelling *yaśśîm* tightens up the metaphor, making the second-colon verb a close counterpart to the first-colon *yartîaḥ*; MT *yaśîm* is flaccid and weakens the metaphor begun in the first colon. [568]

Another candidate for a similar reinterpretation is Job 36 : 13 :

wěḥanpê lēb yaśśîmû (MT *yaśîmû*) *'āp*
lō' yěšawwě'û kî 'ăsārām

But the impious-minded fan ire ;
    they pleaded not when he binds them.

Numerous commentators intuit the sense of this verse, but they must resort to emendations or circumlocutions to convey the meaning of the Hebrew : e.g., " harbor " (Pope), " cherish " (*RSV*), " lay up " (*NAB*). A. S. Peake sums up the dilemma :

The words *lay up anger* are difficult, and many explanations have been given. The meaning seems to be that instead of accepting God's discipline in the right spirit they cherish angry thoughts about it. The second line describes their sullen demeanor under it ; they will not cry to God for help. [569]

---

[567] *Bib* 53 (1972), p. 400.
[568] Ibid.
[569] A. S. Peake, *Job* (The Century Bible ; London : T. C. and E. C. Jack, 1904), p. 299-300.

The difficulties of interpretation disappear and the metaphor becomes clear with the repointing of MT *yaśîmû 'āp* " they lay up, cherish anger " to *yaśśîmû 'āp* " they fan, cause to flare up (God's) anger "; those who do so " expire (*yigwĕ'û*) without knowing. " J. D. Michaelis proffered this suggestion in 1773, based on the Vulgate *provocant iram Dei*. [570] Dahood's parallel suggestion for Job 40 : 23 adds to the cogency of Michaelis' solution of Job 36 : 13.

Repointing *yāśîm* of Job 34 : 14 to *yaśśîm*, from *nśm*, this time with the nuance " to inspire, " clarifies the metaphor of vv 14-15 :

> 'im-yaśśîm (MT yāśîm) 'ēlāyw libbô
> rûḥô wĕnišmātô 'ēlāyw ye'ĕsōp
> yigwa' kol-bāśār yāḥad
> wĕ'ādām 'al-'āpār yāśûb

> If his heart inspired him
>   to take back his spirit and breath,
> All flesh would expire together,
>   and man return to the dust.

With this interpretation, the strong parallelism the poet has created between vv 14 and 15 emerges. In 14a, if God's heart " inspires " (*yaśśîm*) him, then in 15a, all flesh will " expire " (*yigwa'*). In 14b, if the life-giving breath that comes from God returns to him (Gen 2 :7; 3 : 19; Isa 42 : 5; Ps 104 : 29; Qoh 12 : 7), then, in 15b, what remains of man returns to the dust from which it was taken. [571] A similar image of the breath escaping the body at death is found in *UT* 3 Aqht (obv) 24-26. Anat orders *Yṭpn* to slay the hero Aqhat :

> tṣi km rḥ npšh
> km iṯl brlth
> km qṭr baph

---

[570] J. D. Michaelis, *Deutsche uebersetzung des Alten Testament mit Anmerkungen für Ungelehrte : Der erste Teil welcher das Buch Hiobs enthalt* (Göttingen und Gotha, 1773), p. 31. Certain modern commentators have followed Michaelis' lead : Norbert Peters, *Das Buch Job* (Exegetisches Handbuch zum Alten Testament 21 ; Münster : Aschendorff, 1928), p. 159 ; Fridolin Stier, *Das Buch Ijjob : Hebraisch und Deutsch* (München : Kösel, 1954), p. 339 ; J. Lévêque, *Job et son Dieu*, p. 586.

[571] Tromp, *Death and the Nether World*, p. 87-91.

Let his breath escape like wind,
    his soul like vapor,
    like smoke from his nostrils. [572]

This reading of Job 34 : 14 also brings to light another example of the
stylistic device which the Joban poet employs, the use of a verb and
a noun from the same root in the same verse : 14a *nšm*, " to breath,
inspire " ; 14b *nšmh* " breath. "

Job 31 : 25

gloated. Compare the context of *'eśmaḥ* here (N.B., v 24, *zāhāb* " gold "
and *ketem* " fine gold ") with *šmḥ* in *UT* 51 V : 80-82 (and 93-97):

    wbn bht ksp wḥrṣ
    bht ṭhrm iqnim
    šmḥ btlt 'nt

    " So build a house of silver and gold,
    a house of lapis gems ! "
    Rejoice does Virgin Anat.

    yšmḥ parallels *yld* in *UT* 76 III : 36-38, *kibr lb'l (yl)d wrum lrkb
'rpt yšmḥ aliyn b'l* " For a bull to Baal is born, indeed a buffalo to the
Cloud-Rider ; rejoice does Aliyan Baal. " This echoes the collocation
wĕyaldêhem " their children " ... *wĕyiśmĕḥû* " they rejoice " in Job
21 : 11-12.

gloated ... attained. This same collocation, *śmḥ ... mṣ'*, occurs also in
v 29 below and in Job 3 : 22. Dahood ascribes to *mṣ'* in these latter
two verses the only meaning which its cognate in Ugaritic *mṣa/mǵy*
possesses, " to reach, arrive at, attain " ; [573] e.g., Job 3 : 22 :

    haśśĕmēḥîm 'ĕlê-gîl
    yāśîśû kî yimṣĕ'û-qāber

---

[572] The sense of the word *iṭl* is disputed ; cf. Gordon, *UT*, Glossary 142
" breath, gust, " and Caquot, *TO*, p. 439 (n. *d*) " crachat. " Dahood suggests
(private communication) that Ug. *iṭl* = Heb. *'ēšel* " tamarisk, " and that *rḥ
... iṭl* here in 3 Aqht 25 represents the break-up of the composite phrase *rḥ iṭl*
" the scent of the tamarisk " ; compare Heb. *rêaḥ śādeh* " the scent of the field "
(Gen 27 : 27) and *rêaḥ lĕbānôn* " the scent of Lebanon " (Cant 4 : 11).

[573] Dahood, " Northwest Semitic Philology and Job, " p. 57 ; idem, *Psalms
III*, 4th Note on Ps 116 : 3.

Who rejoice at the arrival,
    are happy when they reach the grave. [574]

The conceptual similarity of Job 3 : 22 and 31 : 29 (rejoicing upon
arrival at the grave and rejoicing at the arrival of misfortune upon
one's enemy) with 31 : 25 (rejoicing at the attaining of riches) suggests
that *mṣ'* in the latter verse possesses the same nuance, " to arrive at,
reach, attain. " This interpretation would resolve the difficulty evi-
denced by some versions over the exact sense of *mṣ'* here in v 25. *NEB*
hedges, for instance, by omitting the verb, " if I have rejoiced ... in
the increase of riches "; " had acquired " (*NAB*, Pope), " had gotten
much " (*RSV*), " aveva accumulato " (Fedrizzi). [575]

I gloated ... I saw. The collocation here in vv 25-26, *'eśmaḥ* " I gloated "
... *'er'eh* " I saw, " recalls Job 22 : 19 in which these same two verbs
are parallel, *yir'û ṣaddîqîm wĕyiśmāḥû* " The righteous see and rejoice."

great ... abundance. These same two roots parallel one another in
Isa 17 : 12-13, *kiš'ôn mayim kabbîrîm* " like the roaring of mighty
waters "//*kiš'ôn mayim rabbîm* " like the roaring of many waters. "
    Both words have not only the material sense " many, abundant, "
but in certain contexts they exhibit a temporal connotation, " many
(years) " = " old, ancient. " For instance, Dahood sees *kabbîr* in
Job 36 : 5 as a divine title " the Old One ":

> *hen 'ēl kabbîr wĕlē'* (MT *wĕlō'*)
> *yim'ās kabbîr kōaḥ lēb*

> Though El is the Old One, he is still the Victor;
>   the Old One detests stubbornness. [576]

rab may also have a temporal sense, as in Job 32 : 9, *rabbîm* = " the
aged ":

> *lō'-rabbîm yeḥkāmû*
> *ûzĕqēnîm yābînû mišpāṭ*

[574] Dahood, " Northwest Semitic texts and textual criticism of the Hebrew
Bible, " p. 23, 30.
  [575] *Giobbe*, p. 219. His footnote reads, " ' aveva accumulato '; lett. ' aveva
incontrato. ' "
  [576] Dahood, *Psalms II*², 2nd Note on Ps 75 : 7; Blommerde, *NSGJ*, p. 125.
See also *kabbîr ṣaddîq* " the Venerable Just One " in Job 34 : 17 (Dahood, *Psalms
II*², p. xxiv).

It is not the aged who are wise,
  nor the elders who understand what is right. [577]

In arguing for this meaning of *rabbîm*, Dahood cites *UT* 51 V: 65-66
and Job 4:3:

  rbt ilm lḥkmt
  šbt dqnk ltsrk

  You are aged, O El, and truly wise,
  The greyness of your beard has truly instructed you.

  hinnēh yissartā rabbîm
  wĕyādayim rāpôt tĕḥazzēq

  Look, you have instructed the aged,
    and fortified doddering hands. [578]

These three texts taken together and all dealing with " wisdom "
(Ug. *ḥkm*, Heb *ḥākam*), " instruction " (Ug. *ysr*, Heb. *yasār*), and " old "
(Ug. *dqn*, Heb. *zakēn*) point to the nuance of " age " in the root *rab*.
    Job 26:3 offers itself as another candidate for this sense of *rab*
=" age. " The same context of " instruction " (*yā'aṣtā*, *hôdā'tā*) and
" wisdom " (*ḥokmâ*) as *UT* 51 V: 65-66, Job 32:9, and Job 4:3a
suggests that consonantal *lrb* (MT *lārōb*) contains the noun *rab* " age "
parallel to *ḥokmâ* " wisdom ":

  mah-ya'aṣtā lĕlō' ḥokmâ
  wĕtûšiyyâ lĕrab (MT *lārōb*) *hôdā'tā*

  How can you counsel without wisdom,
  teach success without age?

The parallelism *lĕlō' ḥokmâ* " without wisdom "//*lĕrab* indicates that
the negative particle *lō'* of *lĕlō' ḥokmâ* does duty also for *lĕrab*, thus
the translation " without age. " Contrast, for instance, the circum-
locution to which *BJ*² resorts in v 3b, " come ton savoir est fertile
en ressources. " [579]

---

[577] Dahood, *Bib* 48 (1967), p. 425.
[578] Ibid.
[579] This comes out in English in *JB*, " never at a loss for a helpful suggestion " !

attained.   Compare the parallelism *mǵy//atw* in *UT* 51 IV : 31-32, *ik mǵyt rbt aṯr(t y)m ik atwt qnyt i(lm)* " Why does Lady Ashirat arrive, why comes the Creatress of the gods ?, " with the collocation of these roots in Job 37 : 22-23, *ya'āteh* (MT *ye'ĕteh*) " he brings " [580] ... *mĕṣā'-ĕnūhû* " we have found him. "

Job 31 : 26

I gazed not.   *r'h* " to see " also has the sense " to look at (with pleasure, delight, favor), " [581] and here, as the discussion on Job 31 : 1 brought out, fixing one's eyes upon the idol or manifestation of a god (e.g., the sun, moon, or stars) refers to a cultic act of worship or supplication.

the light as it brightened — the moon.   Most commentators understand *'ôr* " the light " as an alternate name for " the sun " (*'ôr* " the Light [par excellence] "//*yārēaḥ* " the moon "). [582]   Comparison with Job 29 : 2-3, however, suggests that v 26 provides rather an example of delayed identification. [583]   First colon *'ôr* " light " (unidentified) is identified by second colon *yārēaḥ* as " the moon, " " the light, that is, the moon. " [584]
  Both 29 : 2-3 and 31 : 26 exhibit a similar *Wortfeld*, and an examination of the two together reveals that both are referring to the moon and its light :

> *mî yittĕnēnî kĕyarḥê-qedem*
> *kîmê 'ĕlôah yišmĕrēnî*
> *bahillô* (MT *bĕhillô*) *nērô 'ălê rō'šî*
> *lĕ'ôrô 'ēlek ḥōšek*

---

[580] See the discussion of " gold " (*ketem*) above under Job 31 : 24.
[581] E.g, BDB, p. 907b (6.a.).   For *r'h* " to look upon (with favor) " used of Yahweh, see Dahood, *Psalms III*, 1st Note on Ps 106 : 44.
[582] BDB, p. 21a ; Pope, *Job³*, p. 235 ; Driver–Gray, ICC, vol. I, p. 269.
[583] Dahood, *Psalms III*, 1st Note on Ps 105 : 17, comments, " The author of Job is especially fond of this device. "   See also the discussion of " men younger than I " under Job 30 : 1 above.
[584] Dahood suggests that *mā'ôr* in Ps 74 : 16 means " moon " (*Psalms II²*, 2nd Note on Ps 74 : 16) ; " Yours is the day and yours the night, it was you who caused the moon and the sun (*mā'ôr wāšāmeš*) to be. "   He comments, " In other texts *mā'ôr*, ' luminary, ' may denote either the moon or the sun, but here, because it is conditioned by *šemeš*, it bears the conditioned meaning ' moon. ' "   See also Gen 1 : 16, " God made ... the lesser light (*hammā'ôr haqqāṭōn* = ' the moon ') to rule over the night. "

O that I were as in months past,
  in the days when God protected me;
When he made his lamp shine above my head,
  by his light I walked through darkness.

Mention of *yrḥ* (" month "/" moon ") in v 2a suggests that *nērô* " his lamp " in v 3a is the moon rather than the sun: it is by the moon's light that Job can walk through night's darkness without stumbling or injuring himself (v 3b). [585] In *UT* 77 : 15-17 (and 31) the moon (*yrḫ*) is given the same title " lamp of the heavens " (*nyr šmm*; N.B. also the root *hll* in l. 15):

> *lkṯrt hl(l sn)nt*
> *ylak yrḫ ny(r) šmm*
> *'m ḫr(ḫ)b mlk qẓ*

O *Kṯrt*, (daughters) of *hll*, swallows !
The Moon (god), lamp of the heavens, sends a message
To *Ḫrḫb*, king of summer.

Further, the root *hll* which appears in both passages (*bahillô*, MT *běhillô*, [586] and *yāhēl* in 31 : 26) describes the brilliance of the moon in Job 25 : 5 :

> *hēn 'ad-yārēaḥ wělō' ya'ăhêl*
> *wěkôkābîm lō' zakkû bě'ênāyw*

Behold the Eternal: the moon is not bright,
  nor are the stars clean in his sight.

Arabic *'ahalla* (IV form) means " to begin to shine (of the moon), " and *hillēl* = " new moon. "

as it brightened. The root *hll* appears in Ugaritic in the title of the *kṯrt*, " female jubilants, songstresses, Muses ": *kṯrt bnt hll*, " the Kosharot, daughters of *hll*. " [587] Scholars disagree as to which root in Hebrew it is related, *hll* I " to shine, be bright " or *hll* II " to praise,

---

[585] Compare Job 12 : 25a, *yěmašěšû-ḥōšek wělō'-'ôr* " They grope in darkness with no light " (Pope).

[586] See the discussion above under Job 29 : 3, " When he made his lamp shine. "

[587] For its occurrences, see Gordon, *UT*, Glossary 769.

rejoice, "[588] but the recent French translation of the Ugaritic myths comments on *hll* in *UT* 77 : 6 :

> *hll* a été expliqué tantôt par l'arabe *hilâl*, " croissant de lune " tantôt par l'hébreu *hallél*, " celebrer " ; nous préférons la première explication (cf. ligne 42 : " le seigneur à la faucille "). Il est peu surprenant que les Kotharot, qui favorisent les naissances, soient mises en rapport avec la lune croissante ... [589]

Cf. the name of the divine midwife in *UT* 75 I : 14-15, *tlš amt yrḫ*, " *Tlš*, handmaid of the moon. "

For *hll* + *yrḫ* of Job 31 : 26 (and 29 : 2-3) see *UT* 77 : 3-6, *bsǵsǵ špš yrḫ ytkḫ* ... *(lk)ṭrt lbnt hll (snnt)* " When the sun sets, the moon shines ... O *kṭrt*, O daughters of *hll*, the swallows " (also lines 15-16, 38-41).

the light ... the moon. *RSP* I,II,59 records this parallel pair *'ôr* + *yārēaḥ* common to both Hebrew (here and Qoh 12 : 2) and Ugaritic ; e.g., *UT* 77 : 38-39, *ar yrḫ wyrḫ yark* " Let shine the moon, and may the moon shine for you. "

that is. Parsing the waw of *wĕyārēaḥ* as a *waw explicativum* : " the light ... that is, (the light of) the moon. "[590]

waning. The association with *yrḫ* " moon " and the parallelism with *hll* " begin to shine " point to the technical sense " to wane " for *hlk* here, rather than simply " marching " (Pope) or " moving " (*RSV*, *NEB*). LXX translates here *selēnēn de phthinousan* " and the moon waning. " One may now identify the rhetorical figure of merismus in v 26 : by mentioning the " brightening, waxing " (*hll*) of the moon in the first colon and its " waning " (*hlk*) in the second colon, the poet expresses the entire lunar cycle.[591]

Analogous to this use of *hlk* " to wane, disappear " in Job 31 : 26 is its use in Hos 6 : 4b :

---

[588] E.g., for the latter, Dahood, *Psalms I*, 1st Note on Ps 5 : 6 ; idem, *Psalms II*², 2nd Note on Ps 78 : 63.

[589] Caquot, *TO*, p. 392 (n. *h*). See also Aistleitner, *Wörterbuch*, p. 89 (no. 832), *hll* = " Neumondsichel " ; Driver, *Canaanite Myths and Legends*, p. 137 ; Cathcart, *Nahum*, p. 91.

[590] Blommerde, *NSGJ*, p. 29-30.

[591] See also Krašovec, *Der Merismus*, p. 94.

wĕḥasdĕkem ka'ănan-bōqer
wĕkaṭṭal maškîm hōlēk

Your love is like a morning cloud,
    like the dew that goes early away. (*RSV*)

See also Job 7 : 9 and Cant 2 : 11. [592]

Job 31 : 27

Nor was my heart ... seduced.   Deut 11 : 16 repeats this collocation
pth + lēb in cautioning against idolatry, " Take heed lest your heart
be deceived (*pen yipteh lĕbabkem*) and you turn aside to serve other
gods " ; also Hos 7 : 11 ; Ps 78 : 36-37 ; Prov 7 : 7 ; 8 : 5 ; 9 : 4,16 ; Sir
30 : 23.
    The collocation here in vv 26-27 of *hlk + pth* echoes the parallel-
ism of these two verbs in Hos 2 : 16, " I will allure her (*mĕpattêhā*),
and bring her (*wĕhōlaktîhā*) into the wilderness, and speak to her heart
(*libbāh*) " ; cf. also Prov 1 : 10-11 ; 16 : 29.
    C. H. Gordon proposes *pty* as the root of *ypt* " he tups " in *UT*
52 : 39 ; [593] however, both Dahood [594] and Caquot [595] read *ypt* " beautiful " = Heb. *yāpeh* : *il aṭṭm kypt* " El, his two wives are truly beautiful. "

my heart ... my hand.   This same parallelism *lēb//yād* appears, for
example, in Ezek 21 : 12, " every heart (*kol-lēb*) will melt and all hands
(*kol-yadayim*) will be feeble " ; see also Ex 7 : 3-4 ; Isa 66 : 14 ; Ezek
22 : 14 ; Hos 7 : 5-6 ; Pss 10 : 11-12 ; 58 : 3 ; 76 : 6 ; 125 : 3-4 ; Job 17 :
3-4 ; Qoh 9 : 1.

my heart ... my mouth.   The collocation *libbî ... lĕpî* (note also the rhyme)
recalls this same collocation of roots in *UT* 1001 : 3-4 :

    yr klyth wlbh
    ṭn pk bǵr
    ṭn pk bḥlb

---

[592] On *hlk* " to pass away " as a euphemism for dying, see Dahood, *Psalms
II²*, 3rd Note on Ps 58 : 9 ; idem, *Psalms III*, 3rd Note on Ps 125 : 5 ; Pope,
Job³, p. 111 (note on Job 14 : 20a).
    [593] Gordon, *UT*, Glossary 2129.
    [594] *UF* 1 (1969), p. 24.
    [595] *TO*, p. 374.

He shoots (instructs?) his kidneys and his heart.
Repeat does your mouth from the mount,
Repeat does your mouth from the hill.

For the parallelism *lēb//peh* see Jer 23:16, "They speak of visions
from their own minds (*libbām*), not from the mouth of Yahweh (*mippî
yhwh*)"; cf. further, Isa 29:13; Pss 10:6-7; 19:15; 37:30-31;
49:4; 141:3-4; Prov 15:28.

my hand wafted a kiss from my mouth. Most commentators correctly
understand this verse as a continuation from v 26 of Job's abjuration
of idolatry; e.g., Michel comments:

> Because the veneration of the sun and moon were just mentioned
> previously, v. 27b probably refers to the ancient and modern
> custom of blowing a kiss to a distant object of veneration. [596]

However, failure to see that the preposition *lĕ* means "from" in this
case [597] has prompted a variety of emendations and paraphrases.
RSV, for example, reverses subject and object without any explanation: "and my mouth has kissed my hand." But the Qumran Targum
of Job supports the MT: *wnšqt ydy l(pmy)* "et ma main baisait (ma
bouche)." [598] The translation offered here follows Pope's suggestion:

> If the line under discussion actually refers to the "wafting"
> of a kiss with the hand, the grammatical difficulty is easily solved
> by taking the preposition *l-* in the sense of "from" rather
> than "to," "my hand kissed from my mouth." [599]

UT 124:4 provides an interesting parallel: *ydk ṣgr tnšq šptk.* Interpretations vary, but Gordon's version echoes v 27b, "thy hand(s),
little one, kiss thy lips." [600]

---

[596] Michel, *Book of Job*, p. 434 (n. 636). He includes ample lists of biblical
parallels and bibliographical material on this custom in the Ancient Near East.

[597] On *lĕ* "from," see Blommerde, *NSGJ*, p. 21, and Dahood, *Bib* 47
(1966), p. 406.

[598] van der Ploeg, *Le Targum de Job*, p. 48-49.

[599] Pope, *Job³*, p. 235.

[600] C. H. Gordon, *Ugarit and Minoan Crete* (New York: W. W. Norton,
1966), p. 141. But contrast Driver (following Virolleaud's restoration), *Canaanite
Myths and Legends*, p. 68-69, *hn '(nt tuḫ)d ydk ṣgr tnšq šptk* "Behold Anat will
take your hand, O little one, she will kiss your lips"; see also Caquot, *TO*, p. 474.

Job 31 : 28

Though some translations label this verse as a gloss and enclose it in parenthesis, [601] the Qumran Targum preserves clear evidence of its presence in the textual tradition upon which it is based. [602]   The play on words *libbî* " my heart " (v 27) // *lĕpî* " from my mouth " (v 27) // *pĕlîlî* " criminal " (v 28) likewise serves to anchor v 28 into its context.   See also the comments below on the collocation *'ēl* ... *wĕhit'ōrartî* (under " been elated, " v 29).

betrayed.   The collocation *kiḥaštî* " I had betrayed " ... *'eśmaḥ* " I rejoiced " (v 29) echoes this same collocation in Hos 7 : 3 (*yĕśammĕḥû* ... *ûbĕkaḥăśêhem*), in which W. Kuhnigk has recognized the play on words *kḥš* " lie " // *kḥš* (Ug. *kḥṯ*) " throne " : [603]

> *bĕrā'ātām yĕśammĕḥû melek*
> *ûbĕkaḥăśêhem śārîm*

> By their wickedness they elate a king,
>   and by their deceitfulness, princes.

He remarks,

> ... hier, wo es um König und Fürsten geht, beim Wort *kaḥaš* " Lüge, Trug " doch wohl auch *kḥš* (Vokalisierung unbekannt) " Thron " mitgehört werden muss, wie Hosea ja auch sonst mit Doppeldeutigkeiten nicht spart. [604]

on high.   *min* of *mimmā'al* has a local sense here, " in, on, over. " [605]

Job 31 : 29-30 (Strophe Seven)

> I have not gloated at my foe's ruin,
>   nor been elated when evil overtook him;
> I have never let my mouth offend,
>   seeking his life with a curse.

---

[601] E.g., Fedrizzi, *Giobbe*; Alonso Schökel, *Job*.

[602] van der Ploeg, *Le Targum de Job*, p. 48-49; Sokoloff, *The Targum to Job*, p. 64-65.

[603] Kuhnigk, *NSH*, p. 89.

[604] Ibid.

[605] Dahood, *Psalms I*, 2nd Note on Ps 18 : 7; van Dijk, *Ezekiel's Prophecy on Tyre*, p. 87.

Job denies that he has ever returned evil for evil. Delitzsch, Fohrer, and Alonso Schökel treat these verses as a unit.

Job 31 : 29

ruin. *pîd* appears but four times in the Hebrew Bible; e.g., in Prov 24 : 22 it parallels *'ēd* " disaster, " and here *pîd//rā‘* " evil. " Donner and Röllig have identified the word (*ypd*) on the sarcophagus of Ahiram of Byblos (*KAI* 2 : 2): *hn ypd lk* " See, it will bring you ruin. " [606]

been elated. There is no need to emend *hit‘ōrartî* to *hit‘ōdadtî* (from *‘dd* = Ug. *ǵdd* " to comfort, reassure "), as the apparatus of *BHS* advises. [607] Although the basic meaning of *‘ôr* is " to arouse, awaken " (cf. Job 14 : 12 ; 41 : 2), it is also used analogously of stirring up indignation (Job 17 : 8), love and mercy (Job 8 : 6-7, *'ēl ... yā‘îr* " If you seek God ... surely he will rouse himself for you "), and here in 31 : 29 of inspiring elation. The Qumran Targum to Job also supports MT *‘ôr* " to arouse (elation) " by translating *ht‘rrty* with (*wh*)*llt* " I gave praise, exulted. " [608]

Note the collocation here *'ēl* " God " (v 28) ... *‘ôr* " to arouse (elation), " and in *UT* 51 IV : 38-39 :

> *hm yd il mlk yḫssk*
> *ahbt ṯr t‘rrk*

> Behold the love of El the king is
>   moved because of you,
> The affection of the Bull is aroused
>   on account of you. [609]

overtook. Here again, as in Job 31 : 25 above, *mṣ'* evidences the only meaning it has in Ugaritic (*mṣa/mẓa/mǵy*), " to reach, arrive at, at-

---

[606] See *KAI*, vol. II, p. 4-5.

[607] Dahood, *Bib* 38 (1957), p. 319-320, and Blommerde, *NSGJ*, p. 115, read *wĕhit‘ōdadtî* from *‘dd* (= Ug. *ǵdd*) " to comfort, reassure, " for MT *hit‘ōrartî*. They compare the parallelism in Job 31 : 29, *śmḥ//‘dd* (MT *‘rr*), to the collocation of these same roots in *UT* ‘nt II : 25-27 (*tǵdd ... bšmḫt*), *tǵdd kbdh lṣḥq ymlu lbh bšmḫt* " Her liver swells with laughter, her heart fills with gloating. "

[608] van der Ploeg, *Le Targum de Job*, p. 48-49 ; Sokoloff, *The Targum to Job*, p. 64-65, 127.

[609] See also *UT* 49 VI : 31, *il ... y‘r*.

tain. " [610]   A phrase similar to v 29 occurs in Gen 44 : 34, *pen 'ar'eh bara' 'ăšer yimṣā' 'et-'ābî.* Compare, for example, *RSV* " I fear to see the evil that would come upon my father, " with *NEB*, whose translators seem unaware of this possible nuance of *mṣ'* and are forced to paraphrase : " I could not bear to see the misery which my father would suffer. "

Note also the alliteration in this v 29, *mĕśan'î//mĕṣā'ô.*

overtook ... I have never let.   *RSP* II,I,37 records this Ugaritic Hebrew parallel pair (here and 23 : 3 in Job).   *UT* 'nt VI : 11-14 provides yet another example (*mǵy//ttn*):

> *mǵ lqdš amrr*
> *idk al ttn pnm*
> *tk ḥqkpt il klh*
>
> Go, O *Qdš-Amrr* :
> Then you shall surely set your face
> Toward *Ḥqkpt*, which belongs to El.

Although the text of *UT* 128 II : 10-11 is damaged, the collocation there also of *ytn ... mǵy* is clear.   See further, Job 42 : 15 (*nimṣa'//wayyittēn*) : " In all the land no women were to be found (*nimṣĕ'û*; MT *nimṣā'*) as beautiful as Job's daughters and their father gave them (*wayyittēn*) inheritance among their brothers. "

As the editors of 11QtgJob note, [611] the Targum has three to four additional cola between vv 29 and 30 which appear neither in the MT nor in the ancient versions.

Job 31 : 30

I have never.   Understanding the waw of *wĕlō'* as emphatic, thus translating *wĕlō'* as " never. "   L. Prijs first proposed this and Blommerde followed his lead. [612]

let ... offend.   These two roots collocated here (*nātattî lahăṭō'*) parallel one another in Job 1 : 22 (*lō'-ḥaṭa'//wĕlō'-nātan*) :

---

[610] See the discussion of " gloated ... attained " above under Job 31 : 25 ; also, Dahood, *Bib* 47 (1966), p. 277.

[611] van der Ploeg, *Le Targum de Job*, p. 48-49. See also Sokoloff, *The Targum to Job*, p. 127.

[612] L. Prijs, " Ein ' Waw der Bekräftigung ' ? " *BZ* 8 (1964), p. 107 ; Blommerde, *NSGJ*, p. 115.

bekol-zō't lō'-ḥāṭā' 'iyyôb
wĕlō'-nātan tĕpillâ (MT *tiplâ*) *lē'lōhîm*

In all this Job did not sin,
    nor did he allow a curse against God. [613]

See also Job 35 : 6-7 (*ḥāṭā'tā ... titten*).

let ... let. Job 31 : 30-31, *nātattî ... yittēn*, can be added to the list of
examples of the Ugaritic–Hebrew parallel pair *ytn//ytn* in *RSP* I,II,264.
See also Job 6 : 8 (*yittēn ... yittēn*):

mî-yittēn tābô' še'ĕlātî
wĕtiqwātî yittēn 'ĕlôah

O that my entreaty might be granted,
That God might reward my hope. (Pope)

let. Although the text of *UT* 128 II : 9-10 is damaged, it appears to
parallel *št* and *ytn* : *bbth y št 'rb* (- -)*h ytn* " ... dans sa maison il place;
il entre, son (- -), il met. " [614] This same parallelism is found in
Job 38 : 36 (*šāt//nātan*):

mî-šāt baṭṭūḥôt ḥokmâ
'ô mî-nātan laśśekwî bînâ

Who put wisdom in Thoth?
Who gave Sekwi understanding? (Pope)

See also Job 14 : 13 (*yittēn ... tāšît*).

let ... feast. This collocation in vv 30-31, *nātattî ... niśbā'*, recalls the
Hebrew parallel pair *ntn//śb'* of Job 9 : 18 (*yittĕnēnî//yaśbī'anî*):

lō'-yittĕnēnî hāšēb rûḥî
kî yaśbī'anî mammĕrōrîm

He would not let me draw my breath,
But would sate me with bitterness. (Pope)

---

[613] Revocalizing MT *tiplâ* to *tĕpillâ* " prayer, " here used as a euphemism
for its opposite, *'ālâ* " a curse "; e.g., *bārak* " to bless " used in the same way
in Job 1 : 5 and 2 : 9 as a euphemism for " to curse. "

[614] Following Caquot, *TO*, p. 538.

See also Lam 3 : 30, *yittēn*//*yiśbaʿ*.

his life ... from his flesh. These two words collocated in vv 30-31 (*napšô ... mibběśārô*) form a parallel pair in Job 13 : 14, *běśārî* " my flesh "//*napšî* " my life " and 14 : 22, *běśārô*//*napšô* ; see also Job 6 : 11-12 (*napšî ... běśārî*) and 33 : 20-21 (*wěnapšô ... běśārô*).

his life. The parallelism *mišpāṭî* " my right "//*napšî* " my soul " in Job 27 : 2,

> *ḥay-'ēl ḥēsîr mišpāṭî*
> *wěšadday ḥēmar napšî*
>
> As God lives who withholds my right,
> Shaddai who has embittered my soul, (Pope)

echoes the collocation of these same words in *UT* 127 : 34 (//46-47) : *lttpṭ ṭpṭ qṣr npš* " You have not judged the case of the wretched spirit. " Another Ugaritic-Hebrew parallel pair of which *npš* is a member and which appears in Job is *ap*//*npš* ; e.g., 32 : 2 ('*appô*//*napšô*) : *bě'iyyôb ḥārâ 'appô 'al-ṣadděqô napšô mě'ělōhîm* " He was angry at Job because he held himself more righteous than God. " [615] Compare *UT* 2 : 23 (*ap*//*npš*) : *ubapkm ubqṣrt npškm* " whether in your body or in your repentant soul, " [616] and *UT* 3 Aqht (obv) 24-26 (*npš ... ap*), *tṣi km rḥ npšh km iṯl brlth km qṭr baph* " Issues forth like wind does his soul, like a gust his spirit, like smoke from his nostrils. " [617]

Job 31 : 31-32 (Strophe Eight)

> The men of my household have not said,
>   " O that we might feast on his flesh ! "
> The stranger did not sleep in the street ;
>   my door I opened to the traveler.

Job professes innocence of ever having violated the laws of hospitality and thus leaving the stranger at the mercy of those who would

---

[615] See also Job 18 : 4 (*napšô* + *bě'appô*) ; 27 : 2-3 (*napšî ... bě'appî*) ; 36 : 13-14 ('*ap ... napšām*).

[616] See Whitaker, *A Concordance of the Ugaritic Literature*, p. 455, for the parallels to this passage.

[617] In *UT*, Glossary 264 and 1681, Gordon also discusses the term *ap wnpš* in *UT* 5 : 12,15, " which seems to designate a kind of offering. "

abuse him. Delitzsch, Fohrer, and Alonso Schökel treat these two verses together.

Job 31 : 31

household. Literally " tent " (*'ōhel*). Dahood calls attention to the Ugaritic–Hebrew parallel pair *ahl//mšknt* in *RSP* I,II,15. Job 11 : 14 (*taškēn + bĕ'ŏhŏlekā*) and 18 : 15 (*tiškôn + bĕ'ohŏlô*) provide additions to the list of his examples.

Although the relationship between Heb. *šadday* " Most High, the One of the Mountain " and Ugaritic *ḏd* " territory, premises " [618] is unclear, the parallelism between *'ōhel* and *šadday* in Job 22 : 23 should be noted :

> *'im-tāšûb 'ad-šadday tibbāneh*
> *tarḥîq 'awĕlâ mē'ohŏlekā*

> If you return to Shaddai you will be healed.
> Put iniquity far from your tent. (Pope)

This compares with *ḏd//ahl* in 1 Aqht 213-214, *aqrtn bat bḏdk* (*pǵt*) *bat b<a>hlm* " Our hired woman has come into your premises, (*Pǵt*) has come into your tent. " See also the collocation *haśśādeh ... 'ohŏlekā* in Job 5 : 23-24.

flesh. Job offers another example of the parallel pair *yd ... bśr* in Job 12 : 10 (*bĕyādô ... bāśār*) :

> *'ăšer bĕyādô nepeš kol-ḥāy*
> *wĕrûaḥ kol bāśār 'ōšō* (MT *kol-bĕśar-'îš*)

> That from his hand is the soul of every living being,
> and the spirit in all flesh is his gift. [619]

See also *UT* 77 : 8-9 (*lydh ... kl bśrh*). The parallelism in Job 12 : 10, *kol-ḥāy* " every living being "//*kol bāśār* (MT *kol-bĕśar*) " all flesh, " gives some support to the restoration of *(t)ḥwyn* in *UT* 77 : 9, as pro-

---

[618] Gordon, *UT*, Glossary 721. See also Glossary 722, *ḏd* II " breast "; Aistleitner, *Wörterbuch*, p. 321 (no. 2712), *s₂d* " Berg, Gebirge "; Pope, *Job³*, p. 44 (on Job 5 : 17b); R. Clifford, " The Tent of El and the Israelite Tent of Meeting, " *CBQ* 33 (1971), p. 222 (n. 4).

[619] Cf. Dahood, *Psalms III*, 3rd Note on Ps 105 : 32. On the Ugaritic–Hebrew parallel pair *yd ... bśr*, see *RSP* I,II,215.

posed in the recent French translation of the Ugaritic corpus : *kl bšrh
dm a(- - t)ḫwyn* " (Qu'elles) vivifient *toute* sa chair avec le sang. " [620]

O that we might feast.   Following Pope [621] and Dahood [622] who recognize
here that Job affirms his respect of the law of hospitality in protecting
the stranger from homosexual abuse.   Pope remarks,

> The argument that the men of Job's tent are represented as
> expressing the wish that they could find anyone who has not
> yet been filled from Job's rich table does violence both to the
> text and to common sense. [623]

Comparison of this verse with the following v 31 and the episodes of
Gen 19 and Judg 19 makes it clear that this is the type of situation
being referred to here.   MT *lō'* is taken as the intensive *lū'* rather than
the negative particle ; cf. Pope, *ad loc.*   This interpretation is supported
by the Vulgate, " quis det de carnibus eius ut saturemur, " and the
LXX, *tis an dō$_i$ē hēmin tōn sarkōn autou plēsthēnai.*   For further examples of *šb'* in the niphal, see Dahood [624] and Sabottka. [625]

Job 27 : 14b-15b partially parallels *šb'* and *bkh* (*yiśbě'û*//*tibkênâ*) :

wěṣe'ěṣā'āyw lō' yiśbě'û-lāḥem ...
wě'almĕnōtāyw lō' tibkênâ
His offspring will not have food enough ...
His widows will not weep.

Compare *UT* 62 : 9 (*šb'* + *bky*) : *'d tšb' bk* " until she is sated with
weeping. " [626]

---

[620] Caquot, *TO*, p. 392, N.B. notes *l* and *m*.   See also Job 10 : 11-12 (*ûbāśār
... ḥayyîm*) ; 19 : 25-26 (*ḥāy ... ûmibběśārî*) ; 21 : 6-7 (*běśārî ... yiḥyû*) ; 33 : 20-22
(*ḥayyātô ... běśārô ... wěḥayyātô*).

[621] *Job³*, p. 236-237.

[622] *Psalms III*, 5th Note on Ps 102 : 9.

[623] Pope, *Job³*, p. 236.   Further, Pope cites *UT* 3 Aqht (rev) 23-25, " Hear,
O hero Aqhat, / Thou art (my) brother and I (thy sis)ter. — with satiety of
thy flesh —. "   He remarks, " The fragmentary phrase ' with satiety of thy
flesh ' (*b šb' ṭirk*) might refer to the game which the hero would kill with his
bow, but more likely it expresses the (feigned) sexual desire of the goddess for
the young hero " (*Job³*, p. 237).

[624] *Psalms III*, 5th Note on Ps 102 : 9.

[625] Sabottka, *Zephanja*, p. 21-23.

[626] See also Ps 102 : 9b-10b (*šb'* ... *bkh*) : " My Mocker feasts (*niśbā'û* ; MT
niśbā'û, cf. Dahood, *Psalms III*, 5th Note on Ps 102 : 9) on me ... and from
my tears (*biběkî*) I draw my drink. "

Job 31 : 32

did not sleep in the street.   As noted by Pope, " The situation envisaged
here is exactly that elaborated in Gen xix and Judg xix ; cf. especially
Gen xix 2 and Judg xix 20 " (*raq bārĕḥôb 'al-tālan* " ... only, do not
spend the night in the square "). [627]   *UT* 2 Aqht I : 30 describes one
of the duties of a son toward his father : *grš d ʻšy lnh* " who will drive
off those who would abuse his night guest. " [628]

did not sleep ... I opened.   See the remarks above on this same parallel
pair (reversed), *pātûaḥ//yālîn*, in Job 29 : 19. [629]

stranger ... traveler.   The parallel pair *gēr* " stranger "//*'ōrēaḥ* " traveler " occurs in Jer 14 : 8 :

> *lāmmâ tihyeh kĕgēr bā'āreṣ*
> *ûkĕ'ōrēaḥ naṭâ lālûn*

> Why are you like a stranger in the city,
>   like a traveler who turns aside to spend the night ?

This suggests that *'ōraḥ* of *lā'ōraḥ* here in Job 31 : 32 (//*gēr*) is not the
substantive " path, road " but the participle of the form *ō – a*, " tra-
velever. " [630] This is the interpretation of the ancient versions (LXX
panti elthonti ; Vulg. *viatori*, Syriac) and most modern ones (Pope
" traveler, " *RSV* " wayfarer, " *NAB* " wayfarer, " *BJ²*, " au voya-
geur "). [631]

---

[627] Pope, *Job³*, p. 237.

[628] Dahood, *Proverbs and Northwest Semitic Philology*, p. 14.   The parallels are *UT* 2 Aqht I : 48-49 ; II : 3,19.

[629] Under " shone ... walked " in Job 29 : 3, and " open ... lodging " in
29 : 19.

[630] The examples discussed here (*'ōraḥ* " traveler, one who sets out " in
Job 31 : 32, 34 : 11 and Prov 10 : 17 ; *pōʻal* " Maker " in Job 34 : 11) show
that we are dealing with an alternate participle form (*ō – a* for the more common *ō – ē*) created by the presence of a laryngal or resh.   Compare GCK par.
64b and 65c.   Further instances of this phenomenon include *'ōraḥ bĕraglayw
lĕ'* (MT *lō'*) *yābō'* " Marching with his infantry he enters triumphant " (Isa
41 : 3) ; *gôy lō'-qōrā' bišmî* " a nation who did not call upon my name " (Isa
65 : 1) ; *pōʻal 'ôṣārôt bilšôn šāqer* " Who acquires treasures with a lying tongue "
(Prov 21 : 6).

[631] Recognition of this participial form here in 31 : 32 obviates the need to
revocalize MT *lā'ōraḥ* to *lĕ'ōrēaḥ* as, for example, the apparatus in *BHS* proposes.

Dahood has pointed out a similar case in Ps 139 : 2-3 in which
the parallelism *'orḥî* " my departure "//*ribʻî* " my arrival " calls for
the verbal sense of *'rḥ* (infinitive construct in this case) " to depart,
make a journey " rather than the substantive " path, way " :

> *'orḥî wĕribʻî zērîtā*
> *wĕkol-dĕrākay hiskantāh*

> My departure and my arrival you survey,
> and all my travels superintend. [632]

A similar situation obtains in Job 34 : 11, in which *'ōraḥ* is better
translated " setting out, departure " rather than " way, path " :

> *kî pōʻal 'ādām yĕšallem-lô*
> *ûkĕ'ōraḥ 'îš yamṣi'ennû*

> For the Maker of Man will repay him,
> and as a man sets out, so will He bring
> him to his destination.

As Viganò has noted, *pōʻal 'ādām* is the divine title " Maker of Man "
(compare Job 7 : 20, *nōṣēr hā'ādām* " Watcher of Man ") ; [633] *pōʻal* offers
another example of the participle vocalized *ō – a* rather than *ō – ē*.
  This sense of *mṣ'* " to reach, arrive at, attain " (thus the hiphil
here, " to cause to reach, to bring someone to his destination ") was
discussed above under Job 31 : 25 (" gloated ... attained ") and 29
(" overtook "). The subtle contrast here between these two senses
of *'rḥ* " to set out " and *mṣ'* " to arrive, reach " has hitherto been over-
looked by translators : the goal which a person ultimately reaches
(*mṣ'*) is determined by the direction in which he sets out (*'rḥ*); God is
the guarantor of that. Compare Job 34 : 8 three verses earlier which
v 11 echoes by repeating (in reverse order) the roots *'rḥ* (as a verb,
wĕ'āraḥ " he sets out ") and *pʻl* :

> *wĕ'āraḥ lĕḥebrâ ʻim-poʻălê 'āwen*
> *wĕlāleket ʻim-anšê-rešaʻ*

> (Job) who sets out in the company of evildoers,
> and walks with wicked men. [634]

---

[632] Dahood, *Psalms III*, 1st and 2nd Notes on Ps 139 : 3.
[633] Viganò, *Nomi e titoli di YHWH*, p. 52 (n. 97).
[634] Further instances of this parallelism, *'rḥ*//*hlk*, include : Job 6 : 19, *'ōrĕḥôt*

Recognition of this sense of *'rḥ* " to set out, depart " (again the participle form in *ō – a*) in Prov 10 : 17 clarifies the eschatological overtones of the verse :

> *'ōraḥ lĕḥayyim šômēr mûsār*
> *wĕ'ôzēb tôkaḥat mat'eh*

He is heading toward (eternal) life who heeds instruction ;
but he who rejects reproof strays (into Destruction).

On this pregnant sense of " life " (= " eternal life "), see the examples discussed by Dahood in his " Introduction " to *Psalms III*. [635] L. Sabottka comments on *t'h* " to stray (into ruin) " here in Prov 10 : 17 and in Isa 3 : 12 ; 9 : 15. [636]

Job 31 : 33-34 (Strophe Nine)

> If I hid my rebellious acts from you in the Earth,
>   concealing my guilt in Hades ;
> If I feared the rabble clamor,
>   and the scorn of the clans terrified me,
>   so that I kept silent and did not go out the door.

Job foreswears hypocrisy. Even if he were to sin, his attitude is such that he would never dissemble and attempt to hide his failing either from God (v 33) or from his neighbor (v 34). Delitzsch, Fohrer, the Chicago Bible, Alonso Schökel, and Fedrizzi consider these two verses as a unit.

Job 31 : 33

If I hid ... from you in the Earth. In commenting on the difficulties the translator encounters in this verse, Dahood remarks, " The fact that the normally conservative *RSV* emends to *mē'ādām* points up the gravity of the problem created by MT *ke'ādām*, ' like Adam. ' " The

---

(MT *'arḥôt*; cf. Pope, *Job³*, p. 54)//*hălîkōt*; 16 : 22, *'ōraḥ ... 'eḥĕlōk*; 22 : 14-15, *yithallāk* + *ha'ōraḥ*.

[635] In the section entitled, " Death, Resurrection, and Immortality, " p. XLI-LII (N.B., XLV-XLVII).

[636] L. Sabottka, " Is 30,27.33 : Ein Uebersetzungsvorschlag, " *BZ* 12 (1968), p. 242.

solution he offers is to revocalize *kĕ'ādām* to *ke'ĕdōm* " like blood, " the Hebrew *dām* with an aleph preformative. [637] He translates the verse :

> If I covered my crimes like blood,
> Concealing my guilt in my bosom.

Blommerde presents another possibility, seeing in *'dm* the Ugaritic biform *'id* (in the dual, *'idm*) of Hebrew *yd* " hand. " [638] It shares the preposition of parallel *bĕḥubbî* " in my bosom. " His version reads :

> If I concealed my rebellious acts as in my hands (*kĕ'ādēm* ;
>   MT *kĕ'ādām*),
>   hiding my guilt in my bosom. [639]

More recently, Kuhnigk reports that Dahood favors :

> If I concealed my sins like the ground,
>   to hide my guilt in its bosom.

MT *kĕ'ādām* remains unchanged and the yodh of *bĕḥubbî* is understood as the 3rd person singular suffix (" in *its* bosom "). [640]

The solution adopted here takes the kaph of *k'dm* with the previous word as the 2nd person singular dative suffix, *'im-kissîtîkā* " If I have concealed from you. " [641] *'ādām* shares the preposition of its parallel *bĕḥubbî* " in Hades. "

in the Earth. Many examples of *'ādām* (= " earth "), a variant of the more common *'ădāmâ*, have been identified. [642] The latter is sometimes used as a synonym for the netherworld ; Tromp points to Num 16 : 30-32 as an example :

---

[637] Dahood, " The Phoenician Contribution to Biblical Wisdom Literature, " p. 127-128.

[638] See the discussion above under Job 31 : 23, *'ēd 'ēl* " God's hand. " Another possibility is to revocalize *kĕ'ādām* to *kĕ'ōdem* " as a jewel, precious stone " (cf. *'ōdem* " carnelian " in Ezek 28 : 13) : " If I hid my rebellious acts like a precious stone, / concealing my guilt in Hades " ; compare Matt 13 : 44 (*RSV*), " The kingdom of heaven is like treasure hidden in a field, which a man found and covered up ... " (Dahood, private communication).

[639] Blommerde, *NSGJ*, p. 116.

[640] Kuhnigk, *NSH*, p. 283 (n. 82).

[641] Dahood, in a private communication.

[642] Dahood provides an impressive list with recent bibliography in *Psalms III*, 1st Note on Ps 104 : 14 ; see also Kuhnigk, *NSH*, p. 82-83.

If the ground (*'ădāmâ*) opens its mouth (*pāṣĕtâ ... 'et-pîhâ*) and
swallows them up (*blʿ*) and they go down alive into Sheol, then
you shall know that these men have despised Yahweh. And
as he finished speaking ... the ground under them split asunder;
and the earth (*'rṣ*) opened its mouth (*ptḥ*) and swallowed them
up. [643]

This seems to be the connotation here in Job 31:33 of *'ādām* " Earth
(i.e., the lower part of it = the netherworld). " Job denies having
tried to conceal his evil deeds in the region beyond Yahweh's concern
(or control), the region he has given into the control of chthonic deities
such as *Ḥby*. This same theme of hiding one's sin in the *'ădāmâ* recurs
in Gen 4:10-11:

Listen! your brother's blood is crying to me from the
ground (*min-hā'ădāmâ*). And now you are cursed from the
ground (*min-hā'ădāmâ*) which has opened its mouth to receive
your brother's blood from your hand.

See also Job 14:17; 16:18; 20:27. In 14:13, Job asks God to hide
him in Sheol until God's anger relents:

mî yittēn biš'ôl taṣpinēnî
tastîrēnî 'ad-šûb 'appekā

O that you would hide me in Sheol,
        conceal me till your anger withdraws.

my rebellious acts ... my guilt. This Hebrew parallel pair occurs elsewhere in Job 7:21 (*pišʿî//'ăwōnî*); 13:23 (*'ăwōnôt//pišʿî*); 14:17
(*pišʿî//'ăwōnî*); and 33:9 (*pāšaʿ//'āwōn*).

hiding. This word continues the theme of hiding in the underworld;
e.g., Job 40:13a, *ṭomnēm ba'ăpar* (MT *bĕ'āpār*) *yāḥad* " Hide them in
the slime of the Community. " The substantive from the root *ṭmn*
is used as a synonym for the netherworld in 40:13b, *pĕnêhem ḥăbōš*
baṭṭāmûn " bind their faces in the Crypt. " [644]

---

[643] Tromp, *Death and the Nether World*, p. 26-27; for further discussion
refer to *'ădāmâ* in his " Index of Hebrew Words, " p. 233. See also Michel,
Book of Job, p. 435-436 (n. 642).

[644] Dahood, " Northwest Semitic texts and textual criticism of the Hebrew

in Hades. *ḥūbbî*, understood as an epithet for the netherworld (" Hades "), occurs only here in the Old Testament. The usual version is " bosom " (*RSV, NAB, JB*). [645] The translation offered here was suggested by the Ugaritic passage in which El in a drunken vision sees a god (or demon) named *ḥby*, " a pagan deity of the type that gave rise to our familiar image of the devil " : [646] *wngšnn ḥby b'l qrnm wḏnb* " there meets him *Ḥby*, possessor of two horns and a tail " (*UT* 601 : 19-20). This figure appears again in a variant form as *ḥbywn* (MT *ḥebyôn*) [647] in Hab 3 : 4-5 :

> *wĕnōgah kā'ôr tihyeh*
> *qarnayim miyyādô lô*
> *wĕšām ḥbywn* (MT *ḥebyûn*) *'ūzzōh*
> *lĕpanayw yēlek dāber*
> *wĕyēṣē' rešep lĕraglāyw*

> His brightness was like the sun,
> > two wings (horns ?) were at his side,
> > and behold, like *Ḥbywn*'s was his strength.
> Before him went Pestilence
> > and Plague followed close behind.

Ḥby's chthonic character is suggested by his association here with the demons *dāber* " Pestilence " and *rešep* " Plague, " [648] and by the reference to " his strength " (*'ūzzōh*). Cf. Cant 8 : 6, *kî 'azzâ kammāwet 'ahăbâ* " for strong as Death is love " ; *UT* 49 VI : 17-20, *'z mt 'z b'l* " Mot (Death) is strong, Baal is strong. " N.B. also the reference

---

Bible, " p. 27. He also points to Job 3 : 16 and 20 : 26, where *ṭāmûn* = " the Crypt " ; see also idem, " Hebrew–Ugaritic Lexicography XI, " *Bib* 54 (1973), p. 360.

[645] BDB, p. 285b. Contrast Pope, *Job³*, p. 238, who translates it " covert " from √*ḥbh* " to hide, conceal. "

[646] Gordon, *UT*, p. 551.

[647] Other examples of divine names with variant forms include Ugaritic *aliy/aliyn* (cf. Gordon, *UT*, Glossary 1342), Phoenician *'l/'ln* (cf. Donner–Röllig, *KAI*, vol. III, p. 2), and Hebrew *'ēlî/'elyôn* (Dahood, *Psalms I*, 1st Note on Ps 7 : 9 ; *Psalms III*, p. xxxix-xl) and *šadday/šaddayan* (Pope, *Job³*, p. 147-148).

[648] Vulgate translates *dāber* and *rešep* here with *mors* and *diabolus* respectively. Dahood makes reference to Hab 3 : 5 in discussing the motif of " the escort of maleficent angels that goes before Yahweh to prepare his way " : cf. *Psalms II²*, 2nd Note on Ps 78 : 49 ; 1st Note on Ps 78 : 50. See further, ibid., 4th Note on Ps 68 : 5 ; 1st and 2nd Notes on Ps 85 : 14.

here in Hab 3 : 4 to *qarnayim* " two wings (horns?) " (UT 601 : 20,
qrnym). [649] *'ôr* here is " the Light (par excellence) " = " the sun. " [650]
W. Kuhnigk discusses *šām* " behold " in *NSH*, p. 82. *ḥbywn* (MT
ḥebyôn) " like *Ḥbywn* " shares the particle *kĕ* with its parallel in 4aβ
kā'ôr " like the sun. "

    môt " Death " may designate a place [651] as well as a person. [652]
The parallelism here in Job 31 : 33 with *'ādām* " the Earth " suggests
that a local sense for *ḥby* " Hades " best fits the context.   The " Hades "
of Greek mythology has the same flexibility; depending on the context
it may be either the netherworld or the ruler of the netherworld. [653]

If. The context calls for this nuance of *kî*; compare the Vulgate
(*si expavi ad multitudinem nimiam*), *BJ*[2], [654] and the King James Version.   Dahood finds another example of *kî* = " if " in Ps 72 : 12. [655]

Job 31 : 34

I feared.   The parallelism *'rṣ* / / *ḥtt* (here *'e'ĕrôṣ* " I feared " / / *yĕḥittēnî*
" terrified me ") occurs also in Josh 1 : 9, *'al-ta'ărōṣ wĕ'al-tēḥāt* " do
not fear and do not be dismayed. "

    The paronomasia *'rṣ* " terrify " / / *'rṣ* " earth " of Isa 2 : 19 and 21,
bĕqûmô la'ărōṣ hā'āreṣ " when he (Yahweh) rises to terrify the earth, "
and Ezek 30 : 11, " He and his people with him, the most terrible of
the nations (*'ārîṣê gôyim*), shall be brought in to destroy the land
(*hā'āreṣ*), " repeats the same play on words *'rẓ* / / *'rṣ* in UT 49 I : 35-37:

      yrd 'ṭtr 'rẓ
      yrd lkḫt aliyn b'l
      wymlk barṣ il klh

---

[649] On Hab 3 : 4a, *qarnayim miyyādô lô* " two wings were at his side, " see
Dahood, " Ugaritic Lexicography, " p. 95.
  [650] Cf. Dahood, *Psalms I*, 1st Note on Ps 37 : 6; idem, *Psalms III*, 2nd
Note on Ps 104 : 2, 3rd Note on Ps 112 : 4; Holman, *BZ* 14 (1970), p. 56-58;
Pope, *Job*[3], p. 235.
  [651] See above under Job 30 : 23, *môt* " Death " / / *bêt mô'ēd* " the Meetinghouse "; also Tromp, *Death and the Nether World*, Chapter One, " Local Aspects "
(p. 21-79).
  [652] *môt* " Sir Death "; cf. Tromp, *Death and the Nether World*, Chapter
Three, " Personal Aspects " (p. 99-128).
  [653] *New Catholic Encyclopedia*, vol. 6 (ed. M. R. P. McGuire; New York:
McGraw-Hill, 1967), p. 886.
  [654] " Ai-je eu peur de la rumeur publique? "   See also BDB, p. 473a.
  [655] *Psalms III*, 1st Note on Ps 72 : 12.

Comes down does Ashtar the Terrible.
He comes down from the throne of Aliyan Baal
And rules over the whole grand earth. [656]

In *UT* 75 II : 31, '*rẓ* seems to parallel *adr* : *idm adr* (...) *idm* '*rẓ t'r(ẓ)*. Although the derivation of *adr* is disputed, [657] the parallelism here, *adr*//'*rẓ*, should be compared with *bĕma'ărāṣâ*//*babbarzel*//*bĕ'addîrê* (MT *bĕ'addîr*) in Isa 10 : 33-34 :

Behold the Lord, Yahweh Sabaoth
  will lop the boughs with terrifying power
    (*bĕma'ărāṣâ*) ...
He will cut down forest thickets with an ax (*babbarzel*),
  and Lebanon shall fall with its awesome (cedars)
    (*bĕ'addîrê yippôl*). [658]

rabble clamor. The phrase *hāmôr rab* " a great (noisy) crowd " occurs a number of times in the Hebrew Scriptures (e.g., Dan 11 : 11,13 ; 2 Chron 13 : 8 ; 20 : 2,12 ; Isa 16 : 14). *BHS* has wisely deleted the suggestion in the apparatus of *BHK*³ to emend MT *rabbâ* to *rab*. W. Irwin suggests that we have here another example of the frequent occurrence in Ugaritic and Hebrew of the same noun in both masculine and feminine gender. [659] Normally masculine *hāmôn* appears here and in Qoh 5 : 9 as feminine. [660]

---

[656] See also Job 15 : 19-20 (*hā'āreṣ* ... *lĕ'ārîṣ*) ; 30 : 6 and 8 (*ba'ărûṣ* ... *hā-'āreṣ*) ; and Ps 10 : 18, " no more shall the arrogant frighten (*la'ărōṣ*) men from the earth (*min-hā'āreṣ*). "

[657] Gordon, *UT*, Glossary 92, relates it to Heb. '*addîr*. Dahood, *Bib* 38 (1957), p. 62-66, argues that some occurrences of *adr* in Ugaritic and Hebrew derive from *dry* " to cut. "

[658] MT = *bĕ'addîr yippôl*. *RSV* translates, " and Lebanon shall fall with its majestic trees, " noting : " Compare Gk Vg : Heb *with a majestic one*. " Cf. Zech 11 : 2 ('*erez* " cedar "//'*addirîm* " glorious trees "), *hêlēl bĕrôš kî-nāpal 'erez 'ăšer 'addirîm šuddādû* " Wail O cypress, for the cedar has fallen, for the glorious trees are ruined " (*RSV*).

[659] Irwin, *Isaiah 28 – 33*, p. 40.

[660] Qoh 5 : 9 : *ûmî-'ōhēb behāmôn lō' tĕbû'â* " and he who loves gain, it will not come. " *hāmôn* is the feminine antecedent of *tĕbû'â*, an anomalous form which combines the prefix of the imperfect with the suffix of the perfect. A number of examples appear in the El Amarna correspondence ; cf. Cyrus H. Gordon and Edward J. Young, " '*g'lty* (Isaiah 63 : 3), " *The Westminster Theological Journal* 14 (1951), p. 54.

hāmôn " noise " parallels *tĕšū'ôt* " shouts " in Job 39 : 7 ; cf. *wahămônâh* " her multitude " //*ûšĕ'ônâh* " her throng " of Isa 5 : 14 and *šĕ'ôn* " roaring " //*šĕ'ôn* " roaring " //*wahămôn* " turmoil " of Ps 65 : 8.

terrified. Recognition of this root " to be shattered (with fear) " (Heb. *ḥtt* ; Ug. *ḫt'*) in Job 41 : 25 (reading *ḥătā'āt* " flaw, crack, " feminine absolute noun, for MT *ḥāt* [26] *'ĕt*) helps to clarify the meaning of the verse :

> On the earth is not his equal,
>   made as he is without flaw
>   (*he'āśû liblî ḥătā'āt*). [661]

Dahood has recognized this root *ḥtt* " break " in Phoenician also. He proposes reading the Ahiram sarcophagus graffito (*KAI* 2) *ld't hn ypd lk tḥt zn* " Attention ! Behold you shall come to grief if you break (*tḥt*) this. " [662]

The distant parallelism of *ḥtt*//*šbr* in Jer 17 : 18,

> Let them be dismayed (*yēḥattû*)
>   but let me not be dismayed (*'ēḥattâ*) ;
> Bring upon them the day of evil ;
>   destroy them (*šābĕrēm*) with a double
>   destruction (*šibārôn*),

should be compared with the collocation of these two roots in *UT* 49 II : 23 (*tbr ... ḫtu*) : *klli btbr nt'y ḫtu hw* " Like a kid he was crushed by the grinding of my teeth. " [663]

Finally, the roots *śḥq* and *ḥtt*, parallel as verbs in Job 39 : 22 (*yiśḥaq lĕpaḥad wĕlō' yēḥāt* " He laughs at fear and is not dismayed "), are also parallel as nouns in Jer 48 : 39, " Moab has become a derision and a horror (*liśḥōq wĕlimḥittâ*) to all that are round about him. "

so that I was silent and did not go out the door. This same motif appears in the El Amarna letter 226 : 11-14, and comparison of this passage with Job 31 : 34 serves to clarify the difficult *aḫ-r(i-šu)* of line 11 :

[661] Blommerde, *NSGJ*, p. 139.
[662] Dahood, *Bib* 45 (1964), p. 410.
[663] Dahood, *CBQ* 17 (1955), p. 303 ; see also Jer 48 : 38-39, *šābartî* " I have smashed " ... *'êk ḥattâ* " How it is broken. "

ah-$r(i$-$šu)$
ù i-ba-ka-$m(a$ $la)$
(ya)-as-zu-$m(i)$
(i)-na ali-ia

I am silent
and weep, and I do not
go out into my city. [664]

J. Knudtzon translates ah-$r(i$-$šu)$, with some hesitation, "ich trauere." [665] However, comparing the passage with Job 31:34, one might see in ah-ri-$šu$ the counterpart of '$addōm$ "I was silent" and relate it to Heb. $hrš$ "to be silent, dumb."

Job 31:35-37 (Strophe Ten)

O that the Most High would pay attention to me!
   Behold my signature, let Shaddai answer me,
   and my Opponent write an indictment.
Surely on my shoulder I would wear it,
   I would bind it on like a crown.
The number of my steps I would tell him;
   like a prince I would approach him.

These verses represent the climax of Job's Apology, his final plea for a hearing and judgment in the divine presence. In 29:18-20, Job expressed the hope which stood at the center of his former happy life: that God's blessings upon him would be unending, and that his present felicity was but a sign and foretaste of future glory. Vv 35-37 here in chapter 31 echo that same theme. Job implies that the "indictment" ($sēper$) which he demands of God, far from establishing that he is guilty and deserving of the sufferings he has endured, will rather prove his innocence. That document, much like the "Book of Life" ($sēper$ $hayyîm$) mentioned elsewhere in the Old Testament, [666] will be the proof of his guiltlessness ("The number of my steps I

---

[664] Knudtzon, *Die El-Amarna-Tafeln*, p. 764-765.
[665] Ibid.
[666] E.g., Dan 12:1 and Ps 69:29, $yimmāhû$ $missēper$ $hayyîm$ $wĕ'im$ sad-$dîqîm$ 'al-$yikkātēbû$ "Let them be erased from the scroll of life eternal, and not enrolled among the just"; N.B. Dahood's comments on this latter verse in *Psalms II²*, p. 164. See also, idem, *Psalms III*, p. 103-104 (on Ps 109:13).

would tell him ") and his passport to immortality (" like a prince
would I approach him "). Far from being a source of shame by list-
ing his evil deeds, it will be rather a source of pride which he willingly
exhibits to all who would read (" Surely on my shoulder I would
wear it "). The mention of the " crown " (*'ăṭārôt*) in v 36b recalls
Ps 103 : 4-5 :

> Who will redeem your life from the Pit,
>> who will crown you with kindness and mercy,
> Who will imbue your eternity with his mercy,
>> when your youth will be renewed like the eagle's.

Dahood notes on " who will crown you " :

> ... the mention of *šaḥat*, " the Pit, " in the first colon and the
> use of three eschatological terms in the following verse show
> that the psalmist is describing the afterlife wherein Yahweh
> will place crowns on the heads of the just admitted to Para-
> dise. Ps v 13, collocating *ṣaddīq*, " the just man, " and *ta'ṭᵉrennū*,
> the same verb of our context, probably refers to the same practice
> of crowning the blessed in heaven. [667]

See also Ps 21 : 4-5,

> But you set before him the blessings of prosperity,
>> put upon his head a crown of gold.
> Life eternal he asked of you,
>> you gave it to him ;
> Length of days, eternity, and everlasting. [668]

For Job too, his " indictment " will serve as his crown of glory. [669]

---

[667] *Psalms III*, 4th Note on Ps 103 : 4. Note also the collocation here in
Ps 103 : 4 of the crown (of life) with the motif of the phoenix (v 5), " when your
youth will be renewed like the eagle's " (N.B. Job 29 : 18) ; cf. *Psalms III*, 4th
Note on Ps 103 : 5.

[668] Dahood, *Psalms I*, p. 130.

[669] In 19 : 9, Job expresses the fear that his sufferings were a sign that he
had lost this crown : " He has stripped from me my glory, And taken the crown
from my head " (Pope) ; also Sir 15 : 6 (Greek) and numerous New Testament
texts (1 Cor 9 : 25 ; 2 Tim 4 : 8 ; Jas 1 : 12 ; 1 Pet 5 : 4 ; Rev 2 : 10 ; 3 : 11). See
further, E. R. Goodenough, *Jewish Symbols in the Greco-Roman Period*, Volume
Seven, Pagan Symbols in Judaism (New York : Pantheon, 1958), Chapter Four,

A problem which faces translators is the place of these verses. Since their tone is so climactic, many versions transpose vv 38-40 to another part of the chapter so that vv 35-37 may stand at the end. [670]

However, if one examines other climactic passages, such as Job 19:25-27 and 29:18-20, one sees a phenomenon similar to that in 31:35-37. In both of these cases, the chapter reaches a high point not at the end but a few verses from the end. Rather than trying to adjust the poet's style to fit present-day standards, one should appreciate and accept the work on its own terms. E.g., the remarks of S. Terrien on Job 31:38-40:

> One must bear in mind that Aristotelian canons of logic should not be applied to the processes of thinking which are common to Oriental (or Occidental!) poets. Furthermore, the poet of Job himself appears to favor the device of the afterthought (cf. 3:16; 9:32; 14:13; etc.), and he also gives the impression of deliberately placing a climax not at the end but just before the end of a development (cf. 3:23; 7:20; 10:20; 14:15; etc.). He may be unconsciously following a method not unlike that of the Greek tragedies or Shakespeare, for he is wont to terminate the discourses of his characters not with a climactic display of violent emotion, but with a subdued and almost monotonic phrasing which ends and yet does not end in some unfinished suspense of quietness and melancholy (cf., e.g., 10:21-22). The result — if not the conscious intent — of such rhetoric may be a relaxing of the tension which has been produced on the auditors or readers and a subsequent return to a kind of emotional normalcy. [671]

"Victory and Her Crown," p. 135-171. However, the latter seems to overstress the Greco-Roman origin of this motif and thus its late entry (Maccabean Period) into Judeo-Christian literature.

[670] See the introductory comments to the Eleventh Strophe (vv 38-40) below.

[671] Terrien and Scherer, *The Interpreters Bible*, vol. III, p. 1126-1127. See also the comments of Andersen, *Job*, p. 239-240; e.g., p. 240, "The placement of the central idea away from the end (verses 35-37) so that the last lines (38-40), are not the climax, but an echo of a point made earlier in the poem, is a common device."

Job 31 : 35

O that the Most High would pay attention to me ! Reading *mî yittēn lî śām ʿēlî* (MT *mî yittēn-lî šōmēaʿ lî*). Some commentators sense a lacuna in v 35a and suggest inserting *'ēl* " God " to balance *šadday* in 35b. [672] Another possibility, which scouts emending the conso- nantal text, is to recognize in MT *ly šm ʿly* the idiom *śîm lēb lĕ* " to direct the mind toward, to pay attention to, " with an ellipsis of the *lēb*, [673] and the divine title *ʿly* (*ʿēlî*) " Most High. " This reading un- covers another example of the break-up of the composite divine name *ʿēlî šadday* (N.B., *šadday* in v 35b). Thus Job 31 : 35 functions as an inclusion with 29 : 4-5, in which the same composite name occurs :

> When God Most High (*ʿēlî*; MT *ʿălê*) established my tent,
> when Shaddai was still with me. [674]

Job 23 : 5-6 provides another example of *śîm* " to pay attention to " in which *lēb* is omitted ; [675] compare the collocation *ya-ʿănēnî* " he would answer me " ... *yāśim bî* " pay me heed " (23 : 6), with the parallelism of these same two roots in 31 : 35 (*śîm*//*yaʿănēnî*) :

> I would learn what he would answer me (*yaʿănēnî*)
> and understand what he would say to me.
> With his great power would he contend with me ?
> The Victor — would he himself pay me heed (*yāśim bî*) ? [676]

A similar solution commends itself for Job 10 : 20, when one appre- ciates that *yĕšît mimmennî* represents an ellipsis of *yĕšît* (*libbô*) *mim- mennî* " let him turn his attention from me " : [677]

---

[672] E.g., Fedrizzi, *Giobbe*, p. 221, following E. Sutcliffe, *Bib* 30 (1949), p. 71- 72 ; also, Driver–Gray, ICC, vol. II, p. 228-229.

[673] Compare Job 1 : 8 and 2 : 3, " Have you noticed (*hăśamtā libbĕkā ʿal*) my servant Job ? " ; cf. BDB, p. 963b (2.b.).

[674] Blommerde, *NSGJ*, p. 109, and above under Job 29 : 4 (" God Most High "). Contrast the treatment of this verse by M. Dick, *CBQ* 41 (1979), p. 45-49 ; e.g., p. 47, " I interpret the participle *šōmēaʿ* as the equivalent of the earlier desired *môkîaḥ*, the arbitration judge " (in Job 9 : 33).

[675] Cf. Driver–Gray, ICC, vol. II, p. 160 ; see also Isa 41 : 20.

[676] Reading MT *lōʾ* as the divine title *lēʾ* " the Victor. "

[677] Cf. BDB, p. 1011a.

hălō'-mĕʿaṭ yāmay
yaḥădāl yĕšît mimmennî
wĕ'abligâ mĕʿāṭ

Are not my days few?
    Let him cease, turn his attention from me,
    that I may smile a little.

The identification of this same ellipsis (*šāt min* for *šāt libbô min*) offers
to clarify Lam 3 : 8 :

gām kî 'ezʿaq waʾăšawwēaʿ
šāt mittĕpillatî (MT *šātam tĕpillātî*)

Though I call and cry for help,
    he turns his attention from my prayer.

Finally, the striking rhyme (*mî | |lî | |ʿēlî | |tāwî | |yaʿănēnî | |rîbî*) of
Job 31 : 35 draws attention to its climactic importance within Chapters
29 – 31.

my Opponent. The forensic terminology of vv 35 and 37 (*'îš rîbî*
" my opponent, " *'aggîdennû* " I would declare to him, " *'ăqārăbennû*
" I would approach him ") echoes that of Isa 41 : 21-22 :

Set forth (*qārĕbû*) your case (*rîbĕkem*) says the Lord ;
    bring forth your proofs, says the King of Jacob.
Let them bring them and tell us (*wĕyaggîdû*)
    what is to happen. (*RSV*)

write an indictment. RSP I,II,308 compares *wspr ktb* here in v 35
with *UT* 1005 : 8-9, *nqmd mlk ugrt ktb spr hnd* " Niqmad, king of Ugarit,
has written this tablet. " To the discussion on *spr* = " inscription "
in Job 19 : 23 [678] may be added the use of *spr* = " inscription " in
the Sefire Inscription. [679] Of particular interest for Job 19 : 23 is
Sefire I B : 8-9, *w'l tštq ḥdh mn mly spr' znh* " and let not one of the
words of this inscription be silent. " The composite phrase *mly spr*
" the words of the inscription " is broken up in Job 19 : 23 :

---

[678] Blommerde, *NSGJ*, p. 88 ; Dahood, *RSP* I, p. 86 (II Intro 10e) ; Pope,
Job³, p. 143-144 ; Irwin, *Isaiah* 28 – 33, p. 79-80.
[679] Cf. Fitzmyer, *The Aramaic Inscriptions of Sefire.*

Who could cause then my words (*millî*) to be written,
to be engraved in an inscription (*bassēper*). [680]

Further, Fitzmyer restores Sefire I A: 6-7, *wn(ṣb' 'm spr' z)nh šm*
" and the stele with this inscription he has set up, " and Sefire I B: 28,
(*b'd)y' zy bspr' znh* " the treaty which is this inscription. "

Finally, include Job 38: 21 (*yāda'tā* " you know " ... *mispar* " the
number ") in the Biblical references for *RSP* I,II,400, *spr*//*yd'*.

Job 31 : 36

wear ... crown.   Compare *KAI* 60: 1-3, in which the same two roots
appear (*nś'* + '*ṭrt*):

> *tm bd ṣdnym bn'spt l'ṭr 'yt šm'b'l bn mgn*
> *'š nś' hgw 'l bt 'lm ... 'ṭrt ḥrṣ bdrknm 20 lmḫt*

It was resolved by the Sidonians, the members of the assembly,
to crown with a wreath *šm'b'l*, son of Magon, whom the community appointed over the temple ... a golden wreath weighing
fully 20 dareikens.

crown.   At first glance '*ăṭārôt* would appear to be feminine plural.
However, as Blommerde has remarked, " An apparent feminine plural
in -*ôt* may sometimes represent the Phoenician singular ending in
-*ot* ... " [681]   The context here calls for the singular sense " crown, "
as the ancient versions already attest (LXX, Pesh., Vulgate). Recognition of the Phoenician singular in -*ot* does away with the need to
emend '*ăṭārôt* to '*ăṭeret* as *BHK³* and *BHS* suggest. [682]

The same form ('*ăṭārôt*, '*ăṭārōt*) appears in Zech 6: 11 and 14,
in which the context again calls for the singular (N.B., the feminine
singular verb form *tihyeh* in v 14), as the LXX early on recognized:

> Take from them silver and gold, and make a crown ('*ăṭārôt*),
> and set it on the head of Joshuah, the son of Jehozadak, the
> high priest .... And the crown shall be (*wĕhā'ăṭārōt tihyeh*)

---

[680] Cf. Blommerde, *NSGJ*, p. 88.

[681] Ibid., p. 12.

[682] For further examples of the Phoenician feminine singular in -*ot*, see
Blommerde, *NSGJ*, p. 11; M. Dahood, " *Š'RT* ' Storm ' in Job 4,15, " *Bib*
48 (1967), p. 545; idem, *Psalms II²*, 2nd Note on Ps 53: 7.

in the temple of the Lord as a reminder to Helem, Tobijah, Jedaiah, and Hen, the son of Zephaniah.

Now there is no need to emend the MT to 'ặṭeret as BHK³, NAB, [683] and NEB [684] propose.

On the eschatological implications of " crown " see above under the introduction to this Strophe Ten (vv 35-37).

Job 31 : 37

the number. The parallelism in 2 Aqht VI : 27-29, ytn//šlḥ//spr//spr, is echoed by the collocation and parallelism mispār + hannōtēn wĕšō-lēaḥ of Job 5 : 9-10 (See also RSP I,II,269).

the number of my steps. mispar ṣĕʿāday may well form an inclusion with wĕkol-ṣĕʿāday yispôr " and all my steps he counts " in v 4 of this same chapter. Cf. also, lĕpōʿălê-'āwen " evildoers " (v 3) and bĕʿālêhā " its workers " (v 39).

I would tell him. With Bogaert [685] and Blommerde, [686] the suffix in 'aggîdennû is datival.

I would tell him ... prince. Heb. 'aggîdennû ... nāgîd serves as another example of Dahood's observation, " We must grow accustomed to the idea that repetition was a hallmark of Canaanite poetry. " [687] One type of repetition employs the yqtl–qtl or qtl–yqtl sequence of the same verb in successive cola, as Moshe Held first pointed out. [688] The poet of Job often resorted to the juxtaposition of a verb and noun from

---

[683] *Textual Notes on the New American Bible,* p. 450.

[684] Brockington, *The Hebrew Text of the Old Testament,* p. 266. See also the textual notes in the *RSV.*

[685] M. Bogaert, " Les suffixes verbaux non accusatifs dans le sémantique nord-occidental et particulièrement en hébreu, " *Bib* 45 (1964), p. 229.

[686] *NSGJ,* p. 116.

[687] *RSP* I, p. 79-80 (II Intro 6a) ; Dahood, *Psalms II²,* 4th Note on Ps 73 : 8 ; idem, *Psalms III,* in the " Index of Subjects " under " Repetition of the same word in parallel cola " (p. 487).

[688] Moshe Held, " The YQTL-QTL (QTL-YQTL) Sequence of Identical Verbs in Biblical Hebrew and in Ugaritic, " *Studies and Essays in Honor of Abraham A. Neuman* (eds. Meir Ben-Horin, et al. ; Leiden : Brill, 1962), p. 281-290 ; see also van der Weiden, *Le Livre des Proverbes,* p. 38, 96-97 ; Dahood, *UF* 1 (1969), p. 30-32 ; Irwin, *Isaiah 28 – 33,* " Subject Index " under " Repetition " (p. 190).

the same root in successive cola, as the *'aggîdennû ... nāgîd* here in
v 37 shows. Other examples from Job include 4 : 14 (*paḥad*//*hipḥid*),
11 : 18 (*ûbāṭaḥtā*//*lābeṭaḥ*) ; 21 : 3 (*'ădabbēr*//*dabbĕrî*) ; 34 : 14 (*yaššîm*,
MT *yāśîm*//*wĕniśmātô* ; see above " Excursus on p–nun Verbs in Job ") ;
and 34 : 35 :

> Job does not speak (*yĕdabbēr*) from knowledge,
>   his words (*ûdĕbārāyw*) are not from understanding.

See also Gen 28 : 17 (*wayyîrā'* + *nôrā'*) ; Deut 28 : 58 (*lĕyir'â* + *wĕhan.
nôrā'*) ; Obad 5 (*gannābîm*//*yignĕbû*) ; Hab 3 : 17 (*ma'ăśēh*//*'āśâ*)-
Variants of this stylistic device occur in Ugaritic, as in 1 Aqht 194-197 :

> *ltbrkn alk brkt*
> *tmrn alkn mr(rt)*
> *imḫṣ mḫṣ aḫy*
> *akl(m) kly (')l umty*

> Will you not bless me that I may go blessed,
> Strengthen me that I may go strengthened?
> I'll smite him who smote my brother,
> I'll destroy him who destroyed the infant of my mother.

Also, 2 Aqht VI : 28-29 (*aššpr*//*tspr*) :

> *aššprk 'm b'l šnt*
> *'m bn il tspr yrḫm*
> I will cause you to count years like Baal,
> like the son of El you will count months.

prince. On *nagîd* " prince " as a divine title, see L. Viganò. [689]

Job 31 : 38-40 (Strophe Eleven)

> If because of me my land cried out,
>   and in unison its furrows wept ;
> If I ate its yield without paying,
>   or the life of its workers snuffed out ;
> Instead of wheat let thistles sprout,
>   instead of barley, let fire come upon it.

> Ended are the words of Job.

---

[689] *Nomi e titoli di YHWH*, p. 106-109.

Many modern translators transpose vv 38-40 to another part of Chapter 31, but there is no general agreement as to what the " original " order was. Pope places vv 38-40 between vv 8 and 9; *NAB* after v 8 in the order, 8, 38, 39, 40, 1, 9; BJ² between vv 15 and 16; *NEB* between vv 28 and 29; Fohrer between vv 34 and 35. [690] Commenting on this passage, *The Interpreter's Bible* disagrees with this tendency:

> The biblical student, however, must be extremely cautious in tampering with the text. There is no evidence whatever, either from Hebrew MSS or from those of the ancient versions, to support the thesis of a textual disorder at this point. [691]

On the contrary, the most recent evidence on the history of the text of Job, i.e., the Aramaic Targum on Job from Qumran, supports the present order of the verses in the MT. [692] F. I. Andersen remarks on the function of this concluding strophe of Chapter 31:

> Recapitulation in the main style of the oath of clearance is an echo that sustains the mood of the whole speech beyond its proper end in verses 35 ff. [693]

Job 31 : 38

because of me. The 'al of 'ālay is probably best taken in the causal sense here. [694]

If because of me my land cried out. Commentators compare this motif with Gen 4 : 10, " And he (Yahweh) said, ' What have you done? Listen! Your brother's blood is crying to me from the ground (*qôl dĕmê 'āḥikā ṣō'ăqîm 'ēlay min-hā'ădāmâ*). ' " [695] Note also Job 16: 16-18, in which the two verbs parallel here, *tiz'āq* " cried out " // *yib-kāyûn* " wept, " are distantly parallel as nouns, *bekî* " my weeping " (16:16) // *lĕza'ăqātî* " for its cry " (16:18). Job 16:18 reads,

[690] Fohrer, *Das Buch Hiob*, p. 424-426.

[691] Terrien, *The Interpreters Bible*, vol. III, p. 1126.

[692] van der Ploeg, *Le Targum de Job*, p. 50-51; Sokoloff, *The Targum to Job*, p. 66-67.

[693] Andersen, *Job*, p. 244.

[694] Cf. BDB, p. 754a.

[695] Pope, *Job³*, p. 230; Terrien, *The Interpreters Bible*, vol. III, p. 1127; Fedrizzi, *Giobbe*, p. 220.

'ereṣ 'al-tĕkassî dāmî
wĕ'al-yĕhî māqôm lĕza'ăqātî

O earth, cover not my blood,
and let there be no burial place for its cry. [696]

A similar but less well known motif appears in *UT* 49 II: 34-37:

širh ltikl 'ṣrm
mnth ltkly nprm
šir lšir yṣḥ

The birds indeed eat his flesh,
The winged creatures consume the pieces.
Flesh cries out to flesh. [697]

furrows. *telem* " furrow " occurs twice in Job (here and 39: 10) and
three times elsewhere in the Bible. It appears in Ugaritic in *UT*
51 VIII: 4, parallel to *ġr* " mountain ":

idk al ttn pnm
'm ġr trġzz
'm ġr trmg
'm tlm gṣr arṣ

Then indeed set your face
toward Mount *trġzz*,
toward Mount *trmg*,
toward the furrows of the fertile land.

in unison ... wept. The poet reinforces the alliteration *wĕyaḥad ...*
yibkāyûn by preserving the primitive yodh of the root *bkh* (**bky*). [698]

Job 31 : 39

I ate. *'ākaltî*, here parallel with *nāpaḥ* (*hippāḥtî*), is collocated with
the same verb in Job 20: 26: *tĕ'ākĕlēhû 'ēš lō'-nūpāḥ* " An unfanned
flame shall consume him " (Pope).

[696] Understanding the pronominal suffix of *lĕza'ăqātî* as 3rd person masculine
yodh as in Phoenician; cf. Dahood, " Northwest Semitic Philology and Job, "
p. 61-62.
[697] Dahood, *Bib* 52 (1971), p. 341 (n. 2).
[698] Gordon, *UT*, p. 88-89.

ma'ăkal " food " in Job 33 : 20 parallels *lāḥem* " bread " and thus offers a previously unnoticed parallel pair common to both Ugaritic and Hebrew :

wĕzihămattû ḥayyātô lāḥem
wĕnapšô ma'ăkal ta'ăwâ

His desire for bread nauseated him,
    his appetite for choice food. [699]

N.B., *akl//ḥṭṭ//lḥm* in *UT* Krt 80-83 (//172-174) :

'db akl lqryt
ḥṭṭ lbt ḫbr
yip lḥm dḫmš
mǵd ṭdṭ yrḫm

Prepare grain for the city,
Wheat for the house of Hbr.
Let bread be baked for five,
Provisions for six months. [700]

Finally, the parallelism *wayyābō'û* " they came "//*wayyō'kĕlû* " and they ate " of Job 42 : 11 is echoed by their collocation in Job 20 : 21-22, *lĕ'oklô* " from/after his ravening " ... *tĕbô'ennû* " will come upon him. "

its yield. The two words parallel here in v 39, *kōḥāh* " its yield "// *wĕnepeš* " the life, " are collocated in Job 6 : 11 (*kōḥî* " my strength "// *napšî* " my soul ").
The composite phrase *yĕgî'ê kōaḥ* " weary " of Job 3 : 17 is broken up over the two cola of Job 39 : 11 :

---

[699] Understanding both *ḥayyatô lāḥem* and *napšô ma'ăkal ta'ăwâ* as construct chains interrupted by the masculine singular suffix -*ô*. Cf. Blommerde, *NSGJ*, p. 9-10 (III.5. " Suffix between construct chain and its genitive "), and Dahood, *Psalms III*, " Index of Subjects " under " Construct chain with interposing elements " (p. 481).

[700] Parsing *yip* " Let ... be baked " as a niphal jussive paralleling the imperative *'db* " Prepare "; compare *tābî'û* " you shall bring out "//*tē'āpênāh* " they shall be baked " (Lev 23 : 17). On the Ugaritic–Hebrew parallel pair *akl//ḥṭṭ* here in Job 31 : 39-40 (*'ākaltî ... ḥiṭṭâ*), see *RSP* I, II, 25, and Kuhnigk, *NSH*, p. 45-46.

Can you rely on his great strength ($k\bar{o}h\hat{o}$),
   can you leave yuroel bor ($y\breve{e}g\hat{\imath}^{\cdot}ek\bar{a}$) to him?

Again, the break-up of the phrase $k\bar{o}ah\ l\bar{e}b$ " strong of mind ($=$ stub-
born) " in Job 36:5 occurs in Job 9:4:

Be he clever ($h\breve{a}kam\ l\bar{e}b\bar{a}b$) or mighty ($w\breve{e}^{\cdot}amm\hat{\imath}\d{s}\ k\bar{o}ah$),
   Who could defy him unharmed?

snuffed out. The root nph " to breath, expire " appears in Ugaritic
in the word $mphm$ ($\sqrt{nph}$) " bellows " in UT 51: I : 24 where it is
collocated, as here in Job 31: 39, with ksp " silver ":

$hyn\ ^{\cdot}ly\ lmphm$
$bd\ hss\ m\d{s}b\d{t}m$
$y\d{s}q\ ksp\ y\check{s}lh\ hr\check{s}$

Hyn goes up to the bellows,
In the hands of Hss are tongs.
He pours out silver, he hammers gold.

its workers. Understanding $b^{\cdot}l$ here as a biform of $p^{\cdot}l$ " to work, make, "
with the non-phonemic interchange of b for p. Dahood first pointed
this out in his review of Jean Steinmann's *Le Livre de Job.* [701] For
further bibliography, see Blommerde [702] and Michel. [703] The recently
published third edition of Koehler–Baumgartner's *Lexikon* [704] accepts
the equation $b^{\cdot}l = p^{\cdot}l$ here in Job 31: 39, as well as in Isa 54: 5. See
also C. Epping and J. Nelis, *Job.* [705] *NAB* apparently agrees on this
understanding of v 39; it translates $b\breve{e}^{\cdot}\bar{a}l\hat{e}h\bar{a}$ " its tenants " (" If I
have eaten its produce without payment/ and grieved the heart of
its tenants ") with no textual note indicating an emendation to $p\breve{e}^{\cdot}\bar{a}$-
$l\hat{e}h\bar{a}$. [706] Despite the skepticism expressed by some, [707] the consensus

---

[701] *Bib* 41 (1960), p. 303. The Vulgate translates *nepeš bĕ'ālêhā* as *anima*
agricolarum, " the life of the farmers "; *agricola* " farmer " could be taken
either in the sense of " owner " or " worker " of the land.

[702] *NSGJ*, p. 5-6.

[703] *Book of Job*, p. 437 (n. 647).

[704] Baumgartner, *Lexikon*, vol. I, p. 136-137.

[705] C. Epping and J. Nelis, *Job*: uit de grondtekst vertaald en uitgelegd
(De Boeken van het Oude Testament, Deel VII/Boek I; Roermond: J. J.
Romen & Zonen, 1968), p. 138-139.

[706] *Textual Notes on the New American Bible*, p. 377.

[707] E.g., L. Grabbe, *Comparative Philology*, p. 97, states: " ... one must

on $b'l = p'l$ in certain passages is growing and new examples are coming to light; e.g., 1 Chron 4 : 22, Prov 3 : 27. [708]

Job 31 : 40

Instead ... instead. RSP I,II,590 records this example of the Ugaritic–Hebrew parallel pair *tḥt*//*tḥt*. The Ugaritic passage seems to be an order for replacing personnel, " *Y'dd* for the son of *Arbn*, *'bdil* for *Ilmlk*, *Qly* for *B'ln* the metalsmith " (*UT* 1053 : 1-3).

Instead of wheat ... let fire come for it. Although the Qumran Targum on Job is fragmentary at this point, it does preserve these three words, *tḥwt ḥṭ' ... b'šwšh*, thus providing evidence that v 40 in the Hebrew text used by the Targumist in the 2nd century B.C. was in the same position as it is in our present Hebrew text of Job. [709]

wheat. UT 126 III : 5-10 offers a series of word parallels to *ḥṭṭ* " wheat " which finds echoes in the Hebrew Bible (*arṣ*//*šd*//*ḥṭṭ*//*ksm*) :

> *larṣ mṭr b'l*
> *wlšd mṭr 'ly*
> *n'm larṣ mṭr b'l*
> *wlšd mṭr 'ly*
> *n'm lḥṭṭ bgn*
> *bm nrt ksmm*

> Upon the earth rains Baal,
>   and upon the fields rains the Most High.
> Sweet to the earth is Baal's rain,
>   and to the field the rain of the Most High.
> Sweet to the wheat in the garden, [710]
>   to the spelt in the tilled soil.

---

ask whether Ug *b'l* is actually a cognate of *P'L* or really a cognate of *B'L* with a special semantic development in Ug. The latter would appear to be the case, especially if the name *yp'l* in (*UT*) 2027 : 4 does indeed have *p'l* ' make ' as its base. " But M. Dietrich and O. Loretz, " Zur Ugaritischen Lexicographie (I), " *Bibliotheca Orientalis* 23 (1966), p. 130, analyze *yp'l* as *yp'* + *'l*.

[708] Cf. Dahood, *Or* 45 (1976), p. 136-137. Dahood mentions in particular M. Dijkstra, " A Note on 1 Chr. IV 22-23, " *VT* 25 (1975), p. 671-674 (on 1 Chron 4 : 22).

[709] van der Ploeg, *Le Targum de Job*, p. 50-51; Sokoloff, *The Targum to Job*, p. 66-67.

[710] Following Herdner, *CTA*, p. 74 (n. 15), who reads *bgn* where Gordon, *UT*, has *b'n*; see also Caquot, *TO*, p. 561 (n. *l*).

On the Ugaritic–Hebrew parallel pair *ḥṭṭ//ksm*, see *RSP* I,II,177. For *'rṣ* + *ḥṭṭ* in Hebrew, cf. Deut 8:8 (*'ereṣ ḥiṭṭâ ûśĕʿōrâ* " a land of wheat and barley ") and Ps 147:14-15 (*ḥiṭṭîm ... 'āreṣ*).

The parallelism *śd//ḥṭṭ* here in *UT* 126 III:8-9 is repeated in Joel 1:11:

> *hōbî śû 'ikkārîm*
> *hêlîlû kōrĕmîm*
> *ʿal-ḥiṭṭâ wĕʿal-śĕʿōrâ*
> *kî 'ābad qĕṣîr śādeh*

> Be confounded, O ploughmen,
> Wail, O vinedressers,
> Over the wheat and over the barley,
> For the harvest of the field has perished.

See also Gen 30:14, " Reuben went out in the days of the barley harvest (*qĕṣîr-ḥiṭṭîm*) and found mandrakes in the field (*baśśādeh*), " and Jer 41:8.

barley. On the parallelism *my* " water "//*śʿr* " barley " in *UT* 1 Aqht 51,55,199 (*ṭkmt my ḥspt lśʿr ṭl ydʿt hlk kbkbm* " who shoulders the water, who sprinkles dew on the barley, who knows the movement of the stars ") see Deut 8:7-8, *'ereṣ naḥălê māyim ... 'ereṣ ḥiṭṭâ ûśĕʿōrâ* " a land of streams of water ... a land of wheat and barley. "

let fire come upon it. MT *bā'ĕśâ* is a hapax, usually derived from the root *b'š* " to stink " (= " stinking, noxious weeds "). Better balance with the first colon might be achieved by reading *bā'ā 'iśśāh*, " let fire come upon it (i.e., *'ădāmâ* ' the land ' of v 38), " with *bā'ā* " come " paralleling *yēṣē'* " sprout " and *ḥôaḥ* " thorn "//*'ēš* " fire. " *b'* and *'śh* share the consonant aleph, a phenomenon documented by Blommerde [711] and W. Watson; [712] the feminine singular suffix of *'iśśāh* parses as datival, " upon it, " breaking the monotony of three successive genitive suffixes referring to *'ădāmâ* " the land ": *tĕlāmêhā* " its furrows, " *kōḥāh* " its yield, " and *bĕʿālêhā* " its workers. " Compare Job 31:12 above, in which fire (*'ēš*) acts also as an agent in the curse and is collocated with *b'* (*tĕbû'ātî* " my produce ").

---

[711] *NSGJ*, p. 4.
[712] W. Watson, *Bib* 50 (1969), p. 525-533; idem, *Bib* 52 (1971), p. 44-50.

Ended are.   The Qumran Targum's *sp(w)* " are completed " testifies to the presence of this colon (Job 31 : 40c) in the Hebrew text available to the 2nd–1st century translator. [713]

the words.   Pettinato reports that the root *dbr* appears in the bilingual vocabularies found at ancient Ebla in the form *ta-da-bi-ru* " translator. " [714]   C. H. Gordon remarks on this word,

> If Ugarit is sensational in providing evidence for the background of the Hebrew language from the time of Moses and Joshua, what are we to say about the contribution of Ebla, a thousand years earlier — centuries before the earliest date ever proposed for Abraham?
> ... A root that is exclusively Hebrew–Canaanite is *d-b-r* in the sense of " to speak. "   To designate " speaking, " Arabic and even Aramaic use other roots.   Accordingly, it is of special interest that Eblaite employs forms of *d-b-r* for words pertaining to speech. [715]

of Job.   Instead of considering v 40c as a prosaic editorial addition, as many commentators do, [716] one should rather appreciate its inclusive function; N.B., 29 : 1, " *Job* again took up his poem and said. "

[713] van der Ploeg, *Le Targum de Job*, p. 50-51; Sokoloff, *The Targum to Job*, p. 66-67, 128.
[714] Pettinato, *BA* 39 (1976), p. 50.   See also idem, " I testi cuneiformi della biblioteca reale di Tell Mardikh-Ebla : Notizie preliminari sulla scuola di Ebla, " *Rendiconti della Pontificia Accademia Romana di Archeologia* 48 (1975-76), p. 54.
[715] C. H. Gordon, " 1000 Years Before Abraham, " *Midstream* (February 1977), p. 48-49.   See also the comments above on *napšî* " my life, " under Job 30 : 16.
[716] E.g., Pope *Job*³, p. 239; Fedrizzi, *Giobbe*, p. 221; Driver–Gray, ICC, vol. I, p. 277.

Some Conclusions

This concluding section gathers together under topical headings some of the remarks scattered throughout this study which bear upon certain questions often raised concerning Job, such as the language and provenance of the book, the state of the text, the unity of the work, the author, the mythological background, and the teaching.

I. The Translation

New light from Northwest Semitic on the lexicography, grammar, and syntax of Hebrew allows solutions for some long-standing problem verses in Job 29 – 31, suggestions for solutions in others, and unforeseen insight into verses the apparent sense of which was heretofore accepted unquestioningly. Simple comparison of translations such as that of Marvin Pope in his *Anchor Bible* commentary or the present study's version of chaps. 29 – 31 with other recent translations which have generally ignored the relevance of Northwest Semitic (e.g., *NAB*, *NEB*) demonstrates the difference. However, a commentary such as that of Francis I. Andersen [717] shows that scholars are beginning to take cognizance of this approach, even if they do not always fully agree with all of the results.

One might point, for example, to the working hypothesis of the Northwest Semitic method that the consonantal text of the Masoretes is reliable. This contrasts with the tendency of a commentary such as that of G. Fohrer [718] or of a translation such as the *NAB* [719] to

---

[717] *Job: An Introduction and Commentary.* N.B., p. 58, " There can be no doubt that numerous problems in Job have been cleared up by evidence derived from Ugaritic. "

[718] Fohrer, *Das Buch Hiob*, proposes no fewer than 353 emendations and deletions in the Hebrew text of Job. See the remarks of Dahood, *Bib* 55 (1974), p. 381 (n. 1).

[719] *Textual Notes on the New American Bible* proposes emendations and/or deletions in 21 of the 97 verses in chapters 29-31, five transpositions of entire verses or cola, and a drastic rearrangement of the text in the second half of chapter 30: " 30,26: Followed by vv 16a.27b.17b.27a.28 " (see the *Textual Notes*, p. 377).

emend, delete, or rearrange the Hebrew text. But the confidence which the Northwest Semitic method has exhibited in the *textus receptus* has been vindicated by the discovery of the 2nd century B.C. Targum to Job at Qumran. The Hebrew text it follows closely approaches that of the Masoretes. On this point, at least, the second edition of the *Bible de Jérusalem* (1974) shows evidence of a renewed reliance on the MT. [720] On at least one other point of translation, *BJ*[2] exhibits an openness to the results of Northwest Semitic — the recognition of *qwm* as an auxiliary verb denoting inchoate action in Job 29 : 8. [721] *wîšîšîm qāmû ʿāmādû*, which is translated in *BJ* as " et les vieillards restaient debout, " becomes in *BJ*[2], " les vieillards se mettaient debout. "

II. The Language, Provenance, and Date of Job

It is worth quoting again in this context a passage from David Noel Freedman's concluding remarks in his 1969 article, " Orthographic Peculiarities in the Book of Job " :

> The chief implication of the orthographic data with respect to the composition of Job is that the provenance of the book is northern and its date early. Since the Canaanite/Phoenician affinities in poetic style, mythological allusions, vocabulary and syntax have been increasingly recognized by scholars, we may regard the evidence of the orthography as substantiating or corroborating these views. All the evidence fits well with the proposal that Job was a product of the (North) Israelite diaspora some time in the seventh or early sixth century B.C. [722]

More recently, F. I. Andersen, while opting for an even earlier date, also recognizes its northern flavor :

---

[720] See below under " The Text of Job. " C. Larcher, O.P., is named as the translator of the Book of Job for the first edition of *BJ*. The second edition (*BJ*[2]) continues to list C. Larcher, O.P., as the translator for the Book of Job. The editors comment, " Les traductions ont été revues et les notes complétées et révisées. Ce travail a été effectué, avec la collaboration des divers traducteurs, par un comité de révision ... " (*BJ*[2], Les Editions du Cerf, 1974, p. 7).

[721] Dahood, " Northwest Semitic Philology and Job, " p. 68-69.

[722] *Eretz-Israel* 9 (1969), p. 37. See also the remarks of W. F. Albright quoted by Freedman, ibid., p. 43-44.

Our own opinion, which we admit we cannot substantiate, is that the substance of the book took shape during the reign of Solomon and that its normative form was settled by the time of Josiah. An Israelite, rather than Judaean, setting for its most definitive stage, together with its location in northern Gilead, suggest a date around 750 BC, before this community was decimated by the Assyrian Conquests. [723]

The present study has uncovered further data which support Freedman's assertion of a northern milieu and Canaanite/Phoenician affinities. First of all, to the instances of defective orthography documented by Freedman in chaps. 29 – 31 (29 : 1 *wayyōsep*, 30 : 13 *yōʿîlû*, 30 : 19 *hōrānî*, 31 : 20 *ḥălāṣāw*), one may now add the unusual spellings of *běhēmâ* for *běhemʾâ* in 29 : 6, *kī* for *kî* in 30 : 2, *šoršē* for *šoršê* and *lōhămīm* for *lōhămîm* (MT *laḥmām*) in 30 : 4, *nědībātî* for *nědîbātî* in 30 : 15, and *qidděmūnî* for *qidděmûnî* in 30 : 27.

In 1955, William F. Albright wrote, " Ugaritic and Phoenician will ultimately clear up many of its (Job's) lexicographical difficulties. " [724] One of the more striking examples of the accuracy of Albright's assertion is the confirmation from the Ebla tablets of Dahood's equation of Ugaritic *ḥl* " phoenix " in *UT* 125 : 7-8, 107-109, with *ḥôl* " phoenix " in Job 29 : 18. Other words in Job 29 – 31 which have benefited semantically from Northwest Semitic include the name of Job (*ʾiyyôb*) himself in 29 : 1 and 31 : 40, *ʿēlî* " Most High " (29 : 4 ; 31 : 35), *ḥōrep* " Prime " (29 : 4), *ʿzr* " rescue " (29 : 12 ; 30 : 13 ; 31 : 21), *mětallěʿôt* " jaw " (29 : 17), *lēʾ* " powerful " (29 : 24), *bḥr* " to join " (29 : 25), *drk* " assembly " (29 : 25), *ʿrq* " to gnaw " (30 : 4,17), *mš* " swamp " (30 : 4), *ʾrṣ* " town " (30 : 8), *twr* " to watch, spy " (30 : 11), *pa* " and " (30 : 12), *rḥḥ* " (left) hand, palm " (30 : 12), *nts* " to break up " (30 : 13), *gly* " to arrive " (30 : 14), *ʿly* " cauldron " (30 : 17,30), *ʾakzār* " Cruel One " possibly derived from *gzr* " to cut into pieces " (30 : 21), *tūšiwwâ* " victory " (30 : 22), *qwh* " to call, cry out " (30 : 26), *ḥmh* " answer " (30 : 28), *zimmâ* " licentiousness " (31 : 11), *kwn* " to create " (31 : 15), *qēn* " nest (of the arm) = armpit, socket " (31 : 22), *mṣʾ* " to arrive at, reach, attain " (31 : 25,29), *hll* " to brighten, wax (of the moon) " (31 : 26), *hlk* " to wane, dim " (31 : 26), *ḥby* " Hades " (31 : 33).

---

[723] Andersen, *Job*, p. 63-64.

[724] " Some Canaanite-Phoenician Sources of Hebrew Wisdom, " *Wisdom in Israel and the Ancient Near East* (VTSup 3; Leiden : Brill, 1955), p. 13-14, as quoted by Dahood, *Bib* 38 (1957), p. 306.

In addition to the 31 Ugaritic–Hebrew parallel pairs in chaps. 29 –
31 already recorded by *RSP* I and II, the present study has identified
a further eighteen. At least one of these, *bky//ʿgm* in 30 : 25, is a previously unrecognized hapax in Hebrew and Ugaritic,[725] further illustrat-
ing Dahood's comment in *RSP* I,

> So many of the Canaanite pairs encountered in Job are hapax
> legomena in the Bible. These pairs, moreover, usually involve
> words of infrequent occurrence even when used alone. When
> these observations are joined to the fact that Job contains no
> specific quotations from earlier, now canonical, Hebrew litera-
> ture, one may rightly conclude that Job's linguistic and literary
> problems will most profitably be studied within the North-
> west Semitic milieu. [726]

Finally, the specifically Phoenician affinities of Job are demonstrated by the Phoenician–Hebrew parallel pairs *ym//yrḥ* in 29 : 2, *ʿyn
... pnm* in 30 : 11, and *zrʿ//šrš* in 31 : 8; by the rare form of the word
for " city, " *qrt*, in 29 : 7; and by the Phoenician feminine singular
absolute in -*ōt* represented by *ballāhôt* in 30 : 15 and *ʿăṭārôt* in 31 : 36.
Comparison with Phoenician has clarified the semantic value of *gēw*
" community " (30 : 5), *ʾrṣ* " town " (30 : 8), and *millâ* " gibe, joke "
(30 : 9), as well as the sense of the expression *bĕlî-šēm* " of no name,
nameless " in 30 : 8 and the mythological background of 30 : 17 (N.B.,
the Arslan Tash tablets). The discussion under 31 : 18 amply documents the interesting verbal parallels between Job 31 : 18-21 and the
Kilamuwa Inscription (*KAI* 24); both texts delineate the magnani-
mous qualities expected of a community (or national) leader.

III. The Text of Job

The most recent evidence pertaining to the text of the Book of
Job comes from the 2nd century B.C. Targum to Job from Qumran
Cave XI. Comparison of the Targum to the MT indicates that the
Hebrew work which the Targum translated was substantially the same

---

[725] The other *hapax* pairs in these chapters occur in 29 : 6 (*yṣq//rḥṣ* and
šmn//ẓrw). See also Dahood's comments on *my//ṭl* of 29 : 19, *lbš//ktnt* of
30 : 18, and *dl//ytm//almnt* in 31 : 16-17, in Dahood, " Some Rare Parallel
Word Pairs in Job and in Ugaritic, " p. 26-27.

[726] *RSP* I, p. 81.

as the *textus receptus*. [727]   Thus, none of the more recent attempts to
" improve " the Job of the MT through rearrangements, emendations,
or deletions, finds support in the Qumran manuscript.   As F. I. Andersen has written,

> Translators agree that the Hebrew text of Job presents more
> problems than most other parts of the Old Testament.... We
> shall have to be content with such uncertainty for the time
> being ; but the incomplete state of our research should not be
> permitted to diminish our respect for the integrity of the Hebrew
> text.   On the contrary, the difficulties we encounter are them-
> selves a tribute to the fidelity of the Jewish scribes, who rever-
> ently preferred to copy an obscure text exactly rather than
> attempt to clarify it by emendation.   In this they are more
> modest, and more scientific, than many modern critics. [728]

The working hypothesis of the Northwest Semitic approach that the
consonantal text of the Masoretes is reliable allows a translation of the
97 verses of these three chapters with only three emendations of the
consonantal text : *prḥh* for *prḥḥ* in 30 : 12, *bprṣ* for *kprṣ* in 30 : 14,
and *nqd* for *nqr* in 30 : 17.

The recent publication of the *Biblia Hebraica Stuttgartensia* volume
of Job (1974) offers the possibility of comparing *BHS*'s handling of
the text to that of *BHK³*.   The most obvious difference between the
two editions is in the number of suggested emendations and deletions
in *BHK³* which have been dropped in the apparatus of *BHS*.   Examples
which demonstrate the soundness of the *BHS* tendency include Job
29 : 23.   *BHS* deletes the emendation of *wĕyiḥălû* to *wîḥakkû* proposed
in *BHK³*, and the A : B : : B : A word pattern of vv 21-23, *lî* : *wĕyiḥēllû* : : *wĕyiḥălû* : *lî*, confirms the decision of *BHS*.   Other such instances
are noted under 30 : 9,12,16.   Nevertheless, *BHS* unnecessarily retains
a number of suggested changes in the text from *BHK³*.   For example,
the presence of the parallel pair *šbr*//*šlk* in Job 29 : 17 (see Ex 32 : 19 ;
Deut 9 : 17 ; Jon 2 : 4 ; Dan 8 : 7) undermines the proposal to read
'ešlōp for MT *'ašlîk*, and the identification of the participial form
'ōraḥ, vocalized in *ō – a* instead of the usual *ō – ē*, in 31 : 32 argues
against the revocalization to *'ōrēaḥ* advised by the apparatus of *BHK³*
and repeated in *BHS*.   See further comments under 29 : 3,4,21 ; 30 :
13,15 ; 31 : 1,11,21,29.

---

[727] See the remarks of Pope, *Job³*, p. xlv-xlvi.
[728] Andersen, *Job*, p. 16.

The second edition of the *Bible de Jérusalem* (1974) continues to a certain extent the tendency of the first edition to rearrange and emend the text. Despite the evidence of the Qumran Targum, Job 29 : 21-25 is inserted between 29 : 10-11, and 31 : 38-40b is placed between 31 : 15-16. *BJ*² also retains the emendation of *'zr* to *'ṣr* in 30 : 13 and that of *tĕšārēš* to *tiśrōp* in 31 : 12. However, *BJ*² does sound an encouraging note in the evidence it seems to offer of a renewed confidence in the MT. Comparison of a number of changes in the translation between the first and second editions shows that the second edition in these cases adheres more closely to the MT. In 30 : 4, *BJ*² rejects the emendation of the preposition *'ălê* to *wa'ălê* " et les feuilles " (*BJ*), although it fails to recognize the force of *'ălê* " from " in *'ălê-śíaḥ* and translates " *sur* le buisson. " In 30 : 11, " en ma présence " (*BJ*²) is a more accurate translation of *mippānay* than " de leur bouche " of *BJ*. Further examples include 30 : 17b, " et mes rongeurs " (*BJ*²) for *'ōrĕqay* in contrast to *BJ*'s expansion, " les plaies qui me rongent " ; " les jours de souffrance m'ont atteint " (*BJ*²) for MT *qiddĕmūnî yĕmê-'ōnî* compares with *BJ*'s " chaque jour m'apporte la souffrance " in 30 : 27 ; and " O ma sécurité " (*BJ*²) renders the Hebrew *mibṭaḥî* in 31 : 24 more precisely than " C'est toi ma sûreté " of *BJ*. Finally, *BJ*² rejects two of the emendations accepted earlier by *BJ*: that of *'al-yātôm* " contre un orphelin " (*BJ*²) in 31 : 21 to *'ălê-tām* " contre un innocent " (*BJ*) in 31 : 21, and that of *lî* to *'ēl* " Dieu " in 31 : 35.

IV. The Unity of Job

After reviewing the various theories on the composition of the Book of Job, F. I. Andersen comes down on the side which upholds unity of authorship :

> At this distance in time the details of the complex process of literary growth and subsequent transmission of Job will never be known. Arguments for the disunity of the book are not conclusive, and, in spite of numerous difficulties, the Hebrew text is probably in pretty good shape. It is possible that the whole work is the product of a single mind, and insoluble textual problems need not prevent us from making sense of the book as a whole. [729]

---

[729] Ibid., p. 55. On p. 52 (n. 2), he notes " recent votes in favour of the

Indeed, certain distinctive, almost idiosyncratic stylistic devices which appear in both the Dialogues and the Elihu Speeches (and, in some cases, the Yahweh Speeches as well) argue in favor of a common author. One such device is the parallelism between a prepositional phrase and a dative suffix. Job 29 : 16 and 30 : 9 represent examples recorded in the present study. This phenomenon occurs in the Dialogues (3 : 25 ; 6 : 4 ; 15 : 17 ; 20 : 22), in the Elihu Speeches (32 : 14 ; 33 : 5,33), as well as in the Yahweh Speeches (40 : 30 ; 41 : 20-21). The stylistic artifice of " delayed identification " (see 29 : 18 ; 30 : 1,15,22 ; 31 : 6,26) also abounds throughout Job, in the Dialogues (6 : 2 ; 19 : 26 ; 20 : 23 ; 22 : 21 ; 27 : 3) and at least once in the Elihu Speeches (34 : 17). The juxtaposition of a verb and noun from the same root in successive cola (see 31 : 37) represents another frequent device not restricted to specific sections of Job (4 : 14 ; 11 : 8 ; 21 : 3 ; 34 : 14,35). Finally, Dahood comments in *RSP* I,II,51 on the Ugaritic–Hebrew parallel pair '*n*//'*nk* (see above under Job 29 : 15, '*ānî* ... '*ānōkî*) : " This infrequent parallelism in Job 13 : 2 and 33 : 9 may be cited as an argument for the unity of authorship of the main cycle and of the Elihu speeches. "[730]

V.   The Mythological Background in Job 29 - 31

One of the more interesting aspects of these three chapters of Job which this study surfaces is the obvious preoccupation with death and life. The imagery and vocabulary, especially in chapter 30, alludes again and again to Mot, the ruler of the netherworld, into whose grasp Job senses himself slipping. In 30 : 11-14 Job describes his plight in terms of a city under siege by unnamed enemies, and in v 15 these foes are finally identified (" Terror turns on me, pursues my dignity like the wind ; like a cloud my prosperity disappears "). They are none other than the minions of Mot (= Death), " the King of Terrors " (*melek ballāhôt* ; cf. Job 18 : 14). Further possible references to death and the netherworld include *ḥōmer* " mud " of 30 : 19, '*akzār*

---

authenticity of chapters 32 - 37, and therefore of the unity of the whole book " : N. H. Snaith, *The Book of Job : Its Origin and Purpose* (Studies in Biblical Theology, second series, XI, 1968), p. 72-75 ; Robert Gordis, *The Book of God and Man : A Study of Job* (Chicago : University of Chicago Press, 1965), p. 104-116 ; W. F. Albright, as quoted by Freedman, *Eretz-Israel* 9 (1969), p. 44.

[730] See also his comments on the use of the preposition '*al* in Job with the sense " in spite of, despite, " in *Bib* 52 (1971), p. 438.

" Tormentor, Cruel One " of 30 : 21 (a title of Mot, here used pointedly
of God), *māwet ... bêt mô'ēd lĕkol-ḥāy* " Death ... the Meetinghouse of
all the living " in 30 : 23, *rā'* " Evil " and *'ōpel* " Darkness " of 30 : 26,
'ēš ... 'ad-'ăbaddôn " A fire that devours to Perdition " in 31 : 12, and
'dm " the Earth, " *ṭmn* " to hide, " and *ḥŭbbî* " Hades " of 31 : 33.

If concern with death occupies Job in the central section of these
chapters, his resounding affirmation of hope in life appears at the
beginning and at the end. The allusion to the phoenix myth in 29 :
18-20 (N.B., *ḥôl* " phoenix " and *ṭal* " dew ") and the reference to
'ăṭārôt " the crown (of life) " in 31 : 36 make it clear that, in spite
of the threat of death and the apparent desperation of his situation,
his faith and expectancy remain undaunted.

The introduction to the commentary on Job 30 : 2-8 discusses
the relationship of this passage to *UT* 75 and the mythological creatures
described there, the *aklm* " the Eaters " and the *'qqm* " the Devourers. "

Finally, recognition that *bĕtûlâ* of Job 31 : 1 refers to *btlt 'nt* " the
Virgin Anat " [731] resolves a longstanding *crux interpretum*, and reveals
that Job places idolatry first in his catalogue of transgressions in
chapter 31, and not unchaste thoughts and looks.

VI. Motifs

The present study has uncovered or clarified a number of previously unnoticed motifs employed by the poet. Job 30 : 11, for
example, contains the motif of the " evil eye " (" They watch at my
door and eye me "). It makes interesting comparison with the second
Arslan Tash Inscription and its incantations against *rb 'n* " Big-Eye "
and *'yn* " Eyer (with the evil eye). " With the recognition of the
sense of *twr* " watch " in 30 : 11 and *rgl* " spy " in 30 : 12, the motif
of battle and siege in 30 : 11-15 becomes clearer; this contrasts with
the interpretation of some commentators who liken 30 : 12 to a courtroom scene (e.g., Fedrizzi; Dhorme). Identification of the convention
termed " the physiology of tears " by Terence Collins throws light on
30 : 16 and 27. [732] Appreciation of the image of " Mother Earth "
in 30 : 23, 31 : 15, 31 : 33 aids in the interpretation of these verses,

---

[731] Note the parallelism in Job 31 : 1 of *bĕtûlâ* with *'ênāy* " my eyes, "
which may be a play on the name *'nt*.

[732] Collins, *CBQ* 33 (1971), p. 18-38, 185-197.

and *lĕbaddî* " I alone, " parallel with " the poor, " " the widow, "
and " the orphan " in 31 : 16-17 may allude to the *yaḥîd*, " the solitary
man, " who was sometimes included in the list of those exposed to
possible mistreatment. Finally, the discussion under Job 30 : 2-8 notes
the theme of political or social exile into the sparsely populated and
sparsely vegetated areas of the land (N.B., *grš* " to banish " and *nk'*
" to drive out ").

VII. Divine Titles

'ēlî 'ĕlôah ... *šadday* " God Most High ... the Almighty " at the
beginning of Job's Apology (29 : 4-5) forms an inclusion with this
same title, *'ēlî* " Most High " // *šadday* " the Almighty, " at the end
of these three chapters (31 : 35). In 30 : 21, Job addresses God with
a title which is elsewhere (Prov 17 : 11 ; Jer 30 : 14) an epithet of Death,
'akzār " Tormentor, Cruel One " ; *'akzār* may be part of the break-
up of a composite name here in 30 : 21-22, *'akzār* (...) *'ēl* " the Cruel
God, " or " El, the Cruel One. "   *ṭôb* " good " and *'ôr* " light " may
represent divine epithets in 30 : 26 : " the Good One " and " the Light. "
In 31 : 15 the poet has broken up the composite title *lē' 'eḥād* " the
Unique Victor, " and recognition of its now parallel components reveals
the chiastic structure of the verse ; the divine appellative *'ōśēnî* " He
Who made me, my Maker " appears in the same verse.   *'iš rîbî* " my
Opponent " of 31 : 35 may also be considered a divine title.

VIII. Poetic Techniques

A. Chiasmus

M. Dahood has already demonstrated the value of recognizing
chiasmus as a point of style in Job in his article, " Chiasmus in Job :
A Text-Critical and Philological Criterion. " [733] For instance, the
chiastic word pattern in 29 : 21-23, *lî* : *wĕyiḥēllû* : : *wĕyiḥălû* : *lî*, argues
against the emendation proposed by the apparatus of *BHK*[3] (but
happily omitted in *BHS*). Although content suggests that 30 : 11-15
and 16-19 form distinct strophes, the Joban poet has employed a
chiastic word pattern extending over vv 15 and 16 (*hhpk* : *'ālay* :
kĕ : : *kĕ* : *'ālay* : *tištappēk*) to stitch these two sections together. Finally,
appreciation of the A : B : : B : A word pattern (with the play on the

---

[733] See also Ceresko, *UF* 7 (1975), p. 73-88.

roots *klh//'kl*) of 31 : 16-17, *mēḥēpeṣ* : *'ăkalleh* : : *wĕ'ōkal* : *mimmennâ*, in which the *min* of *mēḥēpeṣ* parallels partitive *min* of *mimmennâ* " (none) of it, " indicates that the *min* of *mēḥēpeṣ* also is partitive and that *mēḥēpeṣ* is best translated " *any* desire. " Further examples of this poetic technique occur in 29 : 2 ; 29 : 2-4 ; 30 : 5 ; 30 : 27 ; 31 : 9 ; 31 : 14 ; 31 : 15.

B. Merismus

The recent publication of Jože Krašovec's monograph, *Der Merismus im Biblisch–Hebräischen und Nordwestsemitischen* (Rome, 1977) testifies to the renewed appreciation of this rhetorical figure in Hebrew poetry. A number of examples appear in Job 29 – 31. The two cola of 29 : 7, for instance,

> When I went storming from the city,
> in the broad place set up my seat,

contrast the extremes in Job's behavior in public, from his enthusiasm in rushing out to his work, to his tranquillity and deliberateness when weighty matters were under consideration in the assembly. Job 31 : 8 represents an interesting example of a double merismus hinging on the double parallelism *zrˤ* " to sow, plant "//*'kl* " to eat " and *zrˤ* " to sow, plant "//*šrš* " to uproot. " Recognition of the merismus in 31 : 10 supports the MT against the suggested emendation in the apparatus of *BHK*[3] ; in naming two of the wife's chief roles,

> May my wife grind for another,
> and over her let others bend,

Job expresses the wish that (as a result of the curse) his wife be at the service of others continually, day and night. Finally, the analysis of 31 : 26 identifies the merismus present there : by mentioning the " brightening, waxing " (*hll*) of the moon in the first colon and its " waning " (*hlk*) in the second colon, the poet encompasses the entire lunar cycle. Further discussion of merismus occurs under 29 : 19 ; 29 : 25 ; 30 : 5 and 8 ; 30 : 16-17 ; 31 : 22-23.

C. Delayed Identification.

As was mentioned above under " The Unity of Job, " this stylistic artifice is not limited to one section of the book, but occurs throughout the Dialogues and at least once in the Elihu Speeches. Appreciation

of this device is key to the interpretation of 30 : 11-15 : the unnamed
enemies who besiege Job in 11-14 are identified in v 15 as the minions
of Mot/Death (*ballāhôt* " Terror "). Recognition of the delayed identification in 31 : 26 (" the light ... the moon, that is ") uncovers the
merismus in this verse, as was discussed in the preceding section (" Merismus "). Further examples of this point of style are noted under
29 : 18 ; 30 : 1 ; 30 : 20-22 ; 31 : 6.

D. The Break-up of Composite Phrases

Job 30 : 3-4 presents a good example of this technique. The
separated elements of the composite phrase *ḥăsar-lāḥem* " the lack of
bread " (2 Sam 3 : 29) placed at the beginning of 30 : 3 (*běḥeser*) and
at the end of v 4 (*lōḥămīm*) act as an inclusion. Another instance
occurs in 31 : 9, in which the phrase *'ēšet rē'î* " the woman (= wife)
of my neighbor " (Ex 20 : 17 ; Lev 19 : 16) is broken up over the two
cola of the verse :

If my heart was deceived by a woman (*'al-'iššâ*)
  and at the door of my neighbor (*rē'î*) I lurked.

See also 30 : 1-2 ; 30 : 18 ; 31 : 11 and 13 ; 31 : 19.

E. Ellipsis

In addition to the forms of ellipsis which Northwest Semitic philology has already widely demonstrated, such as double-duty prepositions
and particles, double-duty suffixes, shared articles, and relative clauses
without morphological indicators, [734] Job 29 – 31 contains two examples
of idiomatic phrases with an ellipsis of one of the elements usually
found in that phrase. *lō' yappîlûn* in 29 : 24 is elliptical for *lō' yappîlûn* (*pānîm*) " they did not grow sad, " and *lî śām 'ēlî* of 31 : 35
omits the *lēb* which is ordinarily a part of the expression (*lî śām* [*lēb*]
'ēlî " that the Most High would pay attention to me ").

IX. Remarks on the Message of Job 29 - 31

A. The Chiastic Structure of 29 – 31

The division into three chapters (29, 30, 31) rather obviously
follows the content of this " Speech of Challenge to God " : [735]

---

[734] See the " Appendix I : A Grammar of Job 29 – 31. "
[735] Cf. Fohrer, " The Righteous Man in Job 31, " p. 6.

Here is summed up all that Job wishes to affirm, before God
and men, regarding his situation and the question of his own
responsibility for it. This renewal of the psalm of lament
develops three themes: past happiness (ch. 29), contrasted
with present misery (ch. 30), followed by the oath (ch. 31)
that he is an innocent man. [736]

Besides the linear progression from one chapter to the next which
appears with a cursory reading of the content of chapters 29 – 31,
a closer examination reveals beneath the surface a chiastic structure,
based on the repetition of words and phrases, which reinforces the note
of hope for an unending life voiced by Job near the beginning (29:
18-20) and repeated toward the end (31: 35-37) of his soliloquy.   The
first and most obvious element in this chiastic structure is the name
of Job (*'iyyôb*) in 29:1 and 31:40c.   *mî-yittĕnēnî* of 29:2 and the
divine name *'ēlî ... šadday* " Most High ... Almighty " in 29:4-5 parallel *mî yitten* and *'ēlî//šadday* of 31:35.   The parallel pair *hll//hlk*
and the *'ôr* " light " – *yārēaḥ* " moon " combination in 31:26 echo
the *hll//hlk* and *yrḥ* " moon/month " ... *'ôr* " light " in 29:2-3.   Finally, the content and vocabulary of 31:16-22 recall that of 29:12-17,
as the following list of words which are common to both passages testifies: *ytm* " orphan, " *'zr* " to rescue, help, " *brk* " to bless, " *'bd* " to
perish, " *'lmnh* " widow, " *lbš* " to clothe, " *'yn* " eye, " *'b* " father, "
'bywn " poor, " and *šbr* " to break, shatter. "   This A–B–A pattern
of chapters 29–30–31 in terms of word repetition underlines the A–B–A
pattern of the content (hope – present experience of suffering – hope)
in these same three chapters.   In 29:18-20 Job expresses the hope
which stood at the center of his former happy life, that his present
felicity was but a sign and foretaste of future glory.   In 31:35-37,
he takes up again the same theme, implying that the *sēper* " indictment " will establish his innocence, not his guilt, and thus serve as
his passport to immortality (" like a prince I would approach him ").
Near the center of the soliloquy, in Job 30:20-23 (45 verses preceding
and 48 verses following), Job bursts out in his only direct address to
the deity in the entire three chapters. Here he uses some of the harsh-
est and most terrifying language in the whole book as his complaint
reaches a high point of intensity and drama. [737]

---

[736] R. A. F. MacKenzie, " Job, " *The Jerome Biblical Commentary* (ed.
R. E. Brown, et al.; Englewood Cliffs, N.J.: Prentice-Hall, 1969), vol. I, p. 526-
527.   See also Driver–Gray, ICC, vol. I, p. 245.

Though his poignant description of his present suffering and his direct anguished cry against God form the core of Job's complaint, they are balanced at the beginning and the end by the note of hope; and the poet subtly reinforces the balance by the chiasmus of words and phrases which moves forward through 29:1-17 and reverses in 31:16-40. Despite the forcefulness of his lament, Job never falls into despair.

B. Chiasmus in Job 31

Chapter 31 exhibits its own chiastic structure, as the following chart indicates:

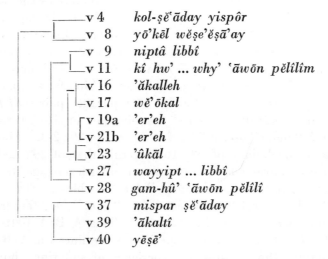

v 4	kol-ṣĕʿāday yispôr
v 8	yō'kēl wĕṣe'ĕṣā'ay
v 9	niptâ libbî
v 11	kî hw' ... why' 'āwōn pĕlîlîm
v 16	'ăkalleh
v 17	wĕ'ōkal
v 19a	'er'eh
v 21b	'er'eh
v 23	'ûkāl
v 27	wayyipt ... libbî
v 28	gam-hû' 'āwōn pĕlîlî
v 37	mispar ṣĕʿāday
v 39	'ākaltî
v 40	yēṣē'

The chiastic pattern focuses on the repetition of the *r'h* almost at the exact center of the chapter (vv 19a and 21b), in the context of Job's disavowal of ever having knowingly (i.e., known through *sight*) failed to help those in distress. This emphasis on *seeing* (*r'h*) may be the poet's artful way of preparing for God's response to Job's challenge, in which Job is reduced to humble silence after having *seen* God for who he really is (Job 42:5-6):

> I had heard of you with the hearing of the ear,
> but now my own eye has seen you (*rā'ătĕkā*);
> Therefore I accept and repent
> upon the dust and ashes. [738]

---

[737] Cf. the discussion in the introduction to the commentary on Job 30: 20-23 above.

[738] For this translation of Job 42:6, see Dahood, *Bib* 55 (1974), p. 382.

C. The Parallel Pairs *hll//hlk* and *ptḥ//lyn*

The parallel pair *hll//hlk* occurs in 29 : 3 (*bĕhillô* " when it shone " // *'elek* " I walked ") and again in 31 : 26 (*yāhēl* " it brightened " //*hōlēk* " waning "). In both verses, *hll* has the sense of " brighten, shine " and refers to the luminous nature of the moon. The context of each verse, however, requires quite a different sense for *hlk*. In 29 : 3, it means simply " to walk, go. " But the stricter parallelism with *hll* " to shine, brighten " (of the moon) in 31 : 26 calls for the translation " to wane " in order to bring out the merismus (*hll* " to wax " // *hlk* " to wane "). The parallel pair *ptḥ//lyn* in 29 : 19 (*pātûaḥ//yālîn*) and 31 : 32 (*yālîn//'eptāḥ*) provides another example of this phenomenon. Although the contexts are quite different, roots " opened out " (*pātûaḥ*) toward water and Job " opening " (*'eptāḥ*) his door to the wayfarer, the poet employs the same word pair. The appearance of a parallel word pair in a verse or passage does not necessarily imply similarity of content or context with other passages in which that same word pair occurs. The use of word pairs served to demonstrate the poet's grasp of the nuances of his language and his skill in utilizing to the fullest the possibilities inherent in it.

It is interesting that these word pairs are repeated, near the beginning of Job's " Challenge to God " (29 : 3,19) and again near the end (31 : 26,32). One is tempted to look for an explanation. In both cases, the activities which these verbs describe (" brighten " // " walk " ; " open " //" lodge ") do not seem to have anything in common, any reason why they should be paired. This problem has a partial solution in the second occurrence of *hll//hlk* in 31 : 26, where the context and parallelism bring out the nuance of " to wane, disappear " in *hlk*. But the activities expressed by *ptḥ* and *lyn* have no obvious connection except that which the creative power of the poet imposes by his skill in the use of the language. Out of the chaotic and disconnected events and activities of human existence, seemingly disparate activities are brought together and make sense together within the context of the poem. The author of Job may be preparing his readers for the message in the Yahweh Speeches. There God affirms, in answer to Job's challenge, that his creative power brings harmony and meaning out of the seemingly chaotic and disconnected happenings in nature, in human history, and in the personal history of each human. Within the context of God's plan every event makes sense and every element has its logical place. Mortal man's vision of this design is limited and incomplete, but God knows what that design is, and that is enough.

D. The Sin of Idolatry

It might be reiterated here what the discussion of 31 : 1-8 brings out, that the first sin of which Job declares himself innocent is idolatry, and not unchaste looks and thoughts, as most commentators would have it.   Twice, then, within this declaration of innocence in Chapter 31, he declares his unswerving loyalty to the one God, in 31 : 1-8 and again in vv 24-28.

Bibliography of Works Cited

Aistleitner, J. *Wörterbuch der ugaritischen Sprache.* Berichte über die Verhand-
lungen der Sächsischen Akademie der Wissenschaften zu Leipzig, Band
106-Heft 3. Berlin : Akademie Verlag, 1963.

Albright, W. F., " The Psalm of Habakkuk, " in *Studies in Old Testament Prophecy.* T. H. Robinson Festschrift, ed. H. H. Rowley. Edinburgh : T. and
T. Clark, 1950, p. 1-18.

——, " Baal-zephon, " in *Festschrift Alfred Bertholet.* Tübingen : Mohr, 1950,
p. 1-14.

——, " Some Canaanite-Phoenician Sources of Hebrew Wisdom, " in *Wisdom
in Israel and in the Ancient Near East* (H. H. Rowley Festschrift), eds.
M. Noth and D. W. Thomas. VTSup 3. Leiden : Brill, 1955, p. 1-15.

——, *Archaeology and the Religion of Israel,* 5th edition. Garden City, N.Y. :
Doubleday Anchor Books, 1969.

——, " The High Place in Ancient Palestine, " VTSup 4 (1957), p. 242-258.

——, " Archaic Survivals in the Text of Canticles, " in *Hebrew and Semitic
Studies. Presented to Godfrey Rolles Driver,* eds. D. Winton Thomas and
W. D. McHardy. Oxford : Clarendon, 1963, p. 1-7.

——, *Yahweh and the Gods of Canaan. A Historical Analysis of Two Contrasting
Faiths.* Garden City, N.Y. : Doubleday Anchor Books, 1969.

Alonso Schökel, Luis, and Ojeda, José Luz. *Job.* Los Libros Sagrados VIII, 2.
Madrid : Ediciones Cristiandad, 1971.

Andersen, Francis I., review of Willibald Kuhnigk's *Nordwestsemitische Studien
zum Hoseabuch,* in *Bib* 57 (1976), p. 573-575.

——, *Job : An Introduction and Commentary.* Tyndale Old Testament Commentaries. Downers Grove, Illinois : Inter-Varsity Press, 1976.

Avishur, Y., " Word Pairs Common to Phoenician and Biblical Hebrew, "
UF 7 (1975), p. 13-48.

Baisas, Bienvenido Q., " Ugaritic '*DR* and Hebrew '*ZR* I, " *UF* 5 (1973),
p. 41-52.

Barré, M. L., " New Light on the Interpretation of Hosea VI 2, " *VT* 28
(1978), p. 129-141.

Baumgartner, Walter. *Hebräisches und aramäisches Lexikon zum Alten Testament,* 2 vols., 3rd edition. Leiden : Brill, 1967, 1974.

Bettenson, Henry, ed. *The Later Christian Fathers.* Oxford Paperbacks 293.
London : Oxford University Press, 1970.

Blommerde, Anton C. M. *Northwest Semitic Grammar and Job.* BibOr 22.
Rome : Pontifical Biblical Institute, 1969.

——, " The Broken Construct Chain, Further Examples, " *Bib* 55 (1974),
p. 549-552.

Boadt, L., " A Re-examination of the Third-Yod Suffix in Job, " *UF* 7 (1975),
    p. 59-72.
Böcher, Otto. *Dämonenfurcht und Dämonenabwehr*: *Ein Beitrag zur Vorge-
    schichte der Christlichen Taufe*. Beiträge zur Wissenschaft vom Alten und
    Neuen Testament 90. Stuttgart: Kohlhammer, 1970.
Bogaert, M., " Les suffixes verbaux non accusatifs dans le sémantique nord-
    occidental et particulièrement en hébreu, " *Bib* 45 (1964), p. 220-247.
Brockington, L. H. *The Hebrew Text of the Old Testament*: *The Readings
    Adopted by the Translators of the New English Bible*. Oxford and Cambridge:
    University Press, 1973.
Brongers, H. A., " Bemerkungen zum Gebrauch des Adverbialen $w^{e'}att\bar{a}h$ im
    Alten Testament, " *VT* 15 (1965), p. 289-299.
Brown, Francis, Driver, S. R., and Briggs, C. A. *A Hebrew and English Lexi-
    con of the Old Testament*. Oxford: Clarendon, 1906.
Burrows, Millar. *The Dead Sea Scrolls of St. Mark's Monastery*: Volume II,
    fascicule 2: Plates and Transcription of the Manual of Discipline. New
    Haven: American Schools of Oriental Research, 1951.
Caquot, A., Sznycer, M., and Herdner, A. *Textes ougaritiques, Tome I*: *Mythes
    et légendes*. Littératures Anciennes du Proche-Orient 7. Paris: Cerf, 1974.
Carmignac, Jean, " Le Complément d'Agent après un Verbe Passif dans l'Hé-
    breu et l'Araméen de Qumrân, " *Revue de Qumran* 9, 35 (1978), p. 409-427.
Cassuto, U. *A Commentary on Exodus*. Translated by Israel Abrahams. Jeru-
    salem: Magnes Press, The Hebrew University, 1967.
— —, *The Goddess Anat*: *Canaanite Epics from the Patriarchal Age*. Translated
    by Israel Abrahams. Jerusalem: Magnes Press, The Hebrew University,
    1971.
Cathcart, Kevin. *Nahum in the Light of Northwest Semitic*. BibOr 26. Rome:
    Biblical Institute Press, 1973.
Cazelles, H., " Positions actuelles dans l'exégèse du Pentateuque, " *De Mari
    à Qumran*: *Festschrift J. Coppens*, ed. H. Cazelles. Bibliotheca Ephemeri-
    dum Theologicarum Lovaniensium 25. Gembloux: J. Duculot, 1969,
    p. 34-57.
Ceresko, A. R., " The A:B::B:A Word Pattern in Hebrew and Northwest
    Semitic, with Special Reference to the Book of Job, " *UF* 7 (1975), p. 73-88.
— —, " The Chiastic Word Pattern in Hebrew, " *CBQ* 38 (1976), p. 303-311.
Christensen, D. L., " Num 21:14-15 and the Book of the Wars of Yahweh, "
    CBQ 36 (1974), p. 359-360.
Clifford, R., " The Tent of El and the Israelite Tent of Meeting, " *CBQ* 33 (1971),
    p. 221-227.
Collins, Terence, " The Physiology of Tears in the Old Testament, " *CBQ* 33
    (1970), p. 18-38, 185-197.
— —, " The Kilamuwa Inscription — a Phoenician Poem, " *Die Welt des Orients*,
    6 (1971), p. 183-188.
Coote, R., " Ugaritic *ph(y)* 'see', " *UF* 6 (1974), p. 1-5.
Cross, F. M., " Leaves from an Epigraphist's Notebook, " *CBQ* 36 (1974),
    p. 486-494.
— —, *Canaanite Myth and Hebrew Epic*. *Essays in the History of the Religion
    of Israel*. Cambridge: Harvard University, 1973.

Cross, F. M., and Saley, R., " Phoenician Incantations on a Plaque from the Seventh Century B.C. from Arslan Tash in Upper Syria, " *BASOR*, 197 (February 1970), p. 42-49.

Dahood, M. J., " The Etymology of *Maltā'ôt* (Ps 58,7), " *CBQ* 17 (1955), p. 300-303.

——, " Some Aphel Causatives in Ugaritic, " *Bib* 38 (1957), p. 62-73.

——, " Some Northwest Semitic Words in Job, " *Bib* 38 (1957), p. 306-320.

——, review of John Steinmann's *Le Livre de Job*, in *Bib* 41 (1960), p. 303.

——, " Qoheleth and Northwest Semitic Philology, " *Bib* 43 (1962), p. 349-365.

——, review of Gillis Gerleman, *Ruth*, in *Bib* 43 (1962), p. 224-5.

——, " Northwest Semitic Philology and Job, " in *The Bible in Current Catholic Thought: Gruenthaner Memorial Volume*, ed. J. L. McKenzie. St. Mary's Theology Studies I. New York: Herder and Herder, 1962, p. 55-74.

——, " An Allusion to Koshar in Ezekiel 33, 34, " *Bib* 44 (1963), p. 531-532.

——, " Hebrew-Ugaritic Lexicography I, " *Bib* 44 (1963), p. 289-303.

——, *Proverbs and Northwest Semitic Philology*. Rome: Pontificium Institutum Biblicum, 1963.

——, " Ugaritic Lexicography, " *Mélanges Eugène Tisserant*, vol. I. Studi e Testi 231. Città del Vaticano, 1964, p. 81-104.

——, review of G. Gerleman *Das Hohelied*, in *Bib* 45 (1964), p. 287-8.

——, " Hebrew-Ugaritic Lexicography II, " *Bib* 45 (1964), p. 393-412.

——, *Ugaritic–Hebrew Philology. Marginal Notes on Recent Publications*. BibOr 17. Rome: Pontifical Biblical Institute, 1965. (*Photomechanical Reproduction* 1976).

——, " Hebrew–Ugaritic Lexicography III, " *Bib* 46 (1965), p. 311-332.

——, *Psalms I*: 1–50, *Introduction, Translation, and Notes*. AB 16. Garden City, N.Y.: Doubleday, 1965.

——, " Hebrew–Ugaritic Lexicography IV, " *Bib* 47 (1966), p. 403-419.

——, " The Phoenician Background of Qoheleth, " *Bib* 47 (1966), p. 264-282.

——, " Congruity of Metaphors, " in *Hebräische Wortforschung. Festschrift Walter Baumgartner*, eds. B. Hartman, et al. VTSup 16. Leiden: Brill, 1967, p. 40-49.

——, " Hebrew–Ugaritic Lexicography V, " *Bib* 48 (1967), p. 421-438.

——, " Nest and Phoenix in Job 29,18, " *Bib* 48 (1967), p. 542-544.

——, " *Ś'RT* ' Storm ' in Job 4,15, " *Bib* 48 (1967), p. 544-5.

——, " Proverbs 8,22-31. Translation and Commentary, " *CBQ* 30 (1968), p. 512-521.

——, " The Phoenician Contribution to Biblical Wisdom Literature, " in *The Role of the Phoenicians in the Interaction of Mediterranean Civilization*, ed. W. A. Ward. Beirut: American University of Beirut, 1968, p. 123-153.

——, " Ugaritic and the Old Testament, " *Ephemerides Theologicae Lovanienses* 44 (1968), p. 35-54.

——, " Hebrew–Ugaritic Lexicography VII, " *Bib* 50 (1969), p. 337-356.

——, " Ugaritic–Hebrew Syntax and Style, " *UF* 1 (1969), p. 15-36.

——, " Hebrew–Ugaritic Lexicography VIII, " *Bib* 51 (1970), p. 391-404.

——, *Psalms III*: 101–150, *Introduction, Translation, and Notes*. AB 17 A. Garden City, N.Y.: Doubleday, 1970.

——, review of *Ugaritica V*, in *Or* 39 (1970), p. 375-379.

——, " Hebrew–Ugaritic Lexicography IX, " *Bib* 52 (1971), p. 337-356.

——, review of *The New English Bible*, in *Bib* 52 (1971), p. 117-123.

——, review of J. Lévêque, *Job et son Dieu. Essai d'exégèse et de théologie biblique*, in *Bib* 52 (1971), p. 436-438.

——, " Phoenician Elements in Isaiah 52 : 13 – 53 : 12, " in *Near Eastern Studies in Honor of William Foxwell Albright*, ed. H. Goedicke. Baltimore/London : Johns Hopkins, 1971, p. 63-73.

——, " The Integrity of Jeremiah 51,1, " *Bib* 53 (1972), p. 542.

——, " Hebrew-Ugaritic Lexicography X, " *Bib* 53 (1972), p. 386-403.

——, " A Note on the Third Person Suffix -*y* in Hebrew, " *UF* 4 (1972), p. 163-164.

——, with the collaboration of Tadeusz Penar, " Ugaritic-Hebrew Parallel Pairs, " in *Ras Shamra Parallels*, Vol. 1, ed. Loren R. Fisher. AnOr 49. Rome : Pontificium Institutum Biblicum, 1972, p. 71-383.

——, " Some Rare Parallel Word Pairs in Job and in Ugaritic, " in *The Word in the World : Essays in Honor of Frederick L. Moriarty, S.J.*, eds. R. J. Clifford and G. W. MacRae. Cambridge : Weston College Press, 1973, p. 19-34.

——, " Hebrew–Ugaritic Lexicography XI, " *Bib* 54 (1973), p. 351-366.

——, " Una coppia di termini ugaritici, " *Bibbia e Oriente* 15 (1973), p. 253-254.

——, *Psalms II* : 51-100, *Introduction, Translation and Notes*. 2nd edition. AB 17. Garden City, N.Y. : Doubleday, 1973.

——, review of Pio Fedrizzi, *Giobbe*, in *Bib* 55 (1974), p. 287-288.

——, " Hebrew–Ugaritic Lexicography XII, " *Bib* 55 (1974), p. 381-393.

——, " Chiasmus in Job : A Text-Critical and Philological Criterion, " in *A Light Unto My Path : Old Testament Studies in Honor of Jacob M. Myers*, eds. H. N. Bream, et al. Philadelphia : Temple University, 1974, p. 119-130.

——, " Northwest Semitic texts and textual criticism of the Hebrew Bible, " *Questions Disputées d'Ancien Testament. Méthode et Théologie*, ed. C. Breckelmans. Bibliotheca Ephemeridum Theologicarum Lovaniensium 33. Gembloux/Louvain : Duculot et Leuven University Press, 1974, p. 11-37.

——, " *Ḥôl* ' Phoenix ' in Job 29 : 18 and Ugaritic, " *CBQ* 36 (1974), p. 85-88.

——, " Ugaritic–Hebrew Parallel Pairs Supplement, " *Ras Shamra Parallels*, vol. II, ed. L. R. Fisher. AnOr 50. Rome : Pontificium Institutum Biblicum, 1975, p. 35-39.

——, " The Emphatic Double Negative *m'yn* in Jer 10 : 6-7, " *CBQ* 37 (1975), p. 458-9.

——, " Jeremiah 5,31 and *UT* 127 : 32, " *Bib* 57 (1976), p. 106-108.

——, review of N. C. Habel, *The Book of Job*, in *Bib* 57 (1976), p. 267-269.

——, review of Michael Sokoloff, *The Targum to Job from Qumran Cave XI*, in *Bib* 57 (1976), p. 269-270.

——, " Hebrew Lexicography : A Review of W. Baumgartner's *Lexikon*, Volume II, " in *Or* 45 (1976), p. 327-365.

——, " Yiphil Imperative *yaṭṭī* in Isaiah 54,2, " *Or* 46 (1977), p. 383-384.

——, " Phoenician–Punic Philology, " *Or* 46 (1977), p. 462-475.

——, " Deuteronomy 33,19 and *UT*, 52 : 61-63, " *Or* 47 (1978), p. 263-264.

——, " Ebla, Ugarit and the Old Testament, " *The Month* (August 1978), p. 271-276.

——, review of L. Grabbe, *Comparative Philology and the Text of Job*, in *Bib* 59 (1978), p. 429-432.

— —, " Ebla, Ugarit and the Old Testament, " *Vetus Testamentum Supplements* 29 (Congress Volume Göttingen 1977; Leiden: Brill, 1978), p. 81-112.

— —, " Stichometry and Destiny in Psalm 23, 4, " *Bib* 60 (1979), p. 417-419.

Das Alte Testament. Einheitsübersetzung der Heiligen Schrift. Stuttgart: Katholischer Bibelanstalt, 1974.

Davies, G. I., " A New Solution to a Crux in Obadiah 7, " *VT* 27 (1977), p. 484-487.

Delitzsch, Franz. *Das Buch Iob*, 2nd edition. Biblischer Commentar über das Alte Testament IV/2, eds. C. F. Keil and F. Delitzsch Leipzig: Dörffling und Francke, 1876.

Dhorme, E., " Ecclésiaste ou Job? " *RB* 32 (1923), p. 5-27.

— —, *Le Livre de Job.* Paris: Lecoffre, 1926.

Dick, Michael Brennan. *Job 31: A Form-critical Study.* Dissertation: The Johns Hopkins University, 1977.

— —, " The Legal Metaphor in Job 31, " *CBQ* 41 (1979), p. 37-50.

Dietrich, M., Loretz, O., Sanmartín, J., " KUN-Š und ŠKN im Ugaritischen, " *UF* 6 (1974), p. 47-53.

— —, and Loretz, O., " Der Prolog des Krt-Epos (CTA 14 I 1-35), " in *Wort und Geschichte: Festschrift für Karl Elliger zum 70. Geburtstag*, eds. H. Gese and H. P. Rüger. AOAT 18. Neukirchen-Vluyn: Neukirchener Verlag, 1973, p. 32-36.

— —, Loretz, O., Sanmartín, J. *Die keilalphabetische Texte aus Ugarit. Einschliesslich der keilalphabetischen Texte ausserhalb Ugarits, Teil 1 Transkription.* AOAT 24. Kevelaer: Butzon und Bercker, 1976.

Dijkstra, M., " A Note on 1 Chr. IV 22-23, " *VT* 25 (1975), p. 671-674.

Di Lella, A. A., review of Tadeusz Penar's *Northwest Semitic Philology and the Hebrew Fragments of Ben Sira*, in *CBQ* 38 (1976), p. 584-586.

Donner, H., and Röllig, W. *Kanaanäische und aramäische Inschriften*, 3 vols., 2nd edition. Wiesbaden: Harrassowitz, 1966-1969.

Driver, Samuel R., and Gray, George B. *A Critical and Exegetical Commentary on the Book of Job*, 2 vols. International Critical Commentary. Edinburgh: T. and T. Clark, 1929.

Driver, G. R. *Canaanite Myths and Legends.* Old Testament Studies 3. Edinburgh: T. and T. Clark, 1956.

Duhm, Bernhard. *Das Buch Hiob.* Kurzer Hand-Kommentar zum Alten Testament. Freiburg, Leipzig, Tübingen: Mohr, 1897.

Epping, O., and Nelis, J. *Job: uit de grondtekst vertaald en uitgelegd.* De Boeken van het Oude Testament, Deel VII/Boek I. Roermond: J. J. Romen & Zonen, 1968.

Fedrizzi, Pio. *Giobbe.* La Sacra Bibbia, ed. S. Garofalo. Torino-Roma: Marietti, 1972.

Fischer, Bonifatio, ed. *Biblia Sancta iuxta Vulgatam Versionem*, 2 vols, 2nd edition. Stuttgart: Württembergische Bibelanstalt, 1975.

Fitzmyer, Joseph, " l^e as a Preposition and a Particle in Micah 5, 1 (5,2), " *CBQ* 18 (1956), p. 10-13.

— —, *The Aramaic Inscriptions of Sefire.* BibOr 19. Rome: Pontifical Biblical Institute, 1967.

Fohrer, Georg. *Das Buch Hiob.* Kommentar zum Alten Testament 16. Gütersloh: G. Mohr, 1963.

——, " The Righteous Man in Job 31, " in *Essays in Old Testament Ethics* (*J. Philip Hyatt, In Memoriam*), eds. J. T. Willis and J. L. Crenshaw. New York : KTAV, 1974, p. 1-22.

Freedman, David Noel, " Orthographic Peculiarities in the Book of Job, " *Eretz-Israel* 9 (William Foxwell Albright Volume ; 1969), p. 35-44.

——, " The Broken Construct Chain, " *Bib* 53 (1972), p. 534-536.

Gaster, Theodor, " A Hang-up for Hang-ups : The Second Amuletic Plaque from Arslan Tash, " *BASOR* 209 (February 1973), p. 18-26.

——, *Thespis : Ritual, Myth and Drama in the Ancient Near East.* New York : Henry Schuman, 1950. New York : Harper Torchbooks, 1966.

Gerleman, G., " Der Nicht-Mensch, Erwägungen zur Hebräischer Wurzel *NBL*, " *VT* 24 (1974), p. 147-158.

Gibson, J. C. L., " Eliphaz the Temanite : Portrait of a Hebrew Philosopher, " *Scottish Journal of Theology* 28 (1975), p. 259-272.

Gilbert, Maurice, " Comment lire les écrits sapientiaux de l'Ancien Testament, " in *Morale et Ancien Testament*, eds. M. Gilbert, et al. Lex Spiritus Vitae I. Louvain-la-Neuve : Centre Cerfaux-Lefort, 1976, p. 131-175.

Ginsberg, H. L. *The Legend of King Keret : A Canaanite Epic of the Bronze Age.* BASOR Supplementary Studies 2-3. New Haven : American Schools of Oriental Research, 1946.

Glasner, Abraham, " Psalm 139 and the Identification of Its Author, " *Beth Mikra* 60 (Jerusalem : Israel Society for Biblical Research, October-December, 1974). English Summary, p. 166.

Goodenough, E. R. *Jewish Symbols in the Greco-Roman Period*, 13 vols. Bollinger Series 37. New York : Pantheon, 1953-1968.

Gordis, Robert. *The Book of God and Man : A Study of Job.* Chicago : University of Chicago Press, 1965.

Gordon, Cyrus H., " Belt-Wrestling in the Bible World, " *Hebrew Union College Annual* 23 (1950-1951), p. 131-136.

——, *Ugaritic Textbook.* AnOr 38. Rome : Pontificium Institutum Biblicum, 1965.

——, *Ugarit and Minoan Crete.* New York : W. W. Norton, 1966.

——, " His Name Is ' One, ' " *Journal of Near Eastern Studies* 29 (1970), p. 198-199.

——, " 1000 Years Before Abraham, " *Midstream* (February 1977), p. 47-52.

Gordon, Cyrus H., and Young, Edward J., " 'g'lty (Isaiah 63 : 3), " *The Westminster Theological Journal* 14 (1951), p. 54.

Grabbe, Lester L. *Comparative Philology and the Text of Job : A Study in Methodology.* Society of Biblical Literature Dissertation Series 34. Missoula, Mont. : Scholars Press, 1977.

Gray, John, " The Massoretic Text of the Book of Job, the Targum and the Septuagint Version in the Light of the Qumran Targum, " *ZAW* 86 (1974), p. 331-350.

——, " A Cantata of the Autumn Festival : Psalm LXVIII, " *JSS* 22 (1977), p. 2-26.

Grelot, P., review of *Le Targum de Job de la Grotte XI de Qumran*, in *Revue de Qumran* 8, 29 (1972), p. 105-114.

Held, Moshe, " The YQTL-QTL (QTL-YQTL) Sequence of Identical Verbs in Biblical Hebrew and in Ugaritic, " in *Studies and Essays in Honor of Abraham A. Neuman*, eds. Meir Ben-Horin, et al. Leiden : Brill, 1962, p. 281-290.

Herdner, Andrée. *Corpus des tablettes en cunéiformes alphabetiques*. Mission de Ras Shamra X, ed. C. F. A. Schaeffer. Paris : Imprimerie Nationale, 1963.

— —, " Remarques sur ' La Déesse 'Anat ', " *Revue des Etudes Sémitiques-Babyloniaca* (1942-1945), p. 33-49.

— —, " Une prière à Baal des Ugaritains en danger, " *Académie des Inscriptions et Belles Lettres* : *Comptes rendus des séances de l'année* 1972, p. 693-703.

Herz, N., " Some Difficult Passages in Job, " *ZAW* 20 (1900), p. 160-163.

Hillers, D. R., review of Lorenzo Viganò's *Nomi e Titoli di YHWH alla Luce del Semitico del Nordovest*, in *CBQ* 39 (1977), p. 576-577.

Holladay, William. *A Concise Hebrew and Aramaic Lexicon of the Old Testament*. Grand Rapids : Eerdmans, 1971.

Holman, Jan, " Analysis of the Text of Psalm 139, " *BZ* 14 (1970), p. 37-71, 198-227.

Huesman, J. " Finite Uses of the Infinitive Absolute, " *Bib* 37 (1956), p. 271-295.

Irwin, W. H. *Isaiah 28 – 33 : A Translation and Philological Commentary*. BibOr 30. Rome : Biblical Institute Press, 1977.

Jeshurun, George, " A Note on Job XXX : 1 (sic), " *Journal of the Society of Oriental Research* 12 (Toronto, 1928), p. 153-154. (The title of this article as it appears in *JSOR* is apparently a misprint and should read, " A Note on Job XXXI : 1. ")

Jongeling, B., " La Colonne XVI de 11Qtg Job, " *Revue de Qumran* 8, 31 (1974), p. 415-416.

— —, Labuschagne, C. J., and van der Woude, A. S., eds. *The Aramaic Texts from Qumran*. Leiden : Brill, 1976.

Joüon, Paul. *Grammaire de l'hébreu biblique*. Rome : Institut Biblique Pontifical, 1923 ; édition photomécanique corrigée, 1965.

— —, " Notes philologiques sur le texte hébreu de Job 1,5 ; 9,35 ; 12,21 ; 28,1 ; 28,27 ; 29,14, " *Bib* 11 (1930), p. 322-324.

Kissane, Edward J. *The Book of Job. Translated from a Critically Revised Hebrew Text with Commentary*. Dublin : Richmond Press, 1939.

Knudtzon, J. A. *Die El-Amarna-Tafeln mit Einleitung und Erläuterungen*. Vorderasiatische Bibliothek 2. Leipzig : Hinrich, 1907-1915.

Koehler, L., and Baumgartner, W. *Lexicon in Veteris Testamenti Libros*. Leiden : Brill, 1953.

Krašovec, Jože. *Der Merismus im Biblisch-Hebräischen und Nordwestsemitischen*. BibOr 33. Rome : Biblical Institute Press, 1977.

Kselman, John S., " Semantic-Sonant Chiasmus in Biblical Poetry, " *Bib* 58 (1977), p. 219-223.

Kuhnigk, W. *Nordwestsemitische Studien zum Hoseabuch*. BibOr 27. Rome : Biblical Institute Press, 1974.

Laurentin, A., " *We'Attāh — Kai Nun*. Formule caractéristique des textes juridiques et liturgiques (à propos de Jean 17,5), " *Bib* 53 (1972), p. 168-197.

Leaney, A. R. C. *The Rule of Qumran and its Meaning. Introduction, Translation and Commentary*. New Testament Library. London : SCM Press, 1966.

Lévêque, Jean, *Job et son Dieu. Essai d'exégèse et de théologie biblique*, 2 vols. Etudes Bibliques. Paris: Lecoffre, 1970.

Lipiński, E., " Le banissement de Yaṣṣib (II Keret VI, 57-58), " *Syria* 50 (1973), p. 38-39.

MacKenzie, R. A. F., " Job, " *The Jerome Biblical Commentary I*, eds. R. E. Brown, et al. Englewood Cliffs, N. J.: Prentice-Hall, 1969, p. 511-533.

McCarthy, Dennis J. *Treaty and Covenant: A Study in Form in the Ancient Oriental Documents and in the Old Testament*, New edition completely rewritten. Analecta Biblica 21A. Rome: Biblical Institute Press, 1978.

McGuire, M. R. P., et al., eds. *New Catholic Encyclopedia*, 15 vols. New York: McGraw-Hill, 1967.

Melamed, E. Z., " Breakup of Stereotype Phrases, " in *Studies in the Bible*, ed. Chaim Rabin. Scripta Hierosolymitana 8. Jerusalem: Magnes, 1961, p. 115-153.

Mendenhall, George. *The Tenth Generation. The Origins of the Biblical Tradition.* Baltimore: Johns Hopkins, 1973.

Meyer, Rudolph, review of *Hebrew and Semitic Studies: Presented to Godfrey Rolles Driver*, in *Orientalistische Literaturzeitung* 62 (1967), col. 371.

——, *Hebräische Grammatik.* Sammlung Göschen, Band 763-765. Berlin: Walter de Gruyter, 1966-1972.

Michaelis, J. D. *Deutsche Uebersetzung des Alten Testament mit Anmerkungen für Ungelehrte: Der Erste Teil Welcher das Buch Hiobs Enthalt.* Göttingen und Gotha, 1773.

Michel, Walter. *The Ugaritic Texts and the Mythological Expressions in the Book of Job.* Dissertation: University of Wisconsin, 1970.

Milik, J. T., review of *Les papyrus araméens d'Hermoupolis et les cultes syrophéniciens en Egypte perse*, in *Bib* 48 (1967), p. 546-622.

Moriarty, Frederick J., " Word as Power in the Ancient Near East, " in *A Light Unto My Path: Old Testament Studies in Honor of Jacob M. Myers*, eds. H. N. Bream, et al. Philadelphia: Temple University, 1974, p. 345-362.

Mowinckel, Sigmund, *He That Cometh.* Translated by G. W. Anderson, Oxford: Blackwell, 1956.

Obermann, J., " An Antiphonal Psalm from Ras Shamra, " *JBL* 55 (1936), p. 21-44.

Oppenheim, A. L., et al., eds. *The Assyrian Dictionary of the Oriental Institute of the University of Chicago.* Chicago/Glückstadt: Oriental Institute/ J. J. Augustin, 1956 ff.

Peake, A. S. *Job.* The Century Bible. London: T. C. and E. C. Jack, 1904.

Peckham, Brian, " The Nora Inscription, " *Or* 41 (1972), p. 457-468.

Penar, Tadeusz. *Northwest Semitic Philology and the Hebrew Fragments of Ben Sira.* BibOr 28. Rome: Biblical Institute Press, 1975.

Peters, Norbert. *Das Buch Job übersetzt und erklärt.* Exegetisches Handbuch zum Alten Testament 21. Münster: Aschendorff, 1928.

Pettinato, G., " Testi Cuneiformi del 3. millennio in paleocananeo rinvenuti nella campagna 1974 a Tell Mardikh-Ebla, " *Or* 44 (1975), p. 361-374.

——, " The Royal Archives of Tell Mardikh-Ebla, " *BA* 39 (1976), p. 44-52.

——, " I testi cuneiformi della biblioteca reale di Tell Mardikh-Ebla: Notizie preliminare sulla scuola di Ebla, " *Rendiconti della Pontificia Accademia Romana di Archeologia* 48 (1975-76), p. 46-57.

— —, " L'Atlante Geografico del Vicino Oriente Antico attestato ad Ebla e ad Abū Ṣalābīkh (I), " *Or* 47 (1978), p. 50-73.

Pettinato, G., and Matthiae, P., " Aspetti amministrativi e topografici di Ebla nel III millennio av. Cr., " *RSO* 50 (1976), p. 1-30.

Pope, Marvin. *El in the Ugaritic Texts.* VTSup 2. Leiden : Brill, 1955.

— —, review of A. C. M. Blommerde, *Northwest Semitic Grammar and Job*, in *Bib* 52 (1971), p. 149-150.

— —, *Job: A New Translation with Introduction and Commentary*, 3rd edition. AB 15. Garden City, N. Y. : Doubleday, 1973.

Prato, Gian Luigi, review of L. Grabbe, *Comparative Philology and the Text of Job*, in *Gregorianum* 60 (1979), p. 173-175.

Prijs, L., " Ein ' Waw der Bekräftigung ' ? " *BZ* 8 (1964), p. 105-109.

Rabin, C. " Three Hebrew Terms from the Realm of Social Psychology, " in *Hebräische Wortforschung. Festschrift Walter Baumgartner*, eds. B. Hartmann, et al. VTSup 16. Leiden : Brill, 1967, p. 219-230.

Rahlfs, Alfred. *Septuaginta*, 2 vols. Stuttgart : Württembergische Bibelanstalt, 1935.

Ringgren, Helmer. *The Faith of the Psalmist.* Philadelphia : Fortress, 1963.

Roth, Wolfgang, " NBL, " *VT* 10 (1956), p. 394-409.

Rowley, H. H. *Job.* The Century Bible, New Series. London : Nelson, 1970.

Sabottka, L., " Is 30,27.33 : Ein Uebersetzungsvorschlag, " *BZ* 12 (1968), p. 241-245.

— —, *Zephanja. Versuch Einer Neuübersetzung mit Philologischen Kommentar.* BibOr 25. Rome : Biblical Institute Press, 1972.

Sarna, N. M., " The Mythological Background of Job 18, " *JBL* 82 (1963), p. 315-318.

Saydon, P., " Assonance in Hebrew as a Means of Expressing Emphasis, " *Bib* 36 (1955), p. 36-50, 287-304.

Segert, Stanislav. *A Grammar of Phoenician and Punic.* Munich : C. H. Beck, 1976.

Seux, M. J. *Epithètes royales akkadiennes et sumériennes.* Paris : Letouzez et Ané, 1967.

Smith, J. M. P., and Goodspeed, E. J. *The Complete Bible : An American Translation.* Chicago : University of Chicago, 1939.

Snaith, N. H. *The Book of Job : Its Origin and Purpose.* Studies in Biblical Theology, Second Series II. London : SCM Press, 1968.

Sokoloff, Michael. *The Targum to Job from Qumran Cave XI.* Ramat-Gan, Israel : Bar-Ilan University, 1974.

Speiser, E. A., " The Stem PLL in Hebrew, " *JBL* 82 (1963), p. 301-306.

Stier, Fridolin. *Das Buch Ijjob : Hebraisch und Deutsch.* München : Kösel, 1954.

Terrien, S., and Scherer, P., " The Book of Job, " *The Interpreters Bible*, vol. 3. New York/Nashville : Abingdon, 1954, p. 877-1198.

Textual Notes on the New American Bible, eds. Louis Hartman and Myles Bourke. Paterson : St. Anthony Guild, 1970.

Traduction oecuménique de la Bible. Paris : Cerf, 1976.

Tromp, Nicolas. *Primitive Conceptions of Death and the Nether World in the Old Testament.* BibOr 21. Rome : Pontifical Biblical Institute, 1969.

Tur-Sinai, N. H. *The Book of Job*: *A New Commentary*, revised edition. Jerusalem: Kiryath Sepher, 1967.

van der Broek, R. *The Myth of the Phoenix According to Classical and Early Christian Traditions*. Etudes préliminaires aux religions orientales dans l'empire roman 24. Leiden: Brill, 1972.

van der Ploeg, J. P. M., et van der Woude, A. S., avec collaboration de B. Jongeling, *Le Targum de Job de la Grotte XI de Qumran*. Leiden: Brill, 1971.

van der Weiden, W. A. *Le Livre des Proverbes. Notes philologiques*. BibOr 23. Rome: Biblical Institute Press, 1970.

van Dijk, H. J. *Ezekiel's Prophecy on Tyre (Ez. 26,1 – 28,19)*: *A New Approach*. BibOr 20. Rome: Pontifical Biblical Institute, 1968.

Vattioni, Francesco. *Ecclesiastico*. *Testo ebraico con apparato critico e versioni greca, latina e siriaca*. Napoli: Istituto Orientale di Napoli, 1968.

Viganò, Lorenzo. *Nomi e titoli di YHWH alla luce del semitico del nord-ovest*. BibOr 31. Rome: Biblical Institute Press, 1976.

Virolleaud, Charles. *La Légende Phénicienne de Danel*. Mission de Ras Shamra 1. Paris: Paul Geuthner, 1936.

Watson, W., " Shared Consonants in Northwest Semitic, " *Bib* 50 (1969), p. 525-533.

— —, " More on Shared Consonants, " *Bib* 52 (1971), p. 44-50.

— —, " Reclustering Hebrew *l'lyd-*, " *Bib* 58 (1977), p. 213-215.

Whitaker, Richard C. *A Concordance of the Ugaritic Literature*. Cambridge: Harvard University, 1972.

Xella, Paolo. *Il Mito di ŠHR e ŠLM. Saggio sulla mitologia ugaritica*. Studi Semitici 44. Rome: Istituto di Studi del Vicino Oriente, Università di Roma, 1973.

Zorell, F., and Semkowski, L. *Lexicon Hebraicum et Aramaicum Veteris Testamenti*. Rome: Pontificium Institutum Biblicum, reeditio photo-mechanica, 1968.

APPENDIX I

A Grammar of Job 29 - 31

I. Orthography

A. Defective spelling

29 : 1 *wysp* for *wyswp* " and (Job) again "
29 : 6 *bḥmh* for *bḥm'h* " with cream "
30 : 2 *k lḥ* (MT *klḥ*) for *ky lḥ* " full vigor "
30 : 3 *' mš* for *'w mš* " or swamp " (MT *'emeš*)
30 : 4 *šrš* for *šršy* " roots "
       lḥmm for *lḥmym* " consuming " (MT *laḥmām* " their food ")
30 : 13 *y'ylw* for *yw'ylw* " they succeed "
30 : 15 *ndbty* for *ndybty* " my dignity "
30 : 19 *hrny* for *hwrny* " he casts me "
30 : 27 *qdmny* for *qdmwny* " confronting me are "
31 : 20 *ḥlṣw* for *ḥlṣyw* " his loins "

B. Single writing of consonants

30 : 19 *w'tmšl k'pr* for *w'tm mšlk 'pr*; reading *wā'ettōm mūšlak 'āpār* " and I perish, flung upon the slime " (MT *wā'etmaš-šēl ke'āpār*)
31 : 40 *b'šh* for *b' 'šh*; reading *bā'ā 'iššāh* " May fire come upon it " (MT *bā'ěšâ*)

II. Phonetics

A. Prothetic aleph

31 : 22 *w'zr'y* " and my arm " (compare *zrw'* in Job 38 : 15 ; 40 : 9)
31 : 23 *'yd* " hand "

B. Interchange of *b* and *p*

    29 : 25 *bāḥar* = *pāḥar* " to gather, assemble "

    31 : 39 *bāʿal* = *pāʿal* " to do, work "

III. Pronouns

A. Third person singular suffix *-y*

    29 : 18 *qinnî* " his nest "

    30 : 18 *kappay* (MT *kĕpî*) " his (two) hands "

    31 : 1 *lĕʿênāy* " in His presence "

    31 : 18 *minnĕʿûrēy* (MT *minnĕʿûray*) " from his youth "

           ʾimmî " his mother "

    31 : 21 *ʿezrātî* " his acquittal "

B. Dative Suffix:

    29 : 16 *ʾeḥqĕrēhû* " I examined for him "

    30 : 9 *nĕgînātām* " a song for them "

    30 : 18 *yĕʾazzĕrēnî* (MT *yaʾazrēnî*) " he loosens from me "

    30 : 22 *ûtĕmōgĕgēnî* " you sweep away from me "

    31 : 18 *guddĕlanî* (MT *gĕdēlanî*) " he was raised by me "

    31 : 33 *kissîtîkā* (MT *kissîtî kĕ*) " I have concealed from you "

    31 : 37 *ʾaggîdennû* " I would tell (to) him "

    31 : 40 *ʾiššāh* (MT *bāʾĕšâ*) " fire upon it "

C. Dative suffix balancing a prepositional phrase:

    29 : 16 *lāʾebyônîm* " to the needy " // *ʾeḥqĕrēhû* " I examined for him "

    30 : 9 *nĕgînātām* " a song for them " // *lāhem* " to them "

IV. Nouns

A. Phoenician singular in *-ot*:

    30 : 15 *ballāhôt* " Terror "

    31 : 36 *ʿăṭārôt* " crown "

B. Free interchange of plural in *-m* and *-n*:

    31 : 10 *ʾăḥērîn* " others " (cf. *ʾăḥērîm* in Job 34 : 24)

C. Nouns appearing in both masculine and feminine genders:

31 : 23 masculine *'êd* ' hand " (+ *pāḥad* " is a dread ") for usually
         feminine *yād*
31 : 33 masculine *'ādām* " earth " for usually feminine *'ădāmâ*
31 : 34 feminine *hāmôn* " clamor " (+ *rabbâ*) for usually masculine
         hāmôn (cf. Isa 16 : 14, etc.)

V. Verbs

A. Denominatives:

30 : 11 *wî'înūnî* (MT *wayĕ'annēnî*) " (they) eye me "
30 : 12 *rōgĕlay* (MT *raglay*) " who spy on me "

B. Passive qal:

30 : 1   *lāšît* " to be set "

C. Privative piel:

30 : 18 *yĕ'azzĕrēnî* (MT *ya'azrēnî*) " he loosens from me "

D. Infinitive absolute used finitely:

30 : 15 *hahăpōk* (MT *hohpak*) " (Terror) turns "

E. Shaphel:

30 : 21 *tašaṭminnî* (MT *tiśṭĕmēnî*) " you make me take cover "

F. Participle in *ō – a*:

31 : 32 *lā'ōraḥ* " to the traveller "

G. Preservation of final *-y*:

30 : 14 *y'tyw* " they come "
31 : 38 *ybkywn* " they wept "

H. The energic mood:

31 : 18 *'anḥennâ* " I guided him "

VI. Prepositions

A. The preposition *lĕ*:

   1. comparative *lĕ*
      30 : 1   *lāšît* " (too poor) to be set "

   2. " from "
      30 : 13   *lāmô* " from them "
      31 : 27   *lĕpî* " from my mouth "

   3. " upon "
      30 : 19   *laḥōmer* " upon the mud "

B. The preposition *min*:

   1. local
      31 : 28   *mimmāʿal* " on high "

   2. partitive
      31 : 16   *mēḥēpeṣ* " any desire "
      31 : 17   *mimmennâ* " (none) of it "

C. The preposition *ʿal*

   1. " from "
      29 : 7   *ʿălê-qāret* " from the city "
      30 : 2   *ʿālêmô* " from them "
      30 : 4   *ʿălê-śîaḥ* " from the bush "
      30 : 16   *ʿālay* " from me "

   2. " before, in the presence of "
      29 : 13   *ʿālay* " (entered) my presence "

   3. " by " (agency with a passive verb)
      31 : 9   *ʿal-ʾiššâ* " (lured) by a woman "

D. The preposition *ʿim*:

   1. " as, like "
      29 : 18   *ʿim-qinnî* " like its nest "

   2. " toward "
      31 : 5   *ʿim-šāwʾ* " toward an idol "

E. The preposition *taḥat* = " among, amidst "

      30 : 7   *taḥat ḥārûl* " amidst the nettles "
      30 : 14   *taḥat šōʾâ* " amidst the havoc "

VII. Particles

A. Emphatic *lū'* (MT *lō'*)

31 : 31   *lū'* (MT *lō'*) *niśbā'* " O that we might feast "

B. waw

1. emphatic waw
    30 : 4   *wĕšoršē* (MT *wĕšōreš*) " the very roots "
    31 : 1   *ûmâ* " never would I "
    31 : 30 *wĕlō'* " I have never "
2. *waw explicativum*
    29 : 12 *wĕlō' 'ōzēr lô* " who had no deliverer "
    31 : 26 *wĕyārēaḥ* " the moon, that is "

C. *kî* :

1. emphatic *kî*
    30 : 2   *kī lēaḥ* (MT *kālaḥ*) " full vigor "
2. *kî* = " if "
    31 : 14 *kî-yiqqôm* (MT *yāqûm*) " if (God) punished "
            kî-yipqōd " if he called to account "
    31 : 34 *kî 'e'ĕrôṣ* " if I feared "

D. Negative *mâ* :

31 : 1   *ûmâ* " I have never "

E. The conjunction *pa* " and "

30 : 12 *pĕraḥâ* (MT *pirḥaḥ*) " and left (hand) "

F. Enclitic mem :

31 : 11 *pĕlîlî*-m (MT *pĕlîlîm*) " criminal "

VIII. Syntax and Poetic Devices

A. Omission of the suffix with names of parts of the body :

30 : 12 *'al-yāmîn* " on my right "

B. Concrete sense of abstract nouns :

29 : 6   *hălîkay* " my foot "
          'ămmūday (MT *'immādî*) " my legs "

31 : 5   *šāw'* " an idol "
         mirmâ " a fraud "
31 : 7   *'aššūrî* " my foot "

C. Break-up of stereotyped phrases:

'ābîkā yāmîm " your aged father "
    Jointly: Job 15 : 10
    Separately: Job 30 : 1 *lěyāmîm ... 'ăbôtām*
'ēšet rē'ekā " the wife of your neighbor "
    Jointly: Ex 20 : 17; Lev 20 : 10; etc.
    Separately: Job 31 : 9 *'iššâ ... rē'î*
birkat 'ōbēd " the blessing of one perishing "
    Jointly: Job 29 : 13
    Separately: Job 31 : 19-20 *'ôbēd ... bērăkûnî*
ḥăsar-laḥem " one who lacks bread "
    Jointly: 2 Sam 3 : 29
    Separately: Job 30 : 3-4 *běḥeser ... lōḥămīm* (MT *laḥmām*)
ṣě'îrê haṣṣō'n " the little ones of the flock "
    Jointly Jer 49 : 20; 50 : 45
    Separately: Zech 13 : 7 *haṣṣō'n//haṣṣō'ărîm*
                  Job 30 : 1 *ṣě'îrîm ... ṣō'nî*
rāb-kōaḥ " great force "
    Jointly: Job 30 : 18
    Separately: Josh 17 : 17 *rab//kōaḥ*
tdmm amht " maidservants' lewdness "
    Jointly: *UT* 51 III : 20-22
    Separately: Job 31 : 11-13 *zimmâ ... wa'ămātî*

D. Conditional sentence without a morphological indicator:

31 : 6   *yišqělēnî* " should he weigh me "

E. Relative clause without *'ăšer*:

29 : 16   *wěrib lō'-yāda'tî* " and the cause of one whom I did not
        know "

F. Ellipsis:

    1. double-duty suffix
        29 : 11   *šāmě'â* " heard me "//*wattě'aššěrēnî* " blessed me "
        29 : 14   *wayělabběšēnî* (MT *wayyilbāšēnî*) " adorned me "//
                 me'îl " my robe "//*ṣānîp* " my tartan "

30 : 11   *petaḥ* (MT *pittaḥ*) " my door "//*mippānay* " my presence "

31 : 18   *minnĕʿûrēy* (MT *minnĕʿûray*) " from his youth "// *kĕʾāb* " as by his father "

ʾimmî " his mother "//*ʾanḥennâ* " I guided him "

2. double-duty prepositions

   a.   *bĕ*

      29 : 6   *bĕḥēmâ wĕṣôrî* (MT *wĕṣûr*) " with cream and balsam "//*ṣôq* (MT *yāṣûq*) " when (rivers of oil) flowed "

      30 : 6   *baʿărûṣ nĕḥālîm* " in the most dreaded of ra-vines "//*ḥōrê ʿāpār wĕkēpîm* " in the holes of the ground and rocks "

      30 : 18   *bĕrāb-kōaḥ* " with great force "//*kappay* (MT *kĕpî*) " with his hands "

      31 : 33   *ʾādām* " in the Earth "//*bĕḥubbî* " in Hades "

   b.   *lĕ*

      29 : 23   *māṭār* " for the rain "//*lĕmalqôš* " for the spring rain "

      30 : 19   *laḥōmer* " upon the mud "//*ʿāpār wāʾēper* " upon the slime and ashes "

3. double-duty particles

   a.   *kĕ*

      29 : 23   *kammāṭār* " as for the rain "//*lĕmalqôš* " as for the spring rain "

   b.   *lōʾ*

      30 : 20   *wĕlōʾ taʿănēnî* " you answer me not "//*watittbōnen* " you ignore me "

   c.   *ʾim-lōʾ*

      30 : 25   *ʾim-lōʾ bākîtî* " did I not weep "//*ʿāgĕmâ* " did not (my soul) grieve "

4. extension of the idiom of the double-duty suffix

   31 : 14   *ʾeʿĕśeh* " I do "//*yiqqōm* (MT *yāqûm*) " (he) punished me "

yipqōd " he called me to account "//*ʾăśîbennû* " I answer him "

5. ellipsis of one element in a set expression

   29 : 24   *lōʾ yappîlûn* (*pĕnêhem*) " they did not grow sad "

31 : 35   *lî śim (lēb) 'ēlî* (MT *lî šōmēa' lî*) " the Most High
        would pay attention to me "

6. shared article

30 : 4   *haqqōṭĕpîm* " plucking " // *lōḥămîm* (MT *laḥmām*) " con-
        suming "

G. Delayed identification

29 : 18   *qinnî ... ḥôl* " his nest ... the phoenix "
30 : 1   *śāḥăqû ... ṣĕ'îrîm mimmennî lĕyāmîm* " they deride me ...
        men younger than I "
30 : 11-15   *yātūrû* (MT *yitriw*) " they watch " ... *wî'înūnî* (MT
        wayĕ'annēnî) " they eye me " ... *šilllēḥû* " they cast
        off " ... *yāqûmû* " (they) rise up " ... *šūllĕḥû* (MT *šilllēḥû*)
        " they are unrestrained " ... *wayyāsōllû* " (they) heap
        up " ... *nātĕsû* " they break up " ... *yō'îlû* " they suc-
        ceed " ... *ye'ĕtāyû* " they come " ... *hitgalgālû* " they ar-
        rive " ... *hahăpōk* (MT *hohpak*) " turns " ... *ballāhôt*
        " Terror "
30 : 20-22   *'ēlêkā* " to you " ... *ta'ănēnî* " you answer me " ... *watit-
        bōnen* " you ignore " ... *tēhāpēk* " you have become "
        ... *tašaṭminnî* (MT *tiśṭĕmēnî*) " you make me take cover "
        ... *tiśśā'ēnî 'ēl* (MT *'el*) " you lift me up, O God "
31 : 6   *yišqĕlēnî* " should he weigh me " ... *wĕyēda' 'ĕlôah* " God
        would know "
31 : 26   *'ôr* " the light " ... *wĕyārēaḥ* " the moon, that is "

H. Distant parallelism :

30 : 1,9   *śāḥăqû* " they deride " ... *nĕgînātām* " a song for them "
        Compare Lam 3 : 14 *śĕḥōq* " a joke " // *nĕgînātām* " a
        song for them "
30 : 18,21   *rāb* " great " ... *'ōṣem* " powerful "
        Compare *UT* 'nt I : 12 and Isa 31 : 1 *rb* " large " // *'ẓm*
        " mighty " (*RSP* I,II,516)
        kōaḥ " force " ... *'ōṣem* " powerful "
        Compare Deut 8 : 17 *kōḥî wĕ'ōṣem yādî* " my power and
        the might of my hand "

I. *casus pendens* :

30 : 2   *gam-kōaḥ yĕdêhem lāmmâ lî* " Yes, the strength of their
        hands — what is it to me ? "

J. Anticlimactic parallelism:

    29 : 2   *kĕyarḥê-qedem* " as in months past "//*kîmê* " as in the days "

K. Repetition:

    1. repetition of the same root in the same verse

        29 : 14 *lābaštî wayĕlabbĕšēnî* (MT *wayyilbāšēnî*) " I put on (righteousness) and it adorned me "

        31 : 37 *'aggîdennû* " I would tell him " ... *nāgîd* " prince "

    2. repetition of the same root as inclusion

        29 : 1, 31 : 40 *'iyyôb* " Job "//*'iyyôb* " Job "

        29 : 3,25   *rō'šî* " my head "//*rō'š* " leader "

        30 : 25,31 *bākîtî* " did I (not) weep "//*bōkîm* " weepers "

        31 : 19,21 *'er'eh* " I saw "//*'er'eh* " I saw "

        31 : 16,23 (paronomasia) *'ăkalleh* " (I) caused to fail "// *'ûkāl* " I could (not) bear "

L. Merismus:

    29 : 7   *bĕṣē'tî śō'ēr* (MT *ša'ar*) " when I went storming "// *'ākîn môšābî* " (I) set up my seat "

    29 : 19   *māyim* " waters "//*ṭal* " dew "

    29 : 25   *wĕ'ēšēb rō'š* " (I) presided as leader "//*wĕ'eškôn* " I tented as king "//*kĕ'āšēr* (MT *ka'ăšer*) ... *yĕnaḥēm* " as a happy man who consoles "

    30 : 5,8   *gēw* " community "//*hā'āreṣ* " the town "

    30 : 16-17 *yĕmê* " days "//*laylâ* " at night "

    31 : 8   *'ezrĕ'â* " I sow "//*yō'kēl* " (another) eat " *'ezrĕ'â* " I sow "//*yĕšōrāšû* " be uprooted "

    31 : 10   *tiṭḥan* ... *'ištî* " may my wife grind "//*wĕ'ālêhā yikrĕ'ûn* " over her may (others) bend "

    31 : 22-23 *tippôl* " fall "//*ûmiśśĕ'ētô* " and the raising of it "

    31 : 26   *yāhōl* " it brightened "//*hōlēk* " waning "

M. Chiasmus:

    29 : 2   *yittĕnēnî* " (who) would give me ": *kĕyarḥê* " as in months ":: *kîmê* " as in the days ": *yišmĕrēnî* " (God) protected me "

    29 : 2-4 *kîmê 'ĕlôah* " as in the days when God ": *nērô* " his lamp ":: *'ôrô* " his light ": *bîmê* ... *'ĕlôah* " as in the days (when) God "

29:21-23   *lî* " to me ": *wěyiḥĕllû* " and (they) waited " :: *wěyi-*
           ḥălû " they waited " : *lî* " for me "

30:4   *haqqōṭĕpîm* " plucking " : *mallûaḥ* " mallow " :: *wĕšorš̄e*
           rĕtāmîm " the very roots of the broom " : *lōḥămîm* (MT́
           laḥmām) " consuming "

30:15-16   *hahăpōk* (MT *hohpak*) " turns " : *ālay* " on me " :
           kārûaḥ " like the wind " :: *kĕ'āb* " like a cloud " : *ālay*
           " from me " : *ti štappēk* " is drained "

30:27   *mē'ay* " my insides " : *rūttĕḥû* " seethe " :: *qiddĕmūnî*
           " are confronting me " : *yĕmê-'ōnî* " days of afflic-
           tion "
           mē'ay : *dāmmû* :: *qiddĕmūnî* : *yĕmê-'ōnî* (*mē* ... ' : *d* ... *mû*
           :: *d* ... *mû* : *mē* ... ')

31:9   *niptâ libbî* " (if) my heart has been lured " : *'al* " by "
           :: *'al* " at " : *petaḥ rē'î* " my neighbor's door "

31:14   *ûmâ* " then what " : *kî* " if " :: *kî* " if " : *mâ* " what "

31:15   *hallē'* (MT *hălō'*) " the Victor " : *babbeṭen* " in the
           belly " : *'āśāhû* " he made him " :: *wayĕkūnennû* " and
           he created us " : *bāreḥem* " in the womb " : *'eḥād* " the
           Unique "

31:16-17   *mēḥēpeṣ* " any desire " : *'ăkalleh* " (I) caused to fail " ::
           wĕ'ōkal " while I ate " : *mimmennâ* " (none) of it "

N. The Verb *qwm*:

1. *qwm* + subjuntive to express purpose
    30:28 *qamtî baqqāhāl 'ăšawwēa'* " I rise in the assembly to
    cry for help "

2. *qwm* as an auxiliary verb to express inchoate action
    29:8 *wîšîšîm qāmû 'āmādû* " the elders began to stand up "

O. " Gathering up " of words in one verse which have appeared
    separately in previous verses:

    31:7 *haddārek* " the way " (= v 4 *dĕrākāy* " my ways "), *'ênay*
    " my eyes " (= v 1 *lĕ'ēnāy* " in His presence "), *hālak*
    " followed " (= v 5 *hālaktî* " I have walked ")

APPENDIX II

Parallel Word Pairs

I. Ugaritic-Hebrew Parallel Pairs in Job 29 - 31

abl ... *bky* " to mourn " ... " to weep "
  Job 30 : 31 *'ēbel* / / *bōkîm*

UT 1 Aqht 163-172 ; Gen 37 : 35 ; Deut 34 : 8 ; 2 Sam 19 : 2 ; Esth 4 : 3 ; Neh 8 : 9

aḫ / / *r'* " brother " / / " friend "
  Job 30 : 29 *'āḫ* / / *wĕrēa'*

RSP I,II,18

uḫryt / / *aṯryt* " afterlife " / / " happiness "
  Job 31 : 7 *'aššūrî* ... *'aḫar*

UT 2 Aqht VI : 35-36

akl / / *akl* " to eat " / / " to eat "
  Job 31 : 17 *wĕ'ōkal* / / *'ākal*

RSP I,II,23

akl / / *ḥṭt* " grain " / / " wheat "
  Job 31 : 39-40 *'ākaltî* ... *ḥiṭṭâ*

RSP I,II,25

akl / / *kly* " to eat " / / " to consume "
  Job 31 : 16-17 *'ăkalleh* + *wĕ'ōkal*

RSP I,II,26

almnt / / *ytm* " widow " / / " orphan "
  Job 31 : 16-17 *'almānâ* ... *yātôm*

RSP I,II,40

um ... *ab* " mother " ... " father "
  Job 31 : 18 *kĕ'āb* / / *'immî*

RSP I,II,47

an / / *ank* " I " / / " I "
  Job 29 : 15-16 *'ānî* ... *'ānōkî*

RSP I,II,51

ar + *yrḫ* " to shine " + " moon "
  Job 29 : 2-3 *kĕyarḫê* ... *lĕ'ôrô*
  Job 31 : 26 *'ôr* / / *wĕyārēaḫ*

RSP, I,II,59

bky / / *'gm* " to weep " / / " to grieve "
  Job 30 : 25 *bākîtî* / / *'āgĕmâ*

UT Krt 26-27

dl ... *ytm* " the poor " ... " the orphan "
  Ps 82 : 3 *dal* / / *yātôm*
  Job 31 : 16-17 *dal* ... *yātôm*

UT 127 : 48-49

dl//ytm//almnt " the poor "//" the orphan "   *RSP*, I,II,153
   //" the widow "
   Job 31 : 16-17 *dallîm//'almānâ//yātôm*

dr'//akl " to sow "//" to eat "   *RSP* II,I,15
   Job 31 : 8 *'ezrě'â//yō'kēl*

hlk ... ḥwš " to walk " ... " to hurry "   *UT* 'nt x IV : 7;
   Job 31 : 5 *hālaktî//wataḥaš*   51 VI : 16-18

yṣq//rḥṣ " to pour "//" to wash "   *RSP* I,II,253
   Job 29 : 6 *birḥōṣ//ṣôq* (MT *yāṣûq*)

yrḥ//ym " month "//" day"   *RSP* I,II,258
   Job 29 : 2 *kěyarḥê//kîmê*

ytm//almnt " orphan "//" widow "   *RSP* I,II,262
   Job 29 : 12-13 *yātôm ... 'almānâ*

ytn//ytn " to give "//" to give "   *RSP* I,II,264
   Job 31 : 30-31 *nātattî ... yittēn*

ktb + spr " to write " + " tablet "   *RSP* I,II,308
   Job 31 : 35 *sēper + kātab*

ktp//bn ydm " shoulder "//" between the   *RSP* II,I,29
   hands " (= " breast " or " back ")
   Job 31 : 21-22 *yādî ... kětēpî*

l//l " to, for "//" to, for "   *RSP* I,II,316
   Job 29 : 15 *lě//lě*

l//lm " to "//" to "   *RSP* I,II,318
   Job 29 : 21 *lî//lěmô*

lb ... aṭr " heart " ... " toward "   *UT* 49 II : 8-9,29-30;
   Job 31 : 7 *'aššūrî//libbî*   Pss 37 : 31; 44 : 19;
        Qoh 7 : 26

lb ... p " heart " ... " mouth "   *UT* 1001 : 3-4
   Jer 23 : 16 *libbām//mippî*
   Job 31 : 27 *libbî ... lěpî*

lbš//ktnt " garment "//" tunic "   *RSP* I,II,330
   Job 30 : 18 *lěbûšî//kūtāntî*

lbš//lbš " to don "//" to don "   *RSP* I,II,331
   Job 29 : 14 *lābaštî//wayělabběšēnî*
   (MT *wayyilbāšēnî*)

lpš ... ksy " garment " ... " to cover "   *RSP* I,II,339
   Job 31 : 19 *lěbûš//kěsût*

lpš ... mizrtm " tunic " ... " double girdle "   *RSP* I,II,340
   Job 30 : 18 *lěbûšî ... yě'azzěrēnî*
   (MT *ya'azrēnî*)

my//*ṭl* " water "//" dew "	*RSP* I,II,352
Job 29:19 *māyim*//*ṭal*	
mlk//*drkt* " kingship "//" dominion "	*RSP* I,II,359
Job 29:25 *darkām* ... *kĕmelek*	
mlk//*yṯb* " to reign "//" to sit enthroned "	*RSP* I,II,360
Job 29:25 *wĕ'ēšēb* ... *kĕmelek*	
mǵy//*ytn* " to reach, obtain "//" to give "	*RSP* II,I,37
Job 31:29-30 *mĕṣā'ô* ... *nātattî*	
mt//*ḥyy* " to die "//" to live "	*RSP* I,II,372
Job 30:23 *māwet*//*ḥāy*	
'bd//*bn amt* " slave "//" son of a hand-maid "	*RSP* I,II,404
Job 31:13 *'abdî*//*wa'ămātî*	
'ḏr + yd " to liberate " + " hand "	*RSP* II,I,46
Job 31:21 *yādî* ... *'ezrātî*	
'yn ... *pn(m)* " to eye " ... " face "	*UT* 'nt IV : 83-84
Jer 16:17 *'ênay*//*millĕpānāy*	
Job 30:11 *wi'înūnî* (MT *wayĕ'annēnî*) ...	
mippānay	
'yn//*rḥq* " to eye "//" to be distant "	*UT* 'nt IV : 83-84
Job 30:10-11 *rāḥăqû* ... *wi'înūnî* (MT *wayĕ-*	
'annēnî)	
'yn//*twr* " to eye "//" to watch "	*UT* 76 II : 27-28
Job 30:11 *yatūrû* (MT *yitriw*)//*wi'înūnî*	
(MT *wayĕ'annēnî*)	
'l//*'l* " upon "//" upon "	*RSP* I,II,418
Job 31:9 *'al*//*'al*	
'ny ... *byn* " to answer " ... " to perceive "	UT 51 V : 120-122
Job 30:20 *ta'ănēnî*//*wattitbōnen*	
pnm ... *ymn* " face " ... " right hand "	*RSP* I,II,461
Job 30:11-12 *mippānay* ... *yāmîn*	
qrt//*ṯbt* " city "//" residence "	*UT* 51 VII : 11-13 (//
Job 29:7 *qāret* ... *môšābî*	*UT* 67 II : 15-16)
rkb//*nša* " to mount "//" to lift up "	*UT* Krt 74-75 (165-
Job 30:22 *tiśśā'ēnî*//*tarkibēnî*	168)
šmn//*ẓrw* " oil "//" balsam "	*RSP* I,II,561
Job 29:6 *wĕṣôrî* (MT *wĕṣûr*)//*šāmen*	
šm' ... *udn* " to hear " ... " ear "	*RSP* I,II,565
Job 29:11 *'ōzen + šāmĕ'â*	
tḥt//*tḥt* " under "//" under "	*RSP* I,II,591
Job 31:40 *taḥat*//*taḥat*	

ṭbr//*npl* " to break "//" to fall "   *UT* 137 : 7-9
   Job 31 : 22 *tippôl*//*tiššābēr*
ṭql ... *mzn* " shekel " ... " weight "   *RSP* I,II,606
   Job 31 : 6 *yišqĕlēnî* ... *bĕmō'zĕnê*

II. Phoenician-Hebrew Parallel Pairs in Job 29 - 31

zr' ... *šrš* " descendant " ... " offspring "   *KAI* 43 : 15-16
   Job 31 : 8 *'ezrĕ'â*//*yĕšōrāšû*
ym//*yrḥ* " day "//" month "   *KAI* 43 : 10-12
   Job 29 : 2 *kĕyarḥê*//*kîmê*
'n ... *pn* " eye " ... " face "   *KAI* 10 : 10-16
   Jer 16 : 17 *'ênay*//*millĕpānāy*
   Job 30 : 11 *wi'înūnî* (MT *wayĕ'annēnî*) ...
      mippānay

III. Hebrew Parallel Pairs in Job 29 - 31

'bl//*bkh* " mourning "//" to weep "   Gen 37 : 35 ; Deut 34 :
   Job 30 : 31 *'ēbel*//*bōkîm*   8 ; 2 Sam 19 : 2 ; Esth
                                                          4 : 3 ; Neh 8 : 9
'zn//*'yn* " ear "//" eye "   Job 13 : 1 ; 28 : 21-22 ;
   Job 29 : 11 *'ōzen*//*'ayin* (MT *'ayn*)   42 : 5
'kl//*nph* " to eat "//" to breathe "   Job 20 : 26
   Job 31 : 39 *'ākaltî*//*hippāḥtî*
'kl//*šrš* " to eat, devour "//" to uproot "   Job 36 : 30-31
   Job 31 : 8 *yō'kēl*//*yĕšōrāšû*
   Job 31 : 12 *tō'kēl*//*tĕšārēš*
'rḥ//*ntybh* " way "//" path "   Judg 5 : 6 (*nĕtîbôt*//
   Job 30 : 12-13 *'orḥôt* ... *nĕtîbātî*   *'ŏrāḥôt*) ; Job 19 : 8
'šh//*ptḥ* " wife "//" door "   Judg 14 : 15 ; Prov 9 :
   Job 31 : 9 *'iššâ*//*petaḥ*   13
'šr//*brk* " to pronounce happy "//" to bless "   Ps 72 : 17 (*wĕyitbārĕkû*
   Job 29 : 11-13 *watĕ'aššĕrēnî* ... *birkat*   //*yĕ'aššĕrûhû*)
byn//*tḥt* " between "//" among "   Ezek 10 : 2
   Job 30 : 7 *bên*//*taḥat*
gm//*ky* " and "//" indeed "   Job 13 : 16 ; 40 : 14
   Job 30 : 2 *gam*//*kî* (MT *klḥ*)
   Job 31 : 28 *gam*//*kî*

gr//*'rḥ* " stranger " // " traveler "   Jer 14 : 8
   Job 31 : 32 *gēr*//*'ōraḥ*
grš//*škn* " to drive out " // " to settle "   Gen 3 : 24 (*wayĕgāreš*
   Job 30 : 5-6 *yĕgōrāšû* ... *liškōn*   // *wayyaškēn*) ; Ps 78 :
      55

drk//*ṣ'd* " way " // " step "   Ps 37 : 23 ; Job 34 : 21 ;
   Job 31 : 4 *dĕrākāy*//*ṣĕ'āday*   Prov 16 : 9 ; 20 : 24
hlk//*pth* " to walk " // " to entice "   Hos 2 : 16 (*mĕpatêhā*//
   Job 31 : 26-27 *hōlēk* + *wayyipt*   *wĕhōlaktîhā*) ; Prov 1 :
      10-11 ; 16 : 29

hll//*hlk* " to shine " // " to walk "
   Job 29 : 3 *bĕhillô*//*'ēlek*
   Job 31 : 26 *yāhēl*//*hōlēk*
zhb//*ktm* " gold " // " fine gold "   Job 28 : 16-17 ; Prov
   Job 31 : 24 *zāhāb*//*ketem*   25 : 12 ; Lam 4 : 1
z'q//*bkh* " to cry out " // " to weep "   Job 16 : 16-18
   Job 31 : 38 *tiz'āq*//*yibkāyûn*
zr'//*yṣ'* " to sow " // " to come out "   Isa 44 : 3 (*zar'ekā*//
   Job 31 : 8 *'ezrĕ'â* ... *wĕṣe'ĕṣā'ay*   *ṣe'ĕṣā'êkā*) ; 48 : 19 ;
      61 : 9 ; 65 : 23 ; Job 5 :
      25 ; 21 : 8

ḥlq//*nḥlh* " allotment " // " heritage "   Job 20 : 29 ; 27 : 13
   Job 31 : 2 *ḥēleq*//*wĕnaḥălat*
ḥm'h//*šmn* " cream " // " oil "   Ps 55 : 22
   Job 29 : 6 *bĕḥēmâ*//*šāmen*
ḥmr//*'pr* " mud " // " dust "   Job 4 : 19 ; 10 : 9 ; 27 :
   Job 30 : 19 *ḥōmer*//*'āpār*   16
yḥl//*dmm* " to wait " // " to keep silent "   Ps 37 : 7 ; 131 : 2-3 ;
   Job 29 : 21 *wĕyiḥēllû*//*wĕyiddĕmû*   Lam 3 : 26
   Job 30 : 26-27 *wa'ăyaḥălâ* ... *dāmmû*
yšb//*škn* " to sit " // " to dwell "   Job 15 : 28
   Job 29 : 25 *wĕ'ēšēb*//*wĕ'eškôn*
kwḥ//*kp* " strength " // " palm "   Judg 6 : 14
   Job 30 : 18 *kōaḥ*//*kāppay* (MT *kĕpî*)
kwḥ//*npš* " strength " // " soul, life "   Job 6 : 11
   Job 31 : 39 *kōḥāh*//*wĕnepeš*
knr//*'gb* " harp " // " flute "   Gen 4 : 21 ; Job 21 : 12
   Job 30 : 31 *kinnōrî*//*wĕ'ūgābî*
ksl//*mbṭḥh* " confidence " // " security "   Job 8 : 14
   Job 31 : 24 *kislî*//*mibṭaḥî*

lb//*yd* " heart "//" hand "
   Job 31 : 27 *libbî*//*yādî*

      Ex 7 : 3-4 ; Isa 66 : 14 ;
      Ezek 21 : 12 ; 22 : 14 ;
      Hos 7 : 5-6 ; etc.

mn'//*klh* " to withhold "//" to waste away "
   Job 31 : 16 *'emna*' //*'ăkalleh*

      Ezek 31 : 15

ndbh//*yš*'*h* " dignity "//" prosperity "
   Job 30 : 15 *nĕdībātî*//*yĕšū*'*ātî*

      Ps 51 : 14

nhh//'*bd* " to lead "//" to perish "
   Job 31 : 18-19 *'anhennâ* ... *'ôbēd*

      Job 12 : 23 (*wayĕ*'*ab-*
      bĕdēm//*wayyanhēm*)

nhl//'*pr* " ravine "//" ground, dust "
   Job 30 : 6 *nĕhālîm* ... '*āpār*

      Job 22 : 24 ('*āpār*//
      nĕhālîm)

npl//*nś*' " to fall "//" to lift up "
   Job 31 : 22-23 *tippôl* ... *ûmiśśĕ*'*ētô*

      Ps 106 : 26 (*wayyiśśā*'
      //*lĕhappîl*)

npš//*bśr* " soul, life "//" flesh "
   Job 31 : 30-31 *napšô* ... *mibbĕśārô*

      Job 6 : 11-12 ; 13 : 14
      (*bĕśārî*//*wĕnapšî*) ; 14 :
      22 ; 33 : 20-21

nqm//*pqd* " to punish "//" to call to account "
   Job 31 : 14 *yiqqôm* (MT *yāqûm*)//*yipqōd*

      Jer 15 : 15

ntn//*ht*' " to give "//" to sin "
   Job 31 : 30 *nātattî* + *lahăţô*'

      Job 1 : 22 (*lō*'-*hāţā*'//
      lō'-*nātan*)

ntn//*śb*' " to give "//" to be satisfied "
   Job 31 : 30-31 *nātattî* ... *niśbā*'

      Job 9 : 18 (*yittĕnēnî*//
      yaśbī'*anî*) ; Lam 3 : 30

'*wl*//'*wn* " wickedness "//" evil "
   Job 31 : 3 '*awwāl*//'*āwen*

      Jer 4 : 15-16 ; Job 11 :
      14 ; 22 : 15

'*wl*//*ş*'*d* " wickedness "//" step "
   Job 31 : 3-4 '*awwāl* ... *şĕ*'*āday*

      Job 14 : 16 (*şĕ*'*āday*//
      '*ōl*, MT '*al*)

'*wr*//'*şm* " skin "//" bone "
   Job 30 : 30 '*ôrî*//*wĕ*'*aşmî*

      Mic 3 : 3 ; Job 10 : 11 ;
      Lam 3 : 4

'*md*//*byn* " to stand "//" to perceive "
   Job 30 : 20 '*āmadtî*//*wattitbōnen*

      Job 37 : 14

'*pr*//'*pr* " dust "//" ashes "
   Job 30 : 19 *ke*'*āpār*//*wā*'*ēper*

      Job 42 : 6

'*şm*//*škb* " bone "//" to rest "
   Job 30 : 17 '*ăşāmay* ... *yiškābûn*

      Job 20 : 11 ; 33 : 19
      (*miškābô*//'*ăşāmāyw*)

'*rş*//*htt* " to fear "//" to terrify "
   Job 31 : 34 '*e*'*ĕrôş*//*yĕhittēnî*

      Josh 1 : 9

'*śh*//*kwn* " to make "//" to establish "
   Job 31 : 15 '*āśāhû*//*wayĕkûnennû*

      Deut 32 : 6 ; Ps 119 :
      73 ; Jer 10 : 12 = 51 :
      15 ; etc.

'*śh*//*šwb* " to make " //" to return, answer "   Job 9 : 12 ; 10 : 9 ; 23 :
   Job 31 : 14 *'e'ĕśeh*//*'ăśîbennû*   13

pš'//*'wn* " rebellious act " //" guilt "   Job 7 : 21 ; 13 : 23 ; 14 :
   Job 31 : 33 *pĕšā'āy*//*'ăwōnî*   17 ; 33 : 9

pth//*'rb* " to lure " //" to lurk "   Prov 1 : 10-11
   Job 31 : 9 *niptâ*//*'ārābtî*

ptḥ//*lyn* " to open " //" to lodge "
   Job 29 : 19 *pātûaḥ*//*yālîn*
   Job 31 : 32 *yālîn*//*'eptāḥ*

ṣdq//*mšpṭ* " righteousness " //" justice "   Ps 72 : 1
   Job 29 : 14 *ṣedeq*//*mišpāṭî*

ṣdq//*tm* " righteousness " //" completeness "   Job 9 : 20 ; 12 : 4 ; 22 :
   Job 31 : 6 *ṣedeq*//*tūmmātî*   3 ; 27 ; 5-6

ṣ'd//*hlk* " to step " //" to walk "   Job 18 : 7-8 ; Prov 4 :
   Job 31 : 4-5 *ṣĕ'āday ... hālaktî*   12 ; 30 : 29 (*ṣā'ad*//*lā-
             ket*) ; Lam 4 : 18

qwh//*yḥl* " to cry out " //" to hope "   Ps 130 : 5
   Job 30 : 26 *qiwwîtî*//*wa'ăyaḥălâ*

r'h//*spr* " to see " //" to count "   Job 28 : 27
   Job 31 : 4 *yir'eh*//*yispôr*

rb//*kbyr* " great " //" abundance "   Isa 17 : 12-13
   Job 31 : 25 *rab*//*kabbîr*

rb//*kwḥ* " many, much " //" force "   Josh 17 : 17 (*rab*//
   Job 30 : 18 *rāb* + *kōaḥ*   *kōaḥ*)

rdp//*'br* " to pursue " //" to pass over "   Isa 41 : 3
   Job 30 : 15 *tirdōp*//*'ābĕrâ*

rwḥ//*'b* " wind " //" cloud "   1 Kgs 18 : 45 ; Qoh
   Job 30 : 15 *kārûaḥ*//*kĕ'āb*   11 : 4

śym//*'mr* " to set, consider " //" to say "   Job 7 : 12-13 ; 22 : 22
   Job 31 : 24 *śamtî*//*'āmartî*

śym//*'nh* " to set, consider " //" to answer "   Job 23 : 5-6
   Job 31 : 35 *śām 'ēlî* (MT *śōmēa' lî*)//*ya'ănēnî*

śmḥ//*r'h* " to rejoice " //" to see "   Job 22 : 19 (*yir'û*//*wĕ-
   Job 31 : 25-26 *'eśmaḥ ... 'er'eh*   *yiśmāḥû*)

šbr//*šlk* " to break " //" to thrust "   Ex 32 : 19 ; Deut 9 :
   Job 29 : 17 *wā'ăšabbĕrâ*//*'ašlîk*   17 ; Jon 2 : 4 ; Dan
             8 : 7

šw'//*'nh* " to call out " //" to answer "   Job 19 : 7
   Job 30 : 20 *'ăšawwa'*//*ta'ănēnî*

špṭ//*nqm* " to judge " // " to vindicate"   1 Sam 24 : 13 (*yišpōṭ*

     Job 31 : 13-14 *mišpaṭ* ... *yiqqôm* (MT *yāqûm*)   //*ûněqāmanî*)

špṭ//*ryb* " to judge " // " to contend "   2 Sam 15 : 4 (*rîb*//*miš-*

     Job 31 : 13 *mišpaṭ* ... *běribām*   *pāṭ*) ; Job 13 : 18-19 ;

                                             23 :   6-7 ;   29 : 14-16 ;

                                             37 : 23

špk//*'ḥz* " to pour out " // " to seize "   Job 16 : 12-13

     Job 30 : 16 *tištappēk*//*yō'ḥăzûnî*

tnym//*y'nh* " jackal " // " ostrich "   Isa 13 : 21-22 ; 34 : 13 ;

     Job 30 : 29 *lětannîm*//*ya'ănâ*   Mic 1 : 8 ; Lam 4 : 3

IV.   Ugaritic-Hebrew Parallel Pairs outside Job 29 - 31

ab ... *yld* " father " ... " to give birth "   *UT* Krt 151-152 (297-

     Job 38 : 28 *'āb*//*hôlîd*   298)

adr//*'rẓ* " mighty " // " terrible "   *UT* 75 II : 31

     Isa 10 : 33-34 *běma'ărāṣâ* ... *bě'addîrê*

akl ... *ḥmd* " to eat, devour " ... " to covet "   *UT* 75 I : 36-38

     Job 20 : 20b-21a *baḥămûdô*//*lě'oklô*

akl//*lḥm* " food " // " bread "   *UT* Krt 80-83 (172-

     Job 33 : 20 *lāḥem*//*ma'ăkal*   174)

akl ... *npl* " to eat, consume " // " to fall "   *UT* 75 II : 36-37

     Job 1 : 16 *nāpělâ*//*watō'kělēm*

il//*ab* " god " // " father "   *RSP* I,II,30

     Job 15 : 10-11 *mē'ābíkā* ... *'ēl*

anp//*npš* " nose, face " // " soul "   *UT* 2 : 14,23,31 ; 3

     Job 32 : 2 *'appô* ... *napšô*   Aqht (obv) 24-26

bšr ... *ḥyy* " flesh " ... " to live "   *UT* 77 : 9 (see Caquot,

     Job 12 : 10 *ḥāy*//*bāśār*   *TO*, p. 392)

gly//*bw'* " to arrive " // " to come "   *RSP* I,II,142

     Job 38 : 16-17 *hăbā'tā* ... *hăniglû*

     Job 41 : 5 *gillâ*//*yābô'*

ḍd//*ahl* " territory, premises " // " tent "   *UT* 1 Aqht 213-214

     Job 22 : 23 *'ad-šadday*//*mě'ohŏlekā*

hlk ... *kly* " to go " ... " to destroy "   *UT* 1 Aqht 195-197

     Job 7 : 9 *kālâ*//*wayyēlak*

ḥmm//*qyẓ* " to be hot " // " summer "   *UT* 1 Aqht 40-41

   Gen 8 : 22 *ḥōm*//*qayiṣ*

ṭbḥ//*gzz* " to slaughter " // " to shear "   *UT* 1153 : 4-5

     Isa 53 : 7 *laṭṭebaḥ* ... *gōzězêhā*

knr//*tp* " lyre "//" drum "   *UT* 602 : 4
   Job 21 : 12 *tōp*//*kinnôr*
my//*š'r* " water "//" barley "   *UT* 1 Aqht 51,55,199
   Deut 8 : 7-8 *māyim*//*ûśĕ'ōrâ*
mǵy//*atw* " to arrive "//" to come "   *UT* 51 IV : 31-32
   Job 37 : 22-23 *ya'ateh* (MT *ye'ĕteh*) ...
   mĕṣā'nūhû
nhqt//*g't* " braying "//"lowing "   *UT* Krt 121-122
   Job 6 : 5 *hăyinhaq*//*yig'eh*
npl//*hwy* " to fall "//" to bow down "   *UT* 137 : 14-15 (30-31)
   Job 1 : 20 *wayyippōl*//*wayyištāḥû*
spr//*yd'* " to number "//" to know "   *RSP* I,II,400
   Job 38 : 21 *yāda'tā*//*mispar*
'l//*ytm* " infant "//" orphan "   *UT* 127 : 48-49
   Job 24 : 9 *yātôm*//*'ūl* (MT *'al*)
qwm//*kr'* " to rise "//" to bow down "   *UT* 76 II : 17-18
   Job 4 : 4 *yĕqîmûn* ... *kōrĕ'ôt*
rpa//*abd* " to weaken "//" to perish "   *UT* Krt 7-8
   Job 26 : 5-6 *hārĕpā'îm* ... *la'ăbaddôn*
šb' + *bky* " to be satisfied " + " to weep "   *UT* 62 : 9
   Job 27 : 14b-15b *yiśbĕ'û* ... *tibkênâ*
šd//*ḥṭt* " field "//" wheat "   *UT* 126 III : 8-9
   Joel 1 : 11 *ḥiṭṭâ* ... *śādeh*
šḥq ... *ṭwb* " to laugh " ... " to return "   *UT* 2 Aqht VI : 41-42
   Job 39 : 22 *yiśḥaq*//*yāśûb*
šyt//*ytn* " to set "//" to give "   *UT* 128 II : 9-10
   Job 38 : 36 *šāt*//*nātan*
škn//*lak* " to dwell "//" to send "   *UT* 51 VII : 44-45
   Job 4 : 18-19 *bĕmal'ākāyw* ... *šōkĕnê*
ṭbr ... *ḥt'* " to break " ... " to vanquish "   *UT* 49 II : 23
   Jer 17 : 18 *'ēḥattâ*//*šābĕrēm*
ṭpṭ ... *npš* " to judge " ... " soul "   *UT* 127 : 34 (46-47)
   Job 27 : 2 *mišpāṭî*//*napšî*

V. Hebrew Parallel Pairs in Job outside Job 29 - 31

'bd//*mwt* " to perish "//" to die "   Job 4 : 20-21
   Job 28 : 22 *'ăbaddôn*//*māwet*
'rḥ//*hlk* " to set out "//" to go "   Job 6 : 19 ; 16 : 22 ; 22 :
   Job 34 : 8 *wĕ'āraḥ*//*wĕlāleket*   14-15

'*th*//*bw*' " to come "//" to enter "   Deut 33 : 2 ; Isa 41 :
    Job 3 : 25 *wayye'ĕtāyēnî*//*yābō*'   22-23,25 ;   Mic 4 : 8 ;
                                                    Prov 1 : 27
bw'//'*kl* " to enter "//" to eat "   Job 20 : 21-22
    Job 42 : 11 *wayyābō'û*//*wayyō'kĕlû*
hmh//*šw*' (*š'h*) " to roar "//" to make a din "   Isa 5 : 14 ; Ps 65 : 8
    Job 39 : 7 *hāmôn*//*tĕšū'ôt*
kbd//*ṣ'r* " to honor "//" to despise "   Jer 30 : 19
    Job 14 : 21 *yikbĕdû*//*wĕyiṣ'ărû*
kwḥ//*mšpṭ* " strength "//" justice "   Job 37 : 23
    Job 9 : 19 *lĕkōaḥ*//*lĕmišpāṭ*
m's//*bḥr* " to reject "//" to choose "   2 Kgs 23 : 27 ; Isa 41 :
    Job 34 : 33 *mā'astā*//*tibḥar*   9 ; Jer 33 : 24 ; Job 7 :
                                                    15-16
nḥm//*dbr* " to reply "//" to speak "   Zech 10 : 2 ; Job 16 :
    Job 15 : 11 *tanḥūmôt*//*dĕbārō* (MT *wĕdābār*) 2-3
śḥq//*ḥtt* " to laugh "//" to dismay "   Jer 48 : 39
    Job 39 : 22 *yiśḥaq*//*yēḥāt*
t'b//'*hb* " to abhor "//" to love "   Ps 119 : 163
    Job 19 : 19 *ti'ăbûnî*//'*āhabtî*

Job 29 - 31 and Tell Mardikh / Ebla

Job 29 : 2   *ntn*   = *wa-ti-nu* (an element in a PN ; Pettinato, *Or* 44, p. 372)

my + *k*   = *mi-kà-ìa* " Who is like Ya " (PN ; TM. 75. G. 336 recto II : 1 ; IV : 14 ; V : 4)

Job 29 : 3   *'wr*   = *si-piš-ar* " Shine, O Sun " (PN ; TM. 75. G. 336 verso VI : 5)

Job 29 : 7   *yṣ'*   = *I-ṣa-Yà* " Yah has gone forth " (PN ; Pettinato, *BA* 39, p. 50)

Job 29 : 11   *šm'*   = *sí-ma-ᵈgu₅-ra* " Hear, O Mountain " (PN ; TM. 75. G. 336 verso II : 3)

Job 29 : 16   *'b*   = *Iš-a-bù* " Gift of the Father " (PN ; Pettinato, *BA* 39, p. 50) *a-bù-ᵈgu₅-ra* " A Father is the Mountain " (PN ; TM. 75. G. 336 recto III : 13)

Job 29 : 18   *ḥwl*   = *aḫ-ḫa-lum* " My Brother is the Phoenix " (PN ; TM. 75. G. 336 recto V : 3)

Job 29 : 20   *ḥdš*   = *é-da-šù* (PN ; Pettinato, *Or* 44, p. 372)

qšt   = *qà-šu* (TM. 74. G. 101 recto II : 1)

Job 29 : 24   *npl*   = *šin₄-pi₅-l(a-nu)* (an element in a PN ; Pettinato, *Or* 44, p. 372)

Job 29 : 25   *bḥr*   = *Be-sû-pi-ḫir* " He has reunited his house " (PN ; Pettinato, *BA* 39, p. 50) ; *Ip-pi-ḫir* " It has been reunited " (PN ; ibid.) ; *ip-ḫur-ìa* (TM. 75. G. 336 recto VI : 9) ; *ip-ḫur-ᵈgu₅-ra* (TM. 75. G. 336 verso V : 9) ; *ip-ḫur-ᵈKU-RA*, *ip-ḫur-ᵈé-da*, *ip-ḫur-Ma-lik* (TM. 74. G. 120 verso V : 4-6)

mlk   = *en-na-Ma-lik* " O King, be gracious " (PN ; TM. 74. G. 120 verso II : 7f. ; TM. 75. G. 336 recto V : 11) ; *en-ṣí-Ma-lik* (PN ; TM. 74. G. 120 verso III : 6f.) ; *eb-du-Ma-lik* (PN ; TM.

74. G. 120 verso V : 1f.) ; *ip-ḫur-Ma-lik* (PN ;
TM. 74. G. 120 verso V : 6) ; *puzur₄-ra-ma-lik*
(PN ; TM. 75. G. 336 recto I : 14 ; VII :
10) ; *a : píl-ma-lik* (PN ; TM. 75. G. 336
recto II : 4) ; *a-kà-al-* [*ma-lik*] (PN ; TM. G.
336 recto VI : 12)

Job 30 : 3 *mš* (MT '*mš*) = *gi-maš-ma*šᵏⁱ " Bog Valley " (place name ;
TM. 75. G. 2231 obv. VI : 15)

Job 30 : 16   *npš*   = *nu-pù-uš-tu-um* (Pettinato, *BA* 39, p. 50)

           '*ḫz*   = *ḫa-zu-um* (Pettinato, *Or* 44, p. 372)

Job 30 : 22   *nś'*   = *na-se*ᴵᴵ " prefect, chief " (TM. 75. G. 336 obv
VI : 5 ; rev I : 10 ; III : 1 ; IV : 4,6,8,10,13 ;
V : 2 ; VIII : 2)

Job 30 : 26   *ṭwb*   = *ṭù-bí-sí-piš* " My good is Shapash " (PN ;
TM. 75. G. 336 recto VII : 6) ; also the PN
ṭù-bí-TI, *ṭù-bí-Da-mu*, *ṭù-bí*-AB (TM. 74. G.
120 recto V : 5-7) ; *ṭù-bí*-BE and *ṭù-bí-Da-lu*
(TM. 74. G. 120 verso I : 2-3)

           '*wr*   = *Ar-Ennum* " the Light is mercy " (PN ; Pet-
tinato, *BA* 39, p. 47)

Job 30 : 29   '*ḥ*   = *sí-piš-a-ḫu* " A brother is Shapash " (PN ;
TM. 75. G. 336 recto I : 11) ; *aḫ-ḫa-lum*
" (my) brother is the Phoenix " (PN ; TM.
75. G. 336 recto V : 3) ; *ar-šè-a-ḫu* (PN ;
TM. 75. G. 336 verso IV : 14)

Job 31 : 6   *tmm*   = *tam-mim* (TM. 74. G. 121 recto I : 1)

Job 31 : 8   '*kl*   = *a-kà-lum* (Pettinato, *BA* 39, p. 50)

Job 31 : 13   '*bd*   = *eb-du-Ma-lik* " Servant of the King " and
eb-du-ᵈRa-sa-ap " Servant of Rasap " (PN ;
TM. 74. G. 120 verso V : 1f., and TM 75. G.
336 verso V : 8) ; *eb-du-ìa* (PN ; TM. 75. G.
336 verso II : 1 ; VI : 7)

Job 31 : 18   '*mm*   = *ù-mu-mu* (Pettinato, *BA* 39, p. 50)

Job 31 : 24   *ktm*   = *ku₈-tim* (TM. 74. G. 119 recto I : 1)

Job 31 : 40   *dbr*   = *ta-da-bi-lu* " translator " (TM. 75. G. 2284)

Indexes

Index of Subjects

A+B+A pattern, 68, 69, 205.
A : B : : B : A word pattern (see also Chiastic word pattern), 29, 66, 74, 99, 127, 128, 134, 152, 198, 202.
Accusative of means, 89.
Accusative of specification, 16.
Adultery, 103, 119, 121.
Ahiram of Byblos, 164, 178.
Aleph preformative, 173.
Alliteration, 50, 148, 165, 188.
" Anticlimactic " parallelism, 9, 227.
Archaic genitive ending, 58.
Archaic -û ending, 85.
Asherah, 115.
Arslan Tash, 61, 75, 197, 201.
Ascending pattern of accents, 63.
Assonance, 45, 50.
Asyndeton, 64.

" Babylonian Theodicy, " 107.
Battle imagery, 63, 64, 201.
  attacking army, 65.
  city under siege, 71, 74, 200.
  storming of a city, 61.
Bedroom = proper place for expression of emotions, 75.
Behemoth, 43.
Belt-wrestling, 78.
BHK³, 10, 12, 21, 28, 29, 55, 59, 63, 66, 73, 105, 109, 121, 142, 177, 184, 185, 198, 202, 203.
BHS, 10, 12, 21, 28, 29, 55, 59, 63, 66, 67, 72, 73, 99, 105, 108, 123, 142, 164, 170, 177, 184, 198, 202.
Biform, 27, 30, 57, 190.
BJ, 51, 89, 142, 195, 199.
BJ², 1, 16, 18, 28, 47, 49, 51, 59, 64, 65, 67, 74, 82, 90, 95, 105, 120, 121,

129, 137, 142, 150, 157, 170, 176, 187, 195, 199.
Blowing a kiss to an object of veneration, 162.
" Bog Valley, " 49.
Book of Life, 179.
Break-up of composite phrase (stereotype phrase, fixed expression), 4, 35, 36, 37, 41, 47, 54, 55, 121, 141, 155, 189, 190, 202, 204, 224.

casus pendens, 45, 226.
Chiasmus, 4, 51, 94, 128, 130, 202, 206, 227.
Chiastic structure, 51, 125, 204, 205, 206.
Chiastic word pattern (see also A : B : : B : A word pattern), 9, 10, 28, 120, 127, 130, 206.
Chicago Bible, 18, 29, 45, 47, 74, 104, 119, 172.
Chthonic deities, 174, 175.
Codex Vaticanus, 76.
Composite phrase, title, divine name, 8, 12, 47, 77, 130, 182, 183, 202.
Compound preposition, 54, 55.
Concrete sense of abstract nouns, 223, 224.
Condition clause without morphological indicator, 112, 224.
Congeneric assimilation, 46.
Congruity of metaphor, 113.
Construct chain with interposing elements, 36, 189.
Covenant, 35.
Crown (of life), 180, 201.
Cultic act of worship, 158.

Index of Authors

Aistleitner, J., 60, 84, 98, 133, 160, 168.

Albright, W. F., 23, 30, 40, 43, 115, 131, 195, 196, 200.

Alonso Schökel, L., 23, 51, 87, 95, 105, 108, 123, 140, 163, 164, 168, 172.

Andersen, F. I., 3, 8, 31, 150, 181, 187, 194, 195, 198, 199.

Avishur, Y., 9.

Baisas, B. Q., 18, 67, 142, 143, 148.

Barré, M. L., 25.

Baumgartner, W., 12, 21, 22, 28, 31, 40, 46, 64, 71, 81, 91, 190.

BDB, 46, 53, 54, 158, 175, 176, 182, 187.

Bettenson, H., 88.

Blommerde, A. C. M., 3, 10, 12, 13, 17, 18, 19, 20, 22, 26, 29, 39, 42, 45, 46, 50, 51, 56, 58, 59, 62, 63, 64, 65, 68, 71, 78, 79, 85, 86, 92, 106, 107, 111, 112, 113, 126, 128, 129, 131, 137, 141, 149, 151, 156, 160, 162, 164, 165, 173, 178, 182, 183, 184, 185, 189, 190, 192.

Boadt, L. 26.

Böcher, O., 43.

Bogaert, M., 185.

Brockington, L. H., 66, 108, 109, 125, 132, 142, 148, 185.

Brongers, H. A., 35.

Burrows, M., 58.

Caquot, A., 15, 27, 47, 48, 50, 62, 66, 133, 144, 151, 155, 160, 161, 162, 166, 169, 191.

Carmignac, J., 120.

Cassuto, U., 60, 79, 147.

Cathcart, K., 8, 40, 50, 55, 57, 69, 160.

Cazelles, H., 96.

Ceresko, A. R., 10, 28, 66, 74, 99, 120, 128, 134, 152, 202.

Christensen, D. L., 115.

Clifford, R., 168.

Collins, T., 73, 74, 95, 138, 201.

Coote, R., 131.

Cross, F. M., 1, 8, 61, 62, 75.

Dahood, M. J., 1, 2, 3, 4, 8, 9, 10, 12, 13, 14, 15, 16, 18, 19, 20, 21, 22, 23, 24, 25, 26, 27, 29, 30, 31, 32, 36, 37, 38, 39, 40, 42, 45, 46, 47, 48, 49, 50, 51, 52, 54, 55, 57, 59, 60, 61, 63, 64, 66, 67, 68, 69, 70, 71, 72, 74, 75, 76, 82, 83, 85, 86, 87, 88, 89, 91, 92, 93, 94, 95, 96, 97, 98, 99, 105, 106, 107, 109, 110, 111, 112, 113, 114, 116, 117, 120, 123, 124, 125, 127, 128, 129, 130, 131, 132, 133, 134, 136, 137, 138, 139, 142, 144, 147, 148, 149, 150, 151, 152, 153, 154, 155, 156, 157, 158, 160, 161, 162, 163, 164, 165, 168, 169, 170, 171, 172, 173, 174, 175, 176, 177, 178, 179, 180, 183, 184, 185, 188, 189, 190, 191, 194, 196, 197, 202, 206.

Davies, G. I., 52.

Delitzsch, Franz, 16, 26, 75, 91, 119, 132, 134, 150, 164, 168, 172.

Dhorme, E., 16, 64, 107, 201.

Dick, M. B., 2, 182.

Dietrich, M., 49, 91, 92, 133, 191.

Dijkstra, M., 191.

Di Lella, A., 3.

Donner H., 9, 164, 175.

Driver, G. R., 48, 50, 66, 84, 112, 147, 160, 162.

Driver, S. R., 25, 41, 50, 53, 55, 59, 79, 82, 89, 91, 94, 95, 105, 113, 121, 134, 146, 147, 150, 158, 182, 193, 205.

Duhm, B., 59.

Epping, O., 190.

Fedrizzi, P., 1, 15, 16, 19, 25, 28, 41,

Index of Biblical Passages

GENESIS

1 : 16	158
1 : 29	117
2 : 7	154
3 : 19	154
3 : 24	41, 53, 233
4 : 6	30
4 : 7	61
4 : 10	187
4 : 10-11	174
4 : 14	41
4 : 21	98, 233
7 : 11	26
8 : 22	141, 236
18 : 5	121
19	169, 170
19 : 2	170
21 : 10	41
23 : 11	105
23 : 18	105
27	38
27 : 27	155
27 : 28	24
28 : 17	186
30 : 14	192
31 : 35	77
37 : 35	98, 229, 232
41 : 32	133
41 : 47	131
43 : 16-17	133
43 : 33	38
44 : 34	165
47 : 24	117
48 : 14	38
49 : 6	27
49 : 21	65

EXODUS

1 : 9-10	40
4 : 31	30
7 : 3-4	161, 234
8 : 22	133
9 : 3	149
17 : 12	150
18 : 13	81
20 : 17	121, 204, 224
21 : 20	129
23 : 6	127
32 : 19	21, 198, 235

LEVITICUS

16 : 10	43
16 : 22	43
19 : 16	204
19 : 32	59
20 : 10	121, 224
20 : 14	123
23 : 17	189
25 : 22	117
26 : 16	117

NUMBERS

13 : 2	62
13 : 16	62, 65
13 : 17	62
14 : 36	62
16 : 30-32	173
21 : 14-15	115
21 : 15b	115
21 : 32	65
23 : 1-2	133
23 : 29-30	133

DEUTERONOMY

1 : 24	65
1 : 33	65
2 : 15	149
6 : 4	130
8 : 7-8	192, 237
8 : 8	192
8 : 17	85, 226
9 : 17	21, 198, 235
9 : 17-18	146
11 : 16	119, 161
13 : 15	133
17 : 4	133
23 : 24-25	51

26 : 5	45
28 : 58	186
32 : 6	132, 133, 234
33 : 2	69, 237
33 : 19	54
34 : 7	46
34 : 8	98, 229, 232

JOSHUA

1 : 9	176, 234
5 : 14	146
17 : 17	77, 224, 235

JUDGES

5 : 6	66, 232
6 : 14	78, 233
6 : 34	19
6 : 38	26
11 : 2	41
11 : 7	41
14 : 15	119, 232
16 : 21	76
19	169, 170
19 : 5	121
19 : 20	170

1 SAMUEL

1 : 15	74
2 : 14	57
2 : 25	123
4 : 18	146
4 : 19	71
5 : 6	149
5 : 11	149
18 : 9	61
19 : 10	57
20 : 30	31
20 : 41	146
24 : 13	129, 236
24 : 16	127
25 : 23	146
28 : 22	121

20 : 18	134	4 : 1	233	9 : 8	124	
20 : 24	105, 111, 233	4 : 3	97, 236	15 : 6	180	
		4 : 18	111, 235	30 : 23	161	
21 : 6	170			43 : 3	98	
21 : 28	45	**ESTHER**		44 : 7	9	
22 : 8	109	4 : 3	98, 229, 232			
24 : 2	96	9 : 1	71	**TOBIT**		
24 : 14	40			8 : 3	43	
24 : 22	164	**DANIEL**		— — — —		
25 : 12	152, 233	1 : 4	116			
25 : 22	50	8 : 7	21, 198, 235	**MATTHEW**		
26 : 26	90	11 : 11	177	4 : 1	43	
27 : 22	76, 97	11 : 13	177	4 : 9	146	
29 : 15	65	11 : 26	146	12 : 43	43	
30 : 29	111, 235	11 : 40	15	13 : 44	173	
31 : 23	57, 144	12 : 1	179	18 : 26	146	
RUTH		**NEHEMIAH**		**LUKE**		
2 : 10	146	8 : 9	98, 229, 232	11 : 24	43	
2 : 14	121					
3 : 7	70	**1 CHRONICLES**		**JOHN**		
4 : 1	144	4 : 22	191	17 : 5	35	
		4 : 22-23	191			
CANTICLES		15 : 1	134	**1 CORINTHIANS**		
1 : 3	40	26 : 10	38	9 : 25	180	
2 : 11	161	28 : 7	134	14 : 25	146	
4 : 11	155			15	26	
8 : 6	175	**2 CHRONICLES**				
		12 : 14	134	**2 TIMOTHY**		
QOHELETH		13 : 8	177	4 : 8	180	
4 : 1	139	14 : 12	146			
5 : 9	177	20 : 2	177	**JAMES**		
7 : 19	40	20 : 12	177	1 : 12	180	
7 : 26	116, 230	20 : 18	146			
9 : 1	161	26 : 14-15	134	**1 PETER**		
11 : 4	72, 235	35 : 6	134	5 : 4	180	
12 : 2	160					
12 : 7	154	**BARUCH**		**REVELATION**		
		4 : 35	43	2 : 10	180	
LAMENTATIONS				3 : 11	180	
2 : 12	73	**SIRACH**		4 : 10	146	
3 : 4	97, 234	3 : 9	12, 119	5 : 14	146	
3 : 8	183	4 : 16	114	7 : 11	146	
3 : 14	58, 59, 226	4 : 16-19	114	11 : 16	146	
3 : 18	46	4 : 17	114	19 : 4	146	
3 : 26	28, 233	4 : 18	114	19 : 10	146	
3 : 30	167, 234	4 : 19	114	22 : 8	146	
		9 : 5	108			

Index of Ugaritic Passages

Index of Other Texts

Index of Hebrew Words

240 ; " Sun " (divine title), 93 ; the Light (= the Sun), 176 ; the light (= the moon), 158.

'*ōzen*, ear, 17.

'*zr*, privative piel, to loosen, 77, 78, 221.

'*ezrôa'*, arm, 143, 147, 219.

'*āḥ*, brother, 97, 240.

'*eḥad*, " the Unique, " 129, 130.

'*ḥz*, to seize, 75, 240.

'*ăḥîrām*, personal name, " My brother is exalted, " 152.

'*aḥar*, after, 116.

'*aḥēr*, another, 121.

'*yd*, '*d*, hand, 148, 173, 219, 220.

'*êd*, ruin, 65.

'*iyyôb*, Job, 7, 196, 205, 227.

'*akzār*, '*akzārî*, " Cruel One, " 81, 83, 84, 196, 200, 201, 202.

'*kl*, to eat, 51, 103, 104, 117, 118, 119, 123, 124, 126, 136, 137, 188, 189, 203, 240.

'*ēl*, God, 39, 81, 86, 182, 202.

'*ālâ*, curse, 166.

'*ĕlôah*, God, 131.

'*ĕlîpaz*, Eliphaz (= " My God is fine gold "), 152.

'*almānâ*, widow, 136, 205.

'*āmâ*, maidservant, 122, 128, 129.

'*ēm*, mother, 139, 240.

'*mn*, hiphil, to take courage, be confident, 30.

'*mr*, to say, call, 150.

'*emeš*, yesterday, last night, 48, 49.

'*ănî*, '*ānōkî*, I, 20, 200.

'*sr*, to bind, 78.

'*ap*, anger, 167.

'*ph*, to bake, 189.

'*ōpel*, darkness, 93, 201.

'*ēper*, ashes, 80.

'*rb*, to lurk, 119.

'*erez*, cedar, 177.

'*rḥ*, to set out, depart, 171, 172.

'*ōraḥ*, road, way, 65, 66.

'*ōraḥ*, traveler, 170, 198, 221.

'*ereṣ*, land, earth, 176, 177, 192 ; town, city, 52, 53, 57, 196, 197 ; nether-world, 124.

'*ūrōt*, " (Elysian) Fields, " 24.

'*ēš*, fire, 118, 123, 124.

'*iššâ*, woman, wife, 119, 121, 204, 224.

'*ēšet rēa'*, a neighbor's wife, 120, 121, 204, 224.

'*āšēr*, happy, a happy man, 32, 116.

'*šr*, to walk, tread ; piel, to lead, 114.

'*āšūr*, foot, 114, 116, 224.

'*th*, to come, 69, 70, 221 ; hiphil, to bring, 151, 158.

bĕ, by (causal), 146 ; from, 137.

bw', to come, enter, 69, 70, 189.

bôš, to be ashamed, 122.

bḥr, to choose, 39.

bḥr, to gather, join, unite, 31, 196, 220, 239.

beṭen, belly, womb, 132, 134.

byn, to pay attention to, look upon' 81, 82, 107.

bên, between, 55.

bêt, *mô'ēd*, Meetinghouse, 88, 201.

bkh, to weep, 92, 98, 169, 187, 188, 197, 221, 227.

bĕkôr, first-born, 38.

bĕlî-šēm, nameless, 57, 197.

ballāhôt, Terror, 60, 70, 71, 204, 220.

bēn, son, 119.

b'l (biform of *p'l*), to do, work, make, 185, 190, 191, 220.

beṣer, gold, 54, 55.

bĕṣûr, upon, 54, 55.

barzel, ax, 177.

brk, to bless, 141, 166, 205.

bāśār, flesh, 167, 168, 169.

btḥ, to trust, 186.

bĕtûlâ, the Virgin (Anat), 107, 108, 201.

gdl, pual, to be raised, trained, 137.

gĕw, community, 52, 53, 57, 197.

gēz, fleece, 141.

gzr, to rip, cut into pieces, 44, 84, 196.

gy', valley, 49.

glh, to arrive, penetrate, 70, 196.

gam, yes, indeed, 46, 56.

gnb, to steal, 186.

g'h, to low, bellow, 54, 56.

gēr, stranger, 170,

grš, to drive out, banish, 41, 53.

dbr, to speak, 186, 240.
dābār, word, message, 96, 193.
dāber, Pestilence, 175.
dal, poor, 134, 135, 136.
dām, blood, 173.
dmh, niphal, to be silent, 179.
dmm, to be silent, 28.
drk, dominion, power, assembly
   (= place where dominion is exercised), 31, 32, 196.
derek, way, 104, 111.

hōwâ, disaster, 69.
hālîk, foot, 12, 114, 223.
hlk, to walk, 104, 111, 112, 171, 172 ;
   to wane (of the moon), disappear,
   vanish, 11, 136, 160, 161, 196, 203,
   205, 207 ; hiphil, to bring, 161.
hll, to shine, brighten, wax (of the
   moon), 10, 11, 159, 160, 196, 203,
   205, 207.
hll, to praise, rejoice, 159, 160.
hāmôn, noise, clamor, crowd, 177, 178,
   221.
hēnnâ, these things, 109.
hpk, to turn, overturn, 71.

zāhāb, gold, 152.
zākēn, old, 157.
zimmâ, lewdness, licentiousness, 122,
   123, 196.
z'q, to cry out, 187.
zr', to sow, plant, 117, 118, 203 ; seed,
   descendant, 197.
zĕrōa', arm, 147.

ḥb', niphal, to be silent/hide, 16, 17.
ḥby, *ḥbywn*, " Hades, " 173, 174, 175,
   176, 196, 201.
ḥdš, to make new, 239.
ḥādāš, new, fresh, 27.
ḥwh, eštafal, to bow down, worship,
   146.
ḥôl, phoenix, 22, 23, 25, 26, 196, 201,
   239.
ḥwš, to hasten, 112.

ḥṭ', to offend, 165, 166.
ḥiṭṭâ, wheat, 189, 192.
ḥay, living, 88, 90, 168, 169.
ḥayyîm, (eternal) life, 25, 172.
ḥkm, to be wise, 157.
ḥălāṣayim, loins, 141.
ḥēleq, allotment, 108.
ḥōm, heat, 141.
ḥmd, to desire, 137.
ḥammâ, answer, 95, 196.
ḥōmer, mud, 79, 200.
ḥeser, lack, 47.
ḥăsar lāḥem, one who lacks bread, 47,
   204, 224.
ḥēpeṣ, desire, 134.
ḥpš, hithpael, to rifle, ransack, plunder, 77.
ḥōr, cave, hole, 55.
ḥōreb, heat, 98.
ḥōrep, prime, 12, 196.
ḥrr, to burn, be hot, 97, 98.
ḥrš, hiphil, to be silent, 179.
ḥārāš, craftsman, 133.
ḥšk, to spare, hold back, 60.
ḥth, to snatch, 50.
ḥtt, to terrify, shatter, 176, 178.

ṭbḥ, to slaughter, 141.
ṭôb, good, 202, 240 ; " the Good One, "
   92, 93 ; merry, 99.
ṭḥn, to grind, 118, 121.
ṭal, dew, 23, 24, 25, 26, 201.
ṭmn, to hide, 174, 201 ; shaphel, to
   cause to hide, take cover, 85, 221.
ṭāmûn, the Crypt, 175.

yāgēa', weary, 189, 190.
yād, hand, 84, 85, 139, 142, 145, 148,
   161, 168.
yād 'ēl, the hand of God, 149.
yd', to know, 90, 184.
yôm, day, 9, 75, 197, 227.
yāḥīd, the Unique, 131.
yāḥîd, the solitary man, 136, 202.
yḥl, to wait for, 28, 29, 94.
ykl, to be able, to bear, 134, 144, 227.
yld, to give birth, 139.
yeled, child, 155.

yāmîn, right hand, 63.
ysd, to found, establish, 12.
ysp, to continue, do again, 7.
ysr, to instruct, 157.
yʻl, to gain, profit, 67, 68.
yaʻănâ, ostrich, 97.
yāpeh, beautiful, 161.
yṣʾ, to go out, 14, 103, 239.
yṣq, to pour, 13.
yqd, to burn, 76.
yrʾ, to fear, 186.
yrḥ, to throw, cast, 79.
yrḥ, moon/month, 9, 11, 158, 159, 160, 197, 205, 227.
yšb, to dwell, 54 ; to sit enthroned, 32.
yěšûʻâ, prosperity, 72, 73.
yātôm, orphan, 134, 135, 136, 139, 142, 143, 205.

kě, as, like, 9, 239.
kbd, to achieve, honor, 37.
kābôd (biform of *kāběd*), liver, innards, 27.
kabbîr, abundance, 156 ; the Old One, 156.
kwn, hiphil, piel, to create, 132, 133, 196.
kōaḥ, strength, 45, 46, 77, 78, 85, 226 ; yield, 189, 190.
kḥš, piel, to betray, 163.
kḥš, throne, 163.
kî, emphatic, 46, 106, 223.
kî, if, 176, 223.
klʾ, niphal, to be kept back, restrained, 134.
klh, to fail, evaporate, 136 ; piel, hiphil, to cause to fail, 134, 135, 136, 144, 203, 227.
kālah = kī lěah, full vigor, 46.
kinnôr, harp, lyre, 98, 99, 108.
kesel, confidence, 152.
kesem, spelt, 192.
kěsût, covering, clothing, 139, 141.
kap, hand, 78, 147.
krʻ, to bend, 121, 122.
ktb, to write, 183.
ketem, fine gold, 152, 240.
kūtōnet, tunic, 77.

kātěp, shoulder-blade, 145.

lě, to for, 20, 120 ; from, 67-68, 162, 222 ; upon, 79, 80, 222 ; against, 120 ; comparative, 39, 40.
lūʾ, emphatic, 169, 223.
lʾh, to be strong, prevail, 89, 131.
lěʾ, powerful, victorious, 29, 30, 196 ; the Victor, the Omnipotent, 110, 111, 127, 129, 130, 151, 182.
lěʾ ʾeḥād, the Unique Victor, 202.
lēb, heart, 103, 116, 119, 161, 162, 190.
lbš, to clothe, put on ; piel, to adorn, 19, 205, 227.
lěbûš, garment, clothing, 77, 141.
lěah, vigor, 46.
lḥm, to consume, eat, 48, 51, 52.
leḥem, bread, 47, 121, 189.
laylâ, night, 75.
lyn, to lodge, spend the night, 11, 26, 170, 207.
lěmô, to, for, 28.
lāmmâ, why, 45.

mâ, negative particle, 105, 223.
mʾûm, spot, 116.
mōʾznayim, scales, 113.
mōʾzěnê-ṣedeq, just scales, 111.
maʾăkāl, food, 189.
mʾs, to reject, 38 ; privative piel, to prefer, accept, 39.
mibṭāḥ, trust, 152.
mhr, to hasten, be quick, 87.
mwg, hiphil, to sweep away, 86.
mûʻāqâ, wasting consumption, gnawing, 48.
môšāb, seat, throne, 15.
mwt, to die, 124 ; Death, 88, 124, 176, 201.
mî, who, 9, 239.
mayim, water, 26, 192.
millâ, gibe, joke, 197 ; word, 121, 184.
malʾāk, messenger, 54.
melek, king, 32, 239.
melek, ballāhôt, King of Terrors, 200.
min, (local sense) in, on, over, 59, 60,

163, 222 ; (partitive) any, none, 134, 203, 222.
mn', to withhold, 134.
mispār, number, 185.
ma'al, above, 108.
mē'îm, innards, intestines, 95.
mṣ', to find, 158, 165 ; to reach, arrive at, attain, 155, 156, 164, 196 ; hiphil, to cause to reach, 171.
měṣûdâ, wilderness, 48.
mārôm, height, 107, 108.
mirmâ, fraud, 111, 224.
maśśā', oracle, utterance, 8.
maś'ēt, raising, lifting, 149.
měśō'â, desolation, 50.
maśśû'ôt, Ruin, 69, 70.
maś, swamp, 43, 49, 196, 240.
māšāl, poem, 8.
mišpāṭ, cause, right, judgment, 45, 127, 128, 167.
mětallě'ôt, jawbone, 21, 196.

nābāl, fool, senseless one, 56, 214.
ngd, hiphil, to declare, tell, 183, 185, 186, 227.
nāgîd, prince, 185, 186.
něgînâ, a (mocking) song, 58, 59, 226.
nědîbâ, nobility, dignity, 66, 72.
nhq, to bray, cry out, 54, 56.
nwp, to wave, shake, raise, 148, 149.
nḥh, to guide, 139, 140.
naḥal, torrent, ravine, 54.
naḥălâ, heritage, 108.
nḥm, piel, to console, 32, 139.
nḥm, to reply, 95, 96.
nk' (*nkh*), to strike, smite, thrust, 57.
ně'ûrôt, youth, 138, 139.
npḥ, to blow, fan, 188, 190.
npl, to fall, 31, 123, 144, 145, 146, 149, 239.
npl pānîm, hiphil, to let fall the face (= to grow sad), 30, 31, 204, 225.
nepeš, life, soul, 74, 75, 167, 189, 193, 240 ; throat, 73, 74.
nqm, to punish, 129.
nēr, lamp, 10, 159.
nś', to lift up, raise, 86, 144, 149, 240 ;

to wear, 184 ; to raise up (the eyes), gaze on, 106.
nāśî' chief, leader, 86.
nšm, to breathe, fan, inspire, 153, 154, 155, 186.
něšāmâ, breath, 155.
nětîbâ, path, way, 66, 67.
ntn, to give, 8, 9, 165, 166, 167, 185, 239.
nts, to break up, 66, 69, 196.
neta', progeny, 119.
ntṣ, to pull down, break down, 66.

sll, to cast up, build a highway, 65.
sôlălâ, road, siege mound, 65.
spr, to count, number, 103, 111, 184.
sēper, indictment, 179, 183, 205 ; inscription, 184.
sēper hayyîm, the Book of Life, 179.

'āb, cloud, 72.
'ebed, slave, servant, 128, 129, 240.
'br, to pass on, 72.
'ăgābîm, applause, 99.
'gm, to grieve, 91, 92, 197.
'ēdâ, (nether) assembly, 88, 89.
'ûgāb, flute, 98, 99.
'awwāl, wicked, 109.
'āwel, wickedness, 135.
'āwôn, iniquity, guilt, 123, 174.
'āwōn pělîlî, criminal iniquity, 103, 104.
'wr, hitpolel, to be elated, 164.
'ôr, skin, 97.
'ōz, strength, 175.
'zr, to rescue, liberate, acquit, 142, 143, 196, 205.
'ēzer, escape, rescue, 68.
'ezrâ, acquittal, 142, 143.
'ăṭārôt, crown, 180, 184, 201, 220.
'yn, to eye, see, 59, 61, 197, 221.
'ayin, eye, 17, 62, 104, 105, 108, 135, 205.
'al, from, 15, 25, 45, 50, 51, 74, 199, 222 ; before, in the presence of, 19, 222 ; at, 120 ; because, 187 ; in spite of, despite, 149, 200 ; by (agency with passive verb), 120, 222.

'*ōl*, wickedness, malice, 109, 110, 111.
'*ūl*, infant, suckling, 135.
'*ĕlî*, cauldron, crucible, 76, 97, 196.
'*ēlî*, Most High, 8, 9, 10, 151, 175, 182, 196, 205.
'*ēlî* '*ĕlôah*, God Most High, 12, 202.
'*lm*, to grow dark, 110.
'*im*, as, like, 26, 222 ; toward, 112, 222 ; from, 108.
'*md*, to present oneself, 81, 82.
'*ammūd*, leg, 14, 114, 223.
'*nh*, to answer, 81, 82, 182.
'*nh*, to conquer, 127.
'*āpār*, clay, slime, dust, 54, 79, 80, 84 ; Dust. 87.
'*eṣem*, bone, 75, 76, 97.
'*ōṣem*, powerful, strong, 75, 84, 85, 226.
'*rṣ*, to fear, dread, 53, 54, 176, 177.
'*rq*, to gnaw, rend, devour, 43, 47, 48, 84, 196.
'*śh*, to do, make, 128, 129, 130, 131, 132, 133, 186.
'*ōśēh*, Creator, 131, 202.
'*śh*, to oppress, squeeze, 131, 132.
'*šq*, to oppress, 139.
'*attâ*, now, 35, 58, 72, 73.

pa, and, 63, 64, 196, 223.
peh, mouth, 161, 162.
pḥd, to tremble, 186.
paḥad, dread, 148.
pîd, ruin, 164.
peleg, channel, river, 14, 54.
pll, to assess, reckon, 122, 123.
pĕlîlî, criminal, assessable, 122, 123.
pānîm, face, 30, 31, 62, 63, 197.
p'l, to work, make, 185, 190, 191.
pō'al, Maker, 170, 171.
pa'am, foot, 114.
pqd, to call to account, 129.
pereṣ, breach, 67, 68.
pešaʻ, revolt, rebellion, 174.
pat, bit, morsel, 121.
pth, niphal, pual, to be lured, deceived, 103, 119, 161.
ptḥ, to open, 11, 26, 207.
petaḥ, door, 62.

petî, fool, simpleton, 119.

ṣe'ĕṣā'îm, offspring, 118, 119.
ṣedeq, just, 113.
ṣûr, back, 55.
ṣôrî, balsam, 13.
ṣiyyâ, desert, 49.
ṣiyyîm, wild beasts, 43.
ṣaʻad, steps, 103, 111, 185.
ṣʻr, to be belittled, disgraced, 37.
ṣāʻîr, young, small, 36, 37, 38.
ṣĕʻîrê haṣṣōʼn, the little ones of the flock, 37, 224.

qdm, to confront, meet, 95.
qāhāl, the (nether) assembly, 90.
qwḥ, to call, cry out, 94, 196.
qwl (biform of *qhl*), to call, assemble, 30.
qwm, to rise, 121 ; to denote inchoate action, 16, 195, 228 ; with subjunctive to express purpose, 97, 228.
qṭp, to pluck, 50, 51.
qayiṣ, summer, 141.
qmṭ, hiphil, to lay low, overcome, 89.
qēn, nest (of the arm) = armpit, socket, 147, 196.
qnh, to create, 132.
qōrāʼ, one who calls, calling, 170.
qrb, to approach, 183.
qeren, horn, 176.
qeret, city, 15, 197.
qešet, bow, 27, 239.

r'h, to see, 111, 140, 156, 206, 227 ; to look at with favor, 158.
rōʼš, head, leader, 227.
rab, many, great, 77, 85, 156, 224, 226 ; great (in years) = aged, 156, 157.
rgl, to spy, search out, 61, 65, 201, 221.
regel, foot, 111, 114.
rdp, to pursue, 72.
rûaḥ, wind, 72.
raḥâ, palm, (left) hand, 63, 64, 196.
rĕḥôb, broad place, 16.
reḥem, womb, 132.
rḥṣ, to wash, 13.
rḥq, to be distant, 59.

Index of Ugaritic Words

ab, father, 39, 139.
ab šnm, " father of years, " 36, 37.
abd, to perish, 125.
ablm, mourners (?), 98.
agzrm, ravenous ones, 84.
'id, hand, 148, 173.
udn, ear, 17.
adr, mighty, 177.
ahl, tent, 168.
'wr, to shine, 160.
aḥdy, he alone, 130.
aḫ, brother, 97.
uḫryt, afterlife, 116.
ayab, personal name, 7.
'kl, to eat, 117, 118, 123, 124, 135, 137 ; grain, 189.
'klm, " Eaters, " 43, 44, 47, 201.
aktmy personal name, " I consider Ya my fine gold, " 152.
il " El, " 39, 164.
aliy, aliyn, " Victor " (title of Baal ; from *l'y*), 115, 175.
almnt, widow, 135, 136.
um, mother, 139.
amt, maidservant, 122, 128.
an, I, 20, 200.
ank, I, 20, 200.
ap, nose, 167.
'py, to bake, 189.
arṣ, earth, 176, 191, 192.
'š, fire, 118, 124.
atw, to come, 158.
iṯl, tamarisk (?), 155.
aṯr, toward, 116.
aṯr b'l, " Leader (?) Baal, " 115.
aṯryt, destiny, happiness, 116.
aṯrt ym, " (the Lady) Who Traverses the Sea, " 115.

bw', to enter, 70.
byn, to perceive, discern, 81.
bky, to weep, 92, 98, 169, 197.
bkr, first-born, 38.
bn, son, 119.

b'l, to make, work, 191.
b'lt šmm rmm, " mistress of highest heaven " (title of Anat), 107.
brk, knee ; denominative verb, to bring to the knees, i.e., to be born, 47.
bšr, flesh, 168, 169.
bt, house, 40.
btlt 'nt, the Virgin Anat, 107, 108, 201.
bṯ, to be ashamed, 122.

gbl, border, 42.
gzz, to shear, 141.
gly, to arrive, penetrate, 70.
g't, lowing (of an ox), 56.
grn, threshing floor, 16.

dl, poor, 135.
dqn, beard, 157.
dry, to cut, 177.
drkt, dominion, 32.
dr', to sow, 117, 118.
ḏd, territory, premises, 168.

hlk, to walk, go, 112, 136.
hll I, to shine, be bright, 159, 160.
hll II, to praise, rejoice, 159, 160.

wld, primae waw form of *yld*, to bear, 47.
wpṯ, to spit, 57.

ḫby, name of a deity or demon, 175.
ḥwy, to bow down, worship, 146.
ḥwy, to live, 168, 169.
ḥwš, to hasten, 112.
ḥṭṭ, wheat, 189, 191, 192.
ḥy, living, 88, 90.
ḥkm, wise, 157.
ḥl, phoenix, 22, 23, 196.
ḥm, heat, 141.
ḥmd, to covet, 137.
ḥrr, to burn, be hot, 97, 98.
ḥrš, to fashion, 133.

ḫšk, to spare, hold back, 60.

ḫsr, to be lacking, to lack, 46.
ḫprt, ewes, yearlings, 12.
ḫr, hole, 55.
ḫt', to crush, 178.

ṭb, merry, 98.
ṭbḫ, to slaughter, 141.
ṭḥn, to grind, 118.
ṭl, dew, 24, 26, 27.

ẓḥq, to laugh, smile, 35.
ẓr, back, 55.
ẓrw, balsam, 13.

yd, hand, 64, 84, 142, 145, 168.
yd il, " the hand of El, " 149.
yd', to know, 90, 184.
yḥd, " the solitary man, " 136.
yld, to give birth, 139, 155.
ym, day, 9.
ymn, right hand, 63.
ysr, to instruct, 157.
ypt, beautiful, 161.
yṣq, to pour, 13.
yrḫ, moon, 9, 159.
ytm, orphan, 135, 136.
ytn, to give, put, set, 165, 166, 185.
yṯb, to sit enthroned, 32.

kwn, G, to be ; L and Š, to bring into
    being, create, 132, 133.
kḥṯ, throne, 163.
kbl, dog, 40.
kly, to deplete, destroy, 135, 136.
knr, lyre, 98, 108.
ksm, spelt, 191, 192.
ksp, silver, 190.
kr', to bow, bend, 121.
ktb, to write, 183.
ktn, garment, 77.
ktp, shoulder, 145.
kṯrt, female jubilants, songstresses,
    159, 160.

l, to, for, 20.
l'y, to overcome, 89.

l'k, to send, 54.
lb, heart, 161, 162.
lbš, to clothe, put on ; garment ; 19,
    77.
lḥm, to dine, eat, 52 ; bread, 189.
lẓr (= l + ẓr), upon, 55.
lyn, to spend the night, 170.
lm, why, 45.
lm, to, for, 28.
lpš, garment, clothing, 19, 77, 141.

mizrtm, a (double) garment, 77, 141.
mhrm, (quick, skilled) troops, 87.
mwt, death, 88.
mzn, weight, 113.
mẓa, variant of mṣa, to reach, arrive
    at, attain, 164.
my, mym, water, 26, 27, 192.
mlbr, desert, 43, 49.
mlk, king, 32.
m', enclitic after the imperative, 95.
mǧy (related to mẓa and mṣa), to reach,
    arrive at, attain, 155, 158, 164, 165.
mpḫm, bellows, 190.
mpḫrt, assembly, 31.
mṣa (related to mẓa and mǧy), to
    reach, arrive at, attain, 155.
mrym ṣpn, " the heights of Saphon, "
    108.
mšknt, dwelling, 168.
mšmš, morass, swamp, 43, 48, 49.

nhqt, braying, 56.
nyr šmm, " lamp of the heavens, " 159.
npl, to fall, 123, 145, 146.
npš, soul, 167.
nṣb, to stand, 82.
nša, to raise, 86, 149 ; to raise (the
    eyes), gaze, 106.
nš' g, to lift up the voice, 8.
nts, to break up, destroy, 66.

spr, to count, 20, 184, 195, 186 ; ta-
    blet, inscription, 183.

'bd, slave, 128.
'gm, to grieve, 91, 92, 197.

Index of Other Words